The Fire *of* Freedom

The Fire *of* Freedom

ABRAHAM GALLOWAY & THE SLAVES' CIVIL WAR

DAVID S. CECELSKI

The University of North Carolina Press
Chapel Hill

This book was published with the assistance of the Blythe Family Fund of the University of North Carolina Press.

Designed and set in Calluna and Calluna Sans by Rebecca Evans
Manufactured in the United States of America

The paper in this book meets the guidelines for permanence and durability of the Committee on Production Guidelines for Book Longevity of the Council on Library Resources.

The University of North Carolina Press has been a member of the Green Press Initiative since 2003.

Cecelski, David S.
The fire of freedom : Abraham Galloway and the slaves' Civil War / by David S. Cecelski.
    p. cm.
Includes bibliographical references and index.
ISBN 978-0-8078-3566-1 (hardback)
1. Galloway, Abraham H., 1837–1870. 2. United States—History—Civil War, 1861–1865—Participation, African American. 3. United States—History—Civil War, 1861–1865—African Americans. 4. United States—History—Civil War, 1861–1865—Secret service. 5. Reconstruction (U.S. history, 1865–1877)—North Carolina. 6. Fugitive slaves—North Carolina—Biography. 7. African American abolitionists—Biography. 8. African American legislators—North Carolina—Biography. I. Title.
E540.N3C37   2012   326'.8092—dc23   [B]   2012012538

16 15 14 13 12   5 4 3 2 1

To Laura

There seems to be more of the unquenchable fire of freedom in the eyes of these people than in those of any other people we have yet visited.

—ROBERT HAMILTON, 16 January 1864

Contents

Illustrations and Maps

Foreword

THIS IS THE STORY OF ABRAHAM H. GALLOWAY (1837–70), A FIERY YOUNG slave rebel, radical abolitionist, and Union spy who rose out of bondage to become one of the most significant and stirring black leaders in the United States during the American Civil War. A freedom fighter in what the *New Orleans Tribune*, the first African American newspaper published below the Mason-Dixon Line, called "a Second American Revolution," Galloway burned with an incandescent passion against tyranny and injustice. His war was not the one that we are accustomed to seeing in history books, however. Galloway's war had little to do with that of Grant or Lee, Vicksburg or Cold Harbor. It had nothing to do with states' rights or preserving the Union. Galloway's Civil War was a slave insurgency, a war of liberation that was the culmination of generations of perseverance and faith. It was, ultimately, the slaves' Civil War.

Prologue

New Bern, North Carolina
May 1863

IN THE THIRD YEAR OF THE CIVIL WAR, A NEW ENGLAND ABOLITIONIST named Edward Kinsley walked the streets of New Bern, North Carolina. The seaport was usually a town of 5,500 inhabitants, but at that moment it overflowed with thousands of fugitive slaves who had escaped from the Confederacy. The setting was one of excess in all things: hardship, disarray, fear, heartbreak, joy. Federal troops crowded into colonial homes and antebellum manors. Downtown buildings lay in charred ruins: retreating Confederates had burned some of them, and a Union general torched others after snipers shot at his sentries. The Confederates had fled so quickly that they left doors banging in the wind, family portraits in front yards, and a piano in the middle of a street. The murmur of sawmills could be heard across the Trent River, the sound of the former slaves building a new city. The days clattered noisily by, and even the stillness of evening was broken by short bursts of ecstasy: slave sisters reunited after a lifetime apart or the arrival of a slave family that had survived a journey of 150 miles. No one breathed easy. New Bern was a sliver of sanctuary for African Americans in the slave South, and the Confederate army threatened to recapture the city at any time.[1]

Kinsley had come to New Bern as an emissary of Governor John Albion Andrew of Massachusetts, an abolitionist leader seeking to recruit an African American brigade for the Union army. He had traveled south rather loosely incognito, listed on the rolls of the Union steamship *Terry* as a personal servant to the brigade's commanding officer, Brigadier General

Edward Augustus Wild. His real mission, however, was to determine if the slaves of the South were willing and ready to fight for their own liberty. In his coat pocket, Kinsley carried travel papers handwritten by President Abraham Lincoln and endorsed by Secretary of War Edwin M. Stanton.[2]

Kinsley's mission had not gone as anticipated, however. He had expected the former slaves to throng to the army's ranks. Only months earlier, long before Lincoln authorized the recruitment of African American troops, 120 local freedmen had petitioned Union commanders for the right to take up arms against the Confederacy. By one account, as many as 1,000 African American men had been drilling in New Bern on their own, eager for a chance to join the fray. But something had changed in recent months. Instead of black men swarming to join the Union army, they avoided the new recruiting office on Middle Street nearly to a man. "Something was wrong," Kinsley realized, "and it did not take [me] long to find out the trouble." All pointed him to one individual, the man whom the slave refugees considered their leader. "Among the blacks," he learned, "was a man of more than ordinary ability . . . named Abraham Galloway."[3]

&

In the spring of 1863, Galloway was a familiar sight in Union army camps in New Bern and in slave communities nearby that were still inside the Confederacy. Born in bondage 100 miles south, by the Cape Fear River, he was an elusive figure who seemed to pass through the enemy's pickets like a ghost. The way he held himself was usually the first thing that strangers noticed about Galloway. Only twenty-six years old, he was a handsome man who primped and preened and was at least a little haughty. He was notorious for his sense of honor and his hair-trigger readiness to defend it, yet he was also renowned for laughing loud and often. His defiant posture and his quickness to lash out at anyone, white or black, Yankee or Rebel, who attempted to stain his honor or who insulted a black man or woman in his presence gave credence to stories of his daring behind enemy lines.

Eventually, Galloway consented to see Kinsley at the home of a local black leader named Mary Ann Starkey. She had watched Kinsley closely since his arrival from Boston, and she had finally taken him aside one evening and told him, as he later recalled, "I want to see you." The next morning she instructed him to come to her home at midnight. She did not mention Galloway by name, but she was expecting, she said, "a couple of friends from the Rebel lines."[4]

When the New England abolitionist arrived that night at midnight,

Starkey greeted him and led him into an attic room. Downstairs, a rugged, older ex-slave named Isaac Felton slipped into Starkey's house through the kitchen door. Starkey called him "Uncle Isaac." A younger black man, John Randolph Jr., followed him through the kitchen door. He, too, had been a local slave before the war. A few minutes later, the kitchen door opened and closed a third time. Upstairs, beneath the slant of the cottage's eaves, Kinsley could see, as he later recounted, "by the dim light of the candle that the room was nearly filled with blacks, and right in front of him stood Abraham Galloway and another huge negro, both armed with revolvers."[5] One of the surviving accounts of that night indicates that the black leaders blindfolded Kinsley downstairs and only removed the blindfold after they had gathered in the attic.[6]

Galloway looked at him from behind a plain wooden table with only the candle and a Bible on it. He was tall and had long, dark hair and a broad, round face with high cheekbones and what one observer later called "flashing brown eyes." He was rather light-skinned, by appearance part Indian, part white, or both. He had no formal schooling and could not read or write well, if at all, but Kinsley recognized immediately that he had come face-to-face with a "very shrewd, smart, accomplished man."[7]

That night the convocation of liberated slaves did not mince words. If the Union intended to make the war a crusade for black freedom, Kinsley would discover no shortage of black recruits in New Bern. With a seemingly reckless strain of bravado in their voices, they promised that they could deliver an entire regiment to Brigadier General Wild in only a few days if Kinsley could convince them that they would indeed be fighting for the abolition of slavery. But if the Federal army planned to use black men like chattel and wage a war merely for the preservation of the Union, that was another story. They bluntly listed their demands: equal pay, provisions for black soldiers' families, schooling for soldiers' children, employment for their wives and mothers who contributed to the effort to bring down the Confederacy, care for their elderly and feeble, and assurances that the Union would force the Confederacy to treat captured blacks as prisoners of war rather than reenslave them or execute them as traitors.[8]

The negotiations between the black leaders and Kinsley lasted late into the night. Some of the discussions, especially those concerning the treatment of black prisoners of war, proved long and contentious. Finally, not long before sunrise, they reached an understanding of what it would take to raise African American regiments in New Bern.

Kinsley later described the next few moments as the most harrowing of his life. While Felton and another of the black leaders held revolvers to Kinsley's head, Galloway compelled Governor Andrew's emissary to swear a personal oath that the Federal army would meet their conditions. After Kinsley did so, at five o'clock in the morning, the former slaves released him into the predawn air. Galloway disappeared again across Confederate lines. Four days later, Starkey sent a boy to find Kinsley and tell him that Union army leaders needed to be ready the next day.[9]

The following evening, a little after midnight, Union soldiers saw torchlight approaching them beyond Fort Totten, on the western side of New Bern. Gradually, they made out grand columns of black men, women, and children marching toward them out of the darkness. The procession stretched far into the night. "It seemed to me that the entire population of the South . . . were marching toward the happy land," Kinsley wrote later. Galloway, Felton, and Randolph headed the line of march. Union pickets parted, and the slaves crossed into freedom, congregated around Fort Totten, and then filed into New Bern. Kinsley, who was prone to exaggeration but generally got the gist of things right, estimated that 4,000 men, women, and children arrived in the city that night. "The next day," he remembered, "the word went forth, and the blacks came to the recruiting station by [the] hundreds and a brigade was soon formed."[10] The more than 5,000 African Americans eventually recruited in the New Bern vicinity, most of them former slaves, became the core of the 35th, 36th, and 37th Regiments, United States Colored Troops, known originally as the African Brigade.[11]

℘

That midnight encounter with Abraham Galloway was always Edward Kinsley's most powerful memory of the Civil War. He described that night in a speech to Union army veterans after the war and more fully in an unpublished memoir that he wrote for his family and friends near the end of his life. The drama, excitement, and fear that he felt that night kept his memory fresh, but so, too, did the realization that he had been afforded a rare glimpse at the inner councils of black southerners at the very hour they first emerged from slavery. Few stories have given such a compelling voice or such a clear face to an African American freedom struggle that occurred in New Bern and other Union-occupied parts of the South during the Civil War, as well as within the Confederacy itself.

Rarely have we glimpsed so vividly what the tens of thousands of African Americans who found asylum in Federal territory during the Civil War did with their new freedom. Students of history have long tended to see the "freedpeople"—or "contrabands," as the Union army called former slaves under Federal occupation—either through the eyes of so many New England missionaries, as downtrodden, helpless souls entirely reliant on white goodwill or, just as misleadingly, as patriotic "good soldiers" blindly devoted to the Union cause and serving unquestioningly under the terms and conditions that Union commanders offered them. To some degree, those viewpoints reflected a disposition toward the character of African American slaves before the Civil War as well, one that emphasized deference, lack of political sophistication, provinciality, and a weak level of organization.

This scene in New Bern hints at a very different view of the slaves' Civil War. Instead of docility, Kinsley witnessed a posture of militancy and defiance. Instead of freedpeople who were fragmented and disorganized, he saw recently liberated slaves who were carefully organized, with a command structure and strong leadership. Instead of their being confused by their first taste of freedom, he saw them acting as thoughtful planners and savvy political strategists. Instead of unquestioning former slaves displaying loyalty to the Union cause, he saw freedpeople attempting to shape the Union cause. Instead of ex-slaves imbibing the politics of white abolitionists or Republicans, he saw people charting their own political course. Instead of black women being spectators to the war, he saw women such as Mary Ann Starkey acting at center stage. And instead of contrabands looking to northern blacks for political guidance, Kinsley glimpsed a new politics emerging out of the struggle against slavery in the South.

ברים

As historian Stephanie McCurry has recently pointed out, the Confederacy was created most fundamentally to protect the rights of white southerners to treat blacks as property. That achievement cut against the grain of history. At a time when the arc of history in the West bent toward more liberal, humanitarian values, the founders of the Confederacy forged the first modern state that defined itself in opposition to democracy and freedom. The country's Founding Fathers, Georgia political leader and Confederate vice president Alexander Stephens declared in March 1861, had built a nation "upon the assumption of the equality of the races." In contrast, he continued, "our new government is founded upon exactly the opposite ideas: its foundations are laid, its cornerstone rests, upon the great truth that the negro is not equal to the white man; that slavery is his natural and moral condition."[12]

Building his argument on the U.S. Supreme Court's *Dred Scott* decision, Confederate president Jefferson Davis asserted that "the condition of slavery is with us nothing but a form of civil government for a class of people not fit to govern themselves." The provisional Congress of the Confederate States of America codified that view in the new nation's constitution in February 1861. The Confederate Constitution made clear that slavery—the right of white men to hold blacks as property without the interference of the state—was the breakaway republic's defining creed.[13] Even in a southern state with comparatively few slaveholders and whose citizens had originally voted against secession, the issue was clear. Independence, North Carolina's governor wrote President Lincoln during the war, "is about the preservation of our political institutions, the principal of which is slavery."[14] While Union leaders were reluctant to define the war as being about slavery, the Confederacy's leaders had no such hesitation—and neither did the slaves.

As long ago as 1935, the great African American scholar W. E. B. Du Bois put the black freedom struggle within the South at the center of the Civil War and Reconstruction in his classic *Black Reconstruction*.[15] At the outset of the war, Du Bois observed, "the Negro himself was not seriously considered by the majority of [white] men, North or South." But by withholding their labor from the Confederacy in their "General Strike," the slaves drained the vigor of the rebellion. Eventually, the South's former slaves also fought for the Union in large numbers; approximately 180,000 blacks, including more than 98,000 recruited in the South, served in the Union army or navy. According to Du Bois, they shaped the very meaning of the war and the fate of the United States of America. His view of the war, however, was far from the standard taught in schools and universities. His work long remained on the margins of American history.

More recently, a new generation of scholars has begun to rediscover that powerful tradition of African American militancy within the Civil War South. They have begun to sketch the outlines of a conflict that was not merely "the Brothers' War" but was one in which black southerners were the driving force behind the struggle against slavery and powerful agents of their own destiny.[16] In important ways, their work creates the space in which we can now make intellectual sense out of African American leaders like Abraham Galloway. At the same time, the scene that unfolded that night in New Bern—and the larger story of Galloway's life that will unfold in the pages to come—brings flesh and bone to that new vision of the Civil War.

For all that story's broader implications about the former slaves and the Civil War, the center of its intrigue for Kinsley remained that "man of more than ordinary ability . . . named Abraham Galloway." Like Kinsley, I, too, found Galloway difficult to get out of my mind after my first encounter with him. After I read Kinsley's reminiscences, the first thing I did was check to see if I could learn more about Galloway in books and journal articles. My inquiries had mixed results. I discovered that he did appear in some historical writings; he was not completely unknown, as I had feared. But there was not very much about him. I found only brief entries on Galloway in several specialized biographical dictionaries and a few short passages about his political life during Reconstruction in broader, scholarly works.[17]

In *Black Reconstruction*, for instance, W. E. B. Du Bois remarks that Galloway was an important figure at a constitutional convention held in North Carolina three years after the war, and in 1967 a pioneering regional historian, W. McKee Evans, wrote powerfully about Galloway in his classic account of Reconstruction in the Cape Fear Valley.[18] Over the last generation, several of the foremost historians of the United States—including John Hope Franklin, Leon Litwack, Eric Foner, and Steven Hahn—have also caught sight of Galloway briefly while chronicling the African American freedom struggle after the Civil War.[19] But those scholars were telling other tales, and when it came to Galloway, they glimpsed only a few striking scenes from the war's aftermath—a quick look here, a telling quote there. They had no way of knowing how much more was there.

With few published sources to guide me, I began my quest to discover Galloway's life by working in widening circles outward from that midnight rendezvous in Starkey's attic. That research led me much farther from New Bern than I had expected, and to a much bigger story than I had anticipated. Over the course of a decade, I pursued Galloway's trail through dozens of archives, libraries, and museums across the United States and beyond. The research was challenging and often frustrating, but always enthralling. Figuratively speaking, I followed Galloway from that candlelit attic to slave camps deep inside the Confederacy. I tracked him to secretive antislavery groups stretching from Ohio to Massachusetts, to John Brown's inner circle, and along a clandestine pathway to freedom that used the nation's seaways. Galloway led me to an astonishing meeting with President

Abraham Lincoln at the White House, but also into a macabre theater of race and retribution inside a Union prison camp.

I followed Galloway as well to New Orleans and up the Mississippi River, where he came to know a betrayal of slaves by the Federal army that fueled his fierce skepticism of the Union's commitment to the African American freedom struggle so evident that night in Mary Ann Starkey's attic. I followed him into sprawling refugee camps, to battlefields littered with the corpses of massacred black soldiers, and into disease-scared cities where the only signs of life seemed to be hearses and funerals. He led me farther to black exile communities on the Canadian frontier and to an antislavery conspiracy that reached all the way to the West Indies. From his childhood to his deathbed, I eventually learned, Galloway lived in a world of clandestine meetings and plots, gunrunners, subterfuge, spies, and assassins.

For a long time, I thought that Galloway was solely a man of the shadows—of slave quarters, dark alleys, and nocturnal missions behind enemy lines. But as I continued my research, I also found him standing before adoring crowds, in the North and the South, that came to hear his impassioned calls for political equality during the Civil War. I also discovered him, during Reconstruction, speaking to great gatherings of the South's freedpeople in convention halls, legislative buildings, and church pulpits. I even came across accounts of him demanding justice and equality from a rooftop, while in the torch-lit streets below, his countrymen and countrywomen rallied to his side. In those same years, I found him fighting the Ku Klux Klan in the streets.

By those diverse routes, Galloway's life revealed a Civil War very different from the one I once thought I knew. What emerged was a vivid portrait of the war from the slaves' point of view and the saga of a remarkable life whose arc has much to teach about slavery, the war, and Reconstruction. Galloway was an extraordinary individual by any measure, but above all he embodied and gave voice to a revolutionary generation of African American activists in the South that has largely been forgotten. Through his life, we can see their dreams for freedom and their passion for justice. In his deeds and his words, we can see their determination to play a decisive role in the downfall of the Confederacy and to build a United States that might live up to its democratic ideals. In the brief, mercurial life of Abraham Galloway, a late-night gathering in a candlelit attic opens the door into an important lost chapter in American history.

The Fire *of* Freedom

1

At River's Edge

ABRAHAM GALLOWAY GREW UP IN A WORLD THAT GAZED OUT TO THE open sea. He was born on 8 February 1837 in a little hamlet of ship pilots and fishermen called Smithville.[1] The village perched at the mouth of the Cape Fear River, twenty-eight miles downriver of Wilmington, North Carolina. At the time of Galloway's birth, Smithville had a population of roughly 800 inhabitants, nearly half of them slaves. Pilots had settled there by the inlet a century earlier so that they could watch for ships signaling for their services as they approached the river's mouth from the Atlantic. Smithville grew up around the cottages of the ship pilots, though no one bothered to lay out the boundaries or incorporate the town until 1792. A small garrison of soldiers was also nearby at Fort Johnston, where the walls were constructed of what its slave builders called a "batter" of sand and oyster shells cooked together. The fort overlooked the river and had played a key part in Wilmington's defenses during the Revolutionary War and the War of 1812.[2]

The Smithville of Galloway's childhood consisted mostly of weathered clapboard cottages, fishing camps, and a few modest summer inns. The only public buildings were the fort, a plain wood-framed courthouse, a small seamen's hospital, and a jail that, judging from a surviving inventory of its inmates, was a second home to a great many of the pilots. There were two churches, Grace Methodist and St. James Episcopal, and a graveyard shaded by live oak trees. Legend had it that one old oak marked the eastern end of an important trading path that ran between the coastal Siouan tribes and the Catawba Indians in the upcountry. Nearby, the last of the local Indian tribes had made their final stand in a battle on a high sand dune called Sugar Loaf in 1718. During Galloway's childhood, river pilots still used Sugar Loaf as a navigational landmark between Smithville and Wilmington.

The village had a casual, seaside air: fishing nets dried in backyards, cows and horses wandered the streets, and gangs of men and boys could always be found lollygagging around the wharf waiting for the next Wilmington or Charleston packet. From a watchtower on the waterfront, pilots kept a lookout for incoming vessels, while slaves plied the river in boats loaded with fish and oysters. Sometimes the slave boatmen sang sea chanteys that they had learned from sailors, such as the one about a beautiful Jamaican mulatto that a Smithville visitor heard slave boatmen croon a few years before Galloway's birth. The visitor wrote the chantey's first lines in his diary: "Oh Sally was a fine girl, oh! Sally was a fine girl, oh!"[3]

At dusk Smithville's residents watched the faint silhouettes of slaves paddling dugout canoes on the river. Many slipped out of rice field canals upriver by night to get off their plantations.[4] Under cover of darkness, they fished and hunted, attended worship services, or visited loved ones. A number cut firewood after finishing their field work and secretly sold it to steamboats moored in the river. Such forays were likely the young Abraham Galloway's first acquaintance with the world of stealth and darkness.

In Galloway's youth, wealthy planters and merchants and their families came to Smithville to get away from the low country, with its swamps and flooded rice fields, during the malaria season. They enjoyed long walks by the waterfront and played about in boats. In the surrounding countryside, the toll of plantation bells marked the rhythm of daily life, but in the village itself, slave life revolved around wind and tide and the comings and goings of ships. Those ships may have inspired in the young Galloway, as they did in Frederick Douglass, visions of liberty and freedom. In his classic account of his boyhood as a slave on Maryland's Eastern Shore and in the port of Baltimore published in 1845, Douglass recalled the "beautiful vessels, robed in purest white" that might "yet bear me into freedom."[5]

❧

Galloway's mother and father also lived by the sea. His mother, Hester Hankins, and his father, John Wesley Galloway, both resided in Smithville.[6] She was a slave; he was a free white man. Born in 1820, Hester Hankins had skin the color of ebony, never learned to read or write, and in legal terms, belonged to a local woman named Louisa Hankins, the widow of a Methodist clergyman who died in a boat capsizing off Oak Island in 1835. Hester Hankins probably worked as a house servant and occasional field

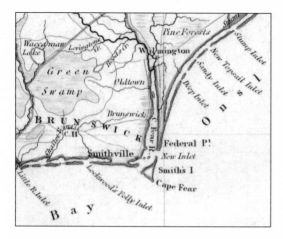

Wilmington, Smithville, and vicinity around the time of Galloway's birth. Detail from Society for the Diffusion of Useful Knowledge, *North America*, sheet 11, *Parts of North and South Carolina* (London: Chapman & Hall, 1844). Originally published in 1833. Courtesy, New Hanover County Public Library, Wilmington, N.C.

hand.[7] How she met Abraham's father remains unclear. All that is known is that she bore her first child when she was seventeen years old. Hester Hankins named her child "Abraham"—his full name was Abraham Harris Galloway—after the great Old Testament nomad who led his followers from Ur to Canaan.[8] She and her son Abraham remained close throughout his life.

The life of Abraham's father is better-documented. John Wesley Galloway's extended family included some of the leading planters in Brunswick County, of which Smithville was the county seat. John Wesley, though, was not a planter but a boatman, a ship's pilot on the Cape Fear River and, sometime after 1850, captain of the Federal lightship moored off Frying Pan Shoals.[9] A dashing, free-spirited young man with penchants for both classical learning and the camaraderie of sailors and fishermen, he was descended from seafarers who had left Scotland to settle in America in the eighteenth century. His ancestors included ship's pilots in Charleston Harbor and a grandfather who led Stamp Act protests against the British and joined the Sons of Liberty during the Revolutionary War. His father left the sea trades, invested in slaves, and built a plantation on the salt marshes of Lockwood Folly River, south of Smithville.

Forsaking his father's life as a planter, John Wesley made his home among the lowly pilots' cottages in Smithville.[10] A tall, lean, broad-shouldered man, he was said to be "strong, manly, attractive." Another of his sons later recalled that their father was "very muscular, active as a kitten, and possessing the kind of courage out of which heroes are made." He added that "in common parlance he would not do to fool with."[11] According to family stories passed down through the generations, John Wesley

Galloway also possessed an exaggerated sense of honor and a stubbornness that bordered on arrogance.[12] He shared many of the aristocratic values of his wealthier cousins, but he never owned much more property than a small lot in Smithville and the six African Americans that he inherited after his father's death in 1826.[13] In a little more than a decade, John Wesley lost or gave up all but one of those slaves. His last remaining slave, Amos Galloway, became Hester Hankins's husband in 1846.

The circumstances of the relationship between John Wesley Galloway and Hester Hankins remain murky. At the time that Abraham was conceived, the summer of 1836, John Wesley was a twenty-five-year-old boatman in the employ of the U.S. Coast Survey, which was constructing a fort on the south side of the main inlet into the Cape Fear River. Though state law and social custom strictly prohibited sexual relationships between slaves and free persons, they were commonplace in Brunswick County, as elsewhere in the South. In the case of John Wesley and Hester, a family bond may have brought them into the same orbit. John Wesley was a second cousin to Hester's owner.

The most striking characteristic of the relationship between Hester Hankins and John Wesley Galloway is that, according to the adult Abraham, John Wesley "recognized me as his son and protected me as far as he was allowed to do so."[14] White men frequently fathered children by slave women in the plantation South, sometimes as part of affairs of the heart but more typically as a product of coercion or rape. For a white man to publicly acknowledge a slave child, however, was a rarity in the antebellum South. John Wesley's recognition of his paternity of Abraham held special significance because it was also a public avowal of his relationship with Hester Hankins. In 1837, when Abraham was born, neither the law, church doctrine, nor local custom encouraged John Wesley to acknowledge or accept any responsibility for an African American son. Quite the opposite was true. John Wesley's public claim of his fatherhood and his efforts to protect his slave son must have been significant to Abraham, perhaps even more so for their rarity.

Abraham's words—his father "protected me as far as he was allowed to do so"—also suggest that he had a rebellious and probably perilous childhood. He obviously needed his father's protection at least occasionally or he would not have been aware of John Wesley's willingness to save him from harm or, for that matter, discovered the limits of his ability to do so. How much protection John Wesley could give Abraham is questionable. If he had been one of the Cape Fear's great planters, the sort of man who oversaw a small fiefdom and on whom an entire neighborhood relied for credit and the use of his rice mill or turpentine distillery, his sway would have been far more considerable. If he chose to do so, such a planter might cast a blanket of protection over a slave child in another man's possession. That was not John Wesley's situation. He was of good family and well respected along the waterfront but scarcely a figure that inspired fear or awe by virtue of his wealth and power. When he shielded Abraham from the whip or the auction block, he did so either by drawing on bonds of family and friendship or by the fierceness of his temper and his capacity to inspire fear in those who crossed him.

Two years after Abraham's birth, in 1839, John Wesley Galloway married the daughter of one of the other ship pilots in Smithville. The couple had eight children together before the Civil War. How much contact the young Abraham had with his younger white half-brothers and half-sisters during his childhood is not known. However, in a legal deposition taken more than half a century after the Civil War, Abraham's widow indicated that her husband had often spoken familiarly of John Wesley's oldest son from his marriage, Alexander Swift Galloway. Swift Galloway, as he was known, was only three years younger than Abraham and seems to have been one of Abraham's playmates when they were children in Smithville.[15]

As the two half-brothers grew older, their fates took very different turns. Along the Cape Fear River a slave child's life was always, to borrow Tennyson's famous phrase, "red in tooth and claw." The fragility of slave families and the hardness of slave children's lives are the dominant themes in court documents, bills of sale, and wills and estate records, but most especially in the accounts of antebellum life written by former slaves.[16] Those firsthand accounts of growing up in slavery on the Lower Cape Fear offer a litany of bloody scenes. Typically, the memoir of the Reverend William H. Robinson, who was born in Wilmington in 1848, recalled how, as a child, he commonly witnessed slave women beaten, abused, and sexually humiliated in public. He saw children whipped. He was only twelve years old when he witnessed a young friend—a fugitive slave—shot to death by bounty hunters. Over the years, the boy lost his father, his mother, and all of his brothers and sisters to the auction block. He himself was beaten severely at least once, probably at the age of nine or ten, when he tried to put himself between his mother and a brutal assailant.[17]

The most powerful scene in his memoir, *From Log Cabin to the Pulpit; or, Fifteen Years in Slavery*, is a vivid account of his sale at the slave market in downtown Wilmington. He was twelve years old at the time. Saying little about his own anguish, Robinson focused instead on the plight of a young mother and her children whom he met in a slave pen where they were kept in the weeks leading up to the auction. The sale itself was traumatic, but what came next was worse. During a long march, in shackles, from Wilmington to a slave market in Richmond, the young Robinson watched the slave trader viciously whip the young mother in front of her children when they could not keep up with the other slaves. In the end, the slave trader sold her toddler and infant away from her so that they would not slow him down. The depth of her sorrow at that moment haunted Robinson for the rest of his life.[18]

That was young Abraham Galloway's world. Unlike Robinson, he never disclosed details of his childhood. But whether his early years closely resembled those of Robinson, were comparatively carefree, or were even worse, his life as a slave ultimately had to separate him from his white half-brother. While Abraham never attended school and never learned to read or write as a child, Swift studied with a master scholar, Walter Gilman Curtis, a tutor on a local plantation and a former Harvard professor. Looking away from the sea for his livelihood, Swift finished his studies and taught school in Smithville just prior to the Civil War. After the fall of Fort Sumter, he enlisted in the Confederate army as a second lieutenant in the 3rd North Carolina Infantry. He was wounded seriously at the Battle of Malvern Hill, but he recovered, joined another infantry unit, and was promoted eventually to captain. Near the war's end, Swift served as superintendent of the Confederate prison camp in Salisbury, North Carolina.[19] All of that time, his older half-brother and childhood playmate was doing everything in his power to bring about the Confederacy's downfall.

☙

Galloway was never his father's property. Instead, a youth named Marsden Milton Hankins held the deed to him, Galloway later said, "from infancy."[20] Hankins was a Smithville lad only seven years his senior.[21] The boy was the son of the Methodist minister who perished in the 1835 boat capsizing off Oak Island—he was one of the few survivors—and he and his mother, Louisa Hankins, remained in Smithville at least until Abraham's birth in 1837.[22] The widow Hankins eventually remarried, giving her hand to Miles Potter, an older planter who owned twenty-two slaves and 400 acres at Town Creek in 1850.[23] In time, Milton apprenticed under a master mechanic and moved upriver to Wilmington to work as a railroad mechanic and engineer. At roughly the same time, probably when he was

Market Street, Wilmington, N.C., 1855. From *Ballou's Pictorial Drawing Room Companion*, 24 February 1855. Courtesy, New Hanover County Public Library, Wilmington, N.C.

ten or eleven years old, Galloway apprenticed as a brick mason in either Wilmington or Charleston, the two closest cities where the demand for skilled building trades was sufficient to require master artisans to take on apprentices. As he grew into maturity, he acquired the traditional arts of brick masonry, which, if a typical apprenticeship, included the crafts of excavating clay from the earth, shaping bricks, firing kilns, and building projects as low as root cellars and as high as church steeples.[24]

By the time that young Galloway became a master brick mason, he had moved to Wilmington to reside with his owner, Milton Hankins. Spurred by skyrocketing world demand for cotton and naval stores, the seaport was booming: exports were rising rapidly, ship and railroad traffic was expanding, an architectural revival was under way, and new immigrants arrived daily. Over the previous decade, Wilmington had become the state's largest city and was, with just under 10,000 residents in 1860, only a little smaller than Atlanta. It was also the state's busiest seaport, as well as the home to a politically conscious, militant class of African American laborers who made their livings on the docks and waterways. More than half the city's population were slaves, many of whom were skilled craftsmen like Galloway. Their political outlook was decidedly sophisticated. Unlike young Abraham, many had learned to read and write, some of them at a clandestine school established by a prosperous free black carpenter named James D. Sampson and run by his daughters.[25] The harbor bustled with schooners bound for New York City and Boston, cotton haulers loading bales for Liverpool, and full-rigged ships carrying barrels of turpentine and pitch all over the world.

Sometime between his wedding in 1851 and 1855, when he first bought property in the city, Milton Hankins began his professional career in Wilmington as a foreman and chief engineer at the shops of the Wilmington & Manchester Railroad. The Hankinses and Galloway settled into a residence in the 800 block of North Fourth Street, near the railroad tracks and a short walk from both the waterfront and the rail yards.[26] The neighborhood was not among the town's most elegant. Free black tradesmen, German shopkeepers, and hundreds of rail yard workers, white and black, free and slave, called it home. With free black builders and mechanics as their immediate neighbors, they resided in a simple, one-story cottage with a front porch facing North Fourth Street, surrounded by a smokehouse, a stable, a dairy, and a slave cabin or two.[27]

Galloway later described Marsden Milton Hankins as a tall, slim, whiskered "man of very good disposition" who "always said he would sell before he would use a whip." He and Hankins were second cousins by marriage, through John Wesley Galloway's family, and familial bonds may have played a part in Hankins's restraint. Abraham later declared that he had been "rocked in a Republican cradle," which, since the antislavery Republican Party was not founded until he was seventeen years old, presumably meant that Hankins and his mother, Louisa, also had some ambivalence about slavery. Whatever her political views, his wife, Mary Ann, was evidently not so even-tempered. Galloway later remembered her as a "very mean woman" who "would whip contrary to [her husband's] orders." Galloway never acknowledged feeling the sting of her lash, but he might have been referring to others. As a young married man, Marsden Milton Hankins owned two additional slaves. They were young female house servants, probably a housekeeper and a cook, who labored directly under his wife's hand.[28]

As a master builder, young Abraham Galloway had the potential to be highly profitable for Hankins. As a tradesman himself, however, Hankins could not closely supervise a slave in a different trade. He consequently left Galloway to seek out brick masonry jobs when, where, and how he pleased so long as he continued to bring $180 a year into the Hankins household. At that time, that was a common arrangement for enslaved builders and mechanics in the South, particularly in southern seaports.[29] Demands on the slave tradesmen usually proved arduous, strictures on mobility were tight, and reprisals for subversive activity were severe; but they still had a greater chance to interact socially and politically beyond the sight of whites than did most other slaves. In Wilmington, many enslaved builders took advantage of that limited degree of latitude. They corresponded with black abolitionists in the northern states, followed news of African American freedom struggles across the Western Hemisphere, and when possible, sheltered fugitive slaves. By their hearths they also instructed children to view the local African American community as their extended family and to look even to black strangers for help in times of trouble. They taught little boys, and girls as well, how to find a hiding place in the canebrakes outside Wilmington, in case they should ever need it, and also where to find concealed scythes with which to fight the bloodhounds that would be put on their trails.[30]

That tradition of slave defiance had deep roots in Wilmington's African American community. A generation before the Civil War, a free black man named David Walker wrote the most powerful statement of the collective political philosophy that arose out of Wilmington and other maritime districts that fringed the Atlantic in the Age of Revolution. Born in Wilmington in or around 1797, Walker lived there as a youth but left the seaport around 1820—about the time that Hester Hankins, Galloway's mother, was born. He eventually settled in Boston, where he opened a secondhand clothes and tailor's shop near the waterfront. Becoming a leader in Boston's abolitionist movement, which at the time was still small and predominantly African American, he wrote one of the founding documents of American antislavery thought. First published in 1829, his pamphlet was titled *Walker's Appeal, in Four Articles: Together with a Preamble to the Coloured Citizens of the World, but in Particular, and Very Expressly, to Those of the United States of America.* Smuggled into southern seaports mainly by black sailors, the *Appeal* called for the equality of all men, regardless of race, and for the abolition of slavery throughout the United States. While that was already an incendiary proposal in that era, Walker did more than plea for the abolition of slavery. Most controversially, he insisted that slaves had the moral right, even the moral obligation, to attain liberty at all costs, including armed struggle. Better to die in open rebellion, Walker counseled the slaves of the South, than to endure another generation in bondage.[31]

Moreover, the *Appeal* did not merely plead with slaveholders for freedom and justice. Instead, Walker demanded them as God-given rights, as natural to the state of humanity as the Declaration of Independence's rights to "life, liberty, and the pursuit of happiness." Walker prophesied calamity in the South if the region's leaders did not forsake a slave economy. The *Appeal* called for the creation of an American society grounded in a spirit of common humanity more respectful of all peoples, including laborers of all races, women, and the poor and destitute. Walker's arguments outraged white southern leaders, who soon blamed the *Appeal* for inspiring the slave Nat Turner's bloody revolt in Southampton County, Virginia, in 1831.

The significance of the *Appeal* derived to an important extent from Walker's revelation of a broader intellectual culture of slave resistance and his articulation of an antislavery political philosophy shared among southern blacks but rarely expressed in writing. To slaveholders, the *Appeal* was an alarming call to action. The most prescient planters conceded that the pamphlet's revolutionary ideals had deep roots in the African American community and particularly in the black communities within southern seaports. That realization left many fearful. Lost on nearly all slaveholders was Walker's earnest plea that the end of slavery need not lead to violence or civil war and, indeed, his hope that blacks and whites might live together one day in peace. "Throw away your fears and prejudices then, and enlighten us and treat us like men, and we will like you more than we do now hate you," Walker pleaded. "Treat us then like men and we will be your friends. . . . The whole of the past will be sunk into oblivion, and we yet, under God, will become a united and happy people." Violence, Walker insisted, was only the last resort of the enslaved.

Reluctant to acknowledge abolitionist ideas originating within the local slave community, Wilmington's white political leaders seemed to find solace in blaming the *Appeal*'s revolutionary ideas on free black sailors from ports outside the South.[32] After confiscating copies of Walker's *Appeal* in Wilmington in 1830 and arresting several slaves, including a tavern keeper named Jacob Cowan, who was caught with 200 copies, the town's leaders also struck out brutally at black seamen, but apparently they did not consider the fact that Walker had been born and raised in their city.[33] Few, if any, recognized that his *Appeal* and its call for armed revolt against slavery expressed a collective vision of African American struggle that arose out of the maritime South.[34]

Copies of the *Appeal* provoked fears of slave insurrection in seaports as far south as New Orleans. The confiscation of copies in Wilmington also triggered a political chain reaction. Local authorities placed severe new restrictions on the mobility of local blacks, free and slave, and harshly curtailed their civil liberties. Homegrown black abolitionists reeled at the drastic new punishments put in place for any free black caught spreading antislavery propaganda or helping slaves to escape from the city. Especially distrustful of black watermen, the Wilmington City Council banned slaves from working on some boats. The North Carolina General Assembly enacted a law in 1830 that quarantined ships employing free black sailors and banned all local African Americans from visiting those vessels, under penalty of thirty-nine lashes. Wary of the politics of free black sailors— "all of them . . . abolitionists," warned a correspondent to a Wilmington newspaper—the deeply rattled legislators made it a crime for them even to speak with local slaves. Five years later, the backlash still reverberated through the corridors of power. At the state constitutional convention in 1835, the delegates rescinded the most fundamental rights of the state's free black citizenry. Freedoms of assembly, worship, voting, speech, travel, and trial by a jury of one's peers all ended. Harsh measures, perhaps, but the state's legislators looked at David Walker's *Appeal* as a declaration of war on the southern way of life. In a sense, they were not mistaken.[35]

The harsh reaction to Walker's *Appeal* dovetailed with the response to Nat Turner's 1831 insurrection in Southampton County, Virginia. Rumors of insurrection raced up and down the Cape Fear River following Turner's revolt. Turner, a messianic slave rebel, had led an uprising of slaves who killed more than sixty whites. When Virginia militiamen thwarted his ambition to spread the rebellion further, Turner hid for nearly two months in the swamps along the North Carolina border. During that time, slaveholders feared that his revolt might still grow into a broader insurrection. Their anxiety led to hysteria and violence throughout much of eastern North Carolina. No place experienced a worse bloodletting than the counties along the Cape Fear River.[36]

In Smithville, where Galloway would soon be born, panic seized a white citizenry terrified by the prospect of a local slave uprising. Whites garrisoned themselves in Fort Johnston and beseeched the state's governor to send arms and troops to protect them from slave rebels. Along the Cape Fear River, planters shackled their slaves, ransacked slave cabins in a search for weapons, and put dozens of suspected insurrectionists to the lash. Some of the most violent suppression occurred in Kenansville, sixty miles north of Wilmington, where local militia tortured twenty-one slaves to compel them to reveal details of an alleged conspiracy. In their agony, the slaves confessed their plot to burn plantations, kill their owners, and march east to plunder and torch Wilmington. Kenansville leaders burned two of the slaves at the stake. In Wilmington, city leaders enacted a curfew for the enslaved and searched their quarters. After interrogating several dozen slaves, they beheaded at least four men and mounted their heads on tall posts along each of the main roads in and out of the city, a warning to those who shared the revolutionary ideals of David Walker. Listening to older slaves describing those dark days, young Abraham Galloway learned the risks of a life dedicated to the struggle for freedom.[37]

2

The Secret Feelings of Their Hearts

IN EARLY 1857, YOUNG ABRAHAM GALLOWAY VOWED TO DEPART THE world of his childhood. At twenty years old, he had lived by the banks of the Cape Fear River all his life and had never traveled more than a day's journey from his friends and family in Smithville and Wilmington. But that spring he and a friend grew determined, they later explained, "that liberty was worth dying for, and that it was their duty to strike for freedom even if it should cost them their lives."[1] His friend was a slave named Richard Eden, a barber by trade and a couple years older than Galloway. While they resided in Wilmington, the two young men grew close enough that they eventually dared "to communicate the secret feelings of their hearts."[2]

A yearning for freedom was not the only reason behind their decision to risk their lives and attempt to escape from Wilmington. Galloway had also been having difficulty earning the wages that Milton Hankins expected of him. A large influx of Irish and German immigrants into the city had tightened the local labor market, increased the competition for building jobs, and exerted a downward pressure on wages. Tensions between enslaved builders and free white tradesmen heightened and occasionally became bitter.[3] The danger for a slave builder like Galloway was greater than merely low wages, however. Galloway's value in dollars represented a significant part of Hankins's total worth, and the young male slave was ultimately his most important asset. If Galloway did not bring enough money into the household, Hankins may have felt compelled to put him up for sale at the local slave market. A strong young man with a skilled trade was worth a great deal, probably in the neighborhood of $1,000 or $1,200, at a time when Hankins's house and lot on Fourth Street had a tax value of less than $100. Under those circumstances, Galloway had good cause to fear his sale to parts unknown.

The fear of sale spurred many slaves to flight. Few would have resented the prospect of being sold more than Galloway, though. He was a prideful, thin-skinned youth, proud of his abilities and prickly about the slightest affront to his dignity. He was also all too familiar with the slave pens downtown, where auctioneers and buyers treated blacks no different from livestock.[4] Like all local slaves, Galloway had seen the caravans of chained black men, women, and children trudging through town along the Post Road.[5] No slave could reliably protect himself or herself from such a fate, but Galloway would have taken great risks to avoid being herded into those slave pens, put on public display on that auction block, or confined in those shackles.

His co-conspirator, Richard Eden, had other considerations in mind when he joined Galloway's bid to gain his freedom. Prior to 1857, Eden had managed to fashion a measure of independence for himself within the seaport. He recalled his owner, a woman named Mary Ormes or Mary Lorens, as "tender hearted," and another contemporary remembered her as "very indulgent with her slaves for the times." With her support, Eden served as the barber at the Carolina Hotel and shared his profits with her. He always "had some spending money by him," a contemporary recalled.[6] Eden had also learned to read and write by trading little pies and banjo songs for lessons with a group of schoolchildren who were devoted to him. They called themselves the "Pie Society."[7]

The relative equanimity of Eden's life changed in 1857. Sometime early that year, Wilmington authorities discovered that he had clandestinely married a free mixed-race woman. Their nuptials broke a state law prohibiting slaves and free citizens, of any color, from marrying.[8] Eden faced a penalty of thirty-nine lashes on his bare back under the terms of the law. Dreading the whip's lash and fearing that he might be torn from his wife's side forever in retribution for his crime, the star-crossed Eden decided that he had little left to lose and grew determined to escape from the seaport.

National political affairs may also have influenced the timing of the young men's decision to flee Wilmington. That spring the U.S. Supreme Court ruled that blacks could never be full citizens of the United States. Widely considered today one of the most extreme misreadings of the Constitution in U.S. history, *Dred Scott v. Sandford* was one of a number of incidents in the late 1850s that smothered African American hopes that the nation would ever rise to its democratic ideals. Scott, a slave, had sued for his freedom and the freedom of his wife and two daughters because they had been held in northern states and territories where slavery was illegal at the time. In the *Dred Scott* decision, however, the country's highest court decreed that Scott did not have legal standing to bring such a suit in a U.S. court of law because the Founding Fathers never intended that black men could be citizens and thus they could not avail themselves of the courts. Among free blacks, *Dred Scott* inspired a wave of emigration out of the United States, principally to Canada, West Africa, and the West Indies. The timing may have been only coincidental, but Galloway and Eden decided to flee the American South and head to Canada almost immediately after the Supreme Court's ruling that the sons and daughters of Africa were, as Chief Justice Roger Taney wrote, "so far inferior that they had no rights which the white man was bound to respect."[9]

Grave dangers lay ahead of them. If their plan went awry, slave hunters would have pursued the two friends with fervor. They shot to kill and frequently employed ferocious hounds especially bred for tracking and catching fugitive slaves. Even white citizens in Wilmington recalled the viciousness of the dogs, in part because they had been known to break their leashes and attack innocent bystanders.[10] If captured alive, the two young African Americans would have received the lashes that Eden was so determined to avoid; it was a torturous punishment that, depending on the whip master's determination, could disfigure, lame, or kill.

Galloway and Eden also had to weigh the possibility of being sold away from Wilmington if they were caught. In the 1850s, sugarcane and cotton planters in the Deep South had a seemingly bottomless appetite for Carolina slave labor. Local masters regularly wielded the threat of a harsher fate to keep their slaves in line.[11] By selling slaves to Alabama, Louisiana, or Mississippi, a Wilmington planter or merchant might make a cautionary tale out of their rebelliousness; the alternative, whipping, left scars that diminished a slave's financial value. The swampy rice fields that they could see just across the Cape Fear River, on Eagles Island, also had a notorious reputation for breaking slave laborers' bodies and souls, but few, if any, of those rice plantations could rival the hardships of the plantations in the Deep South.

Galloway and Eden planned to travel north concealed in a ship's hold, a well-worn maritime passage to freedom. Over the generations, many Wilmington slaves had managed to board sailing vessels and make their way to a free country, but it was far from easy. The way north was risky and dangerous. No reliable numbers exist to show what percentage of fugitive slaves reached the Atlantic, but most—probably the large majority—never made it to the wharf; those who did rarely made it to sea.[12]

Foot of Market Street, Wilmington, N.C., 1873, much as it would have looked when Galloway escaped from the seaport. Rufus Morgan, photographer. Courtesy, New Hanover County Public Library, Wilmington, N.C.

In addition, anyone who helped the two young slaves was taking his or her life into their hands. The penalty for a free sailor convicted of abetting a slave to escape by ship was the hangman's noose. Slaveholders did not always wait for a judge or jury, either. The case of a Wilmington slave pilot named Peter illustrates the point. According to a memoir written by his son, the Reverend William H. Robinson, Peter played a central role in an antislavery underground that had been aiding slaves to escape through the seaport for years. Local authorities watched him carefully, however, and not long before the Civil War, they believed they had the evidence they needed. Convinced of his complicity in the antislavery underground, Peter's owner sold him into the Deep South. His wife and children never saw him again. Not long afterward, according to Robinson, vigilantes murdered one of Peter's co-conspirators, a Quaker oysterman, for his secret efforts to help local slaves escape Wilmington by sea.[13] For everyone's sake, Galloway and Eden had to be cautious.

Perhaps with the help of a slave waterman like Peter, Galloway and Eden identified a ship captain willing to conceal them in the hold of his vessel. The captain hailed from Wilmington, Delaware, and commanded a schooner tied up at the city wharf. The vessel was bound for Philadelphia, in the free state of Pennsylvania. Even if the vessel's master had been recommended to them, Galloway and Eden had to approach him in a delicate manner. Beyond arranging to meet him in the most careful of ways, they had to hold a conversation with him that would not arouse his suspicions in case he was not "true to Freedom." They had to conduct that discussion "in such a way, that even the captain would not really understand what they were up to, should he be found untrue," they told an ally later. The captain quickly understood their intent and did prove to be "true to Freedom."[14] One day in early June, the two young slaves made their way to the wharf.

Out of a habitual caution against implicating co-conspirators, Galloway never disclosed how he and Eden managed to get aboard the schooner. Some fugitive slaves watched the tide, clung to the night, and rowed boats or swam out into the harbor to board vessels. Others made their move in daylight. They relied on blending into the crowds of slaves who trundled cargo and provisions aboard departing vessels, or else they endeavored to join the gangs of black ship's carpenters, caulkers, and blacksmiths making vessels ready for sail. However Galloway and Eden boarded the schooner, the captain hid them in a hold laden with "naval stores"—barrels of tar, rosin, and spirits of turpentine.

Once Galloway and Eden descended into that dark cargo hold, they had no illusions that they were out of danger. Provision inspectors might search the vessel and discover them. Any sailor who found them—and could not be bribed or beaten into holding his tongue—could turn them in for a bounty. Both misfortunes often happened. In addition, the Cape Fear Commissioners of Navigation and Pilotage employed roustabouts to fog seagoing vessels with turpentine smoke in order to drive concealed slaves up onto the top deck. By decree of the Wilmington town council, every ship that called in the port that was bound for a northern state had to be fumigated before the crew weighed anchor.[15]

Harbor inspectors fumigated the ships by burning turpentine dross in their holds. In summertime, local people burned the dregs from turpentine distilleries in cast-iron pots and wooden troughs in order to ward off mosquitoes. The fumigation of ships was probably done in much the same way, except that the inspectors placed their smoldering containers in the lower decks and shut the hatches prior to a vessel's departure. In an enclosed space, the effect would have been much like tear gas. According to Underground Railroad leaders, the turpentine smoke severely damaged the eyes, nostrils, mouth, throat, and lungs. For slaves who refused to come out of hiding, the smoke was said to be lethal.[16]

Galloway and Eden devised an inventive strategy for foiling the fumigators. Prior to boarding the schooner, they fashioned shrouds out of loose-fitting oilcloth and attached drawstrings around their waists. As soon as the smoke began to fill the ship's hold, they intended to cover their heads with the shrouds and draw them tight around their waists. Within the shrouds, they would hold hogs' bladders full of water with which to moisten their mouths and throats and wet towels to cover their nostrils.

Fate spared the two young runaways a life-or-death trial of their plans. The fumigators never appeared aboard the schooner on the day of their departure. That may have simply been a stroke of good luck. More likely, a few pieces of silver had changed hands somewhere along the line. Perhaps their debt to the ship's master was even larger than they realized, or perhaps someone like Peter, the slave pilot, was keeping watch over them as well. In any case, Galloway and Eden still faced peril from turpentine fumes: the vessel's cargo posed nearly as serious a danger as the fumigators. The seams of the barrel staves were not sealed tightly enough to contain the acrid smell of the naval stores. During the voyage, the fumes eventually began to "draw blood" and weaken the stowaways, they later remembered.[17] While they struggled for breath, the schooner sailed down the Cape Fear River, crossed the bar by Smith Island, and disappeared into the Atlantic and the warm, northward currents of the Gulf Stream.

☙

Galloway and Eden survived the passage pained and bloodied, but alive. The captain's vessel sailed north beyond the Chesapeake Bay and, just south of Cape May, moved up the Delaware River. When they were safely across the Mason-Dixon Line and had disembarked in Philadelphia, the two young men found their way to the offices for the Vigilance Committee of Philadelphia. The city's oldest abolitionist society, the Vigilance Committee was one of the busiest way stations for what was popularly known

William Still. From William Still, *The Underground Railroad: A Record of Facts, Authentic Narratives, Letters, etc., Narrating the Hardships, Hair-Breadth Escapes, and Death Struggles of the Slaves in their Efforts for Freedom* (Philadelphia: Porter & Coates, 1872).

as the Underground Railroad. There Galloway and Eden met William Still, one of the country's most prominent African American abolitionists.[18]

William Still was an immensely talented man who, during the Civil War, became a successful stove and coal merchant and eventually one of the nation's first black millionaires. Before the war, though, Still dedicated his life to the abolitionist movement and the Underground Railroad. In 1852, the Pennsylvania Anti-Slavery Society had elected Still its first black chairman and secretary of the General Vigilance Committee. Five years later, he was serving as secretary of the Vigilance Committee of Philadelphia, a branch of the society made up of men who organized, trained, and sometimes armed themselves to protect fugitive slaves and to fight slave catchers and bounty hunters.[19]

Although quite a bit starchier than Galloway, Still had his own legacy of defiance. He had grown up free on a farm in southern New Jersey, the son of a slave woman who had led six of his older brothers and sisters out of slavery in Maryland a decade before his birth. His mother's stories of her life as a slave affected Still deeply. During her two flights from bondage—she was captured and returned to Maryland after her first attempt—she had not been able to bring two of her sons with her. After her escape, her former owner sold the boys into the Deep South. Her sense of loss, and perhaps guilt and misgiving, was an enduring part of her son William's childhood. Born in 1821, he was the youngest of his mother's eighteen children.[20]

As the Vigilance Committee's secretary, Still harbored hundreds of fugitive slaves who came to Philadelphia primarily out of Maryland, Delaware, and Virginia. Galloway and Eden might have stayed at his home on South Street while they recovered from their ordeal. Still also had a large group of local supporters on whom he could have called to care for and conceal the runaways. Some, like Robert Purvis, a wealthy black businessman who had founded the Vigilance Committee in 1837, had secret rooms built into their houses where they could hide runaway slaves when necessary. Many of the Vigilance Committee's supporters worshiped at the Mother Bethel African Methodist Episcopal (AME) Church, where the congregation regularly raised funds to feed and clothe fugitives like the two young men from Wilmington.[21]

Like most fugitive slaves who reached the Vigilance Committee of Philadelphia, Galloway and Eden chose not to linger near the Mason-Dixon Line any longer than necessary. Pennsylvania had outlawed slavery in 1780, earlier than any other state.[22] While that emancipation law was gradual and allowed the state's slaveholders ample time to sell their bondmen into the South, by 1857 approximately 20,000 African Americans called Philadelphia home. Nevertheless, Federal law offered fugitive slaves no shelter in Pennsylvania or elsewhere in the North. Under the provisions of the Fugitive Slave Act of 1850, bounty hunters had the right to seize Galloway and his companion and return them to slavery in Wilmington. Like its counterparts in Boston and New York City, the Vigilance Committee of Philadelphia hired spies, employed informants, and organized militias to foil any slave catcher who crossed the Delaware River in pursuit of a runaway, but the risk was always there.[23]

To play it safe, Still provided Galloway and Eden with railroad tickets as soon as they recovered from their voyage. He also handed them a list of antislavery contacts along the route north, and he may well have furnished a guide to accompany them. Another fugitive slave, a tobacco factory worker from Richmond, Virginia, named John Henry Pettifoot, joined them. Sometime in late June, the three travelers departed from Philadelphia in hopes of making it all the way to Canada.[24] At the request of a Vigilance Committee member, Galloway and Eden left behind two souvenirs: a photograph of Galloway and one of the oilcloth shrouds that they had

Abraham H. Galloway. From William Still, *The Underground Railroad: A Record of Facts, Authentic Narratives, Letters, etc., Narrating the Hardships, Hair-Breadth Escapes, and Death Struggles of the Slaves in their Efforts for Freedom* (Philadelphia: Porter & Coates, 1872).

made to avoid the fumigators in Wilmington Harbor. An etching based on that photograph survives, the only confirmed image of Galloway.

❦

Still directed Galloway and the other two fugitives to a friend of the Vigilance Committee named George Mink, in Kingston, Ontario, just across the Canadian border. Judging from the records that the committee kept over a sixteen-year period for that particular route to freedom, Galloway and his companions probably traveled first to Syracuse, New York, a town built on the salt trade and a booming port since the construction of the Erie Canal three decades earlier had connected Lake Ontario and the Hudson River. The Reverend Jermain Wesley Loguen, a former Tennessee slave who was a teacher and minister in the AME Zion Church, was very likely their contact there. Loguen, the driving force behind Syracuse's Fugitive Aid Society, had worked closely with the Vigilance Committee of Philadelphia for many years. He corresponded frequently with Still and regularly offered his home at the corner of East Genesee and Pine Streets as a shelter for fugitive slaves. By one estimate, Loguen and Syracuse's Fugitive Aid Society sheltered as many as 1,500 fugitive slaves in the generation before the Civil War.[25]

The vigor of Syracuse's antislavery machinery and the nationally renowned rescue of a fugitive slave named William "Jerry" Henry six years earlier, in 1851, had earned the city a reputation for militant opposition to slavery. One of the Syracuse vigilance committee's members, Charles Sedgwick, articulated a prevailing local sentiment. "I must say I had rather hear that one hundred valuable lives were lost," he wrote his wife, "than to hear [that a fugitive slave was apprehended in the North]—No sacrifice of blood is too great to establish the principle that Slaves cannot be hunted & chained & driven off."[26] At a lecture in Syracuse the year after passage of the Fugitive Slave Act, Daniel Webster, then the secretary of state, derided the city as "that laboratory of abolitionism, libel and treason."[27]

Leaving Syracuse, Galloway and his companions likely caught one of the steam packets that traveled the Oswego Canal, a twenty-four-mile-long passage that ran due north from the heart of Syracuse into Lake Ontario. From the canal's mouth on Lake Ontario, the Canadian seaport of Kingston lay only sixty-five miles north-northeast across the eastern edge of the big lake. Galloway's first glimpse of freedom would have been the green hills of Simcoe and Wolfe Islands and the high bluffs of Point Frederick, overlooking the city on the Bay of Quinte. A thousand miles north of Wilmington, Galloway, Eden, and Pettifoot sailed into Kingston beneath the shadow of Fort Henry, a pale yellow limestone fortress that towered over the city. Under the guns of that stronghold, the waters of Lake Ontario emptied in cascading torrents into the St. Lawrence River.

George Mink, their contact in Kingston, was one of Canada's early black business pioneers. The sons of former American slaves, George and his brother, James, boasted Loyalist roots in the Revolutionary era. Their parents had sought shelter in the British colony along with approximately 20,000 other blacks who escaped from slavery during the Revolutionary War. Their father had become a successful coachman in Kingston, and George and James later followed in his footsteps and established a stagecoach line between Kingston and the territory's capital, Toronto, 150 miles to the west. They eventually provided passenger and mail service throughout much of Canada West, which later became part of the province of Ontario, and made small fortunes. By the time that Galloway and his fellows crossed Lake Ontario, James owned a livery, hotel, and tavern in Toronto, while George owned liveries, a tavern, and the Telegraph Motel in Kingston.[28] Galloway would have been hard pressed to find more trustworthy or resourceful friends in all of Canada.

After the American Revolution, the course of slavery had unfolded quite differently in Canada than in the United States. By 1793, Ontario's lieutenant governor, John Graves Simcoe, had led a successful campaign to ban the importation of slaves into Canada and to free on their twenty-fifth birthday all children of slaves born after passage of the law. An act of the Imperial Parliament prohibited slavery throughout the British colonies, including Canada, in 1834, ending the institution forever in the territory that became present-day Ontario. A few weeks later, a crowd of local blacks attempted to break into the Kingston Hotel to liberate a black woman believed to be a slave of a white family visiting from the United States.[29]

In the following years, growing numbers of American slaves sought refuge in Canada West. Their northward migration rose dramatically after the passage of the Fugitive Slave Act in 1850. George Mink was an important, usually behind-the-scenes supporter of those black exiles. As early as 1842, he called Kingston's black leaders together to build support for the British-American Institute, a manual-labor school for former fugitive slaves near Dresden, Canada West. He also marshaled backing for the Dawn Settlement, an exile community of ex-slaves near Chatham.[30]

As a coachman and mail carrier, Mink could inconspicuously arrange passage for the fugitives anywhere in Canada West.[31] Kingston's relatively small black community was close to the U.S. border, though, and that summer slave catchers were crossing into Canada West and attempting abductions.[32] As a consequence, many fugitive slaves chose to continue west to Toronto, home to the territory's largest black community and to at least half a dozen groups dedicated to supporting fugitive slaves. Others headed to one of the planned exile communities like the Dawn Settlement, most of which had been organized by white missionaries from the United States. Yet others headed to the town of Chatham, a political haven for many of the province's most militant antislavery exiles. Though much smaller than Toronto, Chatham was home to the tough-minded Chatham Vigilance Committee and to an important black newspaper, the *Provincial Freeman*. The city sheltered some of Canada's most dedicated black abolitionists, including Martin R. Delany, William Howard Day, Isaac D. Shadd, and the *Provincial Freeman*'s editor, Mary Ann Shadd Cary, the first black woman newspaper publisher in North America. Other fugitive slaves made their way to the town of St. Catharines. Harriet Tubman had lived there, served on the executive committee of the Fugitive Aid Society, and guided hundreds of slaves across the border before she moved to Auburn, New York, in 1857.[33]

As the owner of an inn, livery, and coach business, George Mink was immensely useful to fugitive slaves. His inn provided lodging until they got their feet on the ground; his tavern, meals; his drays, transportation.[34] He had also cultivated the goodwill of the local groups most willing to support fugitive slaves, the Wesleyan-Methodist church and the Kingston Female Benevolent Society. These allies frequently provided financial assistance to fugitives seeking to settle in Canada. His circle of business acquaintances also offered employment for newly arrived runaways. These networks quickly proved helpful to Galloway, Eden, and Pettifoot. On 20 July 1857, Eden wrote William Still in Philadelphia, confirming that the three men had arrived in Kingston in "good health." Eden informed Still that George Mink had already offered Pettifoot a job in one of his businesses and that he—Eden—would soon be opening his own barbershop. He also told Still that Galloway had found work as a brick mason at a daily rate of pay of $1.75 and had begun laying bricks that day.[35]

❧

Galloway explored his first real freedom in Kingston. The booming river port of approximately 15,000 served as capital of the United Counties of Frontenac, Lennox, and Addington. Shipbuilding busied the city most of all. Kingston shipbuilders turned out fleets of merchant vessels, including many of the Great Lakes steamers that hauled coal, limestone, and lumber to Detroit, Chicago, and other ports on the U.S. side of the border. Quarrymen and shipyard workers, most of them Irish, Welsh, or Scottish immigrants, labored everywhere. Galloway heard their brogues in the streets and their songs in the taverns along the river. On the edge of a vast, remote territory of forested lowlands and lake country, the robust city still had some of the feeling of the frontier.

The city's other leading industries, including James Morton's brewery and distillery, one of the largest in North America, catered to miners and shipyard workers. A huge provincial penitentiary, nearly a city unto itself, had also become a Kingston landmark. Galloway saw gangs of the penitentiary's bedraggled inmates marched through the streets on their way to jobs in the vast quarries along the outskirts of the city, as well as to work on a new railroad line that tied Kingston to Toronto and Montreal.[36] On Kingston's roads, Galloway also rubbed shoulders with many native peoples, mainly Cree and Assiboine. Widely scorned and marginalized, they were the first people whom he had encountered in his life who seemed to occupy a lower rung in society than blacks, at least in Canada.[37]

Despite their new liberties, most of the fugitive slaves whom Galloway met in Canada West continued to look southward. "We would rather stay in our native land, if we could be as free there as we are here," Harriet Tubman explained when she still lived in St. Catharines.[38] The world that they knew and the people they loved lay below the Mason-Dixon Line. Many, like Tubman, had come to Canada to escape slavery and quickly turned their efforts to the struggle against slavery back home. To an important extent, they made Canada West the headquarters-in-exile for the continent's black abolitionist movement. The region attracted some of the most ardent and able slave renegades from the South, as well as some of the leading black intellectuals, professionals, and journalists from the northern United States. Along the shores of Lake Ontario, they vigorously debated how best to undermine slavery on the other side of the border.

Though Canada was unquestionably more hospitable than the United States to blacks, Canadian life often disappointed the exiles. Black Canadians enjoyed the full rights of citizenship, the protection of the courts, and voting rights. In most realms of public life, the colonies had even banned segregation by race. Canada's highest courts had also prohibited the extradition of fugitive slaves, providing Galloway and other black exiles a feeling of security unimaginable anywhere in the United States. Canadian law even permitted the marriage of blacks and whites, perhaps the American South's strictest taboo, though interracial marriages do not seem to have been common and were not free of peril. According to a Canadian reminiscence published early in the twentieth century, George Mink's niece married a white man who carried her across the border and sold her into slavery in South Carolina.[39] Canada was not Canaan Land.

Even so, a steady stream of fugitive slaves made their way into Canada West in the summer of 1857. "Six passengers came by Underground Railroad to Chatham one day this week, and more are looked for shortly," reported the *Provincial Freeman*, just as Galloway sailed across Lake Ontario into Kingston.[40] When Galloway disembarked in Kingston, many of Canada West's black exiles had already grown disillusioned with the prospects for racial justice or political equality anywhere in North America. While some sharpened their antislavery efforts in response to the growing racial hostility in the United States, many black exiles had had enough; they had lost faith in the promises of the Declaration of Independence and the Constitution. It was time to get out of North America, they argued.

Galloway arrived in Canada West during the height of that lively, often contentious debate among black abolitionists over the possibilities of redemption for the United States and the wisdom of emigration out of North America. Encouraged most notably by black physician Martin Delany in Chatham, many black leaders pondered anew emigration to Jamaica, Haiti, or the Niger Valley of West Africa.[41] Unlike the campaign by the American Colonization Society to resettle blacks in the West African nation of Liberia a generation earlier, their emigration movement was not organized or endorsed primarily by whites.[42] That earlier generation of whites had seen emigration as a way to relieve the United States of what they considered the divisive burden of its black population, but the new emigrationists instead looked at flight from the United States as an escape from an incurable white supremacy. Led by black activists and by radical white abolitionists of the kind who rode with John Brown in the Kansas Territory, the new emigrationists indicted white supremacy throughout the continent. They also beat the drum for a new black sense of self and a reconstructed nationality for the descendants of the African Diaspora in a hostile world.[43] In Canada West, then, Galloway was not on some far frontier of the abolitionist struggle, but at one of its most vibrant hubs.

3

A Second John Brown

GALLOWAY DID NOT RESIDE PEACEFULLY IN KINGSTON AND LAY BRICKS
for very long. After his escape from bondage and his arrival in Canada West,
he threw himself into the struggle to end slavery in the United States. Between 1857 and 1861, as the United States moved closer and closer to dis-
union and war, he traveled through some of the darkest, most dangerous
corners of the continent's abolitionist movement. We see him, however,
only in fleeting glimpses, and his whereabouts were reported mainly in
rumor and innuendo. According to Robert Hamilton, the African American publisher and editor of New York City's *Anglo-African*, and his confidant in later years, Galloway "wandered all over this country and Canada"
between his first appearance in Kingston and the beginning of the Civil
War.[1]

Risking life and liberty, Galloway made his way back across the border
between the United States and Canada, gave antislavery speeches in Ohio,
and later testified that white abolitionists saved his life there at least once.[2]
He made his way to New England in these first years of his freedom as well.
He visited Massachusetts, where he somehow won the confidence of perhaps the country's most influential white abolitionist, William Lloyd Garrison, the founder of the American Anti-Slavery Society and the editor of
an important journal, the *Liberator*. While in New England, Galloway also
grew close to militant abolitionists who had been key supporters of the
Boston Vigilance Committee and the Boston Anti-Man-Hunting League,
antislavery groups that matched wits, and sometimes fists, with bounty
hunters in pursuit of fugitive slaves. Years later, in the middle of the Civil
War, Galloway entrusted his mother's life to one of them.[3]

Galloway may have also joined one of the militant black abolitionist societies that operated out of Canada West during this period. If he

did, a likely candidate was a mysterious group remembered as the League of Freedom, or simply "the Liberators." According to Richard Hinton, an English radical who was an abolitionist newspaper publisher and one of John Brown's most trusted confidants in the Kansas Territory, as well as a friend of Walt Whitman's, the Liberators moved clandestinely into the free states, particularly Ohio, and endeavored to bring slaves across the Ohio River and guide them north to Canada. At the outset of the Civil War, Hinton wrote, they proved "to be of special use to the Union army," presumably as spies, scouts, or guides inside the Confederacy.[4] Galloway's involvement with the Liberators, or a group like them, would explain one of the great mysteries about his life: why, at the beginning of the Civil War, Union army leaders felt so confident that he was capable of infiltrating the Confederacy.

Whether he was making antislavery speeches or guiding slaves north to Canada, Galloway faced grave dangers when he ventured into the United States. Particularly along the Ohio River, the border between slavery in Kentucky and freedom in Ohio, the black men and women who abetted the escape of slaves from the South risked their lives and their liberty at every turn. Slave hunters and vigilantes patrolled the shoreline, inspected river traffic, and guarded landings and bridges. As a fugitive slave, Galloway realized that he might be captured, prosecuted under the terms of the Fugitive Slave Act of 1850, and returned to slavery. Criminal gangs likewise preyed on people of color, slave and free, along the border. Even if Galloway was not recognized as a fugitive slave, one of those gangs might still have kidnapped him and sold him into slavery in Kentucky or shipped him as far downriver as the slave markets in St. Louis or New Orleans. Passage north over land, for slave runaways and their guides, consequently meant running a gauntlet of armed men, bloodhounds, and informers. If Galloway operated with a group like the Liberators, survival required that he be savvy and cunning, handy with a revolver and a bowie knife, and probably a little cold-blooded.[5]

Galloway demonstrated his passionate commitment to the African American freedom struggle again when he appeared in Boston in the winter of 1860, bound for the black republic of Haiti. At twenty-three years of age, he had been away from his family and friends below the Mason-Dixon Line for more than three years, but he had never stayed in one place long enough to establish a home, begin a family, or leave behind much more than a footprint. He arrived in Boston almost penniless and without even a decent coat to protect him from the chilling sea winds. Wherever he had wandered, and whatever he had seen in his travels across the United States and Canada, he was now one of a small group of revolutionaries determined to use Haiti to carry John Brown's spirit into the belly of the southern states that would soon make up the Confederacy.

But first Galloway had to get through Boston, which was having its own dark night of the soul that winter of 1860–61. Despite a reputation as one of the country's foremost centers of antislavery thought and activism, the city was coming apart at the seams over the issues of slavery, race, and war. As the United States tore itself in half, antiwar mob violence and some of the country's worst race riots prior to the Civil War swept through Boston. The first outbreak of violence occurred on 3 December. That evening, "a diversified mob, composed chiefly of North Street aristocrats and Beacon Street roughs," as the *New York Tribune* put it, attacked the great African American leader Frederick Douglass and other abolitionists at Tremont Temple, a Baptist church.[6] The abolitionists had been holding a public meeting to mark the first anniversary of John Brown's hanging and to address the question How can slavery be abolished? They fought for their lives at Tremont Temple that evening, and then, around midnight, they fought again in the city's streets after having reconvened at the Reverend J. Sella Martin's Joy Street Baptist Church.[7]

According to *Douglass' Monthly*, as the meeting ended, "the street mob took to hunting negroes as they came forth," assaulting many and seriously injuring a few. The sound of breaking glass and sporadic gunfire echoed in the darkened streets as white mobs ransacked the streetcars for "colored victims." Another riot occurred in Boston two weeks later, on 16 December, after Wendell Phillips, one of the nation's most compelling abolitionist orators, gave a lecture at the Music Hall.[8] Galloway may have been in Boston for both the Tremont Temple and Music Hall riots; the records of a local abolitionist society show that he was unquestionably there a few days after Christmas.[9]

While the South teetered on the edge of secession and rioters prowled the streets of Boston, Galloway prepared for the voyage to Haiti. He purchased a suit of clothes in Boston that last week of December, a leading abolitionist noted in a private ledger, "to go with Redpath to Haiti." James Redpath was the principal organizer of an agricultural colony of U.S. and Canadian blacks in the republic of Haiti. A fast-talking, entrepreneurially minded Scottish immigrant, he worked as a crusading antislavery journalist and had been an ally of John Brown's in the bloody guerrilla war over slavery in the Kansas Territory.[10] He was also one of the abolitionists who called the Tremont Temple meeting in Boston. Behind the scenes, Redpath was among several former supporters of Brown who were secretly planning a raid against the American South from a base in Haiti. Galloway bought the suit of clothes with funds advanced him by a young abolitionist named John Curtis, the son of a minister active in the Underground Railroad in Southboro, Massachusetts.[11] The Vigilance Committee of Boston reimbursed Curtis for Galloway's coat at the personal request of William Lloyd Garrison.[12]

On 8 January 1861, Galloway sailed for Haiti. He arrived in Port-au-Prince thirteen days later.[13] Six weeks after that, on 25 February, John Curtis and another young radical, Francis Merriam, also traveled to Haiti on the brig *Mary A. Jones*, alongside forty-seven emigrants bound for Redpath's colony.[14] The new Haitian president, Fabre-Nicholas Geffrard, received them in Port-au-Prince, and most sailed for St. Marc two days later.[15] An erratic and often emotionally unstable young man, Merriam was the grandson of Francis Jackson, treasurer of the Vigilance Committee of Boston. The young Merriam had been one of the few among John Brown's men who escaped after their attack on the Federal arsenal at Harpers Ferry, but he returned to Massachusetts determined to launch another assault on the slave states. Friends and family convinced him to flee back across the Canadian border, which he did with the unlikely help of one of his grandfather's friends, the philosopher Henry David Thoreau.[16]

Boston industrialist and militant abolitionist George L. Stearns was also involved in the Haitian conspiracy. Best remembered today for supplying guns and ammunition that Brown used at Harpers Ferry, Stearns was a ruthless opponent of slavery. Born in Medford, west of Boston, in 1818, he had gone to work at the age of fifteen and grown prosperous in the ship-chandlery business; he later built a factory in Boston and made a fortune in manufacturing lead sheet metal and lead pipe.[17]

During the Kansas Border Wars, Stearns had played a central role in the New England Emigrant Aid Society, which supplied blankets, provisions, and school funds to "Free Soil" settlers. Later, he was a driving force behind the Massachusetts Kansas Committee, which also supported Free Soil settlers, including sending guns and ammunition to antislavery guerrillas. At first, Stearns had believed that political organizing and free elections could win Kansas to his side.[18] By the fall of 1858, however, he had begun to place his support for ending slavery elsewhere—in bloody-minded insurgents like John Brown and the fiery Scotsman James Montgomery, and in Sharps rifles, Colt revolvers, and cash.[19]

Stearns channeled large sums of money and crates of guns and ammunition to Brown and other antislavery fighters in the Kansas Territory, where Free Soil antislavery settlers faced off against the so-called Border Ruffians determined that Kansas would enter the Union as a slave state.[20] Acting the puppet master, buying men's loyalties, and pulling the strings on a secretive web of gunrunners and political agents, he handpicked candidates for political office in Kansas, bankrolled their campaigns, and even sent speeches to his candidates that he expected them to use on the stump. Stearns propped up Free Soil newspapers in Kansas as well, and closer to home, Stearns published antislavery pamphlets under the auspices of the Emancipation League of Boston, which he controlled. He also owned an antislavery daily newspaper, the *Boston Commonwealth*.[21]

Stearns and his wife, Mary—the niece of children's writer, abolitionist, and suffragist leader Lydia Maria Child—both grew close to Brown and his family during the Kansas Border Wars. From their first meeting, George Stearns and John Brown were "like the iron and the magnet," Stearns's son later recalled. After hearing Brown speak, the philosopher Ralph Waldo Emerson wrote that Brown would rather "a whole generation . . . pass away by a violent death, than that one word of" the Golden Rule or the Declaration of Independence "should be violated." Stearns, a friend of Emerson, was made of the same stuff.[22] As Brown turned his attention from Kansas to Harpers Ferry, Stearns bought guns and ammunition for him, helped to support his large family, and when Brown's resolve waivered, promised that he would look after his wife and children if he died in the attack.[23] The wealthy manufacturer never shared Brown's belief that they might ignite a slave insurrection of any size in the South, but his skepticism did not allay his enthusiasm for Brown's kind of antislavery zealotry. His private correspondence sometimes gives the impression that he considered Brown just another of his puppets, a lamb to sacrifice for the greater good of abolishing slavery. However, Stearns always embraced Brown's quixotic attack on Harpers Ferry as a potential catalyst for a civil war to abolish slavery.[24] In the wake of Harpers Ferry, he fled to Canada to avoid a congressional investigation and potential prosecution.

Stearns and a number of John Brown's other supporters had first grown interested in Haiti after learning about the tremendous outpouring of Haitian sympathy for Brown and his family after Brown went to the gallows on 2 December 1859. The black republic's leading newspapers avidly followed both Brown's trial and hanging and lifted him up as a national martyr.[25] After Brown's execution, the country's citizens held three days of mourning, hung flags at half-mast, and draped windows in black. In Port-au-Prince, the nation's leaders held a memorial service at the national cathedral, followed by a long procession to a site on the outskirts of the city known as "The Martyr's Cross." Haitians mourned Brown with similar ardor in Cape Haytien, Jacmel, Gonaïves, and Aux Cayes and raised large sums for the support of his widow and children.[26]

The abolitionist movement in the United States, and particularly the saga of John Brown's raid, held a special importance in Haiti. The martyrdom of Brown and his followers evoked for Haitians the sacrifices that their own ancestors had made more than half a century earlier when they were struggling to defeat troops sent by Napoleon Bonaparte, overthrow French colonial rule, and abolish slavery. Under pressure from southern legislators, Washington had never granted diplomatic recognition to Haiti since its independence. During that time, slaveholding interests in the South had repeatedly called for the United States to invade Haiti, the world's first black republic, and have it annexed to the country as a slave state. To them the continued existence of a country born of an armed slave uprising posed a dangerous example to the black men and women whom they held in bondage. The administration of President Franklin Pierce planned an invasion of Haiti in 1853–54, though it was ultimately canceled. Some in Congress proposed annexation and statehood for Haiti as a slave state as part of a compromise that might balance the entry of a new free state into the Union, probably in the American West.

The flamboyant southern mercenaries and adventurers known as "filibusterers" were also a source of anxiety for Haitian political leaders. Taken from the Spanish *filibustero*, meaning "pirate" or "freebooter," the term referred to private armies whose generals aspired to conquer the U.S. southern neighbors in order to strengthen the slaveholding South, as well as to make their own fortunes.[27] A decade before Harpers Ferry, Haitians had watched warily as the Venezuelan mercenary Narciso López made several attempts to invade Cuba, only seventy-five miles across the Windward Passage from their shores. Supported by southern legislators in the United States, López promised to award the Spanish colony to the U.S. government. Ultimately unsuccessful, he was hanged by the Cubans, who captured him on his final expedition. In 1853, another soldier of fortune, a Mississippian named William Walker, led unsuccessful invasions into the Mexican states of Baja and Sonora. Two years later, he launched another private military expedition, this time a successful takeover of Nicaragua. President Pierce immediately recognized Walker as the country's legitimate ruler. Once entrenched in Nicaragua, Walker began recruiting mercenaries for invasions of Honduras, Guatemala, Costa Rica, and El Salvador. Local forces eventually defeated Walker, too, but slavery might have been restored in all of Central America if he had triumphed.[28]

Haitians grounded their passionate support for John Brown primarily in racial solidarity and a spiritual kinship with their brothers and sisters in the American South. In light of the history of U.S. intervention in Latin America, however, they also possessed a practical desire to weaken the power of slaveholders over U.S. foreign policy. That mutual self-interest was not lost on the Haitian conspirators in the United States. Correspondents to Redpath in 1861 often described Haitian colonization explicitly as a counterbalance to filibustering expeditions such as William Walker's in Nicaragua.[29]

For all their anxiety over a foreign policy shaped by "the Slave Power," many Haitian abolitionists had also grown frustrated with the lack of antislavery militancy in the United States. A letter from Port-au-Prince that appeared in New York City's *Weekly Anglo-African* put a fine focus on that frustration. Signed by a long list of Haitian sympathizers, the letter expressed solidarity with Brown and his supporters but also goaded America's enslaved to be more militant. "We are astonished," they wrote, "that a Spartacus more fortunate than John Brown has not yet risen from the very midst of the slaves in the South." The Port-au-Prince letter concluded, "We believe that the means to abolish slavery is to oppose *force with force*, the most legitimate war being that which man undertakes for the conquest of his *divine rights*."[30] Hearing fervent expressions of the deep affection for Brown in Haiti, the most militant abolitionists in the United States not surprisingly looked to the Caribbean nation as a base for launching another armed attack on the American South.

The origins of the Haitian plot remain obscure but probably reached back to a clandestine meeting at the Ohio farmhouse of John Brown Jr., the firebrand's oldest son, in April 1858. The elder Brown had just returned from a journey to Canada West to recruit guerrillas for the raid on Harpers Ferry. At the Ohio gathering, the Browns and their closest confidants organized a secret society called the Black Strings, whose surviving members would play leading parts in the Haitian conspiracy. In Ohio, the Black Strings pledged to pursue a revolutionary agenda that transcended the coming attack on Harpers Ferry. That vision involved a pan-American movement to unite antislavery struggles throughout the Western Hemisphere. The Black Strings envisioned a new black republic carved out of pieces of the American South, the West Indies, and the parts of Central and South America bordering the Caribbean Sea.

The first step made by the Black Strings did not appear very revolutionary. After Harpers Ferry, the secret group's surviving members founded an agrarian colony of black exiles from the United States and Canada in St. Marc, Haiti, at the mouth of the Artibonite River, on the rocky, southwestern coast of the island of Hispaniola.[31] President Geffrard and his ministers made farmland available for them near a colony of black Louisianans that had already settled in the area.[32] Redpath, Richard Hinton (also a Black String), and Merriam visited Haiti twice in 1859, while Brown awaited his appointment with the hangman.[33] The following year, Redpath published a guidebook on Haiti in order to entice African American emigrants to the country.[34] Several important abolitionists employed by Redpath, including John Brown Jr., recruited settlers for Haiti in Canada West.[35]

At first, Redpath's mission met with a lukewarm response. By the time that Galloway sailed for Haiti, however, even Frederick Douglass, previously a staunch opponent of emigration, showed a new receptiveness. "If we go any where let us go to Haiti," he wrote in *Douglass' Monthly* in January 1861. Douglass now imagined Haiti as a way station and wellspring for the ongoing African American struggle to end slavery. He continued: "Let us go where we are still within hearing distance of the wails of our brothers and sisters in bonds. . . . Let us go to Haiti, where our oppressors do not want us to go, and where our influence and example can still be of service to those whose tears will find their way to us by the waters of the Gulf." Douglass, who had just met with Redpath, added a final word that sheds some light on both the international situation and the abolitionists' dream for Haiti: "Let us be there," Douglass said, "to help beat back the filibustering invaders from the cotton States."[36]

Redpath's "Haitian Colonization Scheme," as the U.S. press dubbed it, received national attention and played a central role in a heated debate among black abolitionists over the prospects for racial equality in the United States versus the promises of emigration. Redpath's other ambitions remained secret until the very eve of the Civil War, however. From the outset of their interest in Haiti, the Black Strings sought to do more there than simply found a black exile community. According to Hinton's private correspondence, his and Redpath's visit to Haiti in the summer of 1859 was contrived fundamentally as an effort to employ a relatively uncontroversial plan—the colony—to mask a far more controversial under-taking. While in Haiti, they investigated the country's potential as a site for the black exile community, but they also journeyed there "in the interest of a more extended insurrectionary or revolutionary movement," as Hin-ton put it. That movement, he continued, "embraced not only a projected uprising of colored American slaves, but the possible organization of . . . a racial nationality in the Gulf States, the mid-continental islands, and por-tions of South America." In short, they were conspiring to use Haiti as a base for creating a black republic extending from the American South to the far corners of the Caribbean Sea.[37]

George Stearns loomed around the plot's edges.[38] But compared to the Black Strings, Stearns had his feet more firmly planted on the ground and approached Haiti with a grim shrewdness and a clear, achievable goal in mind. In his private correspondence and public declarations, Stearns never expressed any enthusiasm for a black exile community or dreams of a black republic stretching from the American South to South America. Instead, as had been the case with his support for Brown at Harpers Ferry, his purpose remained some kind of military assault on the South that might push the United States further toward a civil war over slavery, as Brown's raid, much to his satisfaction, had done. As soon as two of his close associates in Mas-sachusetts, Governor John Andrew and Senator Charles Sumner, assured him that he would not be prosecuted as an accomplice of John Brown, Stearns left Canada and returned to Boston, where he played a role in a second, perhaps even more audacious plan in Haiti.[39]

On his return to Boston, Stearns wasted no time in arranging for the purchase of weapons and gunpowder. He also began to cultivate a rela-tionship with President Geffrard in Haiti. On 11 April 1860, five months after the executioner's trapdoor opened under Brown's feet, Stearns wrote Geffrard, sending him a bronze bust of Brown and declaring, "I was an inti-mate friend of the Hero, and as far as I could aided him in all his endeavors to free that portion of our citizens still restrained in Bondage."[40] Geffrard displayed the bust in Haiti's presidential palace. The only other copy made from the original mold by English sculptor Edwin A. Brackett sat in the Stearns mansion in Medford.[41]

Rumors that Brown's surviving co-conspirators were planning another attack like the one at Harpers Ferry ran rife in the United States while Gal-loway was in Haiti. On 15 March 1861, the *Liberator*, in Boston, reported dismissively on those rumors. William Lloyd Garrison, the newspaper's publisher, was either not aware of the truth behind the rumors, wanted to squelch them so that the Haitian conspirators might proceed safely, or perhaps most likely, simply wanted to put distance between his wing of the abolitionist movement and whatever rash and impolitic actions John Brown's supporters might undertake in Haiti.[42]

The *Liberator*'s headline did not shy from the sensational: "The Designs of Redpath, John Brown, Jr., Fred. Douglas, ETC—A Negro Army to be Formed—A daring Scheme." Referring to newspaper stories in the Midwest and Canada, Garrison's publication described allegations that surviving supporters of John Brown were organizing and arming free blacks in Canada West and the northern states for an attack on the slaveholding South. The newspaper identified Mississippi as their probable target and referred to a *Chicago Times* story that foresaw "a raid upon the South in which all the horrors contemplated by John Brown, Sr., will find full realization."[43]

The *Chicago Times* reported that John Brown Jr. was "arming [black abolitionists] with a view to the invasion of the South [and] that they only awaited the declaration of war to take up their line of march."[44] One of the newspaper's correspondents had apparently got wind of Brown's oldest son recruiting blacks in Canada West but did not realize that two, overlapping plans were afoot, one an exile community, the other a more revolutionary endeavor involving an armed assault on the South. The correspondent did not distinguish that John Brown Jr. was recruiting blacks to join the exile colony in St. Marc. He had gotten the story rather twisted while still capturing the gist of the conspiracy.

Raising the specter of a slave army landing in the Deep South, the newspaper accounts also alleged that Redpath had sought help for the plot from President Geffrard in Haiti and was even "sounding [out] the negroes of that island with a view to raising an army there."[45] Both allegations may have had some truth in them, though Geffrard would never have supported such a plot and risked provoking the ire of the United States. Many newspaper readers no doubt found the story far-fetched and scoffed at the prospects of a small band of armed fanatics posing any real threat to the slave states. Others, however, realized that, in the same spirit as John Brown's raid at Harpers Ferry, such a conspiracy's power lay not in military conquest but in its explosive, divisive impact on American politics and its potential for inciting a civil war over slavery.

According to the newspaper reports, regardless of what state's beaches they might come ashore on, the black exiles and their Haitian allies planned to "force or induce the slaves to join them, pillage, plunder, murder and burn, leaving their track as desolate as the desert, and black with ruin."[46] That, too, was also quite possible. Such millennial ambitions were not out of character for the Black Strings or many of the other radicals who had been close to John Brown. Across the American South, newspapers eagerly reprinted such reports and denounced the conspirators.

Whatever clandestine work he performed in Haiti, Galloway figured in the midst of an intricate chess game unfolding in Port-au-Prince in anticipation of civil war in the United States and a new national government that would forge foreign policy unencumbered by southern legislators for the first time. At the heart of that intrigue lay an emerging, as yet rather inchoate alliance between small groups of militant abolitionists in the United States and the West Indies. Very broadly speaking, that alliance aimed to obtain U.S. diplomatic recognition for Haiti, blunt the rising Spanish interest in the Dominican Republic—slavery was still legal and widespread in Spain's colonies in the West Indies—and draw financial support and possibly even recruits in Haiti and elsewhere for an attack against the American South.

Galloway stayed in Haiti for fifteen weeks. While there, he at least briefly visited the black exile community at St. Marc. He must also have made contacts with the Haitian John Brown Committee and Brown's supporters among Haiti's political leaders. He likely visited Geffrard himself. Galloway may also have had a role in collecting funds raised by the Haitian John Brown Committee and conveying them back to the Brown family's trustees in New York City and Boston. And while plans for any kind of raid on the Deep South apparently remained in only their most formative stages, Galloway had much to do: gaining further insight into the Haitian political scene at the very least but also building closer ties to the country's abolitionists, raising money, recruiting supporters, and laying plans for what he must have known would have been a suicidal assault on the American South.

Galloway returned to the United States on the schooner *Echo* on 1 April 1861. Several months after his departure from the West Indies, a letter from James Redpath to William Lloyd Garrison offered a glimpse at what Galloway did during his time there. Redpath wrote his letter, which first appeared in the *Liberator*, to refute two articles about the St. Marc colony that the newspaper had recently published. Redpath first acknowledged that he and Garrison differed fundamentally in their antislavery tactics.

A bit unfairly, he summarized those differences by asserting that Garrison relied merely on moral suasion to bring about the downfall of slavery, while he, Redpath, sought "to bring physical forces against slavery." Under the circumstances, he wrote, he and Garrison could only agree to disagree: "I recognize the great value of your labors, and your method, but, at the same time, I have faith in another class of workers and of powers."[47] His words do not sound like those of a man devoted to building a peaceful agrarian colony in a remote corner of Haiti.

The Scottish radical next addressed what he considered "slanders of the Haytian people" that had appeared in the *Liberator*. One of these attacks directly concerned Galloway. In several northern newspapers, a mysterious passenger aboard the *Echo* had asserted that Redpath had misrepresented the opportunities and living conditions in St. Marc. This self-styled "friend of free blacks" claimed that the Haitian government required immigrants to work two days a week for the government until their ship's fare was paid. They purportedly received only $3.00 Haitian a day, roughly 25 cents U.S., to establish themselves. The anonymous figure likewise alleged that the Haitian army conscripted the colonists, marched them to the country's frontier with the Dominican Republic, and "put [them] . . . in the front ranks."[48]

The story, which was republished widely, dealt a devastating blow to Redpath's aspirations for the colony at St. Marc. The genuine truths in the story heightened his difficulty; the mysterious passenger's account exaggerated important details, but scarcely all. A significant number of the black colonists had written friends and family in the United States and Canada with credible stories of great hardship, broken promises, religious persecution, and epidemic disease. Some had already forsaken Haiti and returned to their former homes.

The threat of a war between Haiti and Spain compounded the letter's damage to the reputation of Redpath's colony. Hoping to take advantage of the U.S. preoccupation with domestic affairs, Isabella II had new designs on the Dominican Republic and warned Geffrard not to intervene. Some observers even suspected that Spain might lay claim to Haiti, which the country had not held since the Treaty of Ryswick divided the island of Hispaniola between the Spanish and the French in 1697. Few blacks in the United States or Canada would have relished the possibility of settling in a country on the verge of war with a powerful slaveholding power like Spain. Free blacks in both nations closely followed the latest developments in the West Indies.

The letter that alleged Redpath's lack of credibility, the malevolent intent of the Haitian government, and the inhospitality of Haitian society circulated widely. In addition to the *Liberator*, the letter appeared in the *New York Express* and the *New York Tribune* and two Boston papers, the *Journal* and the *Traveler*. In angry reply, Redpath informed the readers of the *Liberator* that "there was *another* passenger by the *Echo*," referring to the schooner's voyage from Port-au-Prince that arrived in New York City on the first of April. That passenger was Galloway. According to Redpath, Galloway returned from Port-au-Prince just prior to the outbreak of civil war. Redpath claimed that Galloway was "personally known to Mr. Garrison" and that, presumably for Garrison and among his circle of Boston abolitionists, "his veracity is undoubted."[49]

According to Redpath, Galloway not only refuted the allegations about St. Marc made by the "friend of free blacks"; he also exposed the gentleman as a Spanish spy, a political agent of Isabella II. Redpath claimed that Haitian authorities had caught and jailed the spy in Port-au-Prince, and they had released him only in order to expel him from the country. If that were true—and it would not be surprising—the spy presumably sought to undermine abolitionists' efforts to improve relations between the United States and Haiti as Spain sharpened its interest in the West Indies. Redpath asserted that Galloway had visited the exile colony just prior to his departure from Haiti and found the immigrants "contentedly working on their free farms." He stated further that Galloway had reported no signs of colonists being impressed into the Haitian army or into work gangs. In his report of Galloway's observations in St. Marc, Redpath said, "The government has not only redeemed *all* of its pledges, but done far more for the emigrants than it promised."[50]

Redpath's letter to the *Liberator* went on to say that Galloway's observations also refuted the Spanish spy's claims of forced labor on public projects. According to Redpath, Galloway conceded that many of the black colonists in St. Marc had donated their labor to construct an irrigation canal from the Artibonite River to the colony. He believed that Haitian officials had granted funds to pay settlers who could not otherwise afford to take unpaid time away from their fields. "This generous act the Spaniard, or dog Noble of the *Express*, now tries to pervert into an act of oppression," Redpath protested.[51] Again, he rested his defense of the troubled colony wholly on his rendition of Galloway's report.

Redpath did not offer a realistic appraisal of the situation in St. Marc, however. His own private correspondence makes clear that living conditions in St. Marc had grown dire by the spring of 1861. Beset by disease, a lack of investment, and poor planning, the St. Marc colonists hovered on the brink of a nightmarish decline. Of course, what Galloway really told Redpath about the Haitian colony is an open question. Redpath was a master propagandist, and no other reports confirm that Galloway endorsed the St. Marc settlement as unambiguously rosy as Redpath claimed.

☙

Galloway came back to the United States only days before the beginning of the Civil War. His return did not immediately signal the Haitian conspiracy's downfall. George Stearns, for one, clearly did not relinquish his support for the plan to launch another armed insurrection against the South from a base in Haiti. That April, while Galloway sailed home on the *Echo*, Stearns sought to purchase a large supply of gunpowder apparently intended for Haiti. However, with several southern states already seceded and war looming, buying gunpowder proved no easy task; state militias, North and South, jostled for powder and armament.[52] At the same time, a figure identified only as a "Mr. H." in Stearns's surviving correspondence hand-delivered a letter to him from John Brown Jr. "*into what is proposed.*" In that letter, the martyr's son informed Stearns that he did not yet feel ready to consider another assault like his father's crusade at Harpers Ferry. He counseled caution. "I still think that our Northern people will have to receive many *severe scourgings* before they will be prepared to even tolerate our methods," he wrote Stearns on 29 April. That same week, Stearns obliquely wrote Frank Sanborn—the distinguished classics teacher among the "Secret Six" who supported John Brown's raid on Harpers Ferry—that "I have a plan of operation which you shall know when we meet."[53]

John Brown Jr. believed that the civil war just breaking out would shortly force the South to "back down and accept terms of compromise which I think the North are still ready to *make* most favorable" or "the outrageous course of the South will soon *abolitionize* the North." He told Stearns that, until more northerners became abolitionists, "I shall not be willing to run *the gauntlet of both North and South.*" He was already turning his efforts toward another channel of antislavery activity: raising a company of "Anti-Slavery men" to serve in the Union army, "trusting that the day is not distant when we can act without being obliged to *fight* the *North* as well as the South." He assured Stearns that he did not want to discourage his father's supporters from undertaking more militant acts. But he had been chastened by the failure of the white northern public to rally around his father. He did not need to say that he, unlike Stearns, had lost a father and two brothers at Harpers Ferry. "The events of the past year or two have perhaps led me to underestimate the Anti-Slavery temper of the North," he conceded.[54]

Even the outbreak of war did not render the Haitian conspiracy obsolete in the eyes of Stearns. He had little faith in the newly elected president, the former Illinois senator Abraham Lincoln. Stearns suspected that Lincoln would settle for peace and the preservation of the Union at any cost, including the continuance of slavery. It was true that, whenever asked about a solution to the country's "Negro problem," Lincoln often demurred and called for the gradual resettlement of free blacks to other countries; the president was nothing if not politic, and the nation's house was deeply divided. Stearns feared that Lincoln favored a political compromise with the Confederacy that would preserve the institution of slavery for the sake of national reunification. As a result, he was not going to abort the clandestine operation in Haiti until the possibility of peaceful compromise vanished.

Stearns did, however, put a temporary hold on the Haitian conspiracy. When he consulted in early May with U.S. Postmaster General Montgomery Blair, who was his only confidant in Lincoln's cabinet, Stearns informed Blair that "we intend . . . to keep quiet." How much Blair knew about the Haitian conspiracy is not clear, but he knew enough to feel relieved by that news. Blair informed Stearns that, in private, his fellow cabinet members believed that a civil war would ultimately lead to the abolition of slavery. He also made clear, though, that the president and the cabinet strongly feared the consequences of any sort of new militant assault along the lines of Harpers Ferry. They believed that such an action would heighten the perception of the war as being fundamentally about slavery. They feared that such a belief would threaten the white northern public's support for the war and might well lead to the secession of border states that had as yet remained faithful to the Union.[55]

Some planning for the Haitian conspiracy went ahead, however. Later that May, John Brown Jr. proffered Stearns a list of more than fifty contacts "who can be relied on to *faithfully* aid in this matter." He also agreed to travel to Windsor, Canada, to solicit funds or recruit men. Even Brown Jr. seemed more optimistic about the northern public by that time. "Nothing is now wanting to bring the people generally right," he told Stearns, "but heavy loss to the North in the first few engagements."[56]

John Brown Jr.'s words seemed prophetic. Stearns, though, did not feel confident enough to forsake the Haitian conspiracy completely until the Battle of Antietam, sixteen months into the war. On 17 September 1862, near Sharpsburg, Maryland, 23,000 casualties, Union and Confederate, marked the most costly single day of fighting in American history. After Antietam, Stearns concluded, the people of the North and the South felt a loss and betrayal so grievous that they no longer required an encore of John Brown's raid at Harpers Ferry to fight to the bitter end. By that time, however, Galloway had already moved on to battlefields no less shadowy but perhaps even more perilous. Long before Antietam, he had left Haiti and disappeared into the Confederacy. Galloway had returned to the United States, as Redpath said of him, *"to go South to incite insurrections."*[57]

4

Spies All Their Lives

GALLOWAY ARRIVED IN NEW YORK CITY FROM PORT-AU-PRINCE ON 1 April 1861, less than two weeks before the shelling of Fort Sumter and the beginning of the Civil War.[1] Immediately, according to James Redpath, he headed into the southern states. Redpath's incendiary assessment of Galloway's purpose—"*to go South to incite insurrections*"—stirred up images of a torch-wielding Nat Turner or John Brown descending on the Confederacy, but his far more behind-the-scenes mission probably posed a greater threat to the Rebel cause. At the recommendation of George Stearns, Massachusetts war leaders had recruited Galloway to serve as a spy inside the Confederacy.[2] His recruitment into the Union spy service marked one of the first signs—and for a long time, one of the few signs—that at least a small number of Union military leaders recognized the potential of the South's slaves to help undermine the Confederacy.

The logic behind Galloway's recruitment was irrefutable. Who better knew how to blend into Confederate society, after all, than a black man born and raised in the South? Who better to infiltrate the Confederacy than an ex-slave who had proven his cunning in escaping to the North? Who could be more trusted than a black man fighting for his people's freedom, and who would be less likely to betray the North for money or out of undisclosed political sympathies? And finally, where better to find demonstrated courage and a familiarity with the arts of subterfuge than in an African American who had been active in the radical abolition movement from Canada West to the West Indies?

The recommendation from Stearns also reveals something important about Galloway on the eve of the war. Needless to say, Stearns had no interest in the meek of heart. He was drawn to abolitionists who shared his apocalyptic fervor, his eagerness to fight, his refusal to abide compromise with the "Slave Power," and his faith that God would forgive sins perpetrated for the sake of destroying slavery. He cared little for abolitionists who mainly made soapbox exhortations, signed heartfelt petitions, or relied on moral suasion to change the hearts of slaveholders. He considered himself a "practical abolitionist," which meant that he did not flinch at the prospect of resorting to violence and war as the path to ending human bondage. Indeed, he celebrated the coming of the war—"Glorious times," he wrote fellow abolitionist Frank Sanborn immediately after the outbreak of hostilities. "They will show that our Republic is worth saving."[3] Galloway may not have agreed with Stearns's political outlook in every respect. Considering his public declarations and private correspondence, however, the Boston industrialist would not have brought Galloway to the attention of Union leaders if he had not shared Stearns's restless sense of urgency, a revolutionary vision of an America without slavery, and a willingness to use all methods available, including violence, to overthrow it.

When he recommended Galloway to the Union's spy service, Stearns also understood that an intelligence agent could not rely on raw courage, fighting ability, or the strength of his antislavery convictions alone. Knee-deep in clandestine affairs and covert plots, Stearns had a discerning view of the qualities necessary in a spy who was intended to infiltrate the Confederacy. He knew that a Union spy would need not only the courage, cunning, and guile displayed by the antislavery guerrillas that he had supported in the Kansas Territory, but also traits not often found among John Brown and his comrades in Kansas: judgment, levelheadedness, and an ability to blend into his surroundings, whether by dissemblance, disguise, or other arts of deception.

Stearns may have first come to know Galloway's talent for covert affairs during the Haitian conspiracy, or the two men might have crossed paths earlier. Stearns may have encountered Galloway first through abolitionist colleagues active along the Ohio River or in Canada West or during some other, unknown sojourn in Galloway's travels prior to the Civil War, perhaps even in the Kansas Territory. But however they met, by the early part of 1861 Stearns had recognized Galloway's potential to make an important contribution to the Union side in the Civil War. Somehow, somewhere, one of the abolition movement's most cold-blooded, demanding, and unsentimental leaders had seen something in Galloway that made him willing to stake his reputation and the lives of his home state's young men on a twenty-four-year-old former slave.

While Galloway was in Haiti, the southern states had seceded from the Union and founded the Confederate States of America. Historian Stephanie McCurry aptly refers to the Confederacy as "the first independent slaveholders' republic in the Western Hemisphere." It was a whole country explicitly founded on African American slavery and, to quote its vice president, "upon the great truth that the negro is not equal to the white man." Indeed, the Confederacy's founders considered their system of human bondage not as some sort of "necessary evil" but as a forward-looking solution to the special dilemmas of democracy, labor, and capital that had caused social disorder in so many other Western countries during the nineteenth century. Galloway had gone to Haiti to strike a blow against slavery, but the birth of such a nation as the Confederacy compelled him to return home as quickly as possible.[4]

Following Galloway's arrival in New York City, events moved quickly on both sides of the Mason-Dixon Line. Immediately after the shooting war started at Fort Sumter, Massachusetts governor John A. Andrew, a dedicated abolitionist who was one of Stearns's most trusted political allies, sent one of his generals, a Lowell attorney and political leader named Benjamin F. Butler, with the 8th Massachusetts Infantry Regiment to reopen communication and rail lines between the Union states and Washington, D.C.[5] The state of Maryland remained Union territory but was hostile and only precariously loyal; Richmond, the Confederacy's new capital, sat scarcely more than a hundred miles south of Washington, D.C. Brigadier General Butler's task was to ensure that Confederate forces did not overrun Washington and checkmate the Union. He did so successfully, although prosouthern mobs in Baltimore attacked his troops with stones and pieces of iron from a local foundry, killing one of his soldiers and startling the soldiers into firing into the crowd.[6]

Less than a week later, on 18 May, President Lincoln's first commanding general, Winfield Scott, ordered Butler, by then promoted to major general, to take command at one of the few remaining Union strongholds in the seceding states: Fortress Monroe in Hampton, Virginia. By that time, Galloway had gone south and evidently joined Butler's command. Galloway answered directly to Butler, according to one of Butler's men, and was said to "possess the fullest confidence of the commanding General."[7] Over the next two and a half years, Galloway served the Union army from the

Chesapeake Bay to the Mississippi River. He traveled extensively behind enemy lines, risked his life on a routine basis, and according to the Union officers with whom he worked most closely, was highly effective. One of those officers, Brigadier General Edward A. Wild, summed up Galloway's service as a spy succinctly in a letter to a colleague in the fall of 1863: "I would like to do all I can for Galloway, who has served his country well."[8]

Not surprisingly, Galloway's duties as a spy consigned the details of his missions to the shadows. He, Butler, and the other Union officers with whom he worked were habitually close-mouthed about exactly where he traveled and what he did. They put little into writing. While Galloway occasionally alluded to his service as a spy in later years, he did so only guardedly and never confided the particulars of his assignments behind enemy lines. Military records are helpful but far from complete. Especially early in the war, before the War Department created a central agency for intelligence gathering, field commanders often kept their spies off the books. Butler frequently paid his spies from Secret Service funds that required little accounting or, even more obscurely, out of his own pocket. That way he did not feel obliged to enumerate bribes, list sources, or detail other illicit payments that might prove awkward to explain in an inspector general's report.

Cloaked in secrecy, a spy's life may not have been a path to glory, but Galloway soon discovered that he could use his position in military intelligence to gain unique insight into the situation of African Americans in the Confederate states. He worked alongside slaves over a broad swath of the enemy's territory. He saw firsthand the aspirations for freedom of his brothers and sisters still in bondage and witnessed their efforts to bring down the Confederacy from within. From his work as a spy, he also came to know the best and worst of the Union army's conduct toward African Americans in the parts of the South that Lincoln's troops first took from the Confederacy. Those experiences shaped his political outlook, compelled him eventually to break with the Union army, and led him ultimately to forsake the shadows for a more public life.

ℭↄ

Located on the southern end of the Chesapeake Bay, Fortress Monroe controlled the deepwater harbor at Hampton Roads and extended the Union army's power far into Confederate territory. The hulking stone fort—the largest in the United States—quickly became a vital entry point for Union troops into the state of Virginia and an important staging ground for naval

"Stampede of Slaves to Fortress Monroe," 1861. From *Harper's Pictorial History of the Great Rebellion*. Courtesy, New Hanover County Public Library, Wilmington, N.C.

operations and intelligence-gathering activities along the coastlines of the Carolinas. Beyond its strategic importance, though, Fortress Monroe also became the crucible in which Butler and the region's slaves first forged the Union army's policy toward the South's enslaved population.[9]

Within days of Butler's taking command at Fortress Monroe, local slaves began to cross into his lines seeking asylum.[10] The major general's orders, however, did not specify their legal status or what he was supposed to do with them. A lack of firsthand experience with the African American freedom struggle hampered him further. Butler was not known as an abolitionist. He had not previously played a leading role in the antislavery movement, and in 1860 he had even briefly supported the presidential candidacy of Jefferson Davis, now the Confederacy's president. Yet the circumstances that he faced at Fortress Monroe compelled him to devise the Union's first policies on the status and treatment of slaves escaping into Union lines.

Despite his conservative leanings and his detachment from abolitionist politics, Butler enacted a series of policies at Fortress Monroe that in many ways were more far-reaching than those proposed by the nation's most radical abolitionists. Whether he did so in consultation with Governor Andrew, Stearns, or even Galloway is not at all clear. However, in providing a haven for slave refugees and extending even modest rights to them, Butler made his first steps toward becoming, among whites, the single most despised leader in the country, both South and North. Among the nation's blacks, on the other hand, he was on his way to becoming the most revered field general in the Union army.[11]

The relationship between Galloway and Butler would not have been possible in most Union commands. That spring, the prevailing opinion was that a northern victory should pose no threat to the rights of southern slaveholders to hold blacks as property. A few days after Butler occupied Fortress Monroe, for instance, Major General George McClellan, later Lincoln's commanding field general, reassured Virginia's Unionists that he would not confiscate their slaves. Indeed, McClellan promised that he would "with an iron hand, crush any attempt at insurrection on their part."[12] Many of the Union's highest-ranking officers shared McClellan's sentiments.

Butler's response to the slaves who sought shelter in his lines was quite different. By the end of May, he was accepting fugitive slaves into his lines and labeling them "contraband of war," so that he was not obliged to return them to the white southerners who claimed them as property. If his troops had acquired a Confederate wagon or a mule, he reasoned, they scarcely would have contacted their owners to return them. Instead, they would have put them to good use. Butler provided the runaways with food, housing, and employment and, to the astonishment of the Confederates, paid them U.S. dollars for their labors. Whether his actions reflected sympathy for the refugees or simple military necessity remains a little vague. At the very least, the Confederacy's use of slave labor to build defenses near Fortress Monroe galled Butler; he intended to deprive Confederate generals of that labor.[13]

As he watched the crowds of black children and the elderly make their way toward Fortress Monroe, Butler saw no choice but to look after them, too, if he accepted black laborers into his lines. As growing numbers of slaves reached Union-held territory, Butler also began to appreciate their military potential. He put them to work building fortifications and supporting his troops as cooks, laundresses, draymen, and other roles. But he also recognized the value of the military intelligence held by the contrabands and acted on it, making him one of the first Union generals to employ former slaves as spies, scouts, and guides.

The potential advantages of using ex-slaves as spies were considerable. Familiar with southern life, able to fade unobtrusively into local slave communities, and accustomed to living by guile and stealth, former slaves like Galloway were uniquely well suited to serve behind enemy lines. "They have been spies all their lives," Union colonel Thomas W. Higginson testified later in the war. A veteran of "Bleeding Kansas," Higginson had a somewhat mixed assessment of the former slaves as soldiers but only enthusiasm for their gifts as intelligence agents. "You cannot teach them anything in that respect," he scoffed. "I should not attempt to give them instructions," he added. "They would be better able to teach me."[14] Higginson realized that the former slaves had practiced dissemblance and stealth all their lives. Almost from birth, they learned to travel furtively at night, to communicate surreptitiously, and to defend themselves. Some of the most creative had even mastered the arts of masquerade, disguise, and forgery.[15]

Another advantage that Galloway and other African Americans had as spies concerned not their experience or gifts for espionage but the ways in which white southerners viewed their slaves and defined the Civil War. As he did so often, the great African American scholar W. E. B. Du Bois got to the heart of the matter in his 1935 classic *Black Reconstruction* when he wrote that, at the war's outset, "the Negro himself was not seriously considered by the majority of [white] men, North or South." A spy could not ask for more than that kind of blindness. More recently, historian Stephanie McCurry has reminded us that whites on both sides of the war viewed the conflict as the "Brothers' War," white man against white man, not one in which slaves were to play a part. In the minds of white America, she writes, it was "the brothers who brought it on in their (divided) capacity as the people, and the brothers assumed it would be theirs to fight." Even the idea that slaves would try to play a role in their own liberation or in the downfall of the Confederacy lay beyond the ken of many southerners, at least early in the war. McCurry quotes as typical a contributor to the *Charleston Mercury* who insisted that planters had no reason to fear their slaves. "They would as soon suspect their children of conspiring against their lives," the newspaper's correspondent declared. Indeed, many southern white leaders argued that slave labor actually gave the Confederacy a military advantage over the Union. While other white southerners recognized the danger and heightened slave patrols and other safeguards against slave resistance, African American spies were still able to take advantage of the blind spot in the white South's collective mind that could not imagine African Americans as agents actively working against the Confederacy.[16]

Working with Butler out of Fortress Monroe, black spies began to deploy their talents against the Confederacy. Reporting directly to one of the Union army's highest-ranking field officers, Galloway seems to have had a uniquely valuable role in Union intelligence-gathering in Tidewater Virginia. But he was not alone. Butler's spy service quickly recruited local blacks, including Norfolk leader Thomas Peake as a spy and infamous fugitive slave George Scott as an army scout. The reach of the department's spy service extended all the way to the Confederate White House in Richmond, where former slave Mary Elizabeth Bowser worked as a servant and Union spy. Feigning illiteracy and taking on a cartoonish "Negro cook" persona, she sent messages to Union leaders throughout the war.[17] Some African Americans served as spies routinely; others were recruited for a single mission, often when Union commanders needed knowledge of the geography and enemy defenses in the neighborhoods where those black men and women had previously been enslaved.[18]

The dangers of serving as a spy were, of course, considerable. Military records do not convey how many black spies died in the line of duty, but certainly many never saw the end of the war. The *Richmond Daily Dispatch* reported the first capture of "negro spies," in Norfolk on 8 August, only two months after Butler occupied Fortress Monroe. Generally speaking, a hangman's noose, not a prison camp, awaited captured spies, no matter their color.[19]

Galloway's ability to keep his own intelligence-gathering activities a secret contributed to his survival. His gift for subterfuge, however, does not make our attempts to chart his covert missions easy. One of the few good clues into the specifics of Galloway's spying activities while based at Fortress Monroe, however, comes from the diary of Union corporal Edmund J. Cleveland. Later in the war, while Corporal Cleveland was serving in the quartermaster department of the supply depot in Beaufort, North Carolina, he wrote that one of the missions that Galloway undertook for Butler was to "scout marine landings" in advance of the invasion fleet launched by Brigadier General Ambrose Burnside against the North Carolina coast in the winter of 1861–62.[20]

Assigning such a mission to a Union operative with Galloway's background made a great deal of sense. He would have had to travel far behind enemy lines by some combination of boat, horse, and foot. He had to go at least sixty miles south of Fortress Monroe, circumvent the Great Dismal Swamp, and cling to the little bays and remote fishing villages scattered between Currituck Inlet and Old Topsail Inlet. Without a topographical engineer at hand, Galloway had to rely on local sailors and pilots for insights about the navigability of inlets, the twists and turns of channels, and details of winds, tides, and currents. For all that information, his most reliable source was slave watermen like those around whom he had grown up in Smithville and Wilmington. Moving south toward the coastal inlets that would make or break the success of the Union invasion, night again became his cover, the local slaves his protectors, and the black pilots and sailors who best knew the local waters his friends, just as their brethren to the south had been when he was a child on the banks of the Cape Fear River.

While investigating landing sites, Galloway may also have recruited slaves to pilot Union vessels during the invasion. The two jobs went hand in hand. In August 1861, Butler and Union naval forces moved south to the North Carolina coast and captured Hatteras Inlet, one of the main passages through the Outer Banks. The following winter, the Burnside expedition moved more earnestly against North Carolina. The Union armada took Roanoke Island, some miles north of Hatteras Inlet, after a battle on 7 and 8 February. In the following weeks, Burnside's forces moved westward and southward into the sounds of North Carolina and attacked the seaports of Plymouth, Washington, New Bern, and Beaufort. The dangers of the state's coastline, with its formidable shoals and shallow, shifting inlets, were legend. Outmanned Confederate defenders counted on having the advantage of local intimacy with those waters. They were disappointed. Repeatedly, slave pilots stepped forward to take the helm and guide the Union invaders past Confederate defenses and safely ashore.[21] The official records of those incidents do not detail how those black watermen came to serve the Union cause, but whoever recruited them had a remarkable ability to instill trust in the men and knew the ways of pilots and the sea.

Galloway would return to eastern North Carolina after Burnside's victory, but he was first called to another part of the Confederacy. Early in 1862, Major General Benjamin Butler was transferred from Fortress Monroe to the Department of the Gulf. On 23 February 1862, Lincoln's new commanding general, Major General George McClellan, ordered Butler to lead "the land forces destined to cooperate with the Navy in the attack upon New Orleans." At the time, New Orleans and all of the Gulf Coast remained in Confederate hands. Butler's became the Union army's first major expedition into the Deep South. Soon after receiving his orders, Butler realized that the discreet gathering of military intelligence would again play a crucial part of his campaign in the Department of the Gulf, and he made sure that Galloway joined him in New Orleans. Butler had to know, however, that he was asking a great deal of his valued spy. By the shores of the Mississippi River, Galloway would be risking his life in a strange land nearly a thousand miles from the place of his birth, in a corner of the plantation South that was unfamiliar to him and inevitably far more dangerous as a consequence.[22]

Galloway's posting to the Deep South would prove to be a turning point in his young life. While he had seen both a suffocating kind of daily suffering and savage atrocity among his fellow slaves along the Cape Fear River and in Tidewater Virginia, he had never witnessed the scale of inhumanity that prevailed on the cotton and sugarcane plantations along the Mississippi River. Slaves composed 90 percent of the population in some Louisiana parishes and Mississippi counties, a far higher percentage than anywhere in Virginia or North Carolina. The level of brutality necessary to subdue those black men, women, and children had few bounds. The region's reputation for cruelty and suffering had spread far and wide before the war. During Galloway's childhood, the streets of Wilmington and Smithville were rife with tales of slave rebels and outlaws who had been sold to the planters in the Gulf States as a cautionary tale for other local slaves. Either Galloway's attachment to Butler, his confidence in the importance of the mission, or his desire for revenge—or all of these things—was very strong.

Backed by troop transports carrying 8,000 soldiers, Butler sailed from Fortress Monroe and arrived at Ship Island, off the mouth of the Mississippi River, on 20 March. Galloway may have traveled with the major general, or he may have sailed a week earlier with one of Butler's officers, a brash young colonel named Halbert Paine, commander of the 4th Regiment, Wisconsin Volunteer Infantry. In any case, Galloway was to be attached to Paine's regiment while he was in the Department of the Gulf.

Though they came from very different backgrounds and homes half a continent apart, Paine and Galloway were cut from the same cloth. Like Galloway, Paine was headstrong, precocious, and quick tempered. Like Galloway, Paine had little patience for military protocol or government policies that interfered with the struggle against slavery. And like Galloway, he could barely contain his rage when anyone, including his superior officers, did not view the war as a crusade to abolish slavery or showed the slightest disregard for the dignity of the contrabands in the South.[23]

Halbert Paine, 4th Wisconsin Infantry.
Courtesy, Wisconsin Historical Society,
WHi-2366.

After suffering a long spell of heat, drudgery, and overcrowding while Butler gathered his forces at Ship Island, Galloway and Paine moved with the 4th Wisconsin up the Mississippi River on 17 April. Along the way, they passed the burning hulks of the two Confederate forts that had guarded New Orleans; Admiral David Farragut's gunboats had just destroyed them to make way for Butler's invasion force. Butler's men reached the landing at the foot of Canal Street in New Orleans on 1 May. Federal troops occupied the seaport for the remainder of the war. Butler made his headquarters at the St. Charles Hotel, in the midst of one of the most welcoming black civilian populations and bitterly hostile white populations imaginable.[24]

Galloway may have been in and out of the St. Charles Hotel for a day or two, but he did not linger in New Orleans for long. His ultimate destination was Vicksburg, Mississippi, more than 200 miles upriver. Perched on high bluffs overlooking the Mississippi River, Vicksburg was all that prevented the Union army from gaining control over the river from its springs in Minnesota all the way to the Gulf of Mexico. More important from a strategic point of view, the fall of Vicksburg would have cut the Confederacy in half. On 12 May, six companies of the 4th Wisconsin, the regiment to which Galloway was attached, steamed north aboard the USS *Ceres* on an expedition to assess Vicksburg's defenses and, if possible, induce the city's surrender.[25]

On that voyage, the river churned at high flood. Galloway and the Union soldiers passed miles of plantations and villages where water had risen to the rooftops. After pausing briefly in Baton Rouge and Natchez, the *Ceres* tied up three miles south of Vicksburg on 18 May. There the mission stalled. Scouting parties, including perhaps Galloway, quickly convinced Admiral Farragut and Brigadier General Thomas R. Williams that the city's defenses were too formidable and that the Rebel troops outmatched them. The Federal vessels withdrew downriver on 26 May, though Galloway may have remained to reconnoiter the city's defenses further.[26]

A snake pit of mortal dangers coiled along that part of the Mississippi River. Whenever behind enemy lines in Mississippi, Galloway had to side-step slave patrols, enemy scouts, Confederate army units, and Rebel guerrillas. Roving bands of flood refugees, slave catchers, and bounty hunters dogged any Union spy or scout, and the white civilian population was universally hostile. The floodwaters only made Galloway's travels in that strange land more perilous.

Two incidents from the Vicksburg expedition proved especially significant to Galloway. First, while he was attached to Halbert Paine's 4th Wisconsin Infantry, he witnessed the fallout from a struggle between Paine and Brigadier General Williams over Union policy toward slaves seeking asylum inside their lines. Following orders from Butler himself, Williams ordered the 2nd Brigade's commanders to turn all fugitive slaves in their lines "out beyond the limits of their respective guards and sentinels." While Paine did not seem to appreciate the fact, when Williams issued that order, he was respecting the chain of command. Unlike at Fortress Monroe, where President Lincoln left Butler to devise his own policy toward the slaves who sought to enter his lines, the president had explicitly ordered Butler to turn away fugitive slaves in the Department of the Gulf. In setting a policy toward the Deep South's slaves, Lincoln hoped that Butler might find a middle ground that would alienate neither northern abolitionists nor southern planters. Lincoln and his generals also worried that the tremendous numbers of slaves on Mississippi River plantations might overwhelm Butler's capacity to care for them and hinder his military operations.[27]

Paine refused to obey Williams's order, a move that must have endeared him to Galloway. In a curtly worded missive to his superior officer, the Union colonel insisted that neither his conscience nor his military judgment would allow him to return slaves to bounty hunters, slave catchers, or "vindictive owners." He reminded the general that "many fugitives . . .

have, upon close examination, given him important military information."[28] Williams took Paine's response as insubordination and little short of treason. He placed the colonel under arrest and confined him to his garrison on 15 June. Outraged, Paine's regiment was soon in a "state of mutiny," one of his soldiers reported. In a dress parade, they marched past the general's headquarters and gave three loud groans for him and three rousing cheers for Paine. Men had been court-martialed for less.[29]

The fugitive slave policy may have made good political sense from Lincoln's point of view and possibly even good military sense, but it could only have strengthened Galloway's distrust of the Union's commitment to the African American freedom struggle. In Mississippi and Louisiana, the young black man observed cotton and sugarcane plantations with thousands of slave laborers. He saw men and women worked to the edge of dying, savagely punished, and horribly deprived. Some of the fugitive slaves who reached Union lines still had chains on their legs, fresh wounds from whippings, and terrible scars that were evidence of a history of rebellion and resistance. Union soldiers encountered many slaves who had come from as far away as North Carolina, Virginia, and Maryland and been sold into the Deep South as a punishment; these fugitives now saw for the first time a chance for freedom and the opportunity to be reunited with their families.[30] To see such black men and women turned away from Union lines and abandoned to the mercy of slave patrols and bounty hunters was not something that a man like Galloway would soon forget or forgive. The only known record of his involvement in Mississippi—a postwar letter from Paine introducing Galloway to the head of the Freedmen's Bureau—does not specify what he witnessed there, but he could not have missed the human consequences of such a far-reaching policy.[31]

&

Galloway soon saw a no less disturbing side of the Union military's efforts in the Department of the Gulf. In June, Butler's forces made another attempt at Vicksburg. Brigadier General Williams permitted Halbert Paine to command the 4th Wisconsin again, though he did not cancel the colonel's court-martial and kept him under house arrest except when the regiment was actually in battle. On 16 June, Paine and his men boarded the steamboat *Laurel Hill* and moved up the Mississippi with approximately 4,000 other soldiers. During that second expedition, Union commanders had no notion of laying siege to Vicksburg. Instead, their military engineers had devised a plan to dig a canal in a muddy oxbow of the Mississippi that, if completed successfully, would allow river traffic to bypass Vicksburg altogether. The canal would give the Union control over the Mississippi without having to touch Vicksburg.

Even before they stuck the first shovel into the swamp mud, Paine's Wisconsin soldiers teetered on their last legs. Only a few days earlier, one of the regiment's other officers wrote that "we could not muster 300 effective men; and of these, not one half could march under the hot sun for two miles without complete exhaustion."[32] Poor rations, bad drinking water, diseases, hard duty, and the suffocating heat of the Mississippi summer had already taken a heavy toll on the regiment. "Butler's Ditch" only increased their misery.

As they grappled with swamp and river, the beleaguered men began to sicken and die. Desperate for laborers, Williams ordered his troops to confiscate 1,000 to 1,200 African American men from local plantations and put them to work on the canal, with the understanding that they would be protected and freed in exchange for their labors. The Mississippi slaves perished as quickly as the troops from Wisconsin. A Union soldier wrote that the slave laborers "died off like an infected flock of sheep."[33] The canal's progress was no greater, either. The engineering proved faulty; the excavation, impossible. Not long after the canal walls collapsed on 11 July, Butler finally gave up and ordered Williams's brigade to withdraw to Baton Rouge. When the Federal troops headed back downriver, however, they left, as a Wisconsin soldier put it, "the deluded negroes that were yet alive . . . to the tender mercies of any one who chose to arrest them."[34] Their prospects must have made Galloway cringe. Arrest, he had to know, was the least of their worries.

After Williams was killed in battle later that summer, Halbert Paine's superior dropped the charges against him and soon promoted him to brigadier general. According to a letter written by Paine in 1866, when he was serving in the U.S. House of Representatives, the Union vessels left behind not only the slave laborers at Vicksburg, but also Galloway. Paine's letter indicated that the Confederates captured Galloway at Vicksburg in 1862.[35] The exact date is uncertain, but the capture most likely occurred during that second expedition up the Mississippi River and the attempt to build "Butler's Ditch." If that is the case, then the black spy either saw, heard, or even experienced firsthand what happened to the abandoned slave laborers who risked their lives to help the Union soldiers and gain their own freedom.

The incident confirmed Galloway's worst suspicions about the Union cause. Of the circumstances of his capture or his treatment in Rebel hands, Paine's 1866 letter said nothing. In addition to his disclosure of the ex-slave's association with his regiment, Congressman Paine indicated only that Galloway could be "trusted implicitly." In the hands of the enemy, his fate unknown to his fellows, Galloway had vanished into the shadows surrounding the muddy banks of the Mississippi.

5

They Will Fight to the Death

A LONG WAY FROM THE MISSISSIPPI RIVER, A VERY DIFFERENT SCENE was unfolding along the salt marshes and quiet bays of the North Carolina coast. Brigadier General Ambrose Burnside's forces had carved out a long slice of the state's coastline running 100 miles north to south that would remain in Union hands for the war's final three years. By taking such a vast territory, Burnside's armada opened a strategic back door to the Confederate capital in Richmond, eliminated a base for privateers and blockade-runners, and deprived the Confederacy of much of the state's agricultural wealth for the remainder of the war. Union commanders would shortly make Beaufort an important supply depot for vessels blockading Confederate shipping in the Carolinas and Georgia. The little seaport also became the main point of entry into the state's interior for Union troops and a launching ground for major naval operations farther south, especially for the invasion of Charleston in 1863 and the long siege of Fort Fisher, at the mouth of the Cape Fear River, in 1864–65.

Burnside's first warships entering Hatteras Inlet set an extraordinary phenomenon in motion: slaves inland began to take their owners' boats and head to the Union invasion force. As soon as New Bern fell in March 1862, the city was, as Burnside said, "overrun with fugitives from the surrounding towns and plantations." Hundreds, then thousands, of African American men, women, and children fled from bondage in Confederate territory to freedom in New Bern, Plymouth, "little" Washington, Beaufort, and Roanoke Island. "It would be utterly impossible . . . to keep them outside of our lines," an overwrought Burnside reported to the secretary of war, "as they find their way to us through woods and swamps from every side."[1]

That boatlift reached deep into the state's interior in a way that suggests that someone had already spread word of the Union army's imminent arrival and heralded the promise of liberty for those who crossed the invading army's lines. The slaves came, they came in large numbers, and they kept coming. A crowd of slaves, "patched until their patches themselves were rags," sailed from the river port of Plymouth all the way to Roanoke Island, a distance of seventy-five miles. "How they succeeded is a wonder to us all," a Yankee soldier exclaimed, reflecting on the stormy weather and rough seas.[2]

On the Chowan River, slaves stole a dinghy and sailed away while their outraged owner took potshots at them from shore. Another night, a slave woman named Juno gathered her children into a dugout canoe and paddled down the Neuse River to New Bern. At Columbia, on the Scuppernong River, a crowd of slaves stole a schooner and sailed to freedom. A little west of there, a black boatman known as "Big Bob" confiscated a vessel and carried sixteen slaves down the Tar River to freedom, then turned and went back upriver for more.[3]

In the seaports captured by Union troops, the scene was one of bedlam and joyous homecoming. Only a few months after Burnside's conquest, an estimated 10,000 former slaves had taken refuge in Union-occupied territory. "Our town is crowded with runaway negroes," a Confederate partisan named James Rumley, in Beaufort, scribbled in his diary later that year. "Not only the able-bodied, but the lame, the halt, the blind and crazy, have poured in upon us."[4] The details of how best to reach Federal territory—what ports were in Union hands, where Confederate power was weakest, what routes were surest—spread quickly through slave communities. At first, few northern or southern observers detected the order behind the great exodus eastward. Eventually, though, even die-hard Confederates who had adamantly refused to forsake a belief in the loyalty of their slaves began to realize that they were not escaping in a haphazard way. "Nearly a hundred crossed the river last night and went into Bertie [County] on their way to Yankee lines," Kate Edmondston, a Roanoke River planter, wrote in her diary later in the war. "So much method do they seem to observe and so well are they piloted that the idea of its being a panic seems to lose ground."[5]

At the first sounds of cannon fire on the Outer Banks, many planters packed their bags and relocated into the state's interior, carrying their slaves with them. Many of those who did not transport their slaves inland

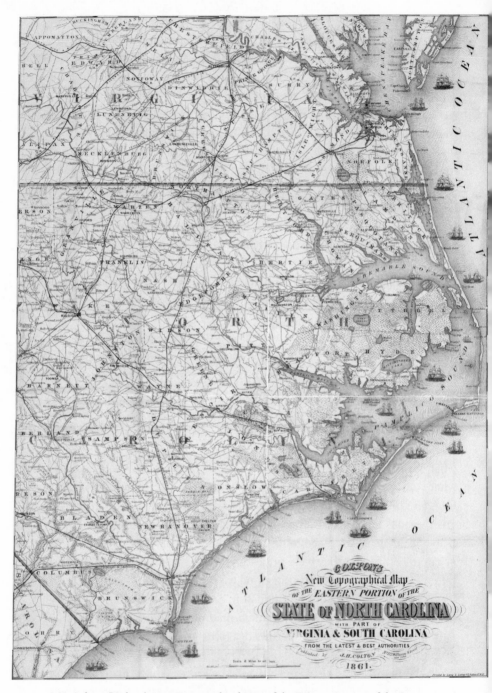

J. H. Colton, "Colton's New Topographical Map of the Eastern Portion of the State of North Carolina with Part of Virginia & South Carolina" (New York, 1861). Courtesy, North Carolina Collection, University of North Carolina Library at Chapel Hill.

"The Effects of the Proclamation—Freed Negroes Coming into Our Lines at Newbern, North Carolina." From *Harper's Weekly*, 21 February 1863. Courtesy, North Carolina Collection, University of North Carolina Library at Chapel Hill.

later regretted the decision. In September 1862 Henry Jones, a slave overseer in coastal Hyde County, informed the plantation's owner that he was losing all control over the slaves. He reported that they had grown "restless, careless, & don't want to work." A few had already fled to Union lines, and Jones had shot "old Pompey." The escaped slaves apparently made contact with Union spies or scouts. Ten days after reporting Pompey's death and the flight of that first group of the family's slaves, Jones wrote that "something like 100 [had] gone off in the last month," 35 in a single night.[6]

News of the Union army's arrival spread into slave communities deep inside the Confederacy. That November a journalist discovered that near Goldsboro, sixty miles within Rebel lines, "the negroes are beginning to manifest . . . a general spirit of insubordination. . . . Almost every day negroes are shot . . . for attempting to run away."[7] Goldsboro planter William Loftin chronicled his family's downfall in letters to his mother. Even before Burnside's troops landed in Beaufort, he wrote her that "a good many negroes are running away" and "all of mine are gone from the oldest to the youngest." Several months later, he reported that his aunt's slaves had also departed, "even old Rose and David." On 2 October 1862, Loftin wrote, "All that I ever had is gone." During a Union raid in January 1863, he began to realize more fully what he was up against. "My boy Tony came up with the Yankees in full uniform saying he was a U.S. soldier. . . . He went to J. H. Bryan's and took his gun away from him. He says he has killed four damned rebels. . . . He had a rifle strapped to his back."[8]

☙❧

Galloway reappeared in New Bern in the midst of that exodus out of slavery. How he survived his ordeal in the Deep South is another mystery in a life full of them. He was illiterate, of course, so he never put into writing how he managed to get away from a Rebel stockade or prison camp in Mississippi, or even how he made the long journey from the heart of the Confederacy to New Bern. He apparently never described the details of the incident publicly, either, or if he did, none of his listeners chronicled his words. A somewhat later edition of New York City's *Anglo-African*, one of the few black-owned and -operated newspapers in the country, proved the only exception. The newspaper alluded rather poetically to Galloway's having been captured "on distant Southern strand" but provided no other details.[9] Most likely, Galloway never told any audience the full story of what happened to him in Mississippi. His life as a slave, a fugitive, and a spy bred in him an abiding caution that rarely, if ever, led him to expound publicly on either the hardships he faced or his most daring exploits.[10]

Galloway's path to New Bern could not have been easy. The city of Vicksburg remained in Rebel hands for another year, until Ulysses S. Grant's long siege finally brought the city to its knees on the Fourth of July 1863. At the time of Butler's final withdrawal from Vicksburg, the closest Union lines lay far down the Mississippi River. However Galloway managed to get out of the Deep South, the journey seemed to have taken a toll on him. Years later, his friend and collaborator the former slave Mary Ann Starkey wrote almost in passing that he had needed her help desperately when he first appeared in New Bern. She may have meant only that he arrived bedraggled and hungry, but another possibility is that he was wounded or sick. Starkey had a reputation as a caring and capable healer and frequently nursed Union soldiers back to health during the war. If Galloway reached New Bern with injuries or a disease that he had contracted in the Mississippi Delta or the Louisiana bayous, she was one of the first individuals to whom local African American leaders would have sent him.

As Galloway recovered from his ordeal in Mississippi, he found himself in a changed city. Prior to the war, New Bern had been a modest backwater seaport where industry and trade centered on the export of timber, naval stores, and agricultural products that had come down the Neuse and Trent Rivers.[11] Now thousands of fugitive slaves made their homes in and around the city, and the fires of Union pickets burned nightly along the waterfront. Thousands of Yankee soldiers also bivouacked in old homes inside the city and in sprawling campgrounds on the town's edges. Across the Trent River, Galloway walked among legions of runaway slaves who were building their own village. They lived, a visitor wrote, in "huts built of split-pine sheathing, with round timber frame; the chimney composed of narrow sticks laid coble-fashion and then plastered with clay."[12] On the New Bern side of the river, he strolled along a waterfront that bustled with ex-slaves working for the Union army and in local fish markets, shipyards, and sailors' taverns.[13]

With its open-air markets, broad piazzas, and the brightly colored dress of the former slave women, New Bern reminded another black newcomer of "Port-au-Prince, Hayti, its aspect and its [racially] mixed population, and its luxuriant breezes."[14] The same thought might have occurred to Galloway, who was no stranger to the Haitian capital. Union ships crowded the harbor, and beyond the wharves and warehouses, the young black man passed fine homes lining wide avenues illuminated at night by gaslights. Each house was surrounded, as a Union soldier wrote home, by "two to twenty negro huts, according to the wealth of the owners." Eyeing the broad streets shaded by oaks laden with Spanish moss, a visiting colonel's wife later described New Bern as having "an air of decayed gentility hanging about it."[15]

New Bern was, above all, a besieged outpost on the margin of a great war. For the remainder of that war, the seaport served as the headquarters for the Union regiments in North Carolina and for the Union blockade of Confederate shipping in the South Atlantic. Rebel lines stood only a few miles away. To the south and west, a broad no-man's-land lay between New Bern and the Confederate towns of Swansboro, Trenton, and Kinston. That territory of uncharted pocosin swamps and remote pine barrens had become a dangerous realm of guerrillas, fugitive slaves, and spies and scouts. New Bern itself was rife with enemy spies and Rebel collaborators as well, and the Confederate army twice mounted assaults to retake the city. Though periodically threatened by Confederate forces, the northern army kept a precarious hold on the port, using it as a base for military excursions into the heart of the state's plantation belt and for a nasty war with Rebel guerrillas.[16]

Seeking shelter in the Union stronghold closest to those plantation districts, the black refugees erected their largest shantytowns along the city's outskirts. Out of those rough-hewn villages arose a great revival of African American political culture, ferment comparable in many ways to the black freedom movement that would come a century later. Unfettered by slavery, the black multitude exulted in the free expression of worship, family, and music for the first time. They organized schools, relief societies, self-help associations, a burial society, and a militia, the last of which was led by a young ex-slave and former army scout named William Henry Singleton. They also established some of the first independent black churches in the South. Andrew Chapel in New Bern, later renamed St. Peters, emerged as the mother church for the African Methodist Episcopal Zion denomination in the South.[17] Those institutions would become cornerstones of black political life for generations.

In those heady first days of freedom, both ex-slaves and antebellum free blacks participated in these African American community institutions. Long before Burnside's troops set foot in North Carolina, New Bern's free blacks and slaves had created a vibrant community. Approximately 1,000 enslaved and free black Methodists worshiped at Andrew Chapel before the war, making it the denomination's second-largest African American congregation in the state. Local blacks had operated at least one school before the war, and strong evidence indicates that they had established other clandestine churches and Sunday schools and possibly a local order of the Prince Hall Masons as well. A small but significant number of that community's leaders were literate and read widely, including national journals; even many who were not able to read and write kept up with national and world events by listening to the stories told by black sailors who had imbibed both strong drink and revolutionary politics in taverns from Bristol to the Bahamas.[18]

Like most southern seaports, New Bern had enjoyed strong commercial ties to the English, Spanish, French, Dutch, and Danish colonies in the Caribbean during the eighteenth century. At that time, slaves from all those islands as well as the seaports of New England, where most of that shipping trade originated, walked New Bern's streets. Over the generations, the lilt of West Indian accents and the cadence of foreign languages had faded within New Bern's black community, but local slaves and free blacks alike had held onto a worldly, cosmopolitan outlook. They continued to communicate secretly with friends and family in distant seaports, kept an attentive ear to what black sailors told them about the African American freedom struggle elsewhere, and maintained a precarious passage of the Underground Railroad that sent at least a few slaves north aboard seagoing vessels.[19]

Free blacks composed an important part of the city's population. Before the war, the little seaport was home to one of the largest free black communities in the South. The free black presence had peaked a generation earlier, between 1790 and 1830. At that time, as many as one in five black residents was free, a relic, to a large degree, of colonial laws that tolerated mixed-race marriages more than did those in neighboring colonies, as well as a state constitution that gave greater rights to free blacks than did other southern states. In New Bern, the free black population included many prosperous artisans, farmers, and shopkeepers, including John Carruthers Stanly, the son of a wealthy white shipping merchant and an Ibo woman born in Africa. A barber, farmer, and shopkeeper, Stanly owned more than 160 slaves and was the largest black slaveholder in the South.[20] His son, John Stuart Stanly, ran a school that drew free black youths from across eastern North Carolina to antebellum New Bern. Though many of the most influential free blacks abandoned North Carolina after a new state constitution curtailed their rights in 1835, they left behind a legacy of intellectual achievement and community leadership that continued to have an important influence on the black community at the time that Galloway arrived there.[21]

Other black leaders were born of the historical moment. Among them were fugitive slaves who escaped from the plantation districts of eastern North Carolina and crossed Union lines to freedom. Those early arrivals to Union lines were an extraordinary lot. The most fervent radicals, the most incorrigible troublemakers, the most militant artisans, and the most defiant slave preachers first risked their lives to reach Union territory. Prior to the war, they were the black Carolinians who had most ardently dared to defy or deceive slavery. Once the war reached their shores, they were the first prepared to take a great leap into the unknown in order to have a chance at freedom.

Inevitably, those black insurgents saw the nature of power in the slave South with the clarity characteristic of outlaws. They perceived its paternalist veneer, its inherent violence, and its grim foundations in ideas of racial purity, sexual domination, and social hierarchy. Many bore scars that they had acquired the hard way as they negotiated plantation discipline

African American Union army scout in New Bern vicinity. From Vincent Colyer, *Report of the Services Rendered by the Freed People to the United States Army, in North Carolina, in the Spring of 1862, after the Battle of Newbern* (New York: Vincent Colyer, 1864). Courtesy, North Carolina Office of Archives and History, Raleigh.

and eluded slave patrols and, once the war began, Rebel troops and the Confederate Home Guard. A few of the hardiest had survived slavery's last years by hiding in remote swamps and subsisting as maroons or marauders: always wary or on the run, usually lonely and living hand to mouth. Eventually, however, many acquired a hardiness and resourcefulness that made them the last souls on Earth that a Rebel scout might wish to encounter on a midnight foray near Union lines.

Like Galloway, some used their local knowledge and hard-earned experience to spy, scout, or guide for the Union army once they reached New Bern. Yankee colonel Simon H. Mix of the 2nd New York Cavalry spoke to their importance in guiding military expeditions into Confederate territory. "In all our expeditions in North Carolina we have depended upon the negroes for our guides, for without them we could not have moved with any safety," a Philadelphia newspaper quoted him that fall. He was especially grateful to have their help in the low country: "Nowhere in the swamps of North Carolina," he said, "can you find a path where a dog can go that the negro does not understand."[22]

Union leaders quickly learned the value of finding contrabands willing to go back into the Confederacy. "Upwards of fifty volunteers of the best and most courageous," wrote Vincent Colyer, superintendent of the poor in New Bern in 1862, "were kept constantly employed on the perilous but important duty of spies, scouts, and guides." He reported that the black operatives "were invaluable and almost indispensable" and testified that "they frequently went from thirty to three hundred miles within the enemy's lines; visiting his principal camps and most important posts, and bringing us back important and reliable information."[23] Galloway, despite the Union army's betrayal of slaves that he had seen in Mississippi, seems to have been chief among them: he traveled behind enemy lines, worked closely with Union generals, and was seen by the black operatives as their leader. More ventured back across enemy lines to rescue friends or family still in bondage and guide them to freedom. Out of the freedpeople's camps, they cast lifelines deep into Confederate territory, retrieving loved ones and expanding and informing the defiant and radical political culture emerging in New Bern.

That was the revolutionary milieu in which Galloway grew into political prominence. No matter how much he had been drawn to the black exile communities of Canada West or to the abolitionist strongholds in the northern states, New Bern placed Galloway in his element again in a way that had not been true since he fled from Wilmington five years earlier. He came from that world, knew its hardships, understood its people, and appreciated their strengths and weaknesses. In their company, Galloway also discovered a new kind of maturity. Prior to that moment, the now twenty-six-year-old youth had lived the kind of rebel's life that required talents for subterfuge: guile, restraint, dissemblance, patience, and the ability to act boldly but carefully under pressure and by oneself. Those gifts served him well as a fugitive, an abolitionist, and a spy. Now Galloway developed a genius for politics. Among North Carolina's freedpeople, he became a grassroots organizer, a coalition builder, and an inspiring orator.

As a spy and a political leader, Galloway seemed to pop up everywhere—and he struck quite a figure. Indeed, as he emerged at least partway out of the shadows, his character and bearing reached the attention of a broader public for the first time. A later description of him written by New York journalist John Dennett gives a good sense of why he rattled white conservatives so profoundly and why he held so powerful an appeal for the newly freed men and women. The ex-slaves had been born into a southern society that upheld white supremacy and tried to deny the existence of interracial sex, associated blackness with ugliness, compelled black men to carry themselves with great deference, and punished any black person who dared to challenge a white man's superior intelligence. Politically and personally, Galloway would have none of it. "His hair was long and black and very curly," Dennett wrote. "He appeared to be vain of its beauty as he tossed it carelessly off his forehead, or suffered it to fall heavily and half conceal his eyes. These were twinkly and slippery, and nearly always half shut, for he laughed much, and then they partly closed of themselves."[24]

Dennett seemed to stumble between being utterly besotted with Galloway and trying to stuff him into an antebellum racial stereotype. "He was a well-shaped man," Dennett noted, "but it was hardly to be discovered as he lolled in his seat, or from the insufferably lazy manner of his walking." But in the end, Dennett could not deny Galloway's magnetism and force. Whenever he rose from his seat and addressed a crowd, Dennett observed, Galloway sprang to life: he stood straight, revealed a commanding voice, and argued eloquently. His "power of sarcasm and brutal invective, and the personal influence given him by his fearlessness and audacity," the journalist conceded, "always secured him a hearing."[25]

That portrait of Galloway came five years later, long after his last days as a Union spy and at a time when age and experience had softened some of his roughest edges. In wartime New Bern, however, he was intense and purposeful. He was strong and broad-shouldered, with a stride that gave ground to no man, black or white. He swaggered, primped, and had a flair for the theatrical that sometimes bordered on the flamboyant. At the time of his rise to leadership in New Bern, he was already renowned, too, for a severe sense of honor and a fearless readiness to defend it, a trait that could only have endeared him to former slaves for whom honor had always been a white man's prerogative. Galloway may also have already gotten into the habit that he displayed later of always carrying a pistol where people could see it in his belt.

Galloway never claimed to be a saint. To the contrary, he sometimes joked that he was anything but, and he usually did so in a sly, self-deprecating way, with a wink and a little chortle, that suggests that he at least wanted his audiences to think him a rogue or a rake. He was, without a doubt, both brazen and steadfast, enormously charming, and like his white southern father, haughty among enemies and, among friends, playful and a little mischievous.

Yet for all his bravado and daring, the young man could not have seemed reckless or foolhardy in wartime New Bern. There was at times a disarming quiet about Galloway. Dennett glimpsed that part of his character when he met him after the Civil War, but he did not appreciate how deeply that part of Galloway was grounded in what it took to survive as a slave, fugitive, and spy. Patience, tact, and wariness had helped Galloway to survive and remained a part of him. All observers agreed with Dennett, too, though, that Galloway laughed loud and often, and his later speeches indicate that he had a wicked, wry sense of humor. In those early days of freedom, when war so often bred a grim callousness to suffering and death, the freedpeople must also have appreciated his playful heart as much as they did his courage and his quickness to stand up for their dignity and self-respect.[26]

Ironically, Galloway possessed many of both the best and the worst traits attributed to the most capable Rebel commanders: their courage and sense of dash and daring, on one hand, but also their pride, temper, rigid sense of honor, and quickness to take offense, on the other. In those respects, he was very much his father's son. Yet his sense of manhood, among other things, was a far cry from that expected of a southern cavalier. Indeed, from his first days in New Bern, Galloway worked closely with black women activists as equals and continued to do so throughout the war. He had an especially close relationship with Mary Ann Starkey, the former slave who had helped him when he first arrived in the city.

Starkey was among the most striking figures in occupied New Bern. A slave until the winter of 1862, when the city fell to Union forces, she was an elegant, genteel hostess with refined tastes for silks and fine linens, a determined social activist, and the mother of two children, including a daughter who, 150 miles west, remained in slavery.[27] During the Union occupation, she also ran a boardinghouse that boasted the city's most sought-after dining room—"the Delmonico of New Bern," one devotee called her establishment, referring to a legendary New York City restaurant. Her dinners were so highly coveted that lower-ranking Union officers jostled for reservations, often, to her regret, leaving disappointed, as army protocol decreed first access to her table as much as her own wishes.[28]

Born in New Bern in 1835 and formerly the property of wealthy local merchant James Bryan, Starkey opened her home as a meeting place for the black women activists of the town. A small adult "reading school" and a Bible school class operated out of her home, and she led a black women's relief society that solicited funds and supplies for refugee families and, later, for black soldiers.[29] As he grew into leadership of the freedpeople in the Union-occupied parts of North Carolina, Galloway supported Starkey's endeavors and frequently worked alongside her. Her surviving correspondence indicates that she saw Galloway often and relied on him heavily, even at times when he was behind enemy lines frequently.[30] He held a unique place of trust and responsibility in the eyes of Starkey and her circle of black women activists.

During that first year of the Union occupation, Starkey also let her home and boardinghouse grow into a front for an array of clandestine activities in which Galloway played a central role. She was especially well placed to collect political and military intelligence. Over the first days of the Union occupation, she had grown close to several of the highest-ranking Union officers in New Bern. Some of them, including the commander of the army invading force, Brigadier General Ambrose Burnside, roomed and boarded with her. Others, especially Colonel Thomas G. Stevenson, the beloved commander of the 24th Massachusetts Volunteers, and Lieutenant Alfred Hartwell, a young Harvard graduate who served in the 44th Massachusetts, became close friends.[31] Most were intimate acquaintances; all were abolitionists who saw the war primarily as one of slave liberation.[32]

The easy mixing of black and white abolitionists gave Starkey's boardinghouse a singular importance in New Bern. No place was better situated for Galloway and his men to pass military intelligence gleaned behind enemy lines to Union officers. Similarly, no place in New Bern was better placed for Starkey, Galloway, and their comrades to gain insight into the Union army's shifting fortunes on the battlefield or its fragile commitment to the African American freedom struggle. Starkey's devotion to "her boys" was genuine, but her friendships with Union officers also made her privy to a great deal of military intelligence that she used to help the African American community. Moreover, at least occasionally, Galloway and his band of black firebrands made their way through shadows and held secret councils in her attic. Beyond the eyes of both Confederate enemies and Union friends, these African American leaders dreamed of revolution and freedom.

Starkey was not surprised when Edward Kinsley arrived in New Bern in late May. Long before the steamship on which Kinsley traveled, the USS *Terry*, dropped anchor, Starkey had learned that a brigadier general named Edward Augustus Wild and the brother of Harriet Beecher Stowe, Colonel James C. Beecher, were coming to New Bern to recruit a black regiment. She had also heard that a "special friend" of President Lincoln's and Massachusetts governor John A. Andrew's accompanied them. That "special friend" was Kinsley, a wool merchant and ardent abolitionist from Cambridge, Massachusetts. On several occasions during the war, Kinsley undertook special assignments of a diplomatic or investigative nature for the governor that required unusual discretion or a particularly delicate touch. Later remembered as the governor's "right-hand man" and as his "friend and trusted confidant," Kinsley seemed to be everybody's best friend, quick to share a flask or his finest cigars with friends and strangers, U.S. senators, and railroad porters alike.[33]

Kinsley traveled to New Bern officially listed on the *Terry*'s rolls, along with an Irish hostler and a black butler named Scipio, as one of Wild's personal servants.[34] A sentimental but restless and sometimes dark-hearted soul, Wild hailed from Brookline, Massachusetts, and had graduated from Harvard Medical School. He was a practicing physician before the war but apparently found the medical opportunities in Boston dull. At heart, he was an adventurer and fighter. Twice arrested as a spy in European wars and later a volunteer in the service of the Omar Pasha in the Crimean War, along the borders of what are now Turkey and Russia, Wild had welcomed the excitement of a war closer to home. By the time that he came south to organize an African American regiment, he had already been wounded at the Battle of Seven Pines and lost an arm at South Mountain. Now he sometimes struggled to stay on his horse because of dizzy spells.[35]

Kinsley was of course not Wild's servant. During the voyage south, he shared the ship captain's table, sat at the general's right hand, and lavished his private stores of fine cigars and raspberry liquors on his dinner companions.[36] The ship's officers and Wild's staff discreetly avoided making inquiries into Kinsley's real purpose for traveling to New Bern. Only Wild knew Kinsley's true reason for being aboard the *Terry*.

When Kinsley arrived in New Bern, the war was not going well for the Union. Just days before, Robert E. Lee had trounced the Union army at Chancellorsville, Virginia. Ulysses S. Grant's army was mired in the muddy trenches around Vicksburg, on the Mississippi River. The recent Federal invasion of Charleston, South Carolina, had been a debacle. With its army beset by death, disease, and deserters, the U.S. Congress had recently passed laws enforcing a military draft. A tremendously unpopular step on the northern home front, the draft sparked widespread dissent. In the coming weeks, antidraft violence would rock northern cities, including riots in New York City that killed 120 blacks, injured an estimated 2,000 more, and incinerated an orphanage for black children.[37] Many northern whites resisted the notion of a war to end slavery or the prospect of black men wearing Union blue.

Desperate for new recruits, President Lincoln had reluctantly authorized the enlistment of African Americans into the Union army. A month before Kinsley's voyage south, the War Department first authorized a black regiment, the 54th Regiment, Massachusetts Volunteer Infantry. A second black regiment, the 55th Massachusetts, was drilling outside Boston and waiting for deployment to the South. Free blacks, not recent slaves, made up those first African American regiments, however, and Lincoln's emissaries had recruited them in a dozen northern states and Canada, not the South. Kinsley's real mission, as he saw it, was to determine if the slaves of the South were willing to fight for their own liberty.

Reports of African Americans in New Bern already petitioning for the right to enlist in the Union army had led Kinsley to expect the local contrabands to greet recruiters with enthusiasm. Instead, they at first avoided Wild's recruiting office. When Kinsley conferred with local black residents in order to understand why the contrabands refused to join the Union army, and what it would take to change their minds, all directed him to Galloway. Finding Galloway, however, was another matter.[38] Kinsley does not seem to have known that Galloway was a Union army spy. In fact, the young black leader may have already parted ways with the Union spy service; he had certainly done so by the fall of 1863, when a letter from Brigadier General Wild described him as a former spy and expressed Union commanders' debt to him.[39] Either way, after holding several meetings with Union officers and local contrabands, Kinsley grew certain that Mary Ann Starkey was the key to reaching Galloway.

Kinsley did everything possible to earn Starkey's trust. One evening in particular, he entertained Wild and two dozen other Union officers at her boardinghouse. He had known many of the officers back home in Massachusetts and hoped that the depth of their antislavery feelings might impress Starkey. While she watched and listened in the background, Kinsley led his fellows in a discussion of the war's aims, the centrality of abolition to their motives for serving in the army, and the bright prospects for former slaves who might join the army's ranks. He understood that Starkey wanted to hear their views discussed frankly and openly, primed by his cigars and whiskey.[40]

What she heard from Kinsley and his colleagues impressed Starkey, but other, smaller things about the Yankee wool merchant also proved significant to her. Perhaps most importantly, at least in Kinsley's eyes, she noticed that he related to the former slaves with unusual sincerity and respect. Unlike most Union officers, no matter what their views on the war's aims and the moral right or wrong of slavery, he spoke to them without condescension or disdain in his voice. One of Starkey's informants, a Reverend Durrell, even visited her kitchen one day to tell her that Kinsley had tipped his cap to him and a large gang of black laborers whom he had passed in town while they trod home with their picks and shovels. The incident had made a deep impression on Durrell. A white man rarely proffered that kind of respect to a black man, no matter what section of the country he called home.[41]

The incident with Reverend Durrell highlighted the kinds of behavior that had led to African American wariness about the Union cause. In occupied New Bern, most Union servicemen of all ranks had fallen into patterns of racial etiquette that were hardly, if at all, different from those that prevailed across the Confederacy. In fact, on seeing Kinsley's gesture of courtesy, a Union colonel with whom he walked that day had chastised him, he later remembered, saying, "Down here we do not pay that respect to negroes which you are showing."[42] Kinsley's good manners and lack of repentance astonished Reverend Durrell and his comrades on the road gang. The black minister later led several of his companions into the recruiting office, though for a time they seem to have been the only enlistees.

According to his appointment diary, Kinsley dined at Starkey's boardinghouse on 19 May and then took tea there four days later.[43] Finally, after watching him closely for nearly a week, Starkey took him aside one evening and told him, as Kinsley later recalled, "I want to see you."[44] Her words sent a wave of euphoria through him. Anxious to find Galloway as soon as possible, Kinsley wanted to meet with her that very night, but she demurred and arranged to see him the next morning. They talked at breakfast the next day, and afterward Starkey instructed him to come by her home at midnight. That was when she told him that she was expecting "a couple of friends from the Rebel lines."[45] She meant, of course, Galloway and a small corps of other local black leaders who could speak for the African American community. She did not say why they risked their lives in Confederate territory. Perhaps they ventured beyond the safety of Union pickets to gain military intelligence for the Federal army. Perhaps they infiltrated distant cities, surveyed bridges or railroads targeted for destruction, or located stores of cotton and other plantation goods that Union army raids might later confiscate in order to weaken the Confederate government. Perhaps they ventured into Rebel territory to rescue men, women, and children still in bondage and lead them to freedom—or all those things. If Starkey knew what they did in the Confederacy, she did not tell Kinsley.

After he had been led into Starkey's candlelit attic, Kinsley found himself face-to-face with Galloway. A crowd of other black men filled the attic. Two of the group's other black leaders stood at Galloway's side. Thirty-five years old, polished, and known for his intelligence, John Randolph Jr.

was a building painter by trade, a minister by calling. Unlike Galloway, he had somehow learned to read and write while still enslaved. His family's roots lay in Washington, North Carolina, the small river port thirty-five miles north, and he had not gained his freedom until the Union army came ashore.[46] The other gentleman, the Reverend Isaac K. Felton, was older, a preacher and old-fashioned exhorter. He was one of the most esteemed African American elders in New Bern; Starkey called him "Uncle Isaac" out of respect for him.[47]

That night the black leaders told Kinsley that they had little faith in Lincoln's commitment to African Americans. Though the president had outlawed slavery in the Confederate States when he issued the Emancipation Proclamation four months earlier, he had not yet taken steps to guarantee their full rights as American citizens. He had not even committed to paying black soldiers the same as white soldiers or to giving black fighters opportunities to rise in the ranks and lead troops in combat. But while Galloway and his companions took those national policy issues seriously, local matters had at least as much to do with their presence in Starkey's attic: the Union occupying force's racial prejudice over the previous year; Yankee pickets who stole money, horses, and other property from fugitive slaves as they escaped from the Confederacy; and the cavalier way that Union officers commandeered the contrabands, but not white Confederates, to build fortifications, dig trenches, and repair bridges and railroads.[48]

Two especially notable incidents involving the Union army's treatment of the contrabands loomed in the minds of the African American leaders that night in Starkey's attic as well. The first had occurred only a few weeks after Yankee troops entered the city, late in the spring of 1862. After a reconnaissance mission into Confederate territory, black Union scouts returned to New Bern and discovered that, while they were gone, government authorities had closed the new African American schools. Considering the freedpeople's thirst for education, the closing of the schools was egregious enough, but Union commanders had also surrendered a young slave woman to a white man who claimed her as his property while they were away. The "young Miss of sixteen" had escaped from "Mr. Bray" and sought asylum with the Union army in New Bern, but the provisional governor that Lincoln had appointed for the Union-occupied parts of the state, Edward Stanly, considered Bray's avowal of loyalty to the Union cause sufficient grounds for restoring his "property" to him.[49]

That capitulation outraged the city's black population. Before the war, Stanly had been a prominent local slaveholder, but he had opposed secession in 1861. After Burnside's successes, Lincoln appointed Stanly to administer civilian affairs in the Union-occupied parts of North Carolina. In appointing Stanly, the president had hoped to hold onto support for the Union among the state's large class of whites who had opposed secession.[50] That might have made good political sense for Lincoln, but it did nothing to reassure the region's blacks about the Union's commitment to ending their enslavement. The news that their new "freedom" could be so fragile and fleeting had sent a shudder through the contraband camps. The incident seemed to reveal a diminishment of the war's relevance to them, a lessening of their sense of sharing in a struggle to abolish slavery, and perhaps even a dissipation of the war's promise of a new America that would offer freedom and justice to all. As the contraband community sought to understand the intentions of Lincoln and the U.S. Congress, they had to notice the erratic and feckless commitment of Union leaders to slave liberation.

In the case of the young woman, the former slaves had also believed that freedom from another kind of tyranny was also at stake. They felt that Bray sought to reenslave the young woman not only for the value of her labor but also in order to have her body for himself. To the contrabands, Governor Stanly's intervention in the matter signaled that he—and, by extension, Lincoln—upheld the rights of white men to exploit black women and girls sexually, a practice that had been endemic to antebellum society in New Bern, as it was throughout the South. Union leaders, they concluded, obviously sided with slaveholders over slaves and did not seek to dismantle a society that tolerated the sexual peonage of black females. Starkey and her circle of women activists would have taken the most umbrage at the incident. Inspired by the young woman's forfeiture, the former slaves seethed with anger and resentment.

For that rugged group of ex-slaves who risked their lives behind enemy lines, and who had later made Galloway their leader, Governor Stanly's decision to return the young slave woman to her antebellum owner was especially abhorrent.[51] Some had just returned to New Bern after traveling, in Vincent Colyer's words, "for a week or more through the marshes, through the pickets of rebel regiments . . . with only a few shillings and a good revolver in their breast."[52] Almost immediately, they demonstrated that they had a collective political sensibility independent of the Union army. On the first night after the slave woman's abduction, twenty of the city's black scouts secretly left New Bern, passed back through Union lines, and disappeared into the Confederacy.[53]

The next morning, Brigadier General John G. Foster recognized at once the nature of the protest and the danger it posed. "The General," Vincent Colyer later told a northern audience, "upon reflection on the effect of thus sending out men who knew everything about the strength and position of his forces, decided that *he would be guided by that act of Congress, which says that no officer of the army shall return a fugitive slave.*" That evening, Foster's soldiers visited the slaveholder's house and liberated the young woman.[54] For the former slaves, the lesson was clear: at every step of the way, they would have to stand up for themselves and compel the Union to make this a war for African American freedom.

Galloway and his brethren who gathered in Starkey's attic that night could not have forgotten another incident, either. This one marked a more decisive rupture with the Union command. In combination with the Union army's betrayal of slaves that he had witnessed in Mississippi, it may also have been the issue that led Galloway to hold back his support for black enlistment in the Union army and led to the necessity of their meeting that night. Indeed, it may have been the final affront that caused him to leave the Union spy service.

At the center of the controversy was a group of contrabands who organized a militia during the fall and winter of 1862–63. William Henry Singleton, who eventually served as a sergeant in the Federal army, later described the raising of that independent black militia in the only African American memoir set in Union-occupied New Bern. A tough, broad-shouldered young man, the son of a slave woman and a white man, Singleton had grown up on a Neuse River plantation forty miles east of New Bern. He had been a field hand most his life, and though repeatedly whipped, he had stubbornly persisted in escaping three times by the time he reached adolescence. As a small child, Singleton learned how to elude slave patrols and bounty hunters and traveled great distances on his own. He had never attempted to escape to the North, however. Instead, he had always returned to his mother's home, or nearby, until the Civil War gave him the opportunity to cross Union lines into New Bern.

After finding asylum in New Bern, Singleton became one of those "best and most courageous" contrabands who served the Union army as scouts, spies, and guides. In Singleton's case, a Union lieutenant colonel, Robert Leggett, employed him as a scout during expeditions into Confederate territory. Singleton resigned from the scouting duties, however, after Leggett told him that the Union army "will never take niggers in the army to fight." In his *Recollections of My Slavery Days*, Singleton recounted that Leggett's remark spurred him to act separately from the Union army. He "hired the

A.M.E. Zion Church at New Bern and commenced to recruit a regiment of colored men." Singleton and his recruits drilled weekly using cornstalks while they waited to be issued rifles.[55] According to Singleton, the militia eventually numbered 1,000 black men. Their drilling began sometime during the autumn of 1862, at least four months before President Lincoln permitted blacks to enlist in the Union army.

The black militiamen expected that they would eventually join the Union army. Their expectations rose immediately after Lincoln issued the Emancipation Proclamation on New Year's Day 1863, which both touted the granting of their freedom as "a fit and necessary war measure" and decreed that freed slaves "of suitable condition, will be received into the armed service of the United States."[56] Hopes flagged later that winter, however, as the War Department moved at an excruciatingly slow pace to arrange for the enlistment of black troops.

As their impatience grew, Singleton's makeshift regiment provoked a great deal of consternation among Union officers in occupied New Bern. Many objected to the cornstalk regiment because the War Department had not yet approved the raising of black regiments. Others opposed the black fighting men because they refused impressments into work gangs and road crews. Still other Union officers and enlisted men found the idea of contrabands serving in the U.S. Army objectionable. They still considered blacks inherently inferior to whites in both intellectual and physical capabilities and did not want them fighting by their sides.[57]

Tensions heightened early in 1863. In a 19 February letter to his headquarters, Lieutenant George F. Woodman, the deputy provost marshal of the Eighteenth Army Corps in New Bern, acknowledged that he had sought confirmation from his superiors that "no authority has been given to any person or persons to raise a Negro regiment." The black men had begun drilling, Woodman reported, after "one colored man," presumably Singleton, "had been told that if he procured the names of one thousand colored men, who were willing to enlist as soldiers, their services might be accepted." The extent to which relations between the Union occupying forces and the contrabands had deteriorated became clear when the provost marshal arrested "about one hundred negroes" among the renegade volunteers until they submitted to being impressed into work gangs.[58] The irony escaped no one in the black community. While Lincoln had to go to greater and greater lengths to induce reluctant white northerners to enlist in the Union army, his officers in New Bern were arresting black men eager to fight for their freedom.

That night in Starkey's attic, Galloway and his comrades also had to take into account another factor: even though they were not allowed to don Union blue, many local contrabands had already been fighting, and sometimes dying, alongside white Union soldiers. In a letter home, for instance, a Yankee infantryman recounted an incident that occurred during a Confederate attempt to recapture little Washington earlier that year. During the Rebel siege, a flatboat full of Union soldiers and a few black scouts attempted a landing at a little peninsula called Rodman's Point. Pinned down by Confederate riflemen, they tumbled back into the boat and lay flat to avoid a spray of gunfire. "'Somebody's got to die to git us out of dis,'" a Union soldier recalled one of the black men saying, "'and it may as well be me!'" The black scout jumped off the flatboat, stood in the mud, and pushed the boat off the bottom before falling into the boat under the force of five bullets. The soldiers were spared.[59]

Galloway, Randolph, and Felton recognized that more than black scouts, guides, and spies had lost their lives while employed by the Union army. Over the last year, ex-slaves had also taken up arms to repel Rebel attempts to recapture the Union-occupied seaports on at least three occasions. Only a few weeks earlier, during a long Confederate siege of little Washington, Union commanders had grown so desperate that they sanctioned the arming of black civilians. To stave off defeat, Union officers forsook official policy and let "100 *negroes armed*" join little Washington's defenders. "It is very noticeable that those who have been opposed to arming blacks have nothing to say *now* against fighting along side of them," a soldier in the 44th Massachusetts wrote from the besieged city to his parents that April. He expressed his sympathy for the black fighters if the city fell. "Us they would parole," he wrote, "them they would murder or still worse return them to their old state of slavery." He concluded, "They will fight to the death."[60] In Starkey's attic, Galloway and the other armed black men sought justice not only for those who might risk their lives on distant battlefields in the coming months, but also for those who had already given their lives.

Most of their demands were straightforward. Before the African American leaders would support Union army enlistment, they wanted assurances that the War Department would outfit and pay black soldiers the same as white Union soldiers. They wanted the Union army to provide housing, provisions, and employment for their families while they were on duty, schooling for their children, and care for their elderly and infirm. The black leaders also sought a pledge that Union leaders would compel the Confederacy to treat any captured black soldiers as prisoners of war, not as fugitive slaves, which would lead to their reenslavement, or as traitors to the Confederacy, which would lead to their hanging. That last demand led to the night's longest and most contentious discussion. According to Kinsley, he eventually promised the black leaders that the Union would ensure that black Union prisoners would receive fair treatment at the hands of the Confederate army, a promise that he could not possibly keep. However, Galloway and his lieutenants had to know that was the case. They may have sought only to demonstrate the issue's importance to them. At least, after discussing the matter so late into the night, Kinsley was not likely to forget the issue when he returned north and met with Lincoln, Andrew, and members of the Massachusetts congressional delegation.[61]

After he compelled Kinsley to swear an oath to stand by their agreement while Felton and one of the other black leaders held revolvers to the poor man's head, Galloway crossed Confederate lines again and was gone for nearly a week. A period of frantic preparations followed, involving Wild's headquarters, the staff of several Union regiments, and the army's Office of the Superintendent of the Freedmen. Little boys ran back and forth across the Trent River railroad bridge, conveying messages between Kinsley and Starkey. Kinsley also accompanied the commander of Union forces in New Bern, Brigadier General John Foster, on a voyage down the Neuse River to inspect a new fort at Wilkinson Point so that they might have the privacy to discuss the agreement that he had brokered with Galloway, Felton, and Randolph. Foster had not inspired confidence in the local ex-slaves, and the abolitionist officers encamped in New Bern judged his support for a black regiment suspect.[62] Kinsley's and Foster's fathers had been boyhood friends in Nashua, New Hampshire, however, and that bond and Kinsley's gentle cajoling apparently won the day.[63]

When Kinsley returned to New Bern after spending the day with Foster, he went directly to Starkey and arranged a meeting with John Randolph Jr. Randolph, who, unlike Galloway, had a wife, children, and a father and mother in New Bern, had remained in town after their meeting at the boardinghouse keeper's home. Kinsley reassured Randolph that black leaders could rely on Foster's support and might now proceed to recruit as many able-bodied black men as possible. He also said, with a wink, that he trusted Randolph's discretion in the matter, even though he did not have a revolver to hold to the black man's head. The comment elicited a laugh from Randolph.[64] Several days later, Galloway, Randolph, and Felton led the long procession of enslaved men, women, and children out of the Confederacy and to safety inside Union lines.

Galloway soon fulfilled his end of the bargain with Kinsley. "The next day," as Kinsley later recalled, "the word went forth," the contrabands surged to Wild's recruiting office, and the brigade's first regiment was soon raised.[65] A letter from one of Wild's officers to the *New Bedford Mercury* shortly announced that "we number more than 600 able-bodied soldiers" and boasted that the new recruits were "not an effete lot of chivalry-tainted bodies, but compact and solid, some of Herculean proportion."[66] Under Wild and his second in command, Colonel James C. Beecher, they were originally known as the 1st North Carolina Colored Volunteers, or sometimes simply as the African Brigade. They were the first of more than 5,000 former slaves who joined the Union army in and around New Bern, and they formed the core of what later came to be called the 35th, 36th, and 37th Regiments, United States Colored Troops.[67] News of Governor Andrew's success at recruiting a black regiment within the original boundaries of the Confederacy spread quickly across the northern states. Within six months, thirty black regiments joined the Union army, most of them also sponsored by northern governors. By war's end, more than 186,000 blacks had served or were serving in the Union army. A sizeable majority were former slaves from the Confederacy.[68]

☙

During that first visit to the South, Edward Kinsley began a relationship with Galloway that lasted throughout the war. They spent a considerable amount of time together at least once more during the war, and they often sent greetings to each other in the letters that Kinsley and Mary Ann Starkey exchanged between 1863 and 1865. Kinsley's fascination with Galloway did not lessen with time. As the decades went by and the Civil War faded into the distant past, Kinsley told the story of his first encounter with Galloway often. The young black leader—that "man of more than ordinary ability," as Kinsley called him—was hard to forget, but much of what made Galloway so memorable to Governor Andrew's emissary had at least as much to do with the glimpse that he had gotten of an African American freedom struggle far larger than Galloway. In a way, the young black leader stood so tall that night in Starkey's attic and strode so confidently into New Bern days later because the freedpeople had been organized far more thoroughly during the war than had generally been recognized in the North or the South.

The black activists who gathered in Starkey's attic that night recognized, of course, that their freedom depended on the defeat of the Confederacy.

African American volunteers for the Union army in New Bern, ca. 1863. From *Frank Leslie's Illusstrirte Zeitung*, 5 March 1864. Courtesy, North Carolina Office of Archives and History, Raleigh.

It was a nation founded on their enslavement, the enslavement of their loved ones, and the enslavement of their descendants into perpetuity. In their eyes, the Confederacy had to be destroyed. They also knew, however, that their struggle was not only with the slaveholders' republic. President Lincoln's first priority, reunification of North and South, and the slaves' first priority, freedom, diverged, but both demanded the destruction of the Confederate States of America. That common goal ensured at least some kind of wartime alliance between Washington, D.C., and African Americans in the South. That common goal did not mean, though, that the fierce tensions between the slaves' aspirations and the Union leadership's ambitions fell by the wayside. Rather, they played out on the national political stage as well as in the candlelit attics of the South.

By the time that Kinsley disembarked in New Bern, the conflicts between the local contrabands and the Union army had led to a breakdown in their relationship. That breakdown proved significant in several ways. First, local African Americans had come to understand that they were fundamentally on their own. In response to that realization, they focused their organizing efforts on developing their own institutions, their own sense of self-reliance, and their own political strength. That was not so much the result of a process of disillusionment—slaves had never had a reason to expect anything more from the U.S. government—as it was a realistic sense of the political moment.

In addition, a cadre of the most committed local black activists, many of whom had served as Union spies, scouts, and guides, increasingly acted independent of the Union army. William Henry Singleton left his job as a Union scout and began to organize an independent black militia. Galloway left the Union spy service and focused on the African American freedom struggle both within and beyond Union lines.[69] In a way, they were guerrillas, freedom fighters as wayward of the Union army's rules and regulations as the Rebel home guards were of Confederate regulars. Like any effective military or guerrilla group, they had developed strong leadership, a clear command structure, a carefully calculated division of responsibilities, and ingenious ways of communicating over long distances. They had engineered systems for calling and holding councils, protecting their secrecy, and defending their members. They knew how to vet potential allies to their cause, as Starkey did Kinsley, and presumably they also had ways of dealing with individuals who failed to prove their trustworthiness. At times, they cooperated with Union officers, but their first duty was to the freedpeople. By the spring of 1863, Galloway consequently found himself at the nexus of an African American political movement that was determined to play a central part in defeating the Confederacy and in making the Union live up to its democratic ideals.

6

My Harte Over Run with Joy

WHEN EDWARD KINSLEY BOARDED THE UNION STEAMER *DUDLEY BUCK* for his voyage home, he must have been both exhilarated and relieved. His mission to aid the recruitment of black soldiers in New Bern had seemed bound to fail until he met Abraham Galloway and his compatriots and agreed to their conditions. Almost instantly, his work in New Bern blossomed. Only a few days before he left for Boston, Kinsley had watched in awe as fugitive slaves marched into New Bern by torchlight with Galloway at their head, claiming a complicated freedom in ramshackle camps where they hoped to build a new world.

Before the *Dudley Buck* could hoist its anchor, however, Kinsley got another powerful message from that half-born world. Just as the steamer prepared to depart, Kinsley heard a clamor from the wharf, where a black woman argued loudly with the guards. When he went to investigate, he found Mariah Hargett, not long ago the slave of the state's provisional Union governor, imploring the soldiers to take her to Kinsley. He waved the men aside and stepped forth to meet her, and she handed him a parcel wrapped in an old *Harper's Weekly*. When he pulled back the tattered paper, Kinsley had to take care not to let the contents spill all over the deck: it was a pile of small coins—three-cent pieces, half-dimes, and precious silver dimes. They had taken up a collection to buy a flag for the new African American regiment, originally named the 1st North Carolina Colored Volunteers. Later renamed the 35th Regiment, United States Colored Troops, the 1st North Carolina was the first of three regiments that eventually made up the African Brigade.

One of the former slave women had written the solicitation for donations. It said, in part, "It is for our good and the good of our Daughters that our husbands and Sons do in List to fight our Battles and gain our

[Liberties]." Concerned about the women's poverty, Kinsley at first refused their gift and insisted that the U.S. government would gladly supply the soldiers with a regimental flag. Dismayed, Hargett did not give up. She insisted that he personally make the arrangements for purchasing the flag with their funds and beseeched him to find a flag as fine looking as those flown by the other Union regiments stationed in New Bern. "We want it as handsome as the flags of the 44th, 45th and 55th," Kinsley later remembered her telling him.[1]

౭ఞ

Once Galloway had thrown his support behind the African Brigade, black men rushed to Union army recruitment meetings in droves. James Rumley, the Confederate loyalist in Beaufort, griped in his diary how "the black traitors are gathering in considerable numbers" to join the army. Rumley described the "horror, or the fiery indignation that burns in [the Rebels'] bosoms . . . when they think of their husbands and brothers and sons who may fall at the hands of the black savages."[2] That summer and fall Galloway did nothing to allay such Confederate hostility. Behind the scenes, Brigadier General Wild wrote, the former spy began to act as a "special and confidential recruiting agent" and as a "recruiting emissary," devoting himself to opening doors for Wild's recruiters in local slave communities and freedpeople's camps.[3] In public, on the other hand, he brazenly articulated a race pride and a political rationale for armed struggle that unnerved die-hard Rebels such as Rumley. At black political rallies held during the Federal occupation, Galloway argued that the former slaves would fight harder and better than white Union soldiers. At one point, he was quoted as saying that although McClellan "failed to take Richmond with 200,000 white soldiers, Butler would soon take it *with twenty thousand negroes*."[4]

More fervently, Galloway contended that the honorable service of the black regiments would compel a victorious Union to grant the former slaves both freedom and political equality. In his vision, black men in blue would win the rights to vote, to serve on juries, to be represented in court by black attorneys, and to run for elected office, all issues around which no political consensus had yet been reached in the North. Galloway's linkage of military service and political equality reflected a growing accord among African American leaders. "Once let the black man get upon his person the brass letters U.S., let him get an eagle on his button and a musket on his shoulder and bullets in his pocket," Frederick Douglass had said, "and there is no power on earth which can deny that he has earned the right to citizenship in the United States."[5] Galloway shared Douglass's conviction. During a speech at a rally celebrating the first anniversary of the Emancipation Proclamation, Galloway told Beaufort's freedmen and freedwomen, as James Rumley remembered his words, "that their race would have not only their personal freedom, but political equality, and if this should be refused them at the ballot box[,] they would have it at the cartridge box!"[6]

While his oratory shocked Confederate loyalists, Galloway got a very different reception from the former slaves. He spoke repeatedly in front of African American audiences in the summer of 1863, and he made a deep impression on those men and women who had so recently lived in slavery. In years to come, he would gain a wider reputation as a moving, eloquent speaker and a fierce debater. But at no time of his life was he a more effective orator than in those first months of freedom on the North Carolina coast. The prodigal ex-slave was always at his best among other former slaves. Impetuous and unafraid, he astonished them with his defiance, but he also amused and beguiled them. One sympathetic critic, a journalist, later bemoaned that Galloway's orations often rambled, shifting in a seemingly unsystematic way from one story or subject to the next, until he found his rhetorical way forward. That manner of speaking frustrated the journalist, who considered Galloway a brilliant but uneducated thinker, but not the crowds of black southerners who gathered to hear him. Eventually, Galloway gathered his thoughts and moved toward a crescendo that usually railed against the injustices of the South and often the North as well, while reinforcing the former slaves' faith in their own powers to reshape their world.[7]

The cadence of his voice and the manner of his speaking were familiar to those African American men and women. No black leader from the North reached them as well. They had grown up in a slave culture that relied not on the written word to convey ideas, but on songs, stories, and sermons. They understood a man who used the same devices to articulate his ideas and express his beliefs. Whether he addressed them from a church pulpit or on courthouse steps, Galloway captured their hearts and stirred their imaginations. Judging by the enthusiastic reception they gave his speeches, they loved how deeply he understood the brevity and hardness of a slave's life yet still stood there before them, laughing and defiant.

☙❧

The summer of 1863 was a season of many perils and much uncertainty for Galloway and the contrabands on the North Carolina coast, but it was also a time of momentous possibility. That was the first summer since President Lincoln had issued the Emancipation Proclamation, which freed the slaves in the states in rebellion. That summer the former slaves could fight for their own freedom wearing the uniform of the United States of America for the first time. Many of the freedpeople could do things that few had imagined prior to crossing into Union lines that year: watch their children attend schools and openly read books; worship in their own churches, spurning the balconies and back rows to which they had been consigned before the war; and even enjoy family reunions and picnics by the shore. For the first time in American history, they also saw themselves as taking part in the political life of their country.

That summer was something of a stolen season as well, rich with the delirium of the new world but still distant from the full price that it would extract. None of the African Brigade had yet left North Carolina to fight and die on far-off battlefields. That summer passed in relative peace, too: Rebel forces made no new efforts to recapture the state's Union-occupied areas. "So quiet was the life in New Bern," a Union veteran recalled, "that it seemed difficult to realize that we were actually in a state of war."[8] Even death seemed to take a bit of a holiday. Though hot and humid, the months passed without any major outbreak of infectious disease. And all summer, newly escaped fugitives entered Union lines almost every day, sometimes in droves when Union forces returned from expeditions into the state's interior. Family reunions, religious revivals, and round after round of political meetings enlivened the nights.

All knew that a great deal of uncertainty and struggle lay ahead, but the former slaves also found much cause for celebration. They held especially grand Fourth of July celebrations that year, including a high-spirited festival on Shackleford Banks, a barrier island several miles east of Beaufort. Four hundred blacks sailed out to the island and spent the day "singing, speaking, promenading and cheering for the Union cause and officers, and groaning for the Confederation," John A. Hedrick, an internal revenue collector in the town, declared.[9]

Some of the festivities raised funds for the support of the families of black men who would soon go to war. Under Mary Ann Starkey's guiding hand, the Colored Ladies Relief Association also solicited donations for the soldiers' families from the New England Freedmen's Aid Society. Starkey and other volunteers often relied on Galloway to bring back these funds on political and fund-raising journeys that he periodically made to Boston and New York City. Edward Kinsley, though he only returned south once

A rare portrait of an African American woman in occupied New Bern. Inscribed "Sylvia, Seamstress of New Berne," the photograph is dated 5 June 1863. Courtesy, Tryon Palace, New Bern, N.C.

or twice, continued to play a special role in support of Starkey's activities in New Bern as well. Late that summer, he sent her $500 worth of hospital supplies for "Wild's *Black Boys*." Starkey's activist women ultimately proved so successful at fund-raising that Galloway carried a donation from them to the "sick and wounded colored soldiers" in Portsmouth, Virginia, on one of his forays to Fortress Monroe. "The ladies here, as everywhere else," a visitor to New Bern wrote, "seem to take the lead in all great enterprises."[10]

The Colored Ladies Relief Association was behind another of the grand celebrations that summer: the presentation of the regimental flag to the first of the regiments raised for the African Brigade. The small bundle of silver coins that Mariah Hargett gave to Kinsley had grown to $150, and Harriet Beecher Stowe, whose brother James was the commander of the regiment, designed the embroidered banner. On the front, the Goddess of Liberty crushed a copperhead snake, while the other side featured a rising sun casting its rays over dark clouds. Above the sun, the seamstresses had inscribed the word "Liberty"; beneath the sun, the words "The Lord is our sun and shield." Boston abolitionists had "consecrated" the flag at a grand meeting at Tremont Temple before sending it south.[11]

The two black women who led the local effort to raise money for the flag, Mariah Hargett and Harriet Filmore, wrote Kinsley on 25 July acknowledging receipt of the banner. "The flag was carried round the Citty and followed by all the colard Ladays and Jentlemen and children," they told him. They compared their struggle for freedom to the flight of the Jews from Egypt and thanked him and their other friends in the North for doing "all they can to Deliver [us] from this Slavish chane." "My harte over Run with Joy," one of them wrote.[12]

Soon thereafter, early on a Thursday morning, the regiment paraded onto the New Bern city green, next to Brigadier General Foster's headquarters. The black soldiers' precision drilling impressed a cheering crowd that reportedly included 400 black women. As president of the Colored Ladies Relief Association, Starkey presented the silk flag to Brigadier General Wild and said a few words, later quoted by the *New York Times* and the *Christian Recorder* in Philadelphia: "As the representative of the Colored Ladies' Relief Association of New Bern, and in their behalf," Starkey said, "I have the honor and the pleasure of presenting to you, for the first North Carolina Colored regiment, this beautiful banner, knowing that wherever they go they will take it with them as an incentive to duty, and when they return they will bring it back with them, to show to us, their friends, that they have stood by it with their lives in the cause of freedom." She concluded: "Take it, and with it the encouragement, and love, and prayers of the women of New Bern."[13]

Wild's reply revealed a great deal about the extraordinary sense of the historical moment and the Christian commitment shared by the African Brigade's white officers and black soldiers. After expressing his gratitude to Starkey for her "widow's mite," he turned to what they all saw as the divine will for the war. "I thank you, and I thank God, who put it into your hearts to do this thing," the general began. Wild continued: "I thank Him who has enabled you to give and us to receive this emblem of the future destiny of your race." The stakes, he said, far exceeded national politics or sectional strife. Their battle to defeat the Confederacy and abolish slavery indicated "the fullness of time has been consummated in this our day and generation." Looking at the gathered crowd of liberated blacks, he thanked God that "you and I are here to witness the dawning of this day, which shall be great in the history of our country, a glorious day of promise in the future of the African race, aye, and for the advancement of civilization throughout the world." Turning back to the hand-stitched banner, Wild closed by saying, "I will now consign it to the care of those who I know will never disgrace it."[14]

After Wild's remarks, the regiment's commander, Colonel James C. Beecher, passed the flag designed by his sister to the regiment's standard-bearer. "I deliver it to you as the most sacred trust that has ever passed through my hands since I was born," he told his men. "I will devote myself to it, and you, I believe, will follow it with a single heart and a strong mind." He then called for three cheers for the flag. "You would have thought a young earthquake had broken loose," Beecher later wrote to a friend. "And when I proposed three more for the women of Newbern you would have thought the old earthquake had come to look for the young one."[15]

The Reverend John N. Mars, an African Methodist Episcopal Zion minister from Connecticut and the regiment's first black chaplain, closed the ceremony with a hymn that he had written for the occasion. Its last stanza proclaimed,

> All men are equal in God's sight,
> The bond, the free, the black, the white;
> He made them all, then freedom gave;
> He *made the* man—man *made the* slave.

As the chaplain closed his song, the black regiment fell into line again and, following their drum and fife corps, marched triumphantly through the city's streets to their encampment across the Trent River. According to Colonel Beecher, "Even the N.Y. Cavalry," a white Union regiment notorious for its ill will toward blacks, "forgot to say 'Nigger.'"[16]

೦ಌ

While the former slaves had much to celebrate that summer, Galloway could not afford to linger long at the festivities. With tens of thousands of blacks joining the Union army, Galloway began to shift his priorities from "the cartridge box" to "the ballot box"—that is, to the achievement of black political equality after the Civil War.[17] That summer he was still seen frequently among the liberated slaves in North Carolina. He remained active with pro-Union political groups and local organizations that defended the rights of black soldiers in Beaufort and New Bern. He spoke frequently at the black churches that had become the heart of political education and community organizing in the freedpeople's camps. He also addressed the mass rallies held by the former slaves on Independence Day and the anniversary of Emancipation Day. At the same time, he continued to assist Union officers to recruit black soldiers and ventured behind enemy lines at least occasionally.[18] He also maintained his ties to his militant abolitionist allies in Boston, including George Stearns, whose machinations had done so much to incite this war. On 26 July he sent two packages, with unknown contents, to Governor Andrew in Boston to forward to Stearns.[19]

His struggle against the Union army's degradation of the former slaves also continued. The raising of the African Brigade and other black regiments certainly signaled a crucial shift in the war's meaning to Galloway and his compatriots, but white supremacist convictions ran deep in the army and compelled him and his circle of black leaders to fight for African American dignity and equality on two fronts. They knew that they had true friends among the Union occupying forces stationed on the North Carolina coast. The close relationships formed with Tom Stevenson, Alfred Hartwell, and other radical abolitionists who made Starkey's boardinghouse their second home had taught them that lesson. Earlier in the war, they had gotten to know and come to respect the sons of some of New England's most prominent abolitionists. But white supremacy nevertheless pervaded the Union ranks, and after experiencing that racism, many of the contrabands never believed that Lincoln's war was their war. While the battle against the Confederacy raged, Galloway was obliged as well to defend black rights on the streets of Union-occupied towns.

A telling incident occurred on the afternoon of 12 July 1863. Galloway was escorting two Union officers attached to Wild's brigade on a recruiting trip to Plymouth, a little port at the place where the Roanoke River flowed into the Albemarle Sound. One was Lieutenant John V. DeGrasse, an African American assistant surgeon and a respected abolitionist from Boston, and the other was the Reverend William A. Green, also from Boston, who had just been appointed but was not yet confirmed as the brigade's first white chaplain.[20]

Plymouth had not fared well during the war. In early 1862, a Union naval bombardment left much of the town in ruins. Fires later destroyed many of its remaining buildings. Union private Warren Lee Goss described Plymouth at that time as a "remnant of what had once been quite a thriving village," observing that "the town consisted of a few tumbled-down houses that had escaped the flames, two or three brick stores and houses . . . a medley of negro shanties . . . and a number of rude frame buildings, made for government use." The private also noted that Plymouth "was a general rendezvous for fugitive negroes," being the gate into Union lines for slaves escaping from plantations throughout the Roanoke River Valley and the swampy counties east of the Chowan River.[21]

Galloway led the two Union officers through Plymouth's charred and

Lieutenant John V. DeGrasse, regimental surgeon, 1st North Carolina Colored Volunteers. Courtesy, Museum of African American History, Boston and Nantucket, MA, USA.

vacant business district to an afternoon worship service and recruitment meeting at the local Episcopal church. Reverend Green presided.[22] After the recessional hymn, Dr. DeGrasse stepped through the church's wrought-iron gate, and the trio began walking up the street, with Galloway and Green lagging well behind, engrossed in conversation. According to a report later filed by Brigadier General Wild, DeGrasse had walked only a short distance from the church when he heard an unfamiliar voice shouting "Lieutenant, lieutenant" behind him. He turned in the direction of the shouts and saw two white Union naval officers rushing toward him. One, it turned out, was John Lakin, master's mate of the USS *Commodore Perry*. The other was Acting Ensign J. R. Peacocks, of the gunboat USS *Southfield*. Both ships lay anchored at Plymouth while doing duty on Albemarle Sound.[23]

Lakin called again to DeGrasse, saying, "Come here! I want to talk to you."[24] Responding to what he considered a tone of insolence and condescension, DeGrasse replied, "Well, what is it?" The naval officers walked up to the black physician and one of them, Lakin, stopped eighteen inches from his face and accusatorily inquired, "You are here recruiting, aren't you?"

Smelling liquor on the man's breath, DeGrasse replied tersely, "I am." Lakin spit out the words, "Who the hell gave you the right to recruit niggers?" The prospect of former slaves serving in the Union army incensed the two drunken white men, as did the sight of DeGrasse in Union dress blues and the black physician's failure to reply in a deferential manner.[25]

"I'll let you know that we did not come here to fight for niggers," Lakin barked, taking a swing at DeGrasse. The doctor leaped backward, so that Lakin's fist glanced off him. As Lakin advanced again, DeGrasse drew his revolver.[26] At that instant, Galloway and Green rushed to the scene. Galloway's first words to his friend were "Why don't you shoot him, Doctor?"

Acting Ensign Peacocks and another white man, an army sergeant named Buckingham who had apparently been drawn to the disturbance, reinforced Lakin at that point. Though DeGrasse already had his weapon drawn, the three white men apparently knew Galloway well enough that they now realized that their real fight was with him. The three men quickly turned to confront Galloway. Peacocks declared, "If you draw your weapon here, I'll blow you through."[27]

"*You* can't blow *anything* through," Galloway replied. Never one to back down from a fight, Galloway knew in this case that if Union army recruiters were going to earn the prestige and influence necessary to build Wild's regiments there in Plymouth, he could not allow white men to berate his fellows in his presence. "I am man enough for either of you," Galloway continued, rolling up his sleeves while turning first toward Lakin.

Green stepped forward and tried to act as peacemaker. He grabbed De-Grasse by the arm and led him away from the impending melee, pleading with him not to shoot any of the Union sailors. He promised to take the matter to Brigadier General Wild, who was on a Union steamer anchored nearby. Realizing that Galloway was poised to pistol-whip a Union naval officer, Green then stepped between Galloway and Lakin and finally drew Galloway away from the sailors.[28] As Galloway, Green, and DeGrasse strode toward the wharf where Wild's steamer was anchored, Lakin, Peacocks, and Buckingham lurched after them, shouting obscenities. "We have got white men enough to fight this war," they bellowed. "We don't want any damned niggers." Wild's report of the incident later listed a number of other comments allegedly made by the Union rowdies, the most memorable of which was "We didn't come out here to fight for the damned niggers no how—These goddamned niggers walking around here with shoulder straps are making them too darned courageous." They kept up their tirade for two blocks to the landing, where Green dragged Galloway and DeGrasse aboard Wild's ship and the men made their complaint.[29]

The African Brigade's commander understood as well as Galloway that to the former slaves such incidents had a symbolic meaning that transcended bruised egos or broken regulations. Wild and one of his junior officers immediately left the ship and confronted the naval officers about the scuffle. Disdainful of any army general who deigned to lead black soldiers, Lakin confessed the facts and railed again, apparently no less vulgarly, against black recruitment in general and against Wild more specifically. Before sunset, Wild had Lakin gagged and escorted to the provost marshal's office. He ultimately delivered him to the commanding officer for the District of the Albemarle, who confined Lakin in the brig.

Wild also demanded that Peacocks go aboard the *Southfield* and turn himself in for arrest, which he eventually did, though not before he threatened retribution against the African Brigade. Meantime, rumor had it that Sergeant Buckingham was inciting a crowd of navy sailors in town against Wild, Galloway, and the African Brigade. Wild, who always enjoyed a battle, brushed off their "sneers and small groans." By nightfall, Wild had demanded that their commanding officer make formal charges against Lakin, Peacocks, and Buckingham on several counts, including conduct unbecoming an officer, swearing, breaking military discipline, causing a public disturbance, and treason. That final charge was the most striking. Wild reasoned that the three men had committed treason, in his words, for "openly discouraging and preventing enlistments in the military service of the U.S."[30]

⧉

Though Galloway apparently avoided more fisticuffs with Union officers, he found no end to his struggles to obtain fair treatment for black soldiers. By the fall of 1863, Major General Butler had returned from New Orleans to his old headquarters at Fortress Monroe and commanded the military districts of North Carolina and Virginia. Galloway now beseeched him to demand from the War Department fairness and equality for black soldiers. Hearing similar complaints from all his black regiments, Butler pushed the secretary of war to pay black recruits salaries and enlistment bounties equal to those of their white counterparts, but his pleas fell on deaf ears.[31]

The murder and abuse of black prisoners of war by Confederate troops also loomed large for Butler and Galloway that fall. Stories of Rebel soldiers killing black prisoners in the field and tales of atrocities against black inmates inside Confederate prison camps, reported by Union spies and Confederate deserters, infuriated both men. As a deadly smallpox epidemic swept Confederate prison camps that winter, the black leaders who counseled Butler underlined the importance of negotiating a prisoner exchange so that the black prisoners could get free of both their white tormentors and smallpox. Butler eventually attempted to negotiate with Confederate leadership via a "flag of truce boat" that plied regularly back and forth across the James River, a move that black soldiers and contrabands applauded.[32] But the Lincoln administration's policies toward black troops still fell far short of real equality and severely damaged recruiting throughout 1863 and beyond. The pay of black soldiers remained less than that of their white counterparts. Blacks could not serve as commissioned officers—except, occasionally, in noncombat roles such as assistant surgeons and chaplains—and Union leaders failed to live up to Lincoln's General Order No. 252, threatening to retaliate an-eye-for-an-eye for Confederate atrocities committed against black prisoners of war.[33] By early December 1863, Major General John G. Peck, a West Point graduate who had worked with Galloway, reported to Butler that African American recruitment in New Bern "is nearly if not quite at a standstill."[34]

Galloway persistently fought for the rights of his recruits, as did other abolitionists elsewhere in the Union-occupied parts of the South. A low point came the following spring when Galloway's old collaborator, George Stearns, resigned his post as the nation's commissioner of negro recruiting. At Governor Andrew's request, Stearns had first led the effort to raise the 54th and 55th Regiments, Massachusetts Volunteer Infantry, the nation's first black regiments. He had done so by raising phenomenal sums from Boston Brahmins and hiring leading black abolitionists across the northern states and Canada as recruiters. Based on his success, President Lincoln had asked him to lead the Union's campaign to recruit black soldiers in 1863. "I continued at my post as long as I could find reason to believe that the government intended to deal honestly with the Negro," Stearns said after his resignation. Black recruitment suffered, he explained, "because they had been treated unfairly and, as far as I know, nearly all representations of these abuses have been allowed to pass unheeded." In an open letter to the *National Anti-Slavery Standard*, Stearns addressed what he saw as the unconscionable consequences of the Union's discriminatory treatment of its black recruits, asking rhetorically, "How long will it take Mr. Lincoln and Mr. Stanton to learn that God has bound up justice to the Negro with the termination of this war!"[35]

The morale of potential black recruits only grew worse. Confederate massacres of black prisoners occurred with alarming frequency. Instead of responding with reprisals in kind, as black southerners urged them to do, War Department officials retaliated against black soldiers who cried out for justice. In April 1864, word of the court-martial of William Walker, a black sergeant in the 3rd South Carolina, reached Galloway and other black leaders across the South. Walker had reportedly declared that he would no longer remain a Union soldier if the War Department continued to pay him $7.00 a month instead of the $13.00 a month that white soldiers received and that he had been promised at the time of his enlistment. His case was only one of many such outrages, but it hit a deeply resonant chord. The symbolism of the discrepancy, not the $6.00 itself, mattered most to Walker and his comrades.

On 25 April, Massachusetts governor Andrew wrote that the Union army leaders "fear the uniform may dignify the enfranchised slave, or make the black man seem like a free citizen, [so] the government means to disgrace and degrade him, so that he may always be in his own eyes, and in the eyes of all men, *only a nigger*." Walker and his entire company showed that they shared the governor's sentiments when they stacked their arms in front of a white captain's tent and refused to report for duty until military authorities addressed their grievances. "He was a smart soldier and an able man," a black correspondent reported, "dangerous as leader in a revolt." A court-martial found Walker guilty of mutiny, and a Florida firing squad shot him dead.[36]

☙

Such outrages infuriated the African American soldiers, but Wild's African Brigade at least knew that they could count on their commanding general. Wild ferociously defended his black soldiers, a quality that must have endeared him to Galloway as well as to his men. While Wild's troops were deployed above Albemarle Sound in northeastern North Carolina that fall, Confederate guerrillas harassed his supply lines, took potshots at his pickets, and ambushed wagon trains. At first, Wild responded with a measure of restraint. But when the guerrillas captured and then hanged one of his black soldiers, he unleashed the regiment's wrath upon them. "Finding ordinary measures of little avail," he later defended himself, "I adopted a more rigorous style of warfare—burned their houses and barns, ate up their livestock, and took hostages from their families."[37]

Wild showed few scruples. The next time that the guerrillas captured a black soldier, he penned a note regarding two of their wives to John Elliott, one of the guerrilla leaders: "Sir: I still hold in custody Mrs. Munden and Mrs. Weeks as hostages for the colored soldier taken by you. As he is treated, so shall they be: even to hanging." Wild was brief but persuasive: "By this time," he reminded the Rebel guerrilla, "you know that I am in earnest." His reputation quickly grew among both Confederate guerrillas and his black fighting men. Edward Kinsley visited New Bern again in January 1864 and wrote back to Governor Andrew at the Massachusetts State House that Wild was "the only Brig. Gen. that is feared by the traitors. He you know goes in for the hanging process." Many black soldiers believed that the Confederacy would have quickly changed its treatment of black prisoners if Lincoln had made Wild's policies universal for even a few days.

At Fortress Monroe, Butler stood by his "hanging general," though he was besieged with vituperative petitions and fiery protests against Wild. Defending him to Secretary of War Edwin Stanton, Butler voiced his approval of Wild's tactics and could not resist boasting that Wild "appears to have done his work with great thoroughness." "I think we are much indebted to Genl. Wild and his Negro troops for what they have done," he told Stanton.[38] Wild and his men grew fiercer and the warfare uglier as they increasingly encountered Confederate regulars who rarely took black prisoners. Surrender, officers and men alike learned, was rarely an option for black soldiers. As the war progressed, that realization led to some very bloody fighting, even by Civil War standards. Near the war's end, after Butler had been transferred and could no longer protect him, Wild faced a court-martial for his reprisals against Rebel troops who had been murdering captive black soldiers in Virginia.[39]

❧

One of the war's most remarkable phenomenon was the enduring faith of African American soldiers despite such mistreatment. For all their trials, black soldiers generally fought with great dedication and effectiveness. "I have given the subject of arming the negro my hearty support," General Ulysses S. Grant wrote to President Lincoln in the summer of 1863. "This, with the emancipation of the negro, is the heaviest blow yet given the Confederacy." Lincoln soon echoed Grant's assessment in a public letter, saying, "Some of the commanders of our armies in the field who have

"Colored Troops, under General Wild, Liberating Slaves in North Carolina."
From *Harper's Weekly*, 23 January 1864. Courtesy, North Carolina Collection,
University of North Carolina Library at Chapel Hill.

given us our most important successes, believe the emancipation policy
and the use of colored troops constitute the heaviest blow yet dealt to the
rebellion." To those who still opposed black military service, Lincoln issued
a scolding: "You say you will not fight to free negroes. Some of them seem
willing to fight for you."[40]

Whatever the arguments over support for the conflict among whites in
the North, the war had always been a liberation struggle for African Americans in the South. Even in the face of abuse and prejudice at the hands of
Union officers and the ruthlessness with which both Rebel regulars and
guerrillas dealt with black prisoners, most black soldiers held onto a prophetic vision of the Civil War that justified their losses and their suffering.

A black sergeant named Charles Brown expressed the prevailing sentiment as well as anyone in the ranks. While encamped near New Bern,
Sergeant Brown wrote that, despite all the calamities faced by his company
due to their race, "I feel more inclined daily, to press the army on further
and further; and, let my opposition be in life what it will, I do firmly vow,

that I will fight as long as a star can be seen, and if it should be my lot to be cut down in battle, I do believe . . . that my soul will be forever at rest." As his regiment marched into battle, Brown said, they sang,

> *We are the gallant first*
> *Who slightly have been tried,*
> *Who ordered to a battle,*
> *Take Jesus for our guide.*[41]

That faith made it easier for the black men in blue to endure their battles against both the Confederacy and the racism that persisted in their own ranks. It also inspired Abraham Galloway's determination, soon to be embraced by a generation of African American veterans, that the freedom they won with the cartridge box would lead them to the ballot box.

7

The Death of a Hero

ALTHOUGH NO LONGER A UNION SPY, GALLOWAY CONTINUED TO travel deep into the Confederacy at least occasionally during the fall of 1863. His contacts behind enemy lines remained extensive even after he turned his attention to black recruitment and political organizing. The far-flung nature of his connections can be measured by his success that November, in Brigadier General Wild's words, at "manag[ing] to get his *mother* sent out of Wilmington, N.C."[1] Wild's astonishment was understandable. Wilmington lay seventy-five miles beyond Union lines and was one of the most heavily fortified and guarded cities in the Confederacy. The seaport's importance to the maintenance of Robert E. Lee's supply lines had ensured the erection of formidable defenses, and a hornet's nest of Rebel spies and detectives swarmed Wilmington to guard against breaches of intelligence. Despite all the traps and precautions, Galloway somehow managed to pluck Hester Hankins from the seaport and spirit her to New Bern.

Galloway found shelter for his mother with Edward Hughes, an African American barber who lived at the corner of Middle and Broad Streets. He then requested Wild's help in getting her from New Bern to Boston. "I would like to do all I can for Galloway, who has served his country well," Wild wrote Edward Kinsley on 30 November 1863.[2] Galloway arranged for his mother to stay in Boston under the protection of John H. Stephenson, one of George Stearns's colleagues and a close family friend of William Lloyd Garrison's. Stephenson, a partner in a millinery firm, had worked for years with abolitionist groups such as the Boston Anti-Man-Hunting League and the Massachusetts Kansas Committee.[3]

The rescue of Hester Hankins says much about Galloway's audacity and his devotion to his mother, but it also reveals the range of his intelligence work behind enemy lines. If he could get an enslaved woman out of Wilmington in the middle of the Civil War, he must have cultivated reliable contacts in the Confederate seaport and established durable lines of communication between Wilmington and New Bern. During his years as a Union spy, an intelligence network of that quality might well have served the Union army in more routine ways: by reporting, for instance, on Rebel troop movements around Wilmington, on the comings and goings of blockade-runners, and on the forts and other defenses that guarded the Cape Fear River. To develop such clandestine relationships, Galloway had presumably drawn on men and women whom he knew during his youth: ship's pilots, riverboat men, fishermen, stevedores, and brick masons and other builders. Most, and perhaps all, of course, were slaves.

⁊

After arranging his mother's safe passage to Boston, Galloway agreed to undertake one final mission as a Union spy. He would not have done this for just any Union general. But shortly after his return to Tidewater Virginia, Ben Butler received reports that the Union prison camp at Point Lookout on Maryland's Eastern Shore housed a sizeable body of Rebel prisoners with Unionist sympathies.[4] Butler bid Galloway to travel to the prison camp and, according to a later newspaper account, "go among the captured Confederates, for the purpose of obtaining the names of those who are loyal to the Union, and who [are] willing and desired voluntarily to subscribe to the oath of allegiance to the Union government."[5]

What it took for Galloway to get inside Point Lookout and make a realistic appraisal of the prisoners' loyalties is hard to imagine. Originally built to house those captured at the Battle of Gettysburg, the prison camp was a grim, dangerous, and unforgiving place. Confederate sentiment remained strong there, and even the highest estimates for the number of Rebel prisoners with Unionist sympathies represented only a small fraction of the prison's overall population. Life was also very cheap inside Point Lookout's parapets, and prisoners had killed one another for causes far less serious than being a Union spy.

Located just above the high-tide line at the end of a marshy peninsula shaped by the Potomac River and the Chesapeake Bay, Point Lookout was framed by a fourteen-foot-high parapet and was divided into sections by a series of muddy streets and drainage canals. Inside those walls, Galloway discovered a world that few would have chosen to enter of their own free will.[6] A plainspoken and quick-witted young prisoner from Martinsville, Virginia, Private G. W. Jones, observed how "every type of humanity was

exhibited . . . —the pious praying, the wicked fighting, the tradesman tricking . . . the thieves stealing [and] all kinds of gaming, from trick cards, keno
[and] lotto, to dice and dumbbells."[7] Other prisoners were less sporting.
They had left battlefields damaged; amputees, the blind, and the shell-
shocked all wandered the grounds.

The prevailing ethic at Point Lookout was "root, pig or die." Private
Jones recalled the constant "scheming, the tricking, the hustling for grub,
the flanking and pointing to the goal for hard-tack and pickled pork, and
trading for rations."[8] The fight for survival was relentless: the camp was
overcrowded; rations were meager; firewood was scarce; blankets and
winter clothing were always in short supply. Forced to drink from con-
taminated wells, the prisoners suffered regularly from dysentery and other
waterborne ailments.

Harsh weather also took its toll. In winter, prisoners froze to death for
lack of beds or blankets; in summer, others died of heat exhaustion. After
a night when he noted that five men in his regiment froze to death, Private B. Y. Malone, one of the "Caswell Boys" from Caswell County, North
Carolina, recorded in his diary that two of his fellows grew "so hungry . . .
that they caught a Rat and cooked him and eat it." Another soldier ate a
dead seagull that washed up on the bay.[9] Men fought, and sometimes died,
over a plug of tobacco or a handful of crackers, the camp's main currencies.
That winter of 1863–64, according to another Rebel prisoner's diary, the
camp's coffin maker built, on average, twelve caskets a day.[10]

Hope, too, was in short supply. Early in the war, Rebel prisoners of war
had often found consolation in the expectation of a Confederate victory
or, at the very least, in the likelihood of their parole and a return to their
families. Neither appeared in the offing at Point Lookout. That winter the
war held at stalemate, with no sign of victory or defeat in sight, and Butler
had halted all prisoner exchanges to protest Rebel atrocities against black
prisoners of war. In a policy that many of the prisoners found even more
disheartening, the camp's commanding officers sometimes posted black
Union soldiers on guard duty, turning Point Lookout into a bizarre and
often disturbing theater of race and retribution where former slaves sometimes guarded former masters.[11] Butler apparently instigated the policy as
one of the few ways that he could exact a bit of revenge for the Confederacy's abuses of black prisoners of war.[12]

Galloway somehow navigated the prison camp's labyrinth of dangers.
He had cunning, but he must also have acted with great delicacy. The official Confederate policy toward soldiers who changed sides treated them

as deserters and traitors. If caught, they faced court-martials and, if found guilty, hanging. At Point Lookout, any Rebel prisoners who revealed a willingness to enlist in the Union army or navy remained beyond the reach of Confederate justice, but they were not exempt from the wrath of their fellow prisoners. Prosouthern sentiment ran high at Point Lookout. Watchful guards could not always prevent Confederate prisoners from meting out their own brand of justice against their fellows whom they believed to be disloyal or traitorous. Galloway had to proceed cautiously for his sake and for theirs.

Galloway must have been successful at Point Lookout. By the middle of December, Butler grew confident enough in the intelligence that he had received from inside the prison camp to suggest an astonishing plan to Secretary of War Stanton. Butler reported to Stanton that a significant number of Confederate prisoners were prepared to swear the oath of allegiance to the United States, if given the opportunity. Butler had also become convinced that many of those men would choose to enlist in the Union army or navy.[13] After a series of setbacks under his command in the Department of the Gulf, Butler did not enjoy a high standing inside Lincoln's cabinet. He would not have risked sending such an incendiary, potentially explosive plan up the chain of command without feeling confident in his sources.

On 21 December, some weeks after Galloway returned south, Stanton instructed Point Lookout commanders to make plans for enlisting prisoners willing to take the Union loyalty oath.[14] Ten days later, just before New Year's Day, Point Lookout guards posted copies of a proclamation offering amnesty to all Rebel soldiers willing to take the oath of allegiance to the United States. By 9 March, 595 prisoners had chosen, as one said, "to swallow the pill," that is, to take the oath of allegiance to the United States and to enlist in the Union army or navy. Three weeks later, the first Point Lookout regiment of "Galvanized Yankees" was officially designated as the 1st United States Voluntary Infantry. (The term "Galvanized Yankees" comes from the way steel changes color when it is galvanized, just as the Rebel soldiers' uniforms changed colors.) Ulysses S. Grant ordered the regiment to the Department of the Northwest, where they garrisoned forts and defended steamboat passengers from the Sioux along the Dakota frontier.[15] A second regiment of Galvanized Yankees recruited at Point Lookout was later also sent west.[16]

೧౩

Soon after rescuing his mother from Wilmington and investigating Union sympathies at Point Lookout, Galloway made his way south again. On or around 1 December, he rendezvoused with Robert Hamilton, a black journalist from New York City, in Norfolk, Virginia. Hamilton published, edited, and wrote for the *Anglo-African*, an influential and widely read newspaper that provided probably the best coverage of the Civil War from the perspective of the nation's blacks. His reporting on black organizing below the Mason-Dixon Line had enthralled his readers and heightened their curiosity about Abraham Galloway and a new generation of young black leaders emerging in the Union-occupied South. Hamilton intended to feed that curiosity by undertaking an extended tour of the Union-held ports along the North Carolina and Virginia coasts. Galloway had agreed to serve as the black journalist's guide.

The two men became friends immediately, though they came from very different backgrounds. Twenty years older than Galloway, Hamilton hailed from a free black family that had been rooted in New York City since the eighteenth century. He had never lived outside the island of Manhattan. He had a passion for the arts, music, and literature, while Galloway had never had the opportunity to learn to read or write. Hamilton also had a reputation as an accomplished musician, and his brother, Thomas, had long been one of black Manhattan's best-known literary figures. Before the war, Thomas Hamilton edited a monthly journal, the *Anglo-African Magazine*, which featured black political writing, poetry, and fiction, including a serialized version of the first black novel written in the United States. Robert had helped his brother edit the magazine until it folded in 1860. He then edited James Redpath's short-lived *Pine and Palm*, largely a mouthpiece for the Haitian emigration movement, and he and Thomas later founded the *Anglo-African*, which quickly became the most influential black journal in the United States.[17]

For all their differences, Hamilton and Galloway also had a great deal in common. Hamilton had been one of Manhattan's foremost black activists throughout the antebellum period. In the 1840s, he campaigned for black voting rights in New York. He played a leading role in the local opposition to the Fugitive Slave Act of 1850, and he remained active in several of the city's civil rights groups right up to the war. During the war, Hamilton's newspaper office doubled as a depot for black army recruitment. Black soldiers peddled subscriptions for Hamilton and read the *Anglo-African* around campfires from the Chesapeake Bay to the Gulf Coast.[18]

In Tidewater Virginia, Hamilton accompanied Galloway to some of the places that the young former slave had gotten to know when he was a spy at the beginning of the war. They visited Norfolk and Portsmouth during the first week of December and then, on 10 and 11 December, toured what was left of Hampton—the town had been burned by retreating Confederates—as well as Benjamin Butler's headquarters at Fortress Monroe. According to Hamilton, they visited local leaders among the former slaves, though he did not name names. Given what is known about Galloway's activities in Virginia, he probably introduced Hamilton to George Scott, the notorious fugitive slave who had become a Union army scout earlier in the war, and also to Thomas and Mary Peake. Thomas, as noted earlier, had served as a Union spy, while Mary ran a clandestine school for black children before the war and served as one of the first teachers in the local contraband schools.

Galloway and Hamilton may also have visited with some of the other local black women activists. Among the most likely doors on which Galloway knocked were those of Annetta M. Lane in Norfolk and Harriet M. Taylor in Hampton, two former slaves renowned for having organized the United Order of Tents, one of the first fraternal lodges for black women in the United States, before the Civil War. Rumor had it that, whatever else it did, the women's group also served as a front for helping local slaves escape to New England and Canada.[19]

Two other black women activists, Clara Duncan and Edmonia Highgate, may also have been on Galloway's visiting list. Duncan, a graduate of Oberlin College, taught in a contraband school in Norfolk. Her leadership in a local crusade against racial segregation on steamships had made her extremely popular among the freedpeople. Highgate, Duncan's good friend, had given up the principalship of a school in Binghamton, New York, to work by her side in Norfolk and Portsmouth.[20] Both women were deeply committed abolitionists and no less devoted than Galloway to Butler. Duncan later joked to Hamilton that she would never agree to teach in any part of the country not under the major general's command.[21]

On the night of 10 December, Galloway escorted Hamilton to a large gathering at Hampton's First Baptist Church. The Reverend William Taylor, a local free black carpenter and "a fiery exhorter" before the war, presided over the meeting. Galloway delivered the keynote address. Hamilton estimated the church's seating capacity at 800 and noted that attendance was "very good but the church was not full."[22] By the next morning, however, word of Galloway and Hamilton's presence had spread; pastors from a coalition of five churches in Hampton and Norfolk invited them to address an organizing convention for a regional black Baptist association, which seems to have gone well. "Although many things are to be seen which make the heart sad," Hamilton reported in the *Anglo-African*, "yet the joys of the present moment must obliterate all sorrows of the past."[23]

☙

At Fortress Monroe the next day, Galloway stood on a Federal dock overlooking the Chesapeake Bay and contemplated the next stage of their tour. He pointed to a light sailing vessel at anchor in the James River and informed Hamilton that the boat was a seagoing ferry that ran between Fortress Monroe and the Union command at Beaufort, North Carolina. They could take passage on the ferry and, if blessed with favorable winds, arrive in Beaufort the next day. Hamilton, however, balked at the prospect of sailing the ocean around Cape Hatteras aboard such a small craft. The dangers of the Outer Banks were legendary, and in the winter months, the prevailing winds made the voyage especially perilous. Reports of two new shipwrecks on the Outer Banks had arrived at Fortress Monroe just in the few days that Hamilton and Galloway had been in Tidewater Virginia.

Galloway wanted to reach Beaufort as quickly as possible, and he did not seem to care about the dangers of wind and tide. Hamilton pleaded with him to take a safer route south. Galloway grudgingly acquiesced to the New Yorker's fears, and the two men sailed a more inland passage, probably taking a Union steamer through the Albemarle and Currituck Canal and across Albemarle Sound to Roanoke Island. From the Federal encampment at Roanoke Island, they could catch a ferry across the Pamlico Sound to New Bern and, in New Bern, a train to Morehead City. During their voyage, Galloway apparently never explained his impatience to Hamilton, but the New York journalist observed his growing restlessness and excitement with every mile.[24]

Morehead City, the terminus of the railroad line, was a sandy, windswept little settlement across the Newport River from Beaufort. A Federal steamer usually ferried passengers back and forth across the river's mouth, but when Galloway and Hamilton stepped off the train, the tide was too low for the passage. Unwilling to wait on the rising tide, Galloway hailed a black fisherman and caught a ride for himself and Hamilton across the channel to Beaufort. "This was not an easy matter," Hamilton remembered, "but these colored pilots know every foot of the way."[25] The fisherman could easily have been one of the slave watermen who had rowed Burnside's troops into Beaufort Harbor almost two years earlier.

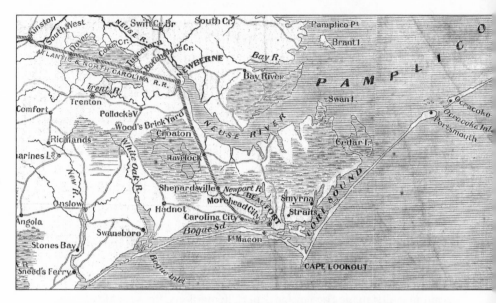

Beaufort, New Bern, and Lower Pamlico Sound, ca. 1862. Detail from "Map of Pamlico and Albemarle Sounds, Embracing Portions of Virginia and North Carolina, with their Strategic Points and Railroad Connections," published in G. Woolworth Colton, *Leslie's Pictorial History of the War of 1861* (New York: Frank Leslie's Publishing House, 1862). Courtesy, New Hanover County Public Library, Wilmington, N.C.

Galloway and Hamilton came ashore at Beaufort on the mudflats of Back Bay, a shallow creek full of oyster reefs rimmed by salt marsh. Galloway led his companion past the neighborhood's old fish houses and docks; through net reels, fish barrels, and wooden sailing boats; and up back streets of sand and oyster shells to the home of a former slave fisherman and his wife, Napoleon and Massie Dixon.[26] At the Dixon house on Cedar Street, Hamilton discovered the mysterious cause of Galloway's haste. In one of the few lighthearted episodes that ever appeared in the *Anglo-African*'s pages, he breezily reported that the dashing young Galloway, otherwise marked in Hamilton's stories by his relentless, all-consuming struggle against slavery and oppression, had lost his heart to a local girl.

Galloway had rushed to Beaufort to marry Martha Ann Dixon. She was only eighteen or nineteen years old, the daughter of slaves, and had been a slave herself until Burnside's forces captured Beaufort in 1862. Meeting the bride-to-be, Hamilton found his new friend's eagerness understandable. "He had wandered all over this country and Canada," Hamilton told his readers, "and only found a priceless gem amid the sands of poor Beaufort."

Galloway and Dixon wed a few weeks later, on 29 December, at her parents' home in Beaufort. The Reverend W. C. Whitcomb, a white Massachusetts chaplain stationed in the little seaport, conducted the ceremony.[27] An inspired Hamilton, not noted for his poetic bent, even penned the couple a few verses that he rather gaily shared with his readers, perhaps against his better literary judgment:

> *Our friend has faced the raging battle,*
> *On distant Southern strand,*
> *And tho' captured mid its rattle,*
> *He ne'er was conquered 'ill by prattle*
> *Of her who dwelt on Beaufort's sand.*[28]

Galloway's bride never attended school as a child but would, in coming years, learn to read and write. At the time of their marriage, she may well have been one of the many older students at Washburn Seminary or one of Beaufort's other contraband schools. Handy with a needle, she later made her living as a dressmaker and seamstress. Women raised among the fishing families of Beaufort typically refined their talents for needle and thread while they stitched fishing nets during long winter nights.[29]

Martha Ann Dixon did not conceal the political convictions that made her a good match for Galloway. In a letter penned less than a month after their marriage and published in the *Anglo-African*, the new Mrs. Galloway extolled the virtues of her hometown's contraband schools and railed against George McClellan's campaign for the presidency and his intention to allow southern planters, in her words, to "get all their niggers back again." In that same letter, she described an altercation between a slave girl and Thomas Duncan, a local sea captain. "It seems," Galloway's wife wrote, "that he wanted her to continue with him as his slave, assuring her that at the end of the war he should get the rest of his 'niggers' back and then she should be free." Mrs. Galloway noted sharply that the woman "most respectfully declined, saying she was free now according to law and President Lincoln's Proclamation."[30]

While in Beaufort, Hamilton was the guest of the Dixons' neighbors, Simon and Eliza Davis. Simon, a shipbuilder, belonged to a legendary clan of part-black, part-Indian, and part-white fishermen, whalers, and boat builders who resided in Beaufort and on the islands to the east.[31] In his newspaper's pages, Hamilton did not say much about Simon Davis, but his wife made a deep impression on him. She carried herself with such striking dignity and defiance, he wrote, that her cowed former owner never dared to strike her. "Having witnessed all the horrors of slavery, the fires of liberty now glow in her eyes with unconquerable luster," Hamilton said. For the *Anglo-African*'s northern readers, his portrait of Eliza Davis reinforced the meaning of freedom to a black woman. For the black soldiers who subscribed to the *Anglo-African*, Hamilton's words reminded them of the stakes for which they fought.[32]

❧

On 16 December, Galloway and Hamilton returned to Morehead City on the ferry and boarded the train for New Bern.[33] Forty miles west, they crossed the Trent River and unloaded Hamilton's bag at the depot in New Bern. There Galloway temporarily left him with Clinton D. Pierson, an exslave who seems to have been a barber and carpenter by trade but who had branched into farming and become a partner in a local grocery store and cotton gin during the Federal occupation. In his newspaper, Hamilton profiled Pierson and several other local African American leaders within Galloway's inner circle.

A short, animated man in his fifties, Pierson was known in New Bern for his boundless energy and his passion for justice. Hamilton compared him to Martin Delany, the brilliant black polymath and political activist who lived in Canada West when Galloway first took refuge there. Delany, though, had never been a slave; Pierson had lived in bondage for half a century, until Burnside's invasion force secured the local seaports. His life had hardly been that of an ordinary bondman, however. His "master was such only in name," he told Hamilton. During his years as a slave, Pierson traveled "wherever he desired, even to New York, and did as he pleased." While still in bondage, he also followed political developments closely and subscribed to national journals. "Our readers will understand precisely what he is," Hamilton commented, reflecting on Pierson's reading habits while a slave, "when we state . . . that he has taken the *Congressional Globe* and the *New York Tribune* for years."[34] The *Globe*, one of the predecessors of the *Congressional Record*, published transcripts of congressional proceedings, including the great debates over slavery and abolition. The *Tribune*, founded by Horace Greeley in 1841, was a radical Republican newspaper and staunchly abolitionist; before the war, the paper counted Karl Marx and Friedrich Engels among its European correspondents.

In subsequent days, Galloway and Pierson gave Hamilton a glimpse of the inner workings of African American politics in New Bern. They took him to worship services at the Christian Church and Andrew Chapel. He visited classes at the contraband schools and described them as "flourishing." A smallpox epidemic had recently led to the quarantine of 250 patients but had finally abated, so the black students again attended classes in large numbers.[35] Hamilton explained that "the number of scholars is very great, and continually augmenting, being fed by escaping bondmen who come from plantations within a radius of sixty miles of this place." He gazed upon the eager students "with emotions indescribable," he wrote. "Study they will, and it is useless for their teachers to tell them to stop, even for a few moments. . . . They appear unconscious of a violation of the command when they open them again."[36]

Among Galloway's colleagues, Hamilton also spent time with Edward H. Hill, an ex-slave and farmer who was the new president of the Society of Thoughtful Children of Greenwood Cemetery, which had just purchased the black community's first hearse. He also visited with John R. Good, a highly esteemed civic leader who had been a free person of color in antebellum New Bern and made his living as a barber before the war. Levin Johnson, a seventy-year-old day laborer, and two brothers, D. H. and Thomas Harris, master building tradesmen who played leadership roles in the local contraband schools, likewise impressed him. All betrayed Hamilton's preconceived notions of antebellum southern blacks as ignorant and unworldly souls. Levin Johnson, for one, confided to Hamilton that he, like Pierson, had taken the *Congressional Globe* while still a slave. Only in the climate of rising political intolerance that developed as the war approached, he told Hamilton, did the New Bern postmaster refuse to deliver his newspaper.[37]

Hamilton remained in New Bern for Christmas. The Sunday evening prior to the holiday, he not only delivered a rousing sermon to a full house estimated at 1,000 persons at Andrew Chapel, but he also sang a solo that was received with much emotion. Back home in Manhattan, Hamilton appeared as a featured vocalist in the choir at Zion Church, the "mother church" for the city's African Methodist Episcopal Zion community. "The John Brown song, as sung by Mr. H.," one of those in attendance at Andrew Chapel remembered, "was entirely different from anything we had ever heard here[,] and the chorus was joined in with much spirit by the whole congregation."[38]

The song was apparently a new version of an already-famous Union marching song, with an unforgettable first two verses and chorus:

John Brown's body lies a-moldering in the grave;
John Brown's body lies a-moldering in the grave;
John Brown's body lies a-moldering in the grave;
His soul is marching on!

Glory, glory, hallelujah! Glory, glory, hallelujah!
Glory, glory, hallelujah! His soul is marching on!

He's gone to be a soldier in the army of the Lord!
He's gone to be a soldier in the army of the Lord!
He's gone to be a soldier in the army of the Lord!
His soul is marching on!

The next evening, Galloway himself called an overflow crowd at Andrew Chapel to order. The black men and women elected John Good to preside over the meeting and chose William Johnson, a local African American grocer, as the recording secretary for the evening. The Reverend Isaac Felton, who had spent so much time behind enemy lines with Galloway, offered the benediction. In a letter to the *Anglo-African*, Johnson later testified, "We often hear our old brother pray, and of course are used to him; but Mr. H declares it the most eloquent prayer he ever heard."[39]

Comparing Andrew Chapel to his home church in New York City, Hamilton expressed astonishment at the degree to which the power of African American abolitionism in the South lifted up a liberating vision of Christianity. He could not have been happier. That night, Hamilton put his whole heart and his lilting baritone into a moving rendition of a hymn called "When Slavery Dies There'll be Freedom." By the time that Good called Galloway to the pulpit, excited men, women, and children packed the aisles and the rear and side walls. Galloway did not disappoint. His speech was "spirited and uncompromising," William Johnson recalled. "He handled secessionists and that still more defeated class, the Copperheads, without gloves, and his speech was received with roars of laughter and great applause." When Galloway returned to his seat, Hamilton again sang "John Brown's Body" before the former slaves returned to their shanty camps along the Neuse and Trent Rivers.[40]

Galloway left Hamilton in Pierson's care while he returned to Beaufort for the Christmas holidays and his wedding. In Galloway's absence, Hamilton addressed at least one other political meeting at Andrew Chapel and a mass celebration of the first anniversary of the Emancipation Proclamation. At the same time, the newlywed Galloway gave "the speech of the day," in the words of a northern missionary who was there, at an Emancipation Day gathering in Beaufort. "All wanted to honor the day which transformed them from things to men," Rev. E. J. Comings wrote from the town. Confederate James Rumley grudgingly scribbled in his diary a few of Galloway's words that day. According to Rumley, Galloway argued passionately for black suffrage and against Major General George McClellan, Lincoln's opponent in the coming presidential election. Rumley also expressed astonishment at Galloway's insistence "that the war would emancipate the poor white man of the south, as well as the blacks."[41]

Thousands of former slaves attended the Beaufort festivities, which included a parade, a political rally, choirs singing, bands playing, worship services, and "a sumptuous feast [that] loaded a table three hundred feet long in the street." A letter written by the Union army's assistant quartermaster in Beaufort and read to the crowd noted what the former slaves could never forget: that the first of January, Emancipation Day, had historically been the day upon which southern slaveholders carried their surplus slaves to the nearest county seat and, as the saying went, "hired them out" to the highest bidders for the coming year, often separating them from spouses, children, parents, and other loved ones. To the former slaves whom he had gotten to know in Beaufort, the assistant quartermaster noted, the first of January had now become their greatest day of celebration, surpassing the first of August, the day in 1834 on which the British Empire had outlawed slavery.[42]

Galloway furnished Robert Hamilton with a copy of the resolutions adopted by the Emancipation Day gathering in Beaufort. The former slaves hailed the day as "the anniversary of our existence as citizens of the United States," and they gave thanks to God "for hearing our cry when in the house of bondage, and for opening to us the door of escape." They expressed appreciation for the opportunity at long last to have their own schools and churches, recognized President Lincoln for the Emancipation Proclamation, and acknowledged "Gen. Butler as the true friend of the colored race, whom God has raised up for the hour." Aware of the doubts that many white northerners had about their readiness for the rights of full citizenship, they declared their determination "by our orderly, temperate, and patriotic conduct to compel even our enemies to acknowledge that we are *worthy of our freedom*." Finally, and perhaps most tellingly, they made clear that they stood more than ready to fight for their liberty. "That since the old flag is committed to our hands as the signal of justice and liberty to ourselves and our children forever," the freedpeople's resolutions concluded, "we will *proudly* bear it aloft in the storm of battle, and show to a doubting world that we choose the *death of a hero* rather than the *life of a slave*."[43]

If Galloway did not pen the meeting's resolutions, they echoed the vow that he had made half a dozen years earlier, when he and a friend secreted themselves in the hold of a northbound ship and emerged from that hiding place not slaves, but free men. The resolutions bore his mark on nearly every word: a twin emphasis on education and political struggle, a conviction that would grow more apparent in the years to come; the confidence in Benjamin Butler, the Union major general to whom he still held a special allegiance; and above all, the defiant willingness to give one's all for freedom—to choose "the *death of a hero* rather than the *life of a slave*." Galloway had made that choice many times in his young life, and not for the last time.

In the pages of the *Anglo-African*, Galloway emerged as an almost larger-than-life figure. Robert Hamilton's travels with Galloway also made a lasting impact on the newspaper's coverage of the African American freedom struggle. The weeks that Hamilton spent with Galloway in Virginia and North Carolina left him almost giddy over the character of black leadership below the Mason-Dixon Line and at the ardor for freedom displayed by the former slaves. Upon his return to New York City, Hamilton increasingly identified the South, not the North, as the wellspring of a new national black politics that had the potential to shape the war and its aftermath. At the same time, the *Anglo-African* portrayed Galloway as the most dynamic and admired black political leader in the South.

Reflecting on his month by Galloway's side, Hamilton also could not forget the yearning for education that he had witnessed among the former slaves. "We will venture to assert that nowhere on the face of the earth will you find a people so situated whose perceptive faculties are so powerfully developed, and who acquire knowledge of letters as rapidly as they do when all restraint is removed," he wrote in a column published on 16 January 1864.[44] The missionaries, teachers, and soldiers from the North who visited the contraband schools echoed Hamilton's assessment of the appetite of the freedpeople for knowledge and their capacity to master reading and writing. In the freedpeople's revolutionary political culture, literacy and politics seemed to reach a mutually reinforcing fever pitch: their first taste of reading and writing opened new ways of interpreting their daily life and political reality, which, in turn, sharpened their desire for more book learning. Hamilton witnessed that relentless drive for intellectual achievement while he toured the North Carolina coast. "The astonishing rapidity with which they acquire a knowledge of letters is a marvel," he observed, "but when you have gone into their cabins and heard their conversation, you no longer wonder that they learn to read in three or four weeks."[45]

For all his admiration for the ex-slaves' political strivings and intellectual accomplishments, Hamilton was also disturbed by much of what he witnessed in the Union-occupied parts of Virginia and North Carolina. He worried, in particular, that the Union army was treating the federally occupied territories "as a step-child." Like many local black leaders, he feared that the Union concentrated too much of its force against Robert E. Lee's army, thus leaving southern seaports now in Union hands vulnerable to attack. He sought to ensure that the vulnerable crucible in which African Americans forged their new politics and sense of citizenship remained protected. Above all, Hamilton expressed outrage that the Union army continued to treat the former slaves with so much racial prejudice and indignity.

Hamilton illustrated his concerns by referring to an incident that occurred on the evening that Galloway and Martha Ann Dixon took their wedding vows in Beaufort. In New Bern that same day, a Union provost marshal's guard, a white soldier, reportedly drove a throng of blacks away from a market sloop that had docked at the town wharf. According to Hamilton, the guardsman told the black crowd "they should not be permitted to buy until the white people were served, asserting at the same time that 'he would as soon shoot a nigger as a rat.'" That scene would have been quite ordinary before the war, of course, and Hamilton conceded that his northern readers might consider the incident a relatively small matter. He reminded them, though, how sparse rations were in New Bern at that time and how desperately the black population needed the food on that sloop.[46]

In the *Anglo-African*, Hamilton recalled the scene's injustice but also how the incident undermined the Union war effort. "The colored people," he reminded his readers, "are, and always have been, loyal, but many of the whites have just returned from rebeldom, and yet these colored Unionists were treated in this base manner, while those who had been trying to take the life of the nation, were thus petted and invited to continue their insults and aggressions on the rights of the loyalists."[47]

Hamilton believed that the preferential treatment of white southerners also had implications for the gathering of military intelligence. When Confederate troops attacked New Bern six weeks later, the city's African American leaders suspected that a white female spy who had fled the town shortly after the incident at the wharf had reported to the enemy forces on the town's defenses. "Is it any wonder that these things should take place while such villains are placed on guard to do provost duty?" asked Hamilton. "The opportunity these scoundrels have to injure the Union cause can only be comprehended by a visit to North Carolina of those who have eyes to see not only causes, but their logical results."[48]

Though Hamilton was distressed by the Union army's conduct, his reports emphasized, above all, the freedpeople's commitment to the freedom struggle. "There is another peculiarity about the people of North Carolina which we thought we observed," he wrote in the *Anglo-African*, "and which we now mention for what it is worth." He continued: "*There seems to be more of the unquenchable fire of freedom in the eyes* of these people than in those of any other people we have yet visited." He did not know why exactly. But he speculated, ironically, that the state's contrabands had received so little help from antislavery societies, religious missions, or black political groups in the North that they had made their own way. "They have been compelled to depend more upon themselves," Hamilton ventured, and "self-dependence among the people has produced its natural results and now, North Carolina is capable of standing alone without aid."[49] Obviously still a little awestruck by his experience among the freedpeople in North Carolina, Hamilton may not have overstated their powers in the end. In the coming weeks, they prepared to carry their "unquenchable fire of freedom" beyond the state's borders and into the larger world.

8

The Meeting with Lincoln

GALLOWAY CARRIED THAT FIRE TO THE WHITE HOUSE IN THE SPRING
of 1864. On 29 April he led a delegation of black southerners to a meeting
with President Lincoln. This extraordinary moment grew out of months of
grassroots organizing and indicated a significant shift in the freedpeople's
political priorities. With thousands of former slaves already serving in the
Union army, Galloway had begun to turn his attention from African American military recruitment to the achievement of voting rights and political
equality after the Civil War. Over the winter of 1863–64, he sought to carry
the radical political culture that had emerged in the federally occupied territories of the South onto a national stage. Like Robert Hamilton, Galloway believed that the fire of freedom burned brightest in the contraband
camps in the Confederate states. By leveraging the power that came with
the Union army's growing reliance on black troops, he and his comrades-in-arms hoped to place the attainment of black political rights at the heart
of the nation's political agenda and compel the Lincoln administration to
endorse their struggle for suffrage and political equality.[1]

President Lincoln had conferred with free black leaders from the North
earlier in the Civil War, but this seems to have been his first meeting with
African American leaders from the South.[2] Those circumstances gave the
gathering a special political significance. Even the character of the delegates themselves indicated its extraordinary character. In addition to Galloway, the black delegates included four of his closest colleagues, Clinton
Pierson, the Reverend Isaac K. Felton, John R. Good, and Edward H. Hill,
all from New Bern or the countryside nearby.[3] The other delegate, Jarvis M. Williams, came from Washington, North Carolina, the little port
on the Tar River. He had been a free person of color before the war and
worked as a baker.[4] Black southerners all, four of them ex-slaves, the del-

egation consisted of a brick mason, two barbers (one also a carpenter), a farmer, a baker, and a preacher, Reverend Felton, whose occupation when enslaved is not known. They were not the White House's typical guests.

Good and Hill barely spoke at the meeting, so awed were they by their surroundings. The splendor of the executive mansion and the graciousness with which Lincoln's butler greeted them took their breath away. The president displayed impeccable manners. He handled himself with the same poise and gentility with which he had welcomed Frederick Douglass to the White House the previous summer. As Douglass recounted, Lincoln was "the first great man that I talked with in the United States freely who in no single instance reminded me of the difference between himself and myself, of the difference of color."[5]

Although Felton was a tough old hand who had repeatedly risked his life behind Confederate lines, the president's hospitality impressed him, too. Even entering the building through the front door astonished him. No white man would have permitted it in New Bern. Throughout the South, the custom that blacks go around to the back door offered a comparatively minor but constant, unalterable, and deadly serious reminder of white supremacy's rule. For all the new things that Felton saw in Washington, Lincoln's simple gesture of respect remained his most lasting impression of the meeting.[6]

President Lincoln did not record what he thought of the group of black leaders who walked through the front door of the White House that day. They were bold, experienced rebels, but rough-hewn and with little schooling. Still, Lincoln was no stranger to self-educated or self-made men. He had known many who had made their names on distant frontiers through great courage and raw genius. The meeting between the president of the United States of America and the representatives of the South's slaves went well, by all accounts. They had a lively and straightforward discussion, earnest but impassioned. According to the black leaders, Lincoln did not act as if he expected deference from them, and they did not give it to him. The scene was one of the war's quiet, almost redemptive little moments, the kind that might convince a soul that it could salvage something good and hopeful about humanity amid all the horrors and bloodletting.

The black southerners presented the president with a petition, signed first by Galloway, that expressed their gratitude for the Emancipation Proclamation. They had not traveled so far, however, merely to thank the president; they came to demand suffrage and political rights. In a gesture that might have seemed brassy, if not downright impudent, Galloway and his colleagues quoted the Declaration of Independence—that "all men are created free and equal." They reminded Lincoln that North Carolina law had allowed suffrage for free blacks from 1776 to 1835, something that many states still in the Union could not boast. They also pointed out that a number of northern states—those, in their words, "most advanced in arts, sciences, and civilization"—had already extended voting rights to black citizens "with eminent success and good results." They argued respectfully, but pointedly, that the Union owed a debt to black Americans for their service in the army and navy. Galloway, always circumspect about his role as a Union spy, wanted nonetheless to make sure that Lincoln understood that he was speaking with black men who had risked their lives for their country. The petition announced that they felt "proud in saying that we have contributed moral and physical aid to our country in her hour of need, and expect so to continue to do until every cloud of war shall disappear, and your administration stand justified by the sure results that will follow."[7]

Above all else, the black leaders sought to convey to the president their fierce commitment to obtaining voting rights. In their eyes, all other political aspirations rested on the right to cast their own ballots. They beseeched President Lincoln, in their petition's words, "to finish the noble work you have begun, and grant unto your petitioners that greatest of privileges, when the State is reconstructed, to exercise the right of suffrage, which will greatly extend our sphere of usefulness, redound to your honor, and cause posterity, to the latest generation, to acknowledge their deep sense of gratitude." The *Anglo-African* later reported that "their interview was a pleasant one and indicated that the black leaders received from Mr. Lincoln assurances of his sympathy and earnest cooperation."[8] The president's assurances did not include a commitment to African American political equality, but Galloway's delegation still considered the meeting a success.

After shaking hands with the president, Galloway and his comrades strode to the Capitol and delivered copies of their petition to members of Congress. In a simple yet significant act, the black southerners walked through the halls of the Capitol, asserting their conviction that they belonged there and had earned the right to have their voices heard in the nation's highest assembly. Now distinguished by the experience of slavery, war, and the first tastes of freedom, their proud figures promised a new dawn in the midst of a bloody war.

The timing of the White House meeting was not accidental. In the spring of 1864, Rebel forces had massacred scores of captured black soldiers on southern battlefields, and the Union's response, or lack of it, had shaken black Americans' faith in Lincoln and the War Department. If the president did not address those concerns in a public way, many abolitionists, both black and white, feared that black enlistments in the Union army would stall, at a crucial juncture when white northern support and white recruitment flagged and Union forces increasingly relied on black recruits.

The most pressing issue for black Americans concerned Confederate policy toward captured black troops and a widespread perception that the Lincoln administration was failing to defend black prisoners of war against Rebel atrocities. Earlier in the war, Jefferson Davis and the Confederate Congress had decreed that black prisoners of war who had formerly been slaves would be reenslaved, put to labor on public works, and returned to their former owners as soon as feasible.[9] That would have been bad enough, but the actual experience of black prisoners in the hands of Rebel troops was often much worse.

James A. Seddon, the Confederacy's secretary of war, explained a rationale behind the brutal treatment of black prisoners the previous summer. In a letter to Robert Ould, who was in charge of prisoner exchanges for the South, Seddon argued that the Union army's recruitment of slaves was "contrary to the usages of civilized nations" and would lead to the unleashing of the "savage passion and brutal appetites of a barbarous race." By resorting to African American fighters, the Union had proclaimed its intent to destroy the South's "social order" and "add to the calamaties of war a servile insurrection": the North obviously desired "that the war shall be one of mutual extermination." Confronted by such an enemy, Seddon indicated that the Confederacy's only choice became "the abandonment of all rules, conventions, mitigating influences, and humanizing usages."[10] Not all Confederate leaders shared Seddon's sentiments, but the murders of black prisoners of war had not occurred in isolation. They reflected a downward spiral in the conduct of the war that affected black and white, northerner and southerner, civilian and soldier, and left few with clean hands.

On the battlefield, Confederates too often treated captured black soldiers with little mercy. By the spring of 1864, Confederate massacres of black soldiers had already occurred at Fort Pillow, Tennessee; Fort Wagner, South Carolina; Milliken's Bend, Louisiana; Poison Springs, Arkansas; and Suffolk, Virginia. Reports of a massacre of wounded black soldiers from the

35th Regiment, United States Colored Troops, formerly the 1st Carolina Colored Volunteers, recruited in New Bern, after an especially bloody battle at Olustee, Florida, had also reached New Bern earlier that year. At Olustee the small number of black soldiers listed as wounded or captured by the Confederate commander, and supplied to his Union counterpart, had already raised eyebrows in Yankee camps. Not for some months more would Union commanders conclude what the surviving black soldiers already knew, that "most of the wounded colored men were murdered on the field."[11] Closer to home, African Americans in New Bern learned that no black man in Union blue could expect to live if captured. That winter, Confederates hanged a black sharpshooter on the north side of the Neuse River after he had surrendered.[12]

The wartime atrocity that hit closest to home for Galloway occurred in Plymouth, North Carolina, the little river port where he had assailed the two Union naval officers the previous year. Late that April, black refugees from Plymouth began to straggle into New Bern. They reported the loss of the town to Rebel forces and a massacre of black soldiers, civilians, and white southern Unionists by Confederate troops commanded by Major General Robert F. Hoke.[13] Leading some 7,000 Rebel troops against approximately 3,000 defenders, Hoke had taken the town after a four-day siege.

Galloway must have winced when he heard that Confederate brigadier general Robert Ransom's brigade had played a leading role in the Battle of Plymouth. Only a month earlier, Ransom's Brigade had taken no prisoners after encountering black troops of the 2nd Regiment, United States Colored Cavalry, at Suffolk, Virginia. "Ransom's Brigade never takes any negro prisoners," one of Ransom's soldiers declared in the *Charlotte Observer* after the incident at Suffolk. One of Ransom's officers, Major John W. Graham, made the same declaration in a letter to his father the month before the Battle of Plymouth. At Suffolk, he wrote, the "ladies . . . were standing at their doors, some waving handkerchiefs, some crying, some praying, and others calling to us to 'kill the negroes.'" He confided to his father, parenthetically, "Our brigade did not need this to make them give 'no quarter,' as it is understood amongst us that we take no Negro prisoners."[14]

A conservative evaluation of the eyewitness reports and a cautious reckoning of the death toll in Plymouth indicate that Rebel soldiers killed more than 100 black people that day. Confederate troops, mainly Ransom's Brigade and cavalrymen led by Colonel James Dearing, executed approximately 25 black prisoners. They also killed 40 other blacks as they sought to escape the battlefield and murdered 40 more who had taken refuge in the swamps nearby. At least a few of the victims were women and children. Several eyewitnesses, including the only African American to leave a first-hand account of the massacre, indicated that the number of victims was much higher.[15]

News of Plymouth's loss and the massacre of black troops there reached Washington slowly. In a message to Lincoln's secretary of the treasury, Salmon P. Chase, on 23 April, David Heaton, the Treasury Department's special agent in New Bern, reported both the town's surrender and the massacre, but he based his report largely on testimony by the first refugees to reach New Bern, not Union field officers.[16] Soon, however, a telegram from the commander of the district's naval forces, Admiral S. P. Lee, confirmed Heaton's message. The news hit hard. It arrived at a time when the Union army's fortunes on the battlefield were sagging. The war was dragging on, and Lincoln's reelection later that year was in doubt.

Militarily, the consequences of losing Plymouth would prove negligible. The Battle of Plymouth was one of the Confederacy's last successes of the war. Only two weeks after taking Plymouth, Hoke's superiors moved him and most of his troops to Virginia, where Grant had launched a major action against the Army of Northern Virginia. Hoke had to abandon his plans to retake other Union-occupied ports on the North Carolina coast, and Federal forces quietly recaptured Plymouth later that fall.

But if the loss of Plymouth had limited strategic consequences, the massacre of black troops had the potential to effect more lasting damage on the Union cause. Many of the nation's black leaders believed that Lincoln's reluctance to retaliate more forcefully for the murder of black prisoners was shameful, as well as a serious blow to the morale of black troops. In their eyes, Lincoln and his generals valued the lives of black soldiers less than those of white soldiers. They could not imagine the president failing to defend white prisoners of war by any means necessary if they were being executed on southern battlefields. Lincoln, though, endeavored to walk a fine line. On one hand, he feared that a fiercer retaliatory posture might dampen white northern support for the war even further, prompt white enlistments to fall yet more, and destroy any remaining hopes for reconciliation with the white South after the war. On the other hand, as the Union casualty count rose and as the white general public increasingly viewed the war as primarily a crusade against slavery, white recruitment dropped precipitously and the Union army's reliance on black troops rose steadily.[17] Under the circumstances, Lincoln no doubt welcomed the opportunity to meet with Galloway's delegation of southern black leaders and the chance to reassure the black South that he was on their side.[18]

☙

After their visit to the White House and Congress, Galloway and at least three of the other men who had met with Lincoln—Pierson, Hill, and Good—traveled across the northern states campaigning for African American voting rights. Their tour attracted little interest in the white press, but it commanded the rapt attention of the black North. The delegation's first public appearance, at New York City's Zion Church, was typical. Chartered in 1801 and considered the "mother church" of African Methodist Episcopal Zionism in the United States, Zion Church sat at the corner of Church and Leonard Streets in Manhattan. A crowd filled the church basement on the evening of 4 May to greet the delegation.[19]

New York City's most prominent AME Zion leaders attended that evening. They included the Reverend Samson Talbot, soon to be elected the city's new bishop, as well as the legendary, and by that time blind and very elderly, Reverend Christopher Rush. Reverend Rush had been one of AME Zionism's founders half a century earlier. In subsequent years, he established churches throughout New York, New Jersey, and Connecticut and served for more than two decades as New York City's AME Zion bishop. Though now part of Manhattan's black elite, the ninety-year-old patriarch of the faith had been born to slave parents near New Bern in 1777 and had never lost touch with family and friends in North Carolina's African American communities.[20]

Reverend Rush gave the invocation that evening, after which the first of Galloway's troupe, Edward H. Hill, stepped forward to address the crowd, albeit reluctantly. A self-educated man, he did not pretend that he was at ease addressing a crowd of Manhattan's most accomplished black leaders. His words came hesitantly at first, but he gradually found his voice. "He said that [slavery] had been a massive wall against which many had pecked," Robert Hamilton, who was there that night, reported, "but John Brown was the only man who had the skill and power to break through it, and he had made the passageway so large that Abraham Lincoln and all his hosts had ample room to pass through." The remark drew "thunderous applause" and "manifestations of great delight."[21]

John Good spoke next. He was also intimidated to address a crowd that included so many distinguished ministers, physicians, and writers. He did not talk for very long, but his physical appearance and manner made a lasting impression on the black Manhattanites. Rigid and cautious in appearance, Good looked worn down by the tragedy and loss that he had witnessed over his lifetime, his whole being somehow evocative of having known profound suffering. Though he had been free by at least 1840, and perhaps all his life, to the audience at Zion Church, he seemed the very embodiment of their oppressed brethren in the South. They recognized him from the caricature of slaves portrayed so often in antebellum slave narratives and other abolitionist propaganda as the helpless victim who needed their aid and guidance, and yet there Good stood: awkward and a little reticent to be sure, but a capable and seasoned political leader who had just come from a personal meeting with the president of the United States. "We were remarkably struck with this gentleman's manner," Hamilton recalled. "He had dwelt amid the horrors of slavery so long, and had seen so much of it that he seemed too full for utterance. Tears and action would have suited him better than words."[22]

Clinton Pierson, the next speaker, related the story of the recent meeting with Lincoln. Unlike Good, Pierson came across as an articulate, sophisticated gentleman and wholly comfortable in front of the audience at Zion Church. To Hamilton, he spoke as if he had been educated in the North and had always been a free man, not a slave reared in the South. "He is a perfect politician," the black editor noted. In a clear, methodical, and detailed manner, if not an especially vivid one, Pierson described what had happened at the White House. He assured the gathering that he had read between the lines of Lincoln's conversation with them and felt confident that the president was committed to black civil rights and full suffrage for the former slaves after a Union victory.[23]

Galloway was the evening's final guest speaker. He addressed the New Yorkers at some length, his words emphasizing the independence and self-reliance of the freedpeople in the Union-occupied parts of North Carolina and Virginia and, at the same time, their urgent need for help from black northerners. Directing his comments to critics of government aid, he told the crowd that hundreds of white people, but only four black men, in occupied Beaufort depended on the army's commissary for charity food. Those four black men, Galloway said, perhaps tongue in cheek, were crippled or blind. "His remarks," Hamilton noted, "besides being exceeding humorous, as well as important, were greeted with peals of laughter and long continued applause." After Galloway left the podium, local leaders made their closing benedictions and appointed a committee to solicit funds with which to buy building supplies to send to the contrabands in

William Benjamin Gould
in late 1870s or early 1880s.
A master craftsman in antebellum Wilmington, Gould
escaped from slavery in 1862,
served in the Union navy, and
was a friend of Galloway's.
Courtesy, New Hanover
County Public Library,
Wilmington, N.C.

Beaufort. Galloway and his companions stayed and visited with their New York brothers and sisters until almost midnight.[24]

Over the next week, Galloway made a number of other public appearances in the North. Mary Ann Starkey wrote Edward Kinsley ten days later to thank him for "bundles you sent to us by Mr. Galloway," indicating that Galloway was in Boston, Kinsley's hometown, where he presumably also visited his mother for the first time since he arranged her escape from Wilmington.[25] He may also have visited other centers of black political life between New York City and Boston. By 11 May, a week after his lecture at the Zion Church, Galloway had returned to New York City. A black sailor, William Gould, commented in his diary that Galloway appeared at the Sullivan Street AME Zion Church; he also mentioned that he had seen Galloway at Robert Hamilton's newspaper offices. Formerly an enslaved master builder in Wilmington, North Carolina, where Galloway had escaped north aboard a ship, Gould had been friends with Galloway there before the war. Gould also escaped from the city, but not until the outbreak of war. In September 1862, he and several other slaves confiscated a boat and rowed out to a Union gunboat, the USS *Cambridge*. Gould immediately joined the Union navy and began his remarkable diary, and he served in the navy until the end of the war.[26]

The first Sunday after Galloway and his delegation arrived home in early June, New Bern's black leaders announced a mass meeting at Andrew Chapel for the purpose of hearing a report on the meeting with President Lincoln. A heavy rain fell from morning until night that Thursday, until rivulets of water flowed down from the town's higher neighborhoods and left puddles in the streets. The throng that gathered at Andrew Chapel still numbered so many that, as a local journalist attested, "they trod one upon another's feet."[27]

Even quite a few white faces appeared in the crowd that night. A correspondent for the *Anglo-African* speculated that some of the white spectators might have been Copperheads curious about the fanfare accorded the local black men who had met with the president. "Their presence, however," the correspondent wrote, "would have been none the less gratifying, even if a few Copperheads should have been there, for they would have had to swallow Galloway's pills in large doses, and one of the peculiarities of his pills are, that they either kill or cure."[28]

Amos York, an African American cooper and preacher, opened the evening's meeting.[29] Rev. Isaac Felton gave a rousing invocation, and the church choir sang a hymn. John Good then stepped into the pulpit and described the delegation's conference with President Lincoln. Good was far more comfortable at Andrew Chapel than he had been at Manhattan's Zion Church. He held the audience rapt as he described in a forceful, plainspoken manner what it was like to sit down with the Great Emancipator and speak to him not as a slave to a master, or as a black man to a white man, but as a man to a man. With his cautious, almost disquieting bearing and haggard, world-worn eyes, Good resembled the majority of the men and women who had crowded into the church that evening. They looked at Good and saw themselves, so the church was filled with a profound sense of excitement and possibility.

For all his enthusiasm for their reception at the White House, however, Good made clear that Lincoln had not acceded to all their demands. Indeed, Lincoln had demurred on their petition's central demand: the right of suffrage after the war. According to Good, the president told them that he sympathized with their yearning for the full rights of American citizenship, but he still insisted that individual states should have the prerogative to determine the rights of their own citizens, black and white, after a Union victory.

The president had not needed to explain what the petitioners knew all too well: the war had seemed stalemated that winter and spring, and Lincoln was facing a serious challenge for reelection from the Union army's former general in chief, Major General George McClellan, the Democratic candidate for president. McClellan, if elected, was considered far more likely to seek a negotiated peace with the Confederacy that would have preserved the institution of slavery. Lincoln and his advisors feared that any greater show of support for black political rights might arouse more northern white opposition to the war and undermine white recruitment and political support for the war, at a time when both had been declining.

Lincoln's reluctance to endorse their demands notwithstanding, most of the former slaves who crowded Andrew Chapel put great store in the fact that Lincoln met with some of their own. "The president received us cordially and spoke with us freely and kindly," Good told them.[30] The president of the United States greeted the ex-slaves—indeed, men that Confederate governments still considered slaves—"freely and kindly," with a respect and hospitality that white people in the South had never shown them. That night they must have felt that they were on the edge of a revolutionary moment in the history of the United States.

Similarly, another member of the delegation, Reverend Felton, emphasized the president's simple decency toward them. That decency, in a way, he said, was more revolutionary than suffrage. "In 1860," he told his friends and neighbors, "to go to the door of the lowest magistrate of Craven County, and ask for the smallest right, would have insulted him, and the offender would have been told to go in at the gate and around the back door. That was the place for 'niggers.'" The black preacher went on: "But 1864 finds us standing at the front door of the executive mansion of the President of the United States!" "What a change!" he exclaimed to a thunderous ovation. The black preacher continued: "He didn't tell us to go 'round to the back door, but, like a gentleman and noble-hearted chief, with as much courtesy and respect as though we had been the Japanese Embassy, he invited us into the White House!"[31]

Andrew Chapel rang with applause and laughter at Felton's words. "And after a lengthy talk with [the president] on matters and things," he said, his voice trembling with feeling, "we again joined hands, took a hearty shake and bid farewell!"[32] Former slaves had walked in the White House's front door! They had shaken the president's hand! Even the black audiences of the North had not been able to appreciate fully what those gestures had meant to Galloway's delegation or what they would mean back home in the South. The church erupted with delight and hope. Putting their hearts into the hymn, the former slaves sang the patriotic song "America," or "My Country, 'Tis of Thee."[33] The song's simple assertion, "My country, 'tis of Thee/Sweet land of liberty," held a singular power and meaning when sung by former slaves in a crowded church in the Civil War South.

After the song's last note faded, Galloway rose from his pew near the front of Andrew Chapel. He spoke from the floor, not the pulpit, and even when a friendly voice to the rear of the church called out and urged him to move into the pulpit, he declined. Galloway promised to speak loud enough to be heard but said that he did not wish to be "exalted so high." He was in fine fettle that evening, lacing his political observations with a sense of satire and sarcasm that ran from beguiling to scalding. According to the *Anglo-African's* correspondent, he "made those laugh who never laughed before," and the crowd's applause frequently interrupted him.[34]

Rather than linger upon the meeting with Lincoln, Galloway set out first to underline that their fate lay most heavily in their own hands. The ballot would not fall down from on high. They could not count on Lincoln to save them. One of the best ways for the former slaves to attract political support was "to show a disposition to help yourselves," he preached. Galloway called upon the community to live up to its own best self: to live lives of personal rectitude and public devotion. Later in his speech, he even said a few words about the responsibility of parents to remain watchful of their children and about the duty of their daughters to be virtuous.[35] His political logic seems impeccable. At twenty-seven years of age, a mere youngster compared with many gathered in the church, Galloway began his essentially radical speech by appealing to the older, more conservative, and more religious ex-slaves among his listeners.

Galloway then turned to the heart of his speech and the cause that led him to the White House: the right to vote and the necessity of agitating for it. Still speaking from the floor of the church, turning first to one side of the crowd, then to the other, he addressed one of the most frequent criticisms made by whites against black suffrage, the alleged corruptibility of black voters. Galloway decried the corruption of white voters whom he had observed in the North. He declared that, in his experience, black northerners had proven far more resistant to vote-buying than their white counterparts. He presumably referred to the powerful role of Tammany Hall in New York City or of the Irish syndicates in Boston. Patriotism and citizenship were the issues when it came to suffrage, he implied, not race.

Suffrage indeed meant everything to Galloway that summer. He understood very well that other battles lay ahead, but the right to vote held the key to them all in his eyes. At Andrew Chapel he made clear that he understood that his audience yearned for more than voting rights. He realized that those gathered there still felt the stings of a hundred daily reminders of their oppression. Local customs decreed, among much else, that black men and women stepped aside for all white pedestrians, waited in line behind all white customers at stores, sat on the exposed lower decks of steamships, and never shared a dining room with whites. They might never occupy a hotel, restaurant, or school with their white neighbors, and they literally risked their lives and their children's lives if they challenged a white man's authority on even the smallest matter. Galloway understood all too well how much the former slaves resented these enduring signs of racial prejudice and hostility. His revolutionary agenda included pushing aside those relics of slavery, but he insisted that they first and foremost stay fixed on voting rights. As for social equality and racial segregation, Galloway told the church that he was willing "to wait a little longer." But, as the *Anglo-African*'s local correspondent quoted him, "he wanted his political rights now."[36]

9

Their Path to Freedom

ON A LOVELY SUMMER DAY IN NEW BERN, GALLOWAY WATCHED THE mustering of the 1st North Carolina Colored Heavy Artillery, one of the African American regiments recruited primarily among the local slaves who had managed to reach Union lines.[1] The scene inspired him to write—or, presumably, to dictate to a literate colleague—his impressions of the black soldiers and their families and send them to William Lloyd Garrison at the *Liberator*. According to Galloway, the regiment's day began with a worship service at its camp on the outskirts of the city. "It was a delightfully pleasing afternoon," he related. He described how "the wives and daughters of the soldiers gaily and some of them very prettily dressed, had collected to attend services with them." After the worship service, the black regiment drilled for the gathered crowd. Galloway walked through their camp and admired its "order and decorum." The soldiers had built their own barracks to take the place of tents, and he reported that the regiment's officers had organized schools in some of the barracks so that the soldiers did not have to go into town to learn reading and writing. "The badge of slavery is superseded by the U.S. uniform," Galloway told the *Liberator*, "and the reading-book and the slate are the accompaniments of these former victims of ignorance wherever they go. They hunger for the 'forbidden fruit' of knowledge with a zest of appetite which imparts marvelous powers of acquisition."[2]

Standing proudly, the black troops lined up in a hollow square on their marching field. Galloway admired how fine they looked and the contrast of their red uniform coats and ebony complexions. Though a late July day in North Carolina had to have been almost unbearably hot and humid, the soldiers stood motionless for more than an hour during the outdoor worship services. "They presented a fine appearance, and one which must disarm the most prejudiced beholder," Galloway observed.

Galloway went on to say that black men who were good soldiers, like those in the 1st North Carolina Colored Heavy Artillery, would surely prove to be good citizens, deserving of the full rights of citizenship and political equality. But his concluding words were not merely an appeal to the goodwill of the *Liberator*'s readers but also, in the fierce poetry in which he intoned them, a warning of his people's devotion to a struggle for freedom that would transcend the Civil War if necessary. Reflecting on that beautiful Sunday afternoon and the regal-looking black soldiers, Galloway said, "None can witness such a scene, and observe their soldier-like bearing, without being impressed with the conviction that this people will cut their path to freedom through the most stubborn obstacles that can beset it—though every step be drenched in rebel blood, in which they will write with the point of the bayonet, on the tablet of this nation, liberty for themselves and their posterity."[3]

Scenes like the mustering of the black troops moved and inspired Galloway that summer of 1864, but he did not focus on local events alone. Increasingly, he and the other local black leaders turned their attention to making an impact on national politics. Galloway had still been in New York City, on the last leg of the tour of the North that followed his meeting with President Lincoln, when the Reverend Henry Highland Garnet put out a call for a national convention of American black leaders in the *Anglo-African*. Garnet was one of the nation's most influential black abolitionists and, from a historian's point of view today, an intellectual precursor to the "black nationalist" political thinkers of the late nineteenth and early twentieth centuries. His call for a national convention would become a signal moment for Galloway and for black America.

Born a slave in Kent County, Maryland, in 1815, Garnet had escaped from the South in 1824 and gone on to study at the African Free School in New York City and at the Oneida Theological Institute, in Whitesboro, New York. By the Civil War, he had become an accomplished minister, teacher, and abolitionist editor. Six feet tall, handsome, and witty, he had always suffered from frail health and had lost a leg following a sports injury that never healed properly. Quick-tempered and defiant, Garnet rarely backed down regarding his rights as a black man and was once even tossed off a train for refusing to sit in a "colored only" section.[4]

Garnet first burst onto the African American political scene in 1843, when, at the National Negro Convention in Buffalo, New York, he stunned

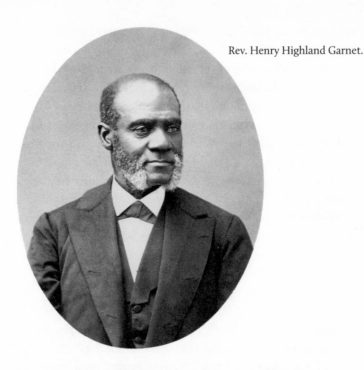

Rev. Henry Highland Garnet.

the crowd with his eloquence and fervor, declaring, in words that echoed David Walker's 1829 *Appeal*, "You had better all die, die immediately, than live slaves, and entail your wretchedness upon your posterity. . . . However much you and all of us may desire it, there is not much hope of redemption without the shedding of blood. If you must bleed, let it come all at once—rather *die freemen, than live to be slaves*."[5]

Although he had supported black emigration from the United States before the Civil War, Garnet advocated for black military service and civil rights during the war. When he issued his call to "the strong men of our people," he had just left his post as a chaplain to New York State's black troops at their training grounds on Rikers Island and accepted the pulpit of the Fifteenth Street Presbyterian Church in Washington, D.C. His proposal for a national black political gathering immediately met with widespread interest. By the spring of 1864, many African Americans, North and South, believed that the time had come to join the far-flung parts of the nation's black community together and begin to imagine the place of blacks in a postwar America. With Vicksburg having fallen the previous summer and Sherman's army pressing the Rebels in Tennessee, they believed that a Union victory was imminent. In their eyes, the time had come to issue a bill due to the white North for the African American contribution to preserving the Union. The question now was only What would that bill be?

In Syracuse, New York, the Reverend Jermain Loguen received Garnet's call and immediately offered to host the convention there. Black leaders soon set a date for a convention that would run from 4 to 7 October.[6] The edition of the *Anglo-African* containing the news reached New Bern while Galloway continued his speaking tour of the North; he may even have met with Garnet while he was in New York City. Without waiting for Galloway to return, New Bern's black leaders announced plans for a mass meeting at Andrew Chapel to discuss their participation in the Syracuse convention. On 2 May, the Reverend James W. Hood, a new AME Zion missionary sent to New Bern by the denomination's New England conference, opened that meeting with song and prayer. John Randolph Jr., the house painter and Methodist preacher who had stood by Galloway's side in Mary Ann Starkey's attic, ascended to the pulpit next. Randolph read aloud the notice of the convention from the *Anglo-African*. The assembly elected Clinton Pierson, who had accompanied Galloway to the White House, to preside for the evening. Pierson named a committee to develop a proposal with respect to Garnet's convention for the full body's consideration. While that committee met in closed session, the Old Benevolent Choir entertained the crowd. When the committee returned, Pierson reopened the night's business, the committee made its proposal, and those in attendance endorsed the national convention and pledged to send delegates to Syracuse representing the black communities of North Carolina.

The African American activists also made plans to hold a larger gathering later that summer to choose the state's delegates to the convention, as well as to write resolutions for the delegates to carry to Syracuse on their behalf. In the meantime, they agreed to invite the freedpeople in Beaufort, little Washington, and Roanoke Island to join in those deliberations. Before adjourning for the evening, they penned a letter to Robert Hamilton at the *Anglo-African* announcing publicly their support for the convention and sharing their resolution "that North Carolina ought and must be represented, and that it is the duty of every man and woman to unite in the free gift of their time, talent, and means to insure this end, as they value the future rise and progress of our race."[7]

Galloway came to New Bern often that summer but rarely stayed long. He traveled to New York City again for political meetings and fund-raising events, and also to Boston, where he met privately with Edward Kinsley and Governor Andrew at the State House, as well as with the state's provost marshal general and George Stearns.[8] At least occasionally, he still acted as an emissary in the recruitment of black soldiers in North Carolina's occupied seaports.[9] He also had to fight another wave of Union army abuses of black refugees, shuttling at least once between New Bern and Fortress Monroe in order to discuss the issue with Major General Butler.[10] He seemed to appear everywhere and at any time, always active and on the run.

Despite his absences, Galloway remained a reassuring presence among New Bern's black political activists. Other black leaders had undertaken the steady labor of organizing the local African American political movement. They worked literally block by block, church by church, town by town. But at a time when potential dangers grounded in far-off capitals and distant battlefields threatened the African American communities of the South, the former slaves gained an important measure of confidence from Galloway's activities. He might come into meetings late and say little, and he often merely kept an eye on the proceedings from afar. But he was there when they truly needed him, whether they were threatened by outside forces or internal divisions, and he was as bold, defiant, and passionate as ever.

ᑎ

The process for selecting delegates to the National Convention of Colored Men of the United States began in earnest on 2 August, with a mass meeting that called for blacks throughout the Union-occupied territories to join the freedpeople of New Bern in their deliberations in the coming weeks. By then, local blacks had fashioned their own brand of a genuinely democratic politics: their deliberations were turbulent, highly spirited, and often fractious. As they gained a greater political confidence and a stronger sense of their personal security, their debates also brought to the fore divisions within the African American community that had previously remained in the background: ideological rifts, contested personal loyalties, regional attachments, religious differences, and perhaps even old antebellum caste lines based on skin color and clan. The summer of 1864, in short, was a full-throated exercise in grassroots democracy. And for all the messiness of local democracy, few could deny that the election of former slaves *by* former slaves to a national convention represented an extraordinary moment in the history of the South.

The next two mass meetings at Andrew Chapel drew ex-slaves from Beaufort, Morehead City, Roanoke Island, little Washington, and of course, all of New Bern's black neighborhoods and contraband camps. Reports on the first convocation differed dramatically. The Reverend James W. Hood, the new pastor at the church—now affiliated with the AME Zion denomination—said that the meeting "broke up in disorder," while local black leaders commented on its "good order, good feeling and perfect harmony."[11] All agreed that they endured wearisomely long debates over eligibility for nomination as a delegate to Syracuse, the kind of argument that is the bane of democratic conventions in every age. The second meeting, while contentious, accomplished more. At that gathering, the black activists elected a delegation to the convention that included three of Galloway's closest colleagues: Clinton Pierson, John Good, and John Randolph Jr. The election did expose a rift, of unknown cause, however, between local African American leaders and a faction led by Hood, who left the meeting feeling marginalized and disgruntled.[12] Galloway does not seem to have been at either meeting and was presumably out of town on other business.

Beyond their own political debates, local blacks confronted a more pressing issue that summer. A fresh rumor circulated that Union army leaders intended to undertake a large, surprise conscription of local black men. Those in the city's black neighborhoods heard that Federal soldiers planned to transport hundreds of local ex-slaves to Virginia battlefields and employ them as forced labor for the Army of the Potomac, as Grant tried desperately to finish off Robert E. Lee in the Richmond-Petersburg Campaign.

The African American men remaining in New Bern apparently wanted none of Lee and Grant's war. Thousands of local ex-slaves had already enlisted in the Union army and navy and were fighting, and often dying, on battlefields in Virginia and elsewhere. Untold hundreds more had willingly volunteered to dig trenches and build fortifications to defend New Bern from Confederate attacks. Some had picked up rifles and hoes to fend off Rebel assaults on the city earlier in the war. By the summer of 1864, though, most of the younger, able-bodied black men already served in the army or at sea. Some of those who had not enlisted were no doubt dismayed by the army's racial prejudice or the way that Union commanders treated black soldiers and laborers in ways that recalled their slavery. After a lifetime in bondage, having no power over where, for whom, or under what conditions they worked, some local freedmen simply felt that they could not abide more forced labor, no matter how noble the cause. Freedom, they reasoned, had to mean the right to control one's own labor and protect and provide for one's family or it meant nothing at all.

With rumors of a conscription afoot in New Bern, much of the city's remaining black male population made itself scarce. "When nine o'clock came," Randolph, Pierson, and Good stated on 24 September, "a colored man could hardly be seen; some had turned to women (at least so far as outward appearance went), some had left and gone to Dixie, and others wandered in the woods." That any would flee for protection "to Dixie" offered a grim reminder of how little faith many ex-slaves had in Lincoln or the Union army. Union forces did, in fact, conscript large numbers of those who did not go into hiding. Union cavalrymen on horseback even chased down some of those black men who took refuge in the forests outside New Bern. They delivered them directly to a steamer waiting at the town wharf, and the ex-slaves soon found themselves digging trenches in Virginia. "Weeks passed," the letter from Randolph, Pierson, and Good attested, "and the people were still in a panic; the Convention and everything else was forgotten."[13]

༼༽

For all the disruption it caused, the conscription crisis was still not the worst calamity that summer. The North Carolina coast also endured one of the most catastrophic yellow fever epidemics in American history. Observers had long feared an outbreak of infectious disease in occupied New Bern. Military camp life was not conducive to good hygiene or proper sanitation even at the best of times. After nearly two years of military occupation, living conditions in and around the seaport had grown notoriously poor. On a tour of the city earlier that spring, Major General Butler himself had noted the unsanitary conditions in the camps. The consequences for political organizing were serious: the contagion raged at its deadliest just when the former slaves began to select their delegates to Syracuse in the early part of September.[14]

The first yellow fever victims were probably in the contraband camps, but they went largely unnoticed by the city's public health officials. The earliest confirmed death was that of a local white druggist, John A. Taylor. The next was a sutler with the 158th New York Volunteers. He was followed by a lieutenant in the Ambulance Corps and then by clerks at the commissary depot at the foot of Craven Street, where heavy rains had left stagnant pools of water under storehouses, creating an ideal breeding ground for the mosquitoes that carried the disease. Soon the disease's symptoms—fever, vomiting, hemorrhaging, and the yellow pallor that accompanied liver failure—could be seen in homes throughout the city.

"Fevers are now sweeping off our people at a rapid rate," Mary Ann Starkey wrote a friend in the North. "Our streets are nearly deserted, and the citizens are quite panic-stricken."[15]

Funeral ceremonies and the movement of horse-drawn hearses through the streets became everyday, all too common occurrences. The town's medical leaders ordered fires lit on street corners to ward off the pestilence. Great towers of billowing black smoke roiled up out of troughs of burning turpentine dross and enveloped the city day and night. To reach the stagnant water underneath the Craven Street wharf, the chief provost marshal ordered the burning of several old warehouses. Lime, which was considered a disinfectant, was also spread throughout the city. On windy days, the ashen-colored lime swirled up in the air like a snowstorm and mixed with the dark black smoke of the turpentine dross, casting a dull grey pall over the city. One soldier described it as "putting Newbern under a regular cloud resembling that hovering over old Plato's Pit," a reference to the allegorical cave that appeared in the Greek philosopher's *Republic*.[16]

Funeral processions passed daily through the Weeping Arches, the marl gateway at Cedar Grove Cemetery that was said to shed tears on hot summer days. Undertakers buried whites among the graveyard's old monuments, while the contrabands buried their own largely in unmarked graves elsewhere. The former slaves mourned their loved ones with songs of grief and loss that lasted late into the night. The sounds of the funeral elegies and cries of the mourners could be heard in the regimental camps, where Union soldiers reported that the lamentations gave them nightmares.[17] The mourning songs even disturbed white missionaries. Though they disapproved of the ecstatic renderings of grief that they heard on the other side of the river, they also grew disheartened by their own lack of power to curtail the death and dying. What, they asked themselves, could their staid hymns and solemn prayers do to stave off the hand of death any better than the haunting melodies that drifted across the Trent?[18]

At its worst, the yellow fever epidemic killed twenty to twenty-five people a day just in New Bern. A "Dead Corps" of volunteers ministered to the sick and removed corpses from their beds. Many of those volunteers also succumbed to the fever. Physicians and surgeons, both civilian and military, were overwhelmed. All but one fell ill, and at least five perished as they cared for the sick.[19] Eventually, authorities canceled even funeral services; Union medical officers considered them too great a public health risk.

By the middle of September, overwhelmed Union officials had begun to evacuate New Bern. Residents shuttered windows, while army commanders canceled church services, shut down schools, and closed most businesses. Boatloads of soldiers and civilians left the wharves for other parts. They moved hospital patients to Federal facilities in Beaufort and transferred sizeable numbers of soldiers to Union camps as far away as Hatteras Island and Fortress Monroe. They deployed soldiers necessary for the defense of the city to camps as far away as feasible in the surrounding countryside. To save the soldiers from the epidemic, Union commanders rushed the 5th Rhode Island Heavy Artillery home early on a forty-day furlough. Their transport was the last ship from New Bern allowed to enter New York Harbor for months without being placed in quarantine.[20] Back in New Bern, the streets fell silent except for funeral wagons. A Union soldier declared that "everything in New Bern has a dead funer[e]al look" and described the epidemic as "a perfect reign of terror."[21]

The white soldiers of the 5th Regiment, Connecticut Infantry had borne much of the responsibility for disposing of the dead during the early part of the epidemic. Their regiment alone lost sixty-seven men.[22] Later, a black regiment, the 1st North Carolina, took over that somber duty. In all, 303 Union soldiers succumbed to yellow fever. Union medical officers estimated the total number of New Bern dead, both military and civilian, at approximately 1,000, though it is unclear if they counted the black civilian deaths in a meticulous way. All observers agreed that the city's contrabands died in far higher proportion than whites, probably due to the closer proximity of their camps to stagnant swamps and marshes, poorer sanitation and drainage in those camps, and more crowded living quarters. Among the dead was Mary Ann Starkey's father.[23]

Though considered a refuge early in the epidemic, the town of Beaufort ultimately fared no better. The little seaport's residents speculated whether the fever arrived via the railroad from New Bern or with the navy sailors massing in the harbor in preparation for the coming attack on Fort Fisher. Either way, the disease left the seaside hamlet a scene of seemingly endless wakes and funerals. Twenty-three members of a single Sunday school class at Ann Street Methodist Church died that fall. The leaders of the town's three contraband schools—the Whipple School, Washburn Seminary, and the Parker School—struggled with the deaths of several teachers. They finally canceled all classes until the epidemic could run its course. One of Beaufort's schoolteachers later recalled that fall as "a time of heat, languor, sickness and death."[24]

The yellow fever epidemic also ravaged other southern seaports, the West Indies, and Bermuda and the Bahamas. One of the casualties was Galloway's father. At the outset of the war, John Wesley Galloway, then fifty-three years old, had organized a Confederate coast guard regiment in Brunswick County. Known as "Galloway's Coast Guard," the volunteers consisted almost exclusively of fishermen, pilots, and sailors. Colonel Galloway and his band of watermen patrolled the beaches south of the Cape Fear River, gave navigational aid and military intelligence to Confederate captains trying to thwart the Union blockade of the river, and at least occasionally, provided the blockade-runners with pilots.[25]

Piloting a blockade-runner, a daring, risky business, demanded a firm hand and steely nerves. It was one of the war's most glamorous occupations but also usually a young man's game. John Wesley Galloway had not piloted a Cape Fear River vessel in a decade, but he agreed to take the wheel of a Confederate blockade-runner, a side-wheel steamer named the *Maria Elena*, after its captain was left with a hold full of cotton by the death of another pilot. Abraham's father apparently did not know that the fever had already spread among the *Maria Elena*'s crew. He died on 16 October off the coast of Bermuda, after successfully piloting the vessel through the Union blockade at the mouth of the Cape Fear River.[26]

The yellow fever epidemic still cast a fearful shadow over life in New Bern when the city's black leaders took steps to mend their political rifts. They had hoped that the national convention in Syracuse might provide an opportunity for unifying the various factions within the occupied territory's black community; instead, the process for selecting delegates had proven divisive. The conscription crisis and the yellow fever epidemic, however, pushed both sides to find common ground and forge a path forward together. They ultimately agreed that they needed a compromise candidate, and only one individual enjoyed sufficient respect from Hood's faction and that of the previously elected delegates. At a mass meeting just prior to the Syracuse convention, Randolph, Good, and Pierson offered their resignations from the Syracuse delegation as a peace gesture and "united with others in selecting Mr. A. H. Galloway as our delegate."[27]

10

God's Free Man

AS GALLOWAY TOOK HIS SEAT AMONG THE 144 DELEGATES AT THE
National Convention of Colored Men of the United States on 4 October
1864, he cut a compelling figure and carried a special kind of moral authority. The convention assembled at Syracuse's Wesleyan Methodist Church
at seven o'clock that evening. Galloway's appearance and the arrival of
the small contingent of other southern delegates had been much anticipated. Galloway was one of only sixteen delegates representing the newly
liberated slaves in the southern states and, with the Reverend Samuel J.
Williams of Roanoke Island, one of two delegates representing North
Carolina.[1] The nation's foremost black leaders, Frederick Douglass and the
Reverend Henry Highland Garnet, also attracted considerable attention,
but the bold young black men who had just come out of the Confederacy
supplied the most powerful new voices at the Syracuse convention.

The national convention in Syracuse represented a historic occasion for
black America. Never before had African Americans gathered in a national
assembly, drawing from both North and South. For the first time, black
American leaders convened to contemplate what race, nation, and freedom
might mean after emancipation, not in some hypothetical way, but after
centuries of bondage, on the verge of slavery's demise. The Syracuse meeting would also give birth to the nation's first truly national civil rights organization, the National Equal Rights League.

The convention marked a crucial opportunity for self-definition for
black America. Its leaders saw African Americans as one people, born of a
particular historical experience. Yet they plainly staked a claim as full American citizens, in part because so many black men had given their lives for
a country that had not regarded them as such. The delegates walked into
the convention hall confident that the United States owed its very survival

to African American soldiers. They defined the political meaning of black military service as a certificate of full citizenship.

On the eve of the convention, a correspondent to the *Syracuse Daily Journal* expressed the prevailing sentiment well: "Many of your readers have heard or read the speeches of Messrs. Frederick Douglass, Henry Garnet, J. Sella Martin, [and] Charles Remond; but they may not be aware how many more there are nearly, if not quite, equal to these." The writer noted that not only the free black leaders of the North had come to Syracuse "to consider questions of gravest importance" and to represent the approximately 225,000 free blacks who resided in the northern states, but so, too, had representatives of "that immense body of people, amounting to not less than four millions, who have been in part, and are to be wholly emancipated from slavery by our awful civil war, and in due time to be incorporated among the constituents of our body politic."[2]

However impressed the *Daily Journal*'s correspondent may have been with the black delegates, not all of Syracuse's citizens welcomed them. The city had a reputation for abolitionism, but it was also home to many Copperheads with antiwar convictions and proslavery beliefs. In early 1861, white protesters had broken up a meeting of the Anti-Slavery Committee of Syracuse and paraded through the city's streets carrying effigies of the Reverend Samuel J. May and Susan B. Anthony, two of the region's best-known white abolitionists.[3] With such sentiments inflamed by the war's tremendous death toll, local abolitionists were not wholly surprised when white residents of the nearby town of Jamesville organized a "McClellan Club" and invited Syracuse's white citizens to a "grand ratification meeting" at Cadogan's Hall on the convention's final night. Anticipating the influx of black delegates, the *Syracuse Courier and Union* opined that the National Convention of Colored Men "will afford a fine opportunity for the Republican Miscegenationists to fraternize with their 'bred'rn and cist'rn.'"[4]

A crowd of whites shouting antiblack slogans did greet the first African American delegates to arrive in Syracuse. Many were strong young men like Galloway, who always traveled with a revolver close at hand. The rowdies kept their distance, and police officers helped to maintain order. At least one incident, however, did go beyond the hurling of racial epithets. A small band of Irishmen accosted Reverend Garnet in front of the St. Charles Hotel. Some disagreement remained, even among black delegates, over exactly what happened. According to Garnet, he and several colleagues had stepped outside to await the arrival of other delegates when four Irishmen approached them. Elegant and always nattily dressed, Garnet walked with a fine, handcrafted cane. Now up in age and always limping on the side of his artificial leg, the less vigorous Garnet looked like an easy mark.[5]

As Garnet recalled, one of the Irishmen tried unsuccessfully to trip him from behind. Another hit him with a hard blow to the chin and knocked him to the ground. Before Garnet's friends could come to his aid, the ruffians had grabbed his cane, his hat, and a bundle of papers that he had been carrying. His friends ran back into the St. Charles to retrieve revolvers from their rooms, but Garnet's assailants had disappeared down the street by the time that they returned. Though Garnet rarely shied from a fight, the incident bothered him profoundly and left him doubting the wisdom of holding the convention in Syracuse.

Garnet later explained why the seemingly minor incident at the St. Charles Hotel troubled him so deeply. The attack brought to mind one of the worst days he had experienced, and one of the freshest wounds to his dignity: the antidraft riots in New York City during the summer of 1863. Spurred by fierce white opposition to the Union's military conscription laws, those riots had lasted for days and resulted in the lynching of 11 blacks, the killing of an estimated 120 civilians in total, the injuring of some 2,000 more, the destruction of the homes of numerous black families, and the torching of an orphanage for black children.[6] Because of Garnet's reputation as a leading black abolitionist, white mobs hunted for him at his home on Mulberry Street. The black minister had escaped the mob, but his memories of blacks burned to death in the streets and hanging from street lamps in New York City had an enduring influence on his outlook on black prospects in America.

At meetings at the St. Charles Hotel, Garnet expressed his fears that he and the convention's other delegates risked more such attacks if they stayed in Syracuse. Others demurred. Led by Frederick Douglass, most delegates argued that the incident required them to stand fast and prove their dignity and courage.[7] The convention ultimately stayed in Syracuse. The assault on Garnet was not forgotten, though. Almost a year later, after the assassination of her husband, Mary Todd Lincoln sent an elegant new walking cane to Garnet as a replacement for the one stolen from him in Syracuse and as a token of her gratitude for his devotion to the late president.[8]

The Syracuse delegates represented African American communities in seventeen states and the District of Columbia and composed the most important gathering of American black leaders held during the Civil War.[9] The country's most distinguished black professionals, scholars, and writers stood in that number. They included physicians John B. Smith of Boston and Peter W. Ray of Brooklyn, as well as John S. Rock, a Boston physician, dentist, and attorney-at-law who had provided medical care to fugitive slaves traveling the Underground Railroad to Canada. Another delegate, William Howard Day, had graduated from Oberlin College, the small Ohio liberal arts institution that was the country's first college to admit black students on a regular basis. A classics teacher, newspaper editor, and lecturer, Day had been a central figure in the campaign against Ohio's discriminatory Black Laws.

Another Ohio delegate, John Mercer Langston, had also graduated from Oberlin. Langston was admitted to the Ohio bar in 1854 and had played leading roles in that state's antislavery societies and in the Underground Railroad. Earlier in the war, he had been one of George Stearns's recruiting agents for the 54th and 55th Regiments, Massachusetts Volunteer Infantry. John P. Sampson, editor of the *Cincinnati Colored Citizen*, one of the country's leading black newspapers, also represented the Buckeye State. Sampson had been born free in Wilmington, North Carolina, and Galloway had known his family well when he lived in the city as a young man. Robert Hamilton, the black newspaperman who had traveled with Galloway in Virginia and North Carolina earlier in the war, represented the black citizens of New York.[10]

Many of the country's most influential black ministers and distinguished men of letters also made their way to Syracuse. The Reverend Sampson White came from the Nineteenth Street Baptist Church, the first black church in Washington, D.C., which he had cofounded in 1839. The Beale Street Baptist Church in Memphis sent the Reverend Morris Henderson, a former slave and its founder and pastor. Another delegate, the Reverend J. W. C. Pennington, had been born a slave in Maryland, escaped, and ultimately played an important role in supporting the rebellious slaves who took over the slave ship *Amistad* while he served as minister at the Talbot Street Congregational Church in New Haven. Another minister at the Syracuse gathering, J. Sella Martin, had returned that winter from a lecture tour of England during which he had lobbied for that nation's support for the Union. Among the leading black scholars at the convention were attorney, poet, and essayist George Vashon and Ebenezer Bassett, principal of the Institute for Colored Youth in Philadelphia. Other educators included Peter H. Clark, Cincinnati's first black public school teacher.[11]

Novelist, playwright, historian, and antislavery activist William Wells Brown was one of the most famous delegates in Syracuse. Raised in slavery in St. Louis, he was working as a riverboatman when he escaped from a steamboat docked at Cincinnati, Ohio, in 1834. He later served for many years as a conductor for the Underground Railroad while a steamboatman on Lake Erie. A renowned lecturer for the American Anti-Slavery Society, Brown wrote what many literary scholars consider the first novel ever published by an African American. Titled *Clotel; or, The President's Daughter* and published in 1853 in London, his novel was believed to be loosely based on the rumors of President Thomas Jefferson's affair with his slave Sally Hemings. Brown's own, rather romanticized autobiography, titled *The Narrative of William W. Brown, a Fugitive Slave, Written by Himself*, stood second only to Harriet Beecher Stowe's *Uncle Tom's Cabin* in shaping the northern public's view of slavery prior to the Civil War.[12]

Not all the delegates arrived in Syracuse as accomplished educators, writers, and professionals, but each had in some way made an important contribution to the African American freedom struggle. One of the lesser-known delegates from Worcester, Massachusetts, Ebenezer Hememway, was perhaps typical. A son of one of the last Worcester Indians and a black man, Hememway worked as the janitor at Worcester city hall, but for years he had also quietly escorted fugitive slaves through central Massachusetts as a conductor on the Underground Railroad.[13]

Though only one in nine delegates hailed directly from the slave South, a much larger number had roots in the region. John D. Richards of Detroit, one of four Michigan delegates, was a prime example. His mother, Maria Louise Moore-Richards, was the daughter of a white Scotsman and a free black woman from Canada, but John had been born in Fredericksburg, Virginia. In 1820, his mother married Adolphe Richards, a prosperous, part-Spanish, part-black, and very light-skinned native of the Caribbean island of Guadeloupe. The couple settled in Fredericksburg. Frustrated at the choice of educating her fourteen children in the city's clandestine black schools or sending them out of the state in order to skirt Virginia laws against teaching blacks to read and write, Moore-Richards moved her family to Detroit after her husband's death in 1851. At least a half-dozen of Fredericksburg's other free black families soon followed her and her children to Detroit. Eventually, the Fredericksburg expatriates became an established enclave in Detroit's black community. By the time that John Richards arrived at the Syracuse convention, he represented two black communities: an exile community of southern blacks in Detroit and the free black community of Fredericksburg. Many delegates shared the complexity of his origins—southern and northern, black, white, and other.[14]

Though small, the group of black women at the convention made their presence felt, and their participation was significant in itself. Most visible were Edmonia Highgate and Frances Ellen Watkins Harper. Highgate, a native of Syracuse, worked as a teacher and nurse among Galloway's circles of political allies in Norfolk and Portsmouth, Virginia. She had come home to Syracuse to recover from yellow fever as well as to attend the convention. Despite her illness, she delivered a moving speech to the full convention on its second night, when the evening's other orators included African American luminaries such as Frederick Douglass and J. Sella Martin. The convention's organizers chose Harper, a popular poet, teacher, and antislavery lecturer who had grown up in a free black family in Baltimore, to deliver the closing remarks on the convention's last night.[15]

From his seat in the convention hall, Galloway could take in the diversity of the country's African American leadership, from George T. Downing, a decorous, self-assured, and very successful entrepreneur who had once aided fugitive slaves in New York City, to the mysterious and dashing young Paschal Beverly Randolph, who had recently been the head of a Rosicrucian temple in San Francisco.[16] Another intriguing delegate, Francis Cardozo, was born free in Charleston, South Carolina, the son of a Jewish businessman and a free black mother. He had managed to study theology at the University of Glasgow, Scotland, and had recently accepted the pastorate of the Temple Street Congregational Church in New Haven.[17]

For all the illustrious—or eccentric—northern black leaders who gathered that first night at the Wesleyan Methodist Church and, on following days, at Weiting Hall, Syracuse's opera house, the eyes of the delegates often turned to the small group of combative young delegates from the South. They stood out, even in that remarkably accomplished crowd: coarser and less polished, but with the swagger and self-confidence of gunfighters.[18] As the convention was called to order, Galloway stood with the other delegates and sang an old Charles Wesley hymn, "Blow Ye the Trumpet, Blow." The first verse and refrain seemed especially suited to the men and women gathered in Syracuse:

> *Blow ye the trumpet, blow!*
> *The gladly solemn sound*
> *Let all the nations know,*
> *To earth's remotest bound:*

The year of jubilee is come!
The year of jubilee is come!
Return, ye ransomed sinners, home.

Following an invocation by Reverend Garnet, the delegates began their business. First came the matter of recognizing the legitimacy of individual delegates to represent the African American communities in their states. The convention's planners had already established the Committee on Credentials, which took up those issues as they arose from the floor. That committee next named a committee for "Permanent Organization," which included one delegate from every state represented at the convention— Galloway was North Carolina's representative—and the Nominating Committee, charged with proposing a slate of officers and a list of committees to oversee the convention's daily business.

After meeting in closed session, the Nominating Committee put forth Frederick Douglass as the convention's president and named sixteen vice presidents, one per state represented, among them Galloway for North Carolina. Taking the president's chair, Douglass also asked Galloway to serve as one of four members of the convention's executive board; he was the only southern delegate represented on that body. Douglass also appointed Galloway to the twenty-five-member Business Committee, charged with overseeing the convention's daily agenda: deciding who would speak when, what committees would be named, and what process for making final resolutions would be followed. That first evening, while Galloway and the other committeemen huddled in closed session, Douglass, Garnet, and William Wells Brown gave speeches welcoming the delegates to Syracuse.[19]

The convention re-adjourned at nine o'clock the next morning at Weiting Hall. The highlight of that second day came when Garnet entered the hall during the afternoon session carrying the battle flag of the 1st Colored Louisiana Regiment. Organized in September 1862, after Butler took New Orleans, the regiment was one of three recruited among free Creoles, not contrabands, and called the Louisiana Native Guards. For a brief time, the Guards had even fought under the leadership of black officers. Captain James H. Ingraham, one of those officers, had brought their flag to Syracuse. The flag symbolized an episode already legendary in the nation's black homes: the Siege of Port Hudson. After Butler's reposting to Fortress Monroe, his replacement in New Orleans, Major General Nathaniel P. Banks, had relegated the Native Guards to building fortifications and performing hostler's duty for white troops. In the spring of 1863, however, the black soldiers finally got an opportunity to prove themselves in battle. As part of the attack on 27 May, the 1st and 3rd Louisiana made a fierce charge across open ground against more than 6,000 entrenched Confederates at Port Hudson, Louisiana. Coordinated with Grant's campaign against the Confederate positions at Vicksburg, Mississippi, the capture of Port Hudson would have afforded the Union control over the Mississippi River from its source to New Orleans. The desperate, almost suicidal charge reached the edge of Rebel fortifications but ultimately failed. The Confederate defenders of Port Hudson would not lay down their arms for another forty-three days, until after the fall of Vicksburg.

Though the Native Guards fell short at Port Hudson, their heroism made a deep impression on the northern citizenry, and the battle also convinced many skeptical Union officers that blacks would make good combat soldiers. Owing to the valiance of the black troops, the charge at Port Hudson became a point of great honor among the country's blacks. One incident in particular, the death of an officer in the unit, Captain André Cailloux, had already become legend. Wounded by artillery fire and dying in the field, Captain Cailloux, according to Garnet, held onto the regiment's flag until Captain Ingraham reached him, took hold of the flag, and moved forward again toward the Rebel batteries. The battle flag that Garnet carried into the hall, he told the delegates, "is even now stained with the blood of the brave Captain Cailloux."[20]

On hearing Garnet's words, Captain Ingraham rose from his seat and bowed to the delegates, who gave him a thunderous ovation. A handsome, young Creole, Ingraham had been a slave until age six and made his home in New Orleans. Garnet called Ingraham to the podium, and the crowd again raised "rousing cheers." He described the battle, the loss of Cailloux, and his pride in the Native Guards. "The whole audience rose," the convention's official proceedings noted, "and united in giving three hearty cheers for Capt. Ingraham, the brave men who were with him, and the battle-flag which they bore." Delegates draped the 1st Louisiana's battle flag across the platform, where it remained throughout the convention.[21]

The evening session began at seven o'clock that night with the delegates singing "The John Brown Song," perhaps better known nowadays as "Glory, Glory Hallelujah."[22] Later that night, Frederick Douglass, by far the nation's most influential and respected black leader, gave the keynote address. Few of the delegates would have stood in his way if Douglass had chosen to play a more dominant leadership role in Syracuse. But Douglass demurred; he seemed to sense that the war, and perhaps age, had changed his role in African American political life. Born a slave in Talbot County, Maryland, in 1818, Douglass had taught himself to read at an early age and escaped from slavery in 1838. He had been the country's foremost black abolitionist for nearly two decades, advocating against slavery as a lecturer, organizer, and writer. Though perhaps best known for his first memoir, *Narrative of the Life of Frederick Douglass, an American Slave*, he had also published several important antislavery newspapers, including the *North Star*, in Rochester, New York. That paper's motto—"Right is of no sex, Truth is of no color, God is the father of us all, and we are all brethren"— captured the essence of his politics and his heart.[23]

A brilliant, often ferocious orator with a resonant baritone, Douglass nevertheless displayed restraint before the crowd in Syracuse. He claimed "that there were younger men behind him upon the platform, who had come up in this time of whirlwind and storm, and who would very naturally give them thunder." He directed his remarks to what he considered the most fundamental question of the meeting: "Why need we meet in a national convention?" Douglass underscored the racial prejudice that dogged their steps in both the South and the North, including, of course, on the streets outside Weiting Hall. "As we pass[ed] to and from this hall," Douglass reminded the delegates, we "constantly endured racial epithets and heard white men barking, 'Where are the damned niggers going?'" But he answered his own question by warning that they could not yet celebrate their victory or, as much as they might like, focus only on seeking the rights of full citizenship after the war. Before giving the stage to J. Sella Martin, Douglass implored the delegates not to forget that they still faced great dangers from political leaders in the North who would settle for peace with the Confederacy "by any means," including the continuance of slavery.[24] Other speakers followed, including Edmonia Highgate, and the evening closed with the singing of "The Battle Cry of Freedom."[25]

Despite the hostility outside the hall, the convention itself displayed a whirlwind of debate, oratory, prayer, and showmanship. During morning and afternoon sessions, the Syracuse delegates argued political issues, developed public resolutions, and handled the convention's business and financial matters. They devoted evenings to oratory and song, calling for one of their number after another to take the stage and address the convention or, in Robert Hamilton's case, to intone a song. The evening speakers covered every aspect of the black freedom struggle and sometimes connected that struggle to other issues of class and power. One of the most influential speakers, Ohio attorney John Mercer Langston, called for the delegates to resist not only slavery but also the "system of oligarchy" that, he argued, led to civil war and that oppressed poor and working-class people of all races. Many of the delegates, perhaps most notably John S. Rock, the Boston physician and attorney, focused their comments on the importance of gaining black suffrage after the war. Other delegates used their moment on the floor simply to bolster morale, instill hope, and urge patience and patriotism.[26] Galloway, for his part, said little on the convention floor. Neither he nor any of the other southern delegates gave evening speeches in Syracuse, though he continued to advocate assiduously in committee meetings and at a host of behind-the-scenes gatherings for the kind of militant political agenda emerging in the contraband camps below the Mason-Dixon Line.

On the convention's third day, Galloway and the other delegates on the working committees began to present their final reports and resolutions for the full convention's consideration. That morning the delegates unanimously passed a landmark resolution adopting the "Declaration of Wrongs and Rights," a document of political philosophy that laid out the moral reasoning and intellectual foundations behind their demands for freedom, suffrage, and the full rights of citizenship. The declaration, which Galloway would soon trumpet North and South, focused on the historical experience of African Americans in the South and called for political equality after the war, rooting its claims in black military service and in equality before God.

The African American leaders modeled the declaration, an extraordinary document, on the Declaration of Independence. Like the Founding Fathers of 1776, the authors did not aspire merely to write a petition of grievances or a list of political demands. Instead, they sought to articulate a philosophical underpinning for the black freedom struggle at that turning point in American history. The convention delegates would soon issue other documents aimed at making specific demands of the government and winning the white North to their cause. The declaration was different: it represented a crucial moment of self-definition for both themselves and their movement.

The "Declaration of Wrongs and Rights" began with the wrongs African Americans had endured. The preamble asserted, "As a branch of the human family, we have for long ages been deeply and cruelly wronged by people whose might constituted their right; we have been subdued, not by the power of ideas, but by brute force, and have been unjustly deprived not only of many of our natural rights, but debarred the privileges and advantages freely accorded to other men." Slavery, they insisted, had not only robbed them of their labor but also denigrated them as human beings. Barred by law from learning "the art of reading God's word," they had been "denounced as incurably ignorant." Blocked from any voice in their own affairs, they observed, "we have been declared incapable of self-government by those who refused us the right of experiment in that direction." But slavery's stigma had not been confined to the plantation South. Looking north, the declaration declared that "we have been denounced as cowards by men who refused at first to trust us with a musket on the battlefield." Slavery, they argued, cut to the heart of their humanity, down to the sanctity of their bodies and their families. "We have been denied the ownership of our bodies, our wives, homes, children, and the products of our own labor," they railed, and "we have been forced to silence and inaction in full presence of the infernal spectacle of our sons groaning under the lash, our daughters ravished, our wives violated, and our firesides desolated, while we ourselves have been led to the shambles and sold like beasts of the field."[27]

Finally, the "Declaration of Wrongs" addressed African American troops and their contribution to the Union war effort. "We have fought and conquered," the black delegates wrote, "but have been denied the laurels of victory." Black men in blue had played a central role in the war, they reasoned, but still awaited reward for their sacrifices. "We have fought where victory gave us no glory," they affirmed, "and where captivity meant cool murder on the field, by fire, sword, and halter; and yet no black man ever flinched." Such men, the authors insisted, had earned the right to citizenship.[28]

The delegates from Syracuse then turned to the rights blacks had earned as American citizens—the "Declaration of Rights." Their words resonated with those of the Founding Fathers in Philadelphia but this time extended to all. "We declare that all men are born free and equal, that no man or government has a right to annul, repeal, abrogate, contravene, or render inoperative, this fundamental principle," the delegates intoned, and "therefore we demand the immediate and unconditional abolition of slavery."[29]

The delegates had moved well past the great antebellum debates over slavery, emigration, and the nature of the Constitution. Their declaration dismissed all discussion of white plans to relocate or colonize blacks after the war and resolved that African American emigration from the United States was untenable. "Here were we born," they stated. "For this country our fathers and our brothers have fought, and here we hope to remain in the full enjoyment of enfranchised manhood, and its dignities." Their citizenship had been bought with blood, they held, and they aspired to defend it with ballots. Now, "as citizens of the Republic," they declared, "we claim the rights of other citizens."[30]

The black leaders justified their claims to those rights as both natural to humanity and ordained by God. These rights, the "Declaration of Wrongs and Rights" concluded, constituted "a portion of what we deem to be our rights as men, as patriots, as citizens, and as children of the common Father. To realize and attain these rights, and their practical recognition, is our purpose." Far more than the American revolutionaries of 1776, black delegates rooted their arguments in their Christian faith. They did not direct their declaration to President Lincoln, the U.S. Congress, or white America. "We confide our cause to the just God, whose benign aid we solemnly invoke," they concluded. "To him we appeal."[31] In the coming weeks, they would gather their numbers to hear the declaration and to vote on its resolutions, not in town halls or government assemblies, but in churches.

Later that day, Galloway joined the Business Committee as it presented a very different document: "An Address to the People of the United States."[32] Directed to the white northern public, the address set forth the grounds for a postwar alliance between southern blacks and northern white Republicans. "Baptized in the best blood of your noblest sons, torn and rent by a strife full of horrors," the address stated, "we ardently hope with you that our country will come out of this tremendous conflict, purer, stronger, nobler, and happier than ever before."[33]

Filling twelve pages in the convention's published proceedings, the "Address to the American People" sought to establish ground for common cause with the white North and reach a mutual acknowledgment that slavery should be abolished and the full rights of citizenship bestowed upon the nation's black citizens after the war. "When great and terrible calamities are abroad in the land, men are said to learn righteousness," the committee's delegates argued, hopeful that the white North had been transformed by war.[34] At the same time, they raised a specter of ruin and disaster if justice did not prevail. They chided both the Democratic and the Republican Parties for their racial prejudices and warned of dire consequences for the nation as a whole if, after the war, the white North reunited with the white South at the expense of the former slaves.

Those in Syracuse even cast a wary eye on old abolitionist publications such as William Lloyd Garrison's *Liberator* and the *National Anti-Slavery Standard* for not more fully embracing the cause of black suffrage. "We may survive the arrows of the known negro-haters of our country; but woe to the colored race when their champions fail to demand, from any reason, equal liberty in every respect!" the address declared.[35] Delegates endorsed President Lincoln's commitment to abolish slavery but still feared that his Republican Party might sacrifice the abolition of slavery in order to reunite North and South if the Union's armies suffered a major defeat or if the party experienced some other unexpected setback. With McClellan Clubs being organized throughout New York State even as they spoke, these fears did not seem unfounded.

Galloway and the other endorsers of the document argued that if the North did not cast its lot with the former slaves, the American Republic would be imperiled. A democracy, they argued, "must have its foundation in the affections of the people: otherwise the people will hinder, circumvent, and destroy it." In the coming years, they asserted, in words that now seem prophetic, defeated white southerners would thoroughly despise the U.S. government, no matter what stance Lincoln and Congress took toward African American political rights. "Every United-States mail-carrier, every custom-house officer, every Northern man, and every representative of the United-States Government, in the Southern States," they warned, "will be held in abhorrence; and for a long time that country [the Confederacy] is to be governed with difficulty. We may conquer Southern armies by the sword; but it is another thing to conquer Southern hate."[36] The black delegates argued further that, if the United States desired friends in the South, the government must build a strong relationship with African Americans. The only way to fortify such an allegiance and secure it against the country's enemies in the South, they reasoned, lay in extending the full rights of suffrage and citizenship to black southerners.

The black leaders also threw down the gauntlet to Republican Party leaders with a blunt statement: "You are sure of the enmity of the masters,—make sure of the friendship of the slaves; for, depend upon it, your Government cannot afford to encounter the enmity of both." Then, in a sentence that reflected the kind of severe sense of southern honor that might have come directly from Galloway, they declared, "To break with your friends, and make peace with your enemies; to weaken your friends, and strengthen your enemies; to abase your friends, and exalt your enemies; to disarm your friends, and arm your enemies; to disfranchise your loyal friends, and enfranchise your disloyal enemies,—is not the policy of honor, but of infamy."[37] The betrayal of black America remained well in the future in the fall of 1864. When it came, however, the nation's black leaders would not be surprised.

The closing of the "Address to the People of the United States" offered words of both reconciliation and warning. "We are among you, and must remain among you," the final paragraph stated, "and it is for you to say, whether our presence shall conduce to the general peace and welfare of the country, or be a constant cause of discussion and of irritation,—troubles in the State, troubles in the Church, troubles everywhere."[38] They had looked into the nation's future and foreseen the racial and sectional strife that dominated so much of American life for the next century and a half.

But they had not accepted the inevitability of that path. "To avert these troubles, and to place your great country in safety from them," the black delegates declared,

> only one word from you, the American people, is needed, and that is JUSTICE: let that magic word once be sounded, and become all-controlling in all your courts of law, subordinate and supreme; let the halls of legislation, state and national, spurn all statesmanship as mischievous and ruinous that has not justice for its foundation; let justice without compromise, without curtailment, and without partiality, be observed with respect to all men, no class of men claiming for themselves any right which they will not grant to another,—then strife and discord will cease; peace will be placed upon enduring foundations; and the American people, now divided and hostile, will dwell together in power and unity.[39]

On that third day of the Syracuse convention, the members of the Business Committee also introduced a series of resolutions concerning some of the most pressing issues of the day. They passed a resolution imploring Congress to treat black soldiers fairly. They encouraged the nation's blacks to settle on public lands in the West. They thanked President Lincoln, his cabinet, and the 37th Congress for rescinding the prohibition on blacks carrying the mail in Washington, D.C., and for abolishing slavery in the District of Columbia. They expressed their appreciation for the Federal government's diplomatic recognition of Haiti and Liberia, the first instances in American history in which the United States had established formal diplomatic relations with black-governed nations. They singled out for praise Major General Benjamin Butler and Massachusetts senator Charles Sumner for their policies toward the contrabands. They also congratulated the War Department, albeit in lukewarm fashion, for taking the first steps toward a policy of retaliation against Confederate troops that treated black prisoners of war as fugitive slaves or traitors.[40]

A youthful portrait of John Mercer Langston, first president of the National Equal Rights League. Courtesy, Oberlin College Archives, Oberlin, Ohio.

The convention's climax occurred with the founding of the National Equal Rights League. As chairman of the Business Committee, Henry Highland Garnet reported a plan for organizing the league early on the convention's third day; the delegates would deliberate their vision for their new creation through much of that day and the next. The publicly stated goals for the league did not appear especially militant: "to encourage sound morality, education, temperance, frugality, industry, and promote every thing that pertains to a well-ordered and dignified life" and "to obtain by appeals to the minds and conscience of the American people, or by legal process when possible, a recognition of the rights of the colored people of the nation as American citizens." Though unaccustomed to that kind of caution, Galloway, Ingraham, and the other southern delegates deemed it politically prudent for the present. From their point of view, the most important details were that the new organization's constitution made every delegate a de facto member of the National Equal Rights League and that the full convention endorsed organizing local and state auxiliaries across the United States.[41] Every returning delegate might then become a league organizer. Galloway, in particular, took this to heart. Far more than most of the delegates in Syracuse in 1864, he believed that grassroots organizing below the Mason-Dixon Line might transform the league into a powerful voice for the millions still in bondage.

On their final morning in Syracuse, the convention's fourth day, the delegates chose officers for the National Equal Rights League. To the consternation of supporters of Henry Highland Garnet, the delegates elected Ohio attorney John Mercer Langston as president. No record of the individual delegates' votes was kept, but Galloway later proclaimed himself a strong supporter of Garnet. Though Galloway had supported Garnet during the convention, Langston and his supporters elected him one of sixteen league vice presidents and asked him to serve as one of the four members of the league's executive board. He was the convention's only delegate elected to two posts.[42] As the convention adjourned, the delegates lifted up an anthem that emphasized the power of the distinctive Afro-Christian vision of liberation that united them beyond all political disagreements and rivalries:

> *From all that dwell below the skies*
> *Let the creator's praise arise*
> *Alleluia, alleluia!*
> *Let the redeemer's name be sung*
> *Through every land by every tongue.*
> *Alleluia, alleluia, alleluia, alleluia, alleluia!*

ᴄᴏ

After the National Convention of Colored Men adjourned on 7 October, Galloway set forth on his second speaking tour of 1864, to stoke support for the National Equal Rights League and underline the crucial nature of the freedom struggle in the South. By then, the reputation of the young ex-spy, war hero, and leader of former slaves from the South had spread throughout the black North. Galloway was invited to address mass meetings in Pennsylvania, Maryland, Massachusetts, New York, and New Jersey. His growing public stature became clear on this tour. At a rally in Baltimore, the crowd "loudly called for" Galloway. Henry Highland Garnet himself introduced the evening's star attraction to the crowd. "In his earnest, straightforward way of putting things," the local correspondent for the *Anglo-African*, probably Garnet himself, wryly observed, Galloway "fairly electrified the audience."[43]

In Baltimore, Galloway told the crowded church that some northern black leaders had criticized him for sharing Garnet's impatience with the Lincoln administration and its tepid support for black political rights. He exclaimed that he proudly embraced the title of "Garnetite." He also found fault with the convention's overall disposition toward the southern delegates. The delegates from the North and West looked at the southerners with admiration and respect, but Galloway protested that they had still slighted them when it came to giving them access to the podium. When money was needed, however, Galloway observed, both the southern delegates and the Garnet supporters "were always called, and always came to the rescue." Stepping back from the convention's turmoil, he discussed the current situation of the freedpeople back home in North Carolina. He also related the story of his capture and imprisonment by Rebel troops in the Deep South earlier in the war. "I am God's free man," Galloway bellowed, "and I feel that I am ready to do all I can to lift up my own oppressed brethren." The black citizens of Baltimore leaped to their feet and roared.[44]

In Newark, New Jersey, Galloway appeared as one of two guest speakers at a mass meeting at the Plane Street Presbyterian Church, the city's first black Presbyterian church, founded in 1835. William Howard Day, one of Newark's two delegates to the convention, reported on what had transpired in Syracuse. In an hour-long oration, Galloway made an impassioned plea for aid to support black communities in North Carolina, in what the *Anglo-African*'s correspondent described as "thoughts that breathe and words that burn."[45]

Several days later, on 12 October, Galloway addressed a mass meeting at Boston's storied Twelfth Baptist Church, the city's so-called Freedom Church. The Twelfth's congregation had been noted for sheltering fugitive slaves before the war and had welcomed many of the nation's most respected abolitionists and freedom fighters into its pulpit, including Harriet Tubman and Frederick Douglass. When Galloway visited the church, the Reverend Leonard A. Grimes served as the minister. Before the war, Grimes had been a free black proprietor of a buggy shop in Washington, D.C., but was caught aiding fugitive slaves and served two years in a Richmond prison before coming to Boston.[46]

Galloway next graced the pulpit at the Zion Church in New York City, where he and his colleagues had spoken that spring after their conference with President Lincoln. Boston minister J. Sella Martin joined him there. After describing his own experiences at the Syracuse convention, Martin called Galloway to address the church's overflow crowd. Once the cheers died down, Galloway reviewed the circumstances of the freedpeople of the South and discussed the difficulties caused by northern recruitment agents that summer. He highlighted the valor of North Carolina's black soldiers at the Battle of Olustee, the Florida battleground where the 35th United States Colored Troops—the first regiment recruited for the African Brigade—took its heaviest losses. In New York and throughout his northern tour, Galloway, more than any of the northern black leaders who shared the floor with him, urged his listeners to organize local chapters of the National Equal Rights League.[47]

Galloway was scheduled to appear the next day in Philadelphia, at the Sansom Street Hall, along with Captain James Ingraham of the Louisiana Native Guards and Sergeant Major Alfred M. Green of the 126th U.S. Colored Troops. At the last minute, however, Galloway was called elsewhere. Galloway and Ingraham did appear together in several other northern cities, however. A former spy could not disclose details, but his service for the Union army was not a secret, and the crowds greeted him as a war hero no less than his colleague from New Orleans. Ingraham, for his part, typically wore his officer's uniform and exhibited a daguerreotype of Lieutenant John H. Crowder, a fellow black officer in the Native Guards who had died at Port Hudson. As he had in Syracuse, Ingraham always displayed the American flag carried at Port Hudson, still stained with the blood of the "immortal Capt. Cailloux."[48] On this tour, at least, African American military service in the Civil War stood at the center of the call for full citizenship for black Americans in their country.

The politics of race pride existed side by side with that call for American inclusion based on military service. Though a Creole and as light-skinned as Galloway, Captain Ingraham was a kindred spirit and always went out of his way to extol black pride and African blood. Before northern audiences, he never failed to point out that his fallen comrade, Cailloux, "was blacker than any man in this audience," a telling point on a number of levels. The black captain addressed both the sacrifices that former slaves made in the Union army and the struggles and accomplishments of the freedpeople back home in the Union-occupied parts of Louisiana. Like Galloway, Ingraham also fiercely defended Benjamin F. Butler, under whom he had served in New Orleans. When he and Galloway appeared together at the Zion Church in New York City, Ingraham unreservedly called Butler "the second savior" and extolled him for the honorable way that he had dealt with black soldiers and contrabands in New Orleans.[49]

The primary goal of those mass meetings was to build national support among blacks for the political agenda laid out by the delegates to the National Convention of Colored Men. From Maine to Missouri, local blacks welcomed the delegates home at such mass meetings and listened carefully to reports of what had occurred in Syracuse. The gatherings featured a full reading of the convention's "Declaration of Wrongs and Rights" as well, followed by requests that the crowds endorse its call for African American political rights and organize their own state and local branches of the National Equal Rights League.[50]

The political discourse on the front pages of the nation's leading newspapers was not as elevated. While the nation's black leaders probed the meaning of the U.S. Constitution and the essence of race, nation, and freedom, the white press in the North was consumed with a vituperative debate over the dangers of "miscegenation" and the threat that Lincoln's reelection posed to the purity of the white race. The subject had been a major issue in coverage of the presidential election all summer and fall. White newspapers featured caricatures such as "The Miscegenation Ball," depicting black women and white Republican men dancing wildly together, or a story published in the *New York World* that fraudulently reported "a negro ball" at the Central Lincoln Club for Republican men and "colored belles."[51]

Those flights of fiction no doubt rankled Galloway as he journeyed across the northern states. African American crowds warmly embraced the "Declaration of Wrongs and Rights" that he and his colleagues had hammered out in Syracuse. White America, however, largely ignored this signal moment in the nation's black history. Syracuse's *Daily Journal*, a Republican paper, considered the assembly "undoubtedly . . . the starting point of a new era in the history of the African race," but that view proved the exception. Even in Boston, the *Commonwealth*, the radical newspaper founded by George Stearns, did not report on the convention, beyond publishing, in its entirety, the convention's "Declaration of Wrongs and Rights."[52]

Not surprisingly, the black press covered the National Convention of Colored Men altogether differently. The *New Orleans Tribune*, newly in business and the first black-owned and -operated daily in U.S. history, emblazoned its front pages with the convention's deliberations. In speaking of the convention, the *Tribune's* editors evoked the founding of the American Republic and compared the gathering in Syracuse to the constitutional convention in Philadelphia in 1776. "The causes which prompted the colonies to revolt against Great Britain," the editors observed, "were not by one fourth as legitimate as the reasons set [forth] in this last peaceful and patriotic declaration." Not only did "Anglo-Africans" reasonably assert their rights, the *Tribune* argued, but they had "come to the rescue of the country," an example of "magnanimity and patriotism [that] finds no parallel in the world's history." The newspaper's editors refused to believe that "the American people will be indifferent to this last Declaration."[53]

The reading of the Syracuse convention's "Declaration of Wrongs and Rights" stirred black audiences across the United States. For many blacks in New England and the mid-Atlantic states who came to hear their delegates report on the convention, the vision of two remarkable young men from the war-torn territories of the old Confederacy touched their hearts nearly as much. They had risked their lives for a Union victory, but neither Galloway nor Ingraham ever confused the Union's cause with the cause of black freedom. Neither ever forgot that the white North's racial prejudice ran deep or that the Lincoln administration's support for civil rights and political equality remained shallow. They never put their race's hopes anywhere except in their own hands.[54] To the black northerners who thronged to see and hear them, they symbolized their people's hopes in the middle of what was still a terrible and uncertain war.

11

Soldiers of the Cross

WHEN HE RETURNED TO NEW BERN, GALLOWAY DISCOVERED WHAT ONE distraught eyewitness called "a city of the dead." The yellow fever epidemic had passed with the coming of the first hard frost, but grief and loss now burdened nearly every family.[1] At the same time, the streets churned with new refugees, orphaned children, and the sick. As the power of the Confederacy crumbled, new waves of slaves fled into the city, far more than could possibly find housing. Many fashioned makeshift shelters out of pine boughs and lived in the surrounding forests. Deserters from Robert E. Lee's Army of Northern Virginia drifted into New Bern and Beaufort as well, many of them hungry and desperate.[2] Black-market smugglers, confidence men, and charlatans of all stripes tried to make a buck before the Confederacy's fall.[3]

Amid that chaos and upheaval, Galloway devoted himself passionately to organizing the Equal Rights League. Only a few days after Lincoln's reelection in November, North Carolina's freedpeople founded a state chapter, apparently the first state chapter of the National Equal Rights League organized anywhere in the United States. As had long been the case, most of the organizing occurred at black churches, including at a big Thanksgiving convocation in Beaufort. By early December, black Carolinians had also established local auxiliary chapters in New Bern, Beaufort, Roanoke Island, and little Washington. Each chapter had approximately 200 members. From outward appearances, they seemed to grow, as Galloway said, "like a gourd in the night," but he knew well that he and his colleagues built on black political organizing that had been occurring in the occupied territories since the arrival of Federal troops in 1862.[4]

The freedpeople made their politics plain in their choice of names for these local associations. They named one after President Abraham Lincoln, to whom many local black activists had grown especially attached since his meeting with Galloway's delegation at the White House. They named another for the Reverend Henry Highland Garnet, the black abolitionist renowned for his strident militancy. The New Bern branch chose to honor the insurgent John Brown and elected Galloway their president. The freedpeople in a fourth auxiliary named their chapter after the Reverend J. J. Clinton, the Philadelphia-born bishop under whose authority Andrew Chapel had come into the AME Zion fold the previous winter.[5]

The four chapters first gathered in a single body—the State League—at Andrew Chapel in New Bern in early December.[6] A few words written by the Reverend James W. Hood in the *Anglo-African* offered the sole record of what occurred at that meeting. Hood indicated only that Andrew Chapel overflowed that night and that Bishop Clinton, who was in town for North Carolina's first AME Zion state conference, gave an inspiring speech. Hood reported that the local leagues were "all in flourishing condition." Later in December, hundreds of freedpeople in Morehead City, the waterfront village just west of Beaufort, founded a fifth local auxiliary in North Carolina—the Abraham H. Galloway Equal Rights League. Hood, who both craved to be a strong leader and respected strong leadership, was pleased. "It is a favorable omen to see that our people have learned to honor their distinguished men," he wrote.[7]

❦

The rise of the Equal Rights Leagues and the vitality of African American political life were on full display on the first of January 1865, the second anniversary of the Emancipation Proclamation. The yellow fever epidemic had not been forgotten, but the moment nonetheless shone with hope and possibility. By the last days of 1864, Robert E. Lee's Army of Northern Virginia was slowly disintegrating under the force of a long, grinding war of attrition with Ulysses S. Grant. Deserters from Lee's army stumbled into North Carolina in tremendous numbers. Sherman's army loomed to the south. Having taken Atlanta in September and Savannah just before Christmas, Sherman was preparing to roar up through the Carolinas.[8]

At the mouth of the Cape Fear River, where Galloway was born, Fort Fisher would fall in only a few days. With the fort's capitulation, Wilmington, the Confederacy's last seaport, would also be lost. The end approached. On the North Carolina coast, black leaders felt confident of the Confederacy's imminent collapse. At the state's founding AME Zion conference in December, the black delegates in New Bern had appointed missionaries to serve for the year of 1865 in Wilmington and Raleigh, though at the time the Confederate flag still flew over both cities. As a sign of their confidence in a Union victory, they even slated Wilmington as the site for their next annual conference.[9]

Emancipation Day 1865 became a coming-out party for the Equal Rights Leagues in North Carolina. The celebration showcased a struggle for equality and justice that had largely remained invisible outside the nation's black communities. Now a new kind of African American political vision exploded onto the scene, one that embraced but rewrote the nation's democratic creed. Simultaneously thoughtful, seasoned, and exuberant, the local chapters of the Equal Rights League celebrated the historic moment and took the opportunity for good-natured competition; they sought to outdo one another to have the finest flags, the most spectacular galas, and the largest delegations. During the week after Christmas, African American school students caught the fever and jostled with one another to make the grandest show for the festivities.

Anne C. G. Canedy, a white teacher at the James School, a contraband school in New Bern, later recalled the thrill of preparing for the big day:

> When we received our invitations to join in the celebration, we knew that banners and badges must be had, even if there were no materials from which to make them. . . . But as our life in New Bern had taught us that bricks can be made without straw, we went to work. All day long, the work of preparation went on . . . and by night . . . with the aid of an old sheet, a little red dress from the second hand clothing department, and some blue cambric, fortunately found at "the store" down town, we had a flag quite good enough for any school to rally around. . . . The trimmings for our flag and banners were not second hand, neither did we have to pay war prices for them; and yet more beautiful decorations we could not ask for—the bright green leaves and brilliant scarlet berries of the southern holly.[10]

The Equal Rights League's Committee on Arrangements also went all out: the members unfurled a large American flag that they had borrowed from the students at the Palmer School, who had purchased it as a gift for the 1st North Carolina Heavy Artillery, another African American regiment. The committee's members arranged free railroad passage for all who wanted to make the journey to New Bern and secured accommodations in local people's homes for them. They erected three stages, hired a band for the day, organized a choir, and invited the region's finest orators to take part. Most visitors were expected to arrive on Saturday afternoon, New Year's Eve. They would stay in New Bern for worship services on Sunday, then celebrate the Emancipation Proclamation's anniversary on 2 January and return home the following day.[11]

ᴄ⁄ͻ

A little after noon on New Year's Eve, a thunderstorm moved down the Neuse River and settled over New Bern. By dusk, a cold rain fell in torrents. The weather did not dampen the spirits of the celebrants arriving in town, however. The Unionist editor of the *Old North State*, a Beaufort newspaper, noted, "As the anniversary of the Emancipation Proclamation of President Lincoln, the day has, to them at least, assumed the sanctity of the 4th of July, and Mr. Lincoln is revered in their hearts as THEIR WASHINGTON." Hundreds of freedpeople arrived in the city. Three hundred black passengers alone alighted from the Morehead City train that evening. They included the bulk of the black activists in the Abraham H. Galloway Equal Rights League and approximately eighty black sailors whose ships lay at anchor in Beaufort Harbor. Other freedpeople arrived on the ferry from Roanoke Island, stepped off lighters from the Outer Banks, and walked or rode into town from the countryside around New Bern.[12]

The rain lifted by morning, and celebrants woke to a hard frost and a clear, cold day. Following church, they attended mass political meetings until late in the evening. The next morning, 2 January, the weather suddenly turned warm and sunny, as North Carolina winters are wont to do, and the participants in the Emancipation Day activities rose early and gathered, each group in its own designated meeting place.

One of the Equal Rights League chapters—records do not indicate which one—prepared for the celebration that morning at Andrew Chapel. During weekdays, the church hosted the Wilde School, another of the city's schools for contraband children. For the Emancipation Day festivities, Anne Canedy and her students made their banners and regalia in the church's upstairs galleries while the league members occupied the main floor. Canedy had never attended a local black political meeting and was riveted by the proceedings below. She later shared her impressions in the pages of the *Freedmen's Journal*, an abolitionist magazine published in Boston by the New England Freedmen's Aid Society.

The church, Canedy wrote, "was crowded with old men and matrons, young men and maidens." The presence of so many black women impressed her deeply. She noted that they had prepared banners for the pa-

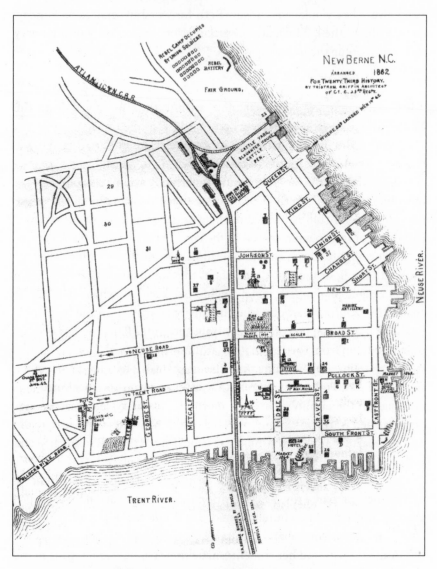

New Bern, N.C., 1862. Andrew Chapel is marked a block north of the Trent River bridge. From James A. Emmerton, *A Record of the Twenty-third Regiment, Mass. Vol. Infantry, in the War of the Rebellion, 1861–1865* (Boston: William Ware & Co., 1886).

rade, stored them by the pulpit, and also laid out red, white, and blue rosettes that would be worn by every member of the league chapter. The chapter's president—if it was the John Brown League, the president was Galloway—called the gathering to order. Those attending began the morning by singing one of the most moving gospel hymns in the Christian canon, "Am I a Soldier of the Cross?"

Am I a soldier of the cross—?
A follower of the lamb?
And shall I fear to own his cause,
Or blush to speak His name?

Must I be carried to the skies
On flowery beds of ease?
While others fought to win the prize,
And sailed through bloody seas?

Are there no foes for me to face?
Must I not stem the flood?
Is this vile world a friend to grace,
To help me on to God?

Sure I must fight, if would reign,
Increase my courage, Lord,
I'll bear the toil, endure the pain,
Supported by Thy word.

Thy saints in all this glorious war
Shall conquer though they die;
They see the triumph from afar
By faith they bring it nigh.[13]

They chose the hymn deliberately. Though they had much cause for celebrating, the former slaves did not look for an easy road ahead. Far from expecting Lincoln, Grant, or the North to hand them freedom, Galloway's people announced their welcoming of struggle and sacrifice as a way of knowing their Savior's suffering better and earning their own path to freedom and justice in this life, heaven in the next life.[14]

That local chapter of the Equal Rights League soon filed out of Andrew Chapel and joined the crowds bound for the old field near Fort Totten known as the 25th Camp Ground, formerly the camp of the 25th Massachusetts Volunteers. There they assembled in a large square. Black soldiers from Union army regiments and the blue-clad sailors from Union naval vessels made up the east side of the square. The Henry Highland Garnet Equal Rights League and the Abraham H. Galloway Equal Rights League shored up the south side. The Abraham Lincoln Equal Rights League and the John Brown League stood together and formed the west side of the square. The Bishop Clinton Equal Rights League arrayed itself on the north side.[15] Four years earlier, the large majority of those at the gathering had been slaves. Field workers, stevedores, ditch diggers, turpentine hands, and threshers had joined sweepers of mule stalls, oystermen, and haulers of manure and lime. Still others had made brick, tended tar kilns, forged iron, stitched sails, or fashioned wheels for drays. None of those laborers, in those days, had any real power to protect their families. None could have made their voices known on the political issues of the day. All had lived from birth with the specter of the auction block hanging over their heads and the heads of their loved ones. Now, with the winter sun shining down on them from the far side of the Trent River, they stood in a new day full of pride and hope.

Within that square, they symbolically protected the next generation. The ranks of soldiers, sailors, and Equal Rights League activists enveloped the student bodies from the eight black schools in New Bern and the surrounding contraband camps: the Palmer School, the Lincoln School, the James School, the Cocke School, the Wilde School, the Russell School, the Harland School, and the Stevenson School. Though most of the pupils were children, adult men and women who had first gained the opportunity for schooling with the coming of the Union troops also joined them. The scholars stood facing the soldiers and sailors, the students from the Palmer School in front and the other seven schools lined up behind them. An estimated 4,000 spectators watched the proceedings.[16]

Galloway had been elected "president" for the day and "commander in chief." He occupied a place of honor on all the celebration's stages and rode in the parade later that day on a fancy dray pulled by horses decorated with ribbons and finery. Galloway generally looked beyond the high moments—meeting with Lincoln, for example—and toward the battles ahead. Perhaps he let down his guard and relished the day, if not for the sake of the honor itself, then for what it said about the affection in which the freedpeople held him.

At the dawn of 1865, Galloway was only twenty-seven years old. One cannot help but wonder what he thought at such a moment after a lifetime of slavery and war. How did he view the elders who still bore scars on their backs that would never let them forget their days in bondage? Or what did he feel when he looked down at the enthusiastic young faces before him and the array of proud black men around him? How did he envision the future when he watched the youngest children, born in war and freedom, who had never known slavery firsthand and who he hoped would grow up in a world of endless possibility? The sight of the great crowd cheering him there by the meeting place of the Neuse and Trent Rivers undoubtedly filled him with pride and wonder.

જી

The proceedings began at nine-thirty that morning. Standing in the fore of the gathered thousands, Galloway gave a signal, and the students from the Palmer School unfurled their beautiful silk flag bought for the soldiers of the 1st North Carolina Heavy Artillery. Caroline Green, one of the Palmer School's young scholars, stepped forward onto the main stage, with Galloway by her side. The picture of grace and poise, she formally handed the flag to the regiment's officers and delivered a short speech. A captain next introduced his commanding officer, who thanked the students for the fine banner and pronounced Green's oration "the greatest that he had ever listened to."[17]

For the black troops in the square, the flag ceremony and the cheering crowd held special meaning after so many months when they had felt unappreciated by the Union army and by the nation for which they fought. Many in the 1st North Carolina Heavy Artillery still bristled with indignation at their mistreatment. "I have been an enlisted man for the space of eleven months," Sergeant Waldron of Company C wrote, "and have yet to receive the first cent for my services." Like most black soldiers, Waldron did not complain about picket duty, poor rations, or the dangers of battle. He accepted the fact that, if captured, Confederate troops were likely to kill him. Those were simply the realities of a black soldier's life. But the unequal wages and discriminatory treatment that he faced within his own army and the racial slurs that he heard from white Union soldiers provided a never-ending source of ire. Waldron remained particularly troubled when Union officers discriminated against his family. "Our wives occasionally visit us," he wrote, "but are compelled to ride in old freight cars, while Copperheads and professed Unionists are treated with every consideration." He and his men were "far from being satisfied with our condition," he added, but "all the same, the boys perform their duties with alacrity and cheerfulness."[18]

The organizers of the Emancipation Day ceremony could not undo the racial prejudice experienced by the 1st North Carolina Heavy Artillery, but they could remind the black soldiers how much their service meant to the former slaves. They had a special affection for a number of the regiment's men who played important roles in New Bern prior to their enlistment. Sergeant Robert Morrow, for example, had been a body servant of Confederate brigadier general J. Johnston Pettigrew and had accompanied his master first to school at the University of North Carolina in Chapel Hill and then to a teaching post at the U.S. Naval Observatory in Washington, D.C. Along the way, Morrow managed to acquire what one observer called "a decent education." He had fled a Tyrrell County plantation and entered the Union lines during a Rebel attack on New Bern in the winter of 1862–63. Not long after escaping from Pettigrew, Morrow opened a school at Fort Totten and taught the freedpeople there until he enlisted in May 1864. He had died a few months earlier, during the yellow fever epidemic, but the local freedpeople had not forgotten him or his school.[19] Many of the other black soldiers had played similarly valuable roles in the community.

Taking the podium, Galloway directed the assembly into a line "profusely strewn with banners rich and beautiful," one witness recalled. The black soldiers of the 1st North Carolina Heavy Artillery led the procession. The band, the speakers for the day, and the Equal Rights League chapters from New Bern, Beaufort, Morehead City, little Washington, and Roanoke Island marched behind them. A freedpeople's choir came next, followed by the students from the eight local schools.[20] By the thousands, they marched into downtown New Bern on Pollock Street, wound their way through the city's business district, and then turned north along the Neuse River past the wharves and warehouses on East Front Street. The parade then turned back west to the City Park.

At the City Park, the crowd reassembled, and Galloway's old friend and fellow renegade Rev. Isaac Felton, named grand chaplain for the day, offered a stirring prayer. Galloway then delivered the keynote speech. No record of his Emancipation Day speech has survived, but, according to Rev. James Hood, "he handled Copperheads and all other kinds of reptiles without gloves, and not withstanding some of his remarks were like gall to many of the bystanders, yet they were obliged to applaud him."[21]

Following Galloway's speech, James E. O'Hara, the African American principal of the Palmer School, read aloud the Emancipation Proclamation. A native of New York City and the son of an Irish merchant and a West Indian woman, he was only twenty years old but had served as a teacher and principal in New Bern since coming south in 1862. For two years, O'Hara had watched the freedpeople, some of them only days out of slavery, display an almost desperate craving for knowledge. Slave women had traded quilts for tutoring. Burly sawmill workers whipped out their Common Readers during lunch breaks. Others had forsworn work boots or groceries in order to buy books or to pay their fair share of a school's bill for lamp oil. O'Hara knew full well how much the Emancipation Proclamation meant to such students, and the crowd must have heard how much the students meant to him as he read Lincoln's words: "That on the first day of January, in the year of our Lord one thousand eight hundred and sixty-three, all persons held as slaves within any State or designated part of a State, the people whereof shall then be in rebellion against the United States, shall be then, thenceforward, and forever free."[22]

A reading of letters of support from Republican leaders around the country followed: Galloway's colleague Robert Hamilton in New York City; Henry Highland Garnet, now in Washington, D.C.; Rev. J. C. Gibbs, pastor of the First African Presbyterian Church in Philadelphia; and U.S. senator Samuel C. Pomeroy of Kansas.[23] After those endorsements, a procession of black religious leaders from several different churches addressed the crowd. Their presence on the platform marked the key roles that their churches had played in the local African American political movement. Between the orations, the band and choir performed. Since the crowd had stood on cold, damp ground for nearly two hours, black leaders adjourned the celebration at that point. Young and old dispersed, dried off in their quarters, and then gathered in boardinghouses, churches, and local homes for festive dinners.[24]

That night they crowded into the city's churches and renewed their celebration of Emancipation Day. The main program that had been cut short that afternoon continued at Andrew Chapel, where a white colonel, B. S. Pardee, of the Union recruiting service, made a speech emphasizing the important role that African Americans who volunteered for the army in New Bern had played in the war. "Mr. Lewett," the principal of another of the local freedpeople's schools, recited a poem that he had written for the occasion. The festivities lasted late into the night, until the crowds filed out into the cold night air, exultant in the glory of God, their deliverance from slavery, and all that they had accomplished since New Bern had fallen to Union forces nearly three years earlier.[25]

The vast majority of the black men and women who celebrated Emancipation Day had been slaves, denied of any semblance of liberty or equality, when the war began. They could not study the Bible without breaking the law, worship in their own churches, swear an oath in a court of law, or protect their children from the auction block. Now they had built their own schools and churches, organized their own benevolent societies, and served in their nation's army and navy. Having fought for their freedom, they now stood together in Equal Rights Leagues and anticipated a future as American citizens. They believed that their blood sacrifices had earned them a place at the heart of the great experiment in democracy that was the United States of America.

Perhaps even Galloway, after such a spectacular day, allowed himself a tiny glimmer of hope for the future. The war neared a triumphant end, American slavery teetered on the brink of collapse, and the Equal Rights Leagues seemed poised to carry the freedpeople's democratic vision into the nation as a whole. He might even have imagined a coming day of rest, when he might not always be fighting enemies on every side. The thousands of freedpeople who celebrated Emancipation Day that second day of January 1865 reveled in the glory of the moment and the brightness of their futures. They shared a deep pride for what they had accomplished and a profound hope for all that they might attain. Never again would any commemorations of the Emancipation Proclamation have so much to celebrate.

In This Land We Will Remain

LESS THAN TWO WEEKS AFTER THE EMANCIPATION DAY CELEBRATION in New Bern, Union forces finally captured Fort Fisher. Not long after, they occupied Smithville, the village of Galloway's birth. The fall of Fort Fisher gave the Union control over the Cape Fear River and cut off the Confederacy's last major supply line to Robert E. Lee's troops in Virginia. The Union's military progress now proceeded swiftly. Sherman's army had taken Savannah, Georgia, just before Christmas and would soon move northward through the Carolinas. African American activists felt the end of the slaveholding republic approaching rapidly. The war's ultimate meaning, as a struggle for their liberation, also seemed clear to them. That was especially true after 31 January, when the U.S. Congress passed the Thirteenth Amendment to the Constitution: the amendment abolished slavery and involuntary servitude, except as punishment for a crime, throughout the country. Fifteen state legislatures ratified the amendment almost immediately.

While the Union and Confederate armies staggered to the war's end, African Americans gathered in New Bern for a two-day celebration of the Thirteenth Amendment and its progress through the state legislatures. On 16 February, Galloway welcomed a standing-room-only crowd into Andrew Chapel. The Reverend James W. Hood, the presiding minister, called the house to order. The assembly named Galloway and the Reverend Isaac Felton honorary vice presidents for the celebration and, on Galloway's motion, accepted Hood as secretary. That night they sang hymns, beginning with "Blow Ye the Trumpet, Blow"; heard a moving invocation by Reverend Felton; and listened to several speeches, including an opening oration by Galloway.[1] The following night, New Bern's black residents passed resolutions expressing their support for the Thirteenth Amendment.

Leaders of the AME Zion church played especially significant roles at those gatherings.[2] Three of the seven committee members appointed to draft resolutions were AME Zion ministers, and the final resolutions strongly reflected their influence. The dominant theme was the guiding hand of a loving God over the affairs of men. "To God we will give songs of praise," they wrote, "and pay humble adoration to His glorious Name, who is the source of all our blessings, and who has put it into the hearts of our rulers to deal justly, love mercy, and work righteousness before all people."[3] Their words signaled their humbleness before God but also revealed a worldview shared by many southern blacks that interpreted their liberation from slavery, their survival, and the Union victory in terms of Old Testament prophecy and New Testament salvation and redemption. To the 4 million slaves in the South, the great African American historian W. E. B. Du Bois later wrote, "God was real. They knew Him. They had met Him personally in many a wild orgy of religious frenzy, or in the black stillness of the night."[4]

To guide their exodus from slavery, the gathering resolved, God had made "his Excellency, Abraham Lincoln . . . the mainspring of the grand machinery which has worked out the freedom of millions of bondmen." They testified, "A superintending and over-ruling Providence has brought the rulers of this nation to see the necessity of making the Federal Constitution what its framers intended it should be, viz: a wall of defense to every free institution, and a safeguard of liberty to all who make its wings their trust." While acknowledging that they did not yet share in the full rights of U.S. citizenship, they pledged, "We are now more than ever willing to make every sacrifice to sustain the Federal government in its efforts to put down this wicked slaveholders' rebellion, and to destroy the cause of discord in our beloved country."[5]

Galloway did not place his hopes for righteousness and justice in God in the same way that the AME Zion leaders did. Grounded at least as deeply in the revolutionary ideals of Tom Paine, Toussaint L'Ouverture, and David Walker, he closed the celebration of the Thirteenth Amendment's congressional passage with an impassioned oration. While he spoke, ushers passed baskets around the church for donations to buy subscriptions to Robert Hamilton's newspaper, the *Anglo-African*. Galloway intended the subscriptions to go to black soldiers still serving in the 35th Regiment, United States Colored Troops, the black unit raised in New Bern two years earlier.[6] The collection provided an important reminder that the war still raged, and not far from where they stood.

The Federal occupation of Wilmington, 1865. From *Frank Leslie's Illusstrirte Zeitung*, 27 February 1865. Courtesy, New Hanover County Public Library, Wilmington, N.C.

Five days later, on 22 February, Union soldiers—including many battle-hardened black troops—marched into Wilmington and occupied the city where Galloway had escaped from slavery a mere eight years earlier. Before abandoning the city to the Yankees, Rebel soldiers searched black homes and abducted a number of younger slaves, but within a couple of weeks most escaped again. The city's black residents reportedly harbored hundreds of Union prisoners of war who had fled from Confederate troops during the siege of Fort Fisher, twenty-eight miles downriver. The retreating troops threatened to torch any house in which they found a Union prisoner hiding, but they did not have time to make good on the threat. One of the first visitors to the seaport after the Confederate retreat heard that "most every colored person's house in Wilmington contained from three to four."[7]

As Union troops crossed the Cape Fear River into Wilmington, a throng of local blacks followed in their wake and showered them with gifts of bread, water, and tobacco. The crowd greeted a Wisconsin black regiment with giddy cheers as the soldiers marched down streets strewn with colorful banners and stepped to the triumphant beat of bugles and drums. The sight of black men in uniform carrying rifles astonished the city's black residents. They rushed to the long columns of black troops, where some of them were lucky enough to discover long-lost sons, brothers, or children. The soldiers soon became the toast of black Wilmington. "The striking qualities of these people seem to be entertaining the friends of the army," a visiting correspondent for the *Anglo-African* noted, adding that "they are willing at any time to divide or share the last they have."[8] He was also impressed that "the colored people in general are well-informed, and considering the circumstances under which they have labored, no city can boast of a more intelligent class." The visitor credited secret schools run by a group of local black women before and during the war for that high degree of culture. He listed Kate Curran, Fannie Sampson, and Mary Day as among those teachers and lauded them for "possessing rare accomplishments."[9]

Shortly thereafter, in early March, Sherman's army crossed into the North Carolina sandhills. Thousands of liberated slaves trailed behind his columns; some had trudged up cart paths and mud roads all the way from Atlanta and Savannah. In mid-March, at Bentonville, a crossroads ninety miles north of Wilmington, Sherman's army drove off the forces of Brigadier General Joseph Johnston, one of the last Confederate armies still in the field. The Union victory at Bentonville opened Sherman's path to Raleigh and the way forward to join Grant's campaign against Lee in Virginia.[10] In eastern North Carolina, African American activists grew only more certain that the Confederacy was in its death throes. They kept a close eye on the fortunes of its last armies and continued to channel their political aspirations into the local Equal Rights Leagues.

The internal deliberations of the local Equal Rights Leagues remain obscure during this period, but surviving correspondence gives a glimpse of one of the New Bern meetings during the first week of March. According to letters from Mary Ann Starkey, the John Brown League gathered in New Bern at that time to present a gift to Galloway, the league's president. Their inspiration for the gift originated with the birth of his and Martha Ann's first child, John, on 16 December. After John Galloway's birth, the John Brown League decided to purchase an engraved family Bible for Galloway in honor of his service to the league. For a former slave in 1865, one whose family had never been recorded in censuses or listed on deeds, birth certificates, or death records, having a Bible to record a son's name and his lineage, marriage, and death held a special significance. Starkey had written Edward Kinsley in Boston during the first week of January and requested that he purchase an appropriate Bible and let her know the cost so that the league could reimburse him. To spare the group's coffers, Kinsley arranged for a group of Massachusetts army veterans who had served in New Bern to donate the precious gift.[11]

On a Saturday evening in early March, the John Brown League held a ceremony to bestow the Bible on Galloway. Starkey wrote Kinsley, characterizing the gathering as "large and very spirited." One of the local league's youngest activists, Laura Bryan, presented the Bible to Galloway, saying, "Mr. Galloway: Allow me to present to you in behalf of the Union League of Ward 11, Boston, Massachusetts, this sacred volume. May you peruse its pages with earnest prayer, carefully treasuring in your heart its precious truths. God grant that its blessed promises may win your feet into that straight path which leads to our Father's bright mansions above."[12] Other speakers rose to praise him as well, and Galloway thanked his companions in a short speech.[13]

After honoring their president, the John Brown League turned to political issues. The pressing question of the day was whether they should call a statewide freedpeople's convention in Raleigh. The league's members had discussed whether or not the moment had arrived for such a gathering at their last meeting, and they continued a lively debate on the issue well into the evening. They ultimately decided, in Starkey's words, "that it would be impolitic to go [to Raleigh] immediately." However, the mere fact that they considered holding a statewide African American political convention at that time was remarkable.[14] Sherman's troops would not capture the state capital for more than a month. Lee's army was still in the field. Yet New Bern's black leaders had grown so impatient to expand their political movement that they looked ahead to the day of a Union victory and seriously considered convening in a state capital that would be freshly liberated from the Confederacy.

They did not have to wait long for the liberation of their brethren in Raleigh. Beginning in the first days of April, events that proved crucially important to the African American freedom struggle not only in North Carolina but across the nation occurred in rapid-fire succession. On 3 April, Richmond, the Confederacy's capital, fell to Union troops. Less than a week later, on 9 April, Lee surrendered the Army of Northern Virginia to Ulysses S. Grant at Appomattox Court House, a crossroads in the Virginia foothills. On 13 April, Sherman's army entered Raleigh. The next day, John

Wilkes Booth shot President Lincoln at Ford's Theater in Washington, D.C. Two weeks later, Sherman accepted the surrender of Johnston's army at the Bennett family's tobacco farm west of Raleigh, near a hamlet and railroad depot called Durham. The slaveholders' republic had fallen. Union agents captured the Confederacy's president, Jefferson Davis, in early May and imprisoned him at Fortress Monroe.[15]

While African Americans in the South had much to celebrate, the assassination of President Lincoln dealt a stunning blow. Though not a supporter of the president until late in the war, Galloway joined the nation's other black leaders at the grim procession of Lincoln's body from the White House down Pennsylvania Avenue to its public viewing in the rotunda of the Capitol Building on 19 April. He also agreed to serve on the executive board of the National Lincoln Monument Association. Headed by the Reverend Henry Highland Garnet, the association dedicated itself to raising funds for a "Colored People's National Monument" honoring the slain president. Back home in New Bern, Galloway's old comrade-in-arms the Reverend Isaac Felton gave a sermon comparing the fallen president to patriarchs beloved by God. "When the light in the East was discernible," Felton intoned, "and the day about breaking, God took Father Abraham up."[16]

Galloway could not dwell long on the president's death or on what possibilities for black America might have passed with him. In North Carolina, as throughout most of the old Confederacy, African American life quickly resumed the urgency of a guerrilla war, and neither he nor other local activists could afford to hesitate in their labors. His old friend Mary Ann Starkey may have expressed best the mix of grief and resoluteness that existed in black communities. "There is little heart left for rejoicing [over the war's end] since the sad news of the death of our President," Starkey wrote a friend on 20 April. She continued: "It must be all right, as God permitted it, but it does seem very hard to us—were it not for the thought that there was one over our nation whom death nor disease can never affect, discouragement would indeed fill our hearts."[17]

In the aftermath of the Confederacy's surrender and Lincoln's assassination, Galloway and his compatriots continued to focus on expanding the Equal Rights League into new parts of the state and on advocating for voting rights and political equality. Neither came easy. With the fall of the Confederacy, new multitudes of African Americans gained freedom, left the places of their servitude, and headed into towns such as New Bern and Beaufort. At times, the local black activists felt consumed simply by their efforts to find food, clothing, and shelter for the refugees who poured down upon them. At one point, in April, the circumstances of the refugees in New Bern grew so dire that black leaders formed a twelve-person committee, divided the town into wards, and went begging door-to-door on their behalf. "My time is mostly occupied now in endeavoring to care for the refugees," Starkey, who was one of the twelve, wrote. "The suffering is not nearly relieved yet," she said.[18]

Beyond meeting the refugees' basic needs, Starkey and other African American leaders also helped them find loved ones from whom they had been separated during slavery. In a letter to Edward Kinsley, Starkey mentioned one such case, an old friend of hers "from Dixie"—presumably the Deep South—who had been sold away from New Bern when she was twelve. In the years since Starkey last saw her, she had grown to adulthood and become a mother. At the end of the war, Starkey's friend made her way home to New Bern to search for her mother, who, it turned out, now lived in New York. Starkey raised the funds necessary for her friend to travel north and reunite with her mother, but she knew that she would need much more help and some luck to find her children. "Since she was sold from her mother she has had four children and some of them have been sold, she knows not to whom or where they are," Starkey wrote.[19] Many other men, women, and children also made their way to New Bern and looked to African American leaders there to help them find family and friends.[20]

Local needs did not present the only challenge for the Equal Rights League activists. By 10 May, when the "Colored Men of the State of North Carolina" sent a petition to Lincoln's successor, Andrew Johnson, a dramatic shift in the political outlook for the country's former slaves had also occurred. The petition's wording was highly deferential; the black leaders would never have addressed such an obsequious letter to Lincoln. Yet, though humble in phrasing, the petition stated its central aim forthrightly: "We want the privilege of voting," the petitioners declared. They continued: "It seems to us that men who are willing on the field of danger to carry the muskets of a republic, in the days of Peace ought to be permitted to carry its ballots." They sought the right to vote prior to any elections in the states of the former Confederacy, but, concluding with a deferential posture, added, "The whole question we would humbly submit to your better judgment."[21]

Though worded cautiously, the petition marked the first formal contact between the state's black leaders and President Johnson. It was, then, fundamentally a calling card: *we are here*. The ex-slaves realized that the

Tennessean had been a slaveholder and had a checkered past with respect to supporting African American civil rights. They knew that he had thus far failed to support their right to suffrage or any fundamental reconstruction of the Confederacy.[22] Nevertheless, they wanted to appeal to the new president's better self. Their calling card was a courtesy, and they penned their petition politely. Behind their good manners, the state's black leaders sought to understand whether or not their war for liberation had really ended at Appomattox Court House.

⌘

Despite the change in the national political winds, Equal Rights League activists continued to press for voting rights and to broaden their movement beyond the formerly Union-occupied parts of the North Carolina coast. One place where they had success immediately was Wilmington. Galloway had been in and out of Wilmington often during that spring. Judging by how quickly local chapters of the Equal Rights League emerged in the city, he might have even reached Wilmington before Union troops in February. As a spy, he had worked clandestinely with the city's black citizens during the war, and he had the opportunity to draw on his relationships in his old hometown to build a local presence for the league. His success was evident by the first week of May, when Salmon P. Chase, the chief justice of the U.S. Supreme Court and previously Lincoln's secretary of the treasury, visited Wilmington as part of a southern tour. In his private diary, Chase noted that the city's former slaves had already organized three Equal Rights League chapters.[23] Black activists told him that they counted as many as 600 local members and that, to his surprise, one-third of them were women. The chief justice wrote that the league's leaders informed him that they sought "Education, Improvement and Suffrage."[24]

The sudden revelation of such African American political strength sent tremors through Wilmington during the summer of 1865. On 3 June, North Carolina's provisional governor, Williams Woods Holden, issued a proclamation counseling the state's black residents to lower their expectations for suffrage and other political rights. Wilmington blacks paid his proclamation little heed. "The proclamation of your Excellency has been read to them," Wilmington's white political leaders complained to Holden that summer, "and they still insist that they are entitled to all the social and political rights of white citizens."[25] A petition from the white ex-mayor and board of commissioners to the governor later in the summer declared, "Our own colored population are assuming a somewhat dictatorial spirit, and insolent." The white leaders described black political organizing as an "insurrectionary movement" and protested that the National Equal Rights League chapters "had even petitioned for a role in the city's governance."[26]

A few weeks later, leading white citizens in Wilmington begged the governor to send them a hundred Spencer rifles or navy revolvers so that they could protect themselves from their former slaves. Complaining of a black militancy that, if not checked, "will end in the subversion of order and the disruption of civil authority," they also asked Holden to prevail upon the War Department to withdraw black troops from Wilmington.[27] Holden soon sent a copy of the petition to President Johnson and requested that the commander in chief order the removal of all black soldiers from Wilmington.[28]

Holden had good reasons to expect Johnson's sympathy. In Wilmington, African American activists sought the full rights of citizenship and strived to bend the government to their more inclusive vision of southern society. Johnson, on the other hand, supported a policy toward the South—"Presidential Reconstruction," it came to be called—that would readmit Confederate states to the Union without upending their social orders, other than ending slavery. He did not support black voting rights, much less more radical measures such as land redistribution.[29] The ultimate shape of the South's reconstruction remained far from clear, however, and the petitioners' anxiety reflected the strength of African American political organizing in Galloway's hometown during those first months of freedom.

⳹

For all the early successes in Wilmington, the towns of New Bern and Beaufort continued to act as the central points for black political organizing in North Carolina. New Bern and an adjacent freedpeople's camp, James City, remained especially important. After Appomattox, Federal officials ordered the state's contrabands to disband their camps and return the land to their antebellum owners. At Beaufort, Plymouth, little Washington, and Roanoke Island, the freedpeople reluctantly complied with the government orders, though many had no homes to which they could go or any land upon which they might make a living.[30]

The occupants of James City, however, did not relinquish their claim so easily. By the shores of the Trent River, just opposite New Bern's wharf district, the former slaves refused to surrender their new homes, shops, and fields to the property's antebellum owner, James Bryan. They not only did not surrender the contraband camp, but they also successfully fended

Union generals addressing a meeting at a church in James City, 1866. From *Harper's Weekly*, 9 June 1866. Courtesy, New Hanover County Public Library, Wilmington, N.C.

off state troops and local militias sent to evacuate them. They would go on to fight the removal in the courts, and by force of arms when necessary, for decades.[31]

Those former slaves who had lived under the Federal occupation had developed political, educational, and religious institutions that gave them a long head start in confronting postwar life. For all its hardships—or perhaps because of them—the Federal occupation had been a very effective "rehearsal for Reconstruction," to borrow the title of Willie Lee Rose's groundbreaking history of the freedpeople in South Carolina.[32] In parts of the Confederacy that had not fallen to Union forces until the war's last days, African Americans often found it harder to disentangle themselves from the web of slavery, hesitantly trying out new rights for the first time and taking their first steps as free men and women. That was not the case in the coastal communities that had been occupied by the Union army, however. In those African American communities, the freedpeople moved steadfastly to shape the politics of Reconstruction.

Galloway remained in the thick of that political ferment, exhibiting, as one journalist said of him, an "exceedingly radical and Jacobinical spirit" that resonated deeply among local African Americans.[33] When more than 2,000 former slaves celebrated the Fourth of July in 1865 in a Beaufort parade organized by the Salmon P. Chase Equal Rights League—the local chapter's name having been changed, apparently, in honor of the Supreme Court justice's visit to the seaport that spring—Galloway delivered the keynote address. An incensed James Rumley, the Confederate loyalist, called Galloway's words "a most incendiary harangue" and was appalled that he called for "all equal rights before the law, and nothing more."[34]

Not surprisingly, a few weeks later, on 28 August, Galloway emerged, a correspondent for the *New York Times* put it, as the "leading spirit" of a mass meeting of black citizens who assembled in New Bern to shape a political agenda for the postwar era. At the time, a smallpox epidemic was taking the lives of three or four blacks a day in the town, but African American leaders believed that they could not delay further. The convention served as one of the first such gatherings of former slaves held anywhere in the country. In a long keynote address, Galloway called for voting rights and public schooling. "We want to be an educated people and an intelligent people," he told the crowd. In a double-edged declaration that echoed his words of two years before, he also argued that "if the Negro knows how to use the cartridge box, he knows how to use the ballot box."[35]

The centrality of education in Galloway's speech was especially noteworthy. When he listed his demands, the young black leader placed education as a higher priority than suffrage. "We want to read and write and acquire those accomplishments which will enable us to discharge the duties of life as citizens," he asserted, a compelling thing to say for a man who had never learned to read or write.[36]

Galloway went on to announce that he sought "free suffrage," by which he meant the right to vote without any test of education or property ownership. However, he also acknowledged the rising power of reactionary political forces in the nation, and he indicated that he remained willing to compromise, if necessary, with those who opposed black suffrage. From the pulpit, he declared himself prepared to accept limiting the franchise to those who had been educated, presumably those who could pass a literacy test, as long, he said, as it applied equally to blacks and whites. "And I tell you," he told the wildly applauding crowd, "that if this is done, one half the white people of North Carolina will be debarred from voting."[37]

If public schooling and suffrage accounted for Galloway's central demands at the New Bern convention, he also touched on other political issues, including the question of social equality. The *New York Times* correspondent, who noted that Galloway was "an eloquent orator and a general favorite with those who know him," quoted him as responding to white men's expressions of fears about the dangers of racial intermixing by saying, "Why, Sir, if you could only see him slipping around at night, trying to get into negro women's houses, you would be astonished!" A voice in the back of the hall called out, "That's the truth, Galloway."[38]

The mass meeting in New Bern also addressed the white backlash against the freedpeople and the violent, undemocratic nature of the postwar society that had begun to emerge with Presidential Reconstruction. The black New Bernians, led by Galloway, resolved "that the many atrocities committed upon our people in almost every section of our country . . . clearly demonstrate the immense prejudice and hatred on the part of our former owners toward us." They decried "the enforcement of the old code of slave laws that prohibits us from the privileges of schools, that deny us the right to control our families, [and] that reject our testimony in courts of justice." Outraged at the working conditions that prevailed on local farms and plantations, they accused whites of postponing the payment of wages to black laborers "till their crops are laid by and then driving us off, refusing longer to give us food and shelter."

The delegates also detailed a litany of violent acts that had been committed against black men and women who challenged the antebellum racial code. They listed "whipping, thumb-screwing and not infrequently murdering us in cold blood." Their vision was not merely a society without such brutality, however. "In our judgment," they concluded, with more than a measure of understatement, a system of government that allows such atrocities and enforces antebellum racial codes "comes far short of being a republican form of government and needs to be remodeled."[39]

The New Bern assembly appointed Galloway and two other former slaves, John Randolph Jr. and George W. Price Jr., an ambitious young minister's son who had escaped from Wilmington in 1862, to issue a call for a statewide freedpeople's convention in Raleigh a month later, on 29 September.[40] Local black activists had contemplated holding such a gathering for more than half a year but had chosen to wait until a greater measure of peace and security had been achieved in the state's interior.[41] By the late summer of 1865, their world was scarcely less chaotic or dangerous, if at all, than it had been earlier in the year, but Galloway and his colleagues in the Equal Rights League found their patience exhausted: the time to bring together African American leaders from across the state had come.

The convention's organizers printed 1,500 circulars to send into the state's interior. On 8 September, they also appealed to black citizens in newspaper announcements under the banner "Freedmen of North Carolina, Arouse!!" Galloway, Randolph, and Price opened their call with a few lines from the great abolitionist poet John Greenleaf Whittier: "Lo! The waking up of Nations, From Slavery's fatal sleep, the murmur of the Universe, Deep, calling unto deep." They then turned to the Old Testament and Isaiah, declaring, "These are the times foretold by the Prophets when a Nation shall be born in a day." The three men announced that the moment for which the nation's former slaves had been waiting had arrived: "Four million of chattels, branded mercantile commodity, shake off the bands, drop the chains, and rise up in the dignity of men."[42]

Their words resonated in African American communities throughout the state. They instructed black Carolinians to assemble in every township to "speak their views," to put out their own calls for district meetings to elect delegates, and then to come together to choose delegates to Raleigh. Each county would have the same number of delegates as it had state legislators. "Rally, old men; we want the counsel of your long experience," they concluded their appeal. "Rally, young men; we want your loyal presence and need the ardor of youth to stimulate the timid. And may the Spirit of our God come with the people to hallow all our sittings, and wisely direct all our actions."[43]

Their call for a statewide political convention made many inland black leaders anxious. Raleigh's black leaders especially worried that Galloway and his colleagues in New Bern had intentionally scheduled the convention to overlap with the state's constitutional convention, which was due to meet in Raleigh at the same time. "They are more cautious and moderate in their demands," a correspondent for the *Christian Recorder*, the AME church's Philadelphia journal, observed of Raleigh's black leaders, "while the delegates from below seemed disposed to demand every thing in the way of civil rights."[44]

Overruling more cautious black leaders in the state's interior, the coastal chapters of the National Equal Rights League soon met and chose delegates. Two weeks after the New Bern gathering, black activists also convened in Tarboro, an old cotton port on the Tar River. Attracting former slaves from the heart of the state's cotton plantation belt, their mass meeting apparently became the first to select delegates to Raleigh in a section of the state that had still been part of the Confederacy at war's end.[45] Back in New Bern, the Equal Rights Leagues met at Andrew Chapel and selected their own delegates to the state convention. They chose Galloway, John R. Good, John Randolph Jr., and an AME minister from the North, the Reverend George A. Rue.[46]

Three days before Governor Holden called to order a state constitutional convention dominated by the antebellum aristocracy, Galloway called to order 117 black delegates representing forty-two North Carolina counties—out of a total of eighty-nine at that time. They gathered at the Loyal African Methodist Episcopal church, by then known in Raleigh as "the Lincoln Church" for the bust of the fallen president displayed next to its altar. Although no women actively served as delegates, the convention's organizers set aside half the church's galleries for women, an unheard-of policy at the state's white political conventions.[47]

Few of the delegates who gathered at the Lincoln Church dressed so finely as their white counterparts across town. Some had passed the collection plate to obtain a railroad ticket. Many, including Reverend Rue, had slipped out of their hometowns quietly in order to avoid violence at the hands of white mobs.[48] Without giving details of what kind of crowd or conspirators had attempted to waylay him, Rue reported that he barely survived his passage through Goldsboro, a sprawling market town between New Bern and Raleigh where major rail lines crossed and travelers often changed trains. "I have just made my escape," he wrote the editors of the *Christian Recorder*. He also declared that he did not see how other black convention delegates could pass through Goldsboro without the intervention of the U.S. army.[49]

Even conditions in New Bern had deteriorated into a kind of guerrilla war between liberated slaves and their former masters. Compared with Goldsboro or Wilmington, though, the two sides were more evenly matched. That summer, black leaders protested vociferously that returning Rebel soldiers who "vent their spite upon the defenseless blacks" had been made police officers. Confederate army veterans also attempted to intimidate or harass the black soldiers still encamped there. That was usually a mistake. As Rue observed, "When they touch one of these boys . . . , it is pound for pound, drop for drop, and death for death."[50]

An incident on the New Bern–Roanoke Island ferry highlighted the explosiveness of life along the uncertain new color line. That fall, the ferry's captain—"a notorious villain," who, it was said, "always acted inhumanely toward colored people"—tried to compel several African American soldiers in the 1st D.C. Colored Regiment to forsake the vessel's upper deck on the passage from New Bern to Roanoke Island. Before the war, the upper deck of steamboats had strictly been reserved for white patrons. When the black soldiers refused to go below, the captain allegedly hurled a torrent of racial epithets at them. The soldiers held themselves in check for that moment but retaliated once they reached the island. One morning at dawn, they rowed out to the ferry, snuck aboard, and captured the captain and his clerk. According to a letter to the *Anglo-African*, they carried them ashore, tied them to a pine tree, whipped them with a leather belt, and to add insult to injury, robbed them of their money. Ultimately, the black soldiers let them get away, but only after making sure that their captives had learned a lesson about the new color line.[51]

⁓

At their constitutional convention in Raleigh, the state's white conservatives sought to reimpose the antebellum social order. While they drafted so-called Black Codes to bar African Americans from political life, the black delegates across town at the Lincoln Church articulated a profoundly more democratic vision of southern society. "We are living in an important era in the history of the world," a black newspaper exclaimed that fall about a similar convocation of former slaves in Georgia. The black delegates in Raleigh shared that sense of urgency and that feeling of momentous possibility. At their assembly, they demanded the full rights of citizenship, public schools, equal protection under the law, the regulation of working hours, and the abolition of all laws "which make unjust discriminations on account of race or color."[52]

The political views of the black delegates ranged widely from strident militancy to fearful accommodation. The more radical delegates from New Bern and Beaufort dominated the early stages of the convention, however. Several shone with special brilliance in Raleigh. As the gathering's convener, Galloway appointed John Good, his trusted colleague from New Bern, as the convention's temporary president. Delegates elected John Randolph Jr. as the convention's secretary. Most importantly, the Reverend James W. Hood, the AME Zion leader, was elected chairman of the convocation. Hood's presidential address was generally conciliatory, appealing to white goodwill and cautioning the freedpeople to move deliberately. But he also emphasized the delegates' demands for the rights to vote, to testify in courts of justice, to serve on juries, and to be represented in court by black counsel. Coming from the presiding elder of the state's AME Zion congregations, Hood's cautious advice carried a great deal of weight.

The delegates from Raleigh and elsewhere in the state's interior tended to be self-selected men, not ones elected by local assemblies or local chapters of the National Equal Rights League. Most, but not all, were less politically radical and strident than Galloway and his allies. One of the convention's most thrilling orators, James H. Harris, was such a figure. Born a slave in Raleigh but set free in 1848, he had studied at Oberlin College before the war, gotten involved in militant antislavery groups in Canada, and traveled as far as the West Indies and Africa in search of a country where a black man could live his life with dignity. Galloway may well have met him during his sojourn in Canada West. Harris had been one of the few blacks at the 1858 gathering in Chatham, Canada West, where John Brown had first attempted to recruit black militants for his raid on Harpers Ferry. Eloquent and silky-smooth in his demeanor, he had returned home to Raleigh soon after the war's end.[53]

Harris made perhaps the convention's most critical motion. On the second afternoon, he moved that they make the gathering a "mass convention," which meant that, regardless of their credentials, "all who had come in good faith as delegates . . . [could] take their seats." The motion reflected a compromise that had already been reached behind closed doors between the "representative delegates"—that is, those, like Galloway, who had been elected by local Equal Rights Leagues or some other mass meeting—and blacks who came from parts of the state where they had not been free long enough to have developed their own political groups to send representative delegates to the convention. On practical grounds, the decision to include "all who had come in good faith" made a great deal of sense and was probably essential to holding a truly statewide convention. The potential dangers were serious, however. At stake was the future of the state's Equal Rights Leagues and their commitment to grassroots organizing, democratic process, and a radical politics born in the freedpeople's camps. The radical delegates had to understand the risks, and their willingness to support Harris's motion signaled the importance that they placed on extending their political movement as quickly as possible beyond its origins on the state's coast.

For all the extraordinary African American leaders in Raleigh, none made a deeper impression on black delegates or white observers than Galloway. He delivered the keynote speech on the convention's first night and played a pivotal role in nearly every debate. "Perhaps the most remarkable person among the delegates," northern journalist John Richard Dennett observed, was "a light-yellow man whose features seemed to indicate that there was a cross of Indian blood in his veins." He marveled at Galloway's vanity as he tossed his long black hair off his forehead, remarked on the sparkling glint in his eye, and noted how he laughed frequently. He found little that was lighthearted in Galloway's manner, however, when he rose to address the delegates. "When he spoke . . ., he stood erect, using forcible and graceful gestures. His voice was powerful, and, though an illiterate man, his speaking was effective." In Dennett's eyes, Galloway's fierce passion and excoriating wit made him an imposing and often intimidating figure on the convention floor.[54]

During the convention, Galloway made his influence felt on every issue. Another of his orations proved the highlight of an overflow gathering of convention delegates and black Raleigh residents one night at the Lincoln Church. The *Journal of Freedom*, a new Raleigh newspaper founded by two black men, J. Q. A. Crane and Edward P. Brooks, extolled Galloway's speech that night for "advocating equal rights, and a moderate, conservative course in demanding them," a rare characterization of a Galloway speech. Their words indicated that the *Journal of Freedom* was either very radical or that Galloway remained willing to reach out to the state's more cautious black leaders.[55] The *Journal*'s editors noted that his speech, along with those of the evening's other two speakers, James Harris and Isham Swett, of Cumberland County, "while in the main consisting of framed arguments, were interspersed with good bits and genuine wit, and were well received."[56]

Throughout the freedpeople's convention, Galloway fought for the radical political agenda that had emerged out of the contraband camps and Equal Rights Leagues. He brazenly made the cases for suffrage, civil liberties, prohibitions against peonage, workplace rights, full equality within the court system, and a statewide system of public schools that would serve black children. Even more impatiently, he insisted that they must never defer to white rule or accept the antebellum ways of power and privilege. They had fought too long and too hard not to stand with a proud bearing and unbent spirits in this new world that they had played so important a part in creating.

Yet Galloway's defiance of white authority alarmed more cautious black delegates, and the freedpeople's convention ultimately struck a more conciliatory posture. That emerged most clearly when the majority of convention delegates endorsed an open letter to the constitutional convention on the other side of Raleigh. Oddly enough, they selected Galloway, along with James Harris and John Good, to inquire if Governor Holden might address the African American convention and to hand-deliver the open letter to the white convention's leaders. As Galloway had opposed with all his heart so much of the letter's contents and almost groveling tone, he must have accepted the task in a very special spirit. Governor Holden declined the invitation.

Much of the open letter was simply mendacious. The language echoed the dissembling double-talk that many antebellum slaves had fine-tuned to conceal their inner thoughts and secret acts. "Though it was impossible for us to remain indifferent spectators of [the Civil War]," one of the first paragraphs read, "you will do us the justice to admit that we have remained throughout obedient and passive, acting such part only as has been assigned us, and calmly waiting upon Providence." In the fantasy woven by the letter writers, blacks had done nothing to gain their own freedom—not served as Union soldiers, sailors, spies, guides, and scouts; not "stolen themselves" from southern planters; and not organized radical political groups throughout the occupied territories. They had instead merely been "obliged to serve in the camp, to build fortifications, and raise subsistence for the confederate army." The authors did not pretend that they had not dreamed or prayed for freedom—only that they had not acted on those dreams and prayers: "Do you blame us that we have . . . prayed for the freedom of our race?" they asked.[57]

The convention's open letter might be construed as an unavoidable evil, an embarrassing concession, a galling surrender, or merely a tactical feint, the equivalent of the actions of the slave who "shucked and jived" in front of his or her master and then, out of master's sight, orchestrated a runaway plot or a revolt. But the issues in the open letter revealed a great deal about how elemental the African American freedom struggle had become that fall. Containing no mention of suffrage, civil rights, or equal protection under the law, the letter instead beseeched the constitutional convention to consider the most basic rights of the former slaves. "Our first and engrossing concern in our new relation," it stressed, "is how we may provide shelter and an honorable subsistence for ourselves and [our] families." Half a year after Appomattox, many southern whites still did not recognize the Emancipation Proclamation or the Thirteenth Amendment as valid and legitimate. They refused to pay wages to their black employees, withheld a fair share of their crops from them, and sometimes bound them in peonage, denying them the freedom to move from job to job or place to place. The letter highlighted especially the trials of single black mothers. "Women with families of children, whose husbands have been sold, have died or have wrongfully deserted them, have in some cases been driven away from the homes where, under slavery, they have spent a lifetime of hard service. Is it just or Christian thus to thrust out upon the cold world helpless families to perish?"[58]

Family issues assumed paramount importance. The black delegates at the Lincoln Church emphasized the need to educate black children. They urged the state's new legislature to devote funds for the care of black orphans, the infirm, and the disabled who no longer had the protection of family or a plantation slave community. "We invoke your protection for the sanctity of our family relations. Is this asking too much?" they addressed the white convention's delegates and the future legislature. They also sought their assistance in reuniting black families that had been separated either "by war or by the operations of slavery."[59]

The letter ended with a declaration of an attachment to their homes and communities, no matter the blood spilled or the trauma that they had known in them. "Though associated with many memories of suffering, as well as of enjoyment," they stated, "we have always loved our homes and dreaded as the worst of evils, a forcible separation from them. Now that freedom and a new career are before us, we love this land and people more than ever before. Here we have toiled and suffered; our parents, wives and children are buried here; and in this land we will remain unless forcibly driven away."[60]

The most compelling aspect of the black convention's open letter to the constitutional convention lay not in its contents, but in the messengers. One could consider it a little act of genius. The black delegates might have chosen a group of quiet, little-known black men of impeccably deferential manners and humble bearings to deliver their pleading letter to Governor Holden and his fellows. Instead, they chose James Harris, a black militant who had known John Brown, and John Good, who had met with President Lincoln in 1864. Above all, they dispatched Galloway, by then perhaps the most notorious black leader in the South and certainly in the state, famed for the revolver at his hip and for his unremitting fierceness. Galloway may have been delivering a letter full of antebellum good manners and foot-shuffling prose, but the state's aristocracy recognized full well a threat when they saw it: they could accept the letter's appeal to their goodwill and paternalism or they would once more find themselves at war with Galloway and his insurgent brethren.

At the Lincoln Church, the state's black leaders concluded by resolving to reconstitute themselves into the North Carolina Equal Rights League. They adopted a constitution that supplanted that of the state Equal Rights League organized in New Bern a year earlier, when "the state" really only meant the federally occupied territory in and around New Bern, Beaufort, and several outlying contraband camps. The new constitution's preamble read, "Feeling the stern necessity of encouraging a well ordered and dignified life, and emulating the efforts of the friends of Equal Rights in New Berne [sic], looking to the same end, therefore we are met in concert with the determination to organize more permanently, consolidating all efforts looking to our general elevation, operating in harmony with the National League or any other national organization looking forward to the same end."[61]

They thus folded the extraordinary organizing efforts undertaken in the state's contraband camps into what the convention delegates hoped would become a more powerful, statewide Equal Rights League. The delegates elected James Harris to the presidency of the state league and agreed to relocate its office from New Bern to Raleigh.[62] The election of Harris as president, the Equal Rights League's statewide focus, and its shift away from the militancy and radical political culture that had developed in the contraband camps figured as momentous decisions whose repercussions delegates did not fully appreciate at the time. In combination with the inability of the National Equal Rights League's northern leadership to reach out to the South effectively, they would leave former slaves isolated from one another and their brethren in the North just when they desperately needed unity and strength.[63]

As they left the capital, the majority of the delegates believed that their adherence to a more conciliatory posture and to black leaders who put their faith in God and the state's antebellum rulers offered the wisest choices under difficult circumstances. Sometimes patience really amounted to the better part of valor, they believed, and their patience, as much as anything else, had carried them through slavery. They may not have yet been ready for Galloway, but few would forget him or fail to tell stories about him when they returned to homes besieged by white terror. Galloway may have frightened them, for they knew how white conservatives would react to such an insurgent, but he also gave voice to a vision of freedom born in bondage that might yet be their own best salvation and their nation's saving grace.[64]

13

Loud Calls for Galloway

ABRAHAM AND MARTHA ANN GALLOWAY LEFT THE HOME OF MARTHA Ann's parents in Beaufort and moved to Wilmington, North Carolina, sometime after the Raleigh freedpeople's convention in the fall of 1865. The move marked the beginning of a kind of political exile for him. After the convention's delegates chose a more cautious course, Galloway disappeared from public life for more than a year. He removed himself from state and national groups in which he had previously been a leading figure and does not seem to have been involved in the new incarnation of the North Carolina Equal Rights League. He did not even attend the first annual convention of the National Equal Rights League in Cleveland, Ohio— although, to be fair, virtually no southern blacks did—or the second statewide freedpeople's convention in Raleigh in October 1866.[1]

Judging by what happened in Raleigh, the majority of the state's black leaders wanted to take a more cautious and conciliatory approach to Reconstruction politics than Galloway. For the time being, at least, they remained far more willing to give the Johnson administration and the state's white leadership time to recognize the justice of their demands for political equality. The economic hardships of postwar life and the relentless violence directed at African Americans shaped their outlook as well. For most former slaves, survival was challenge enough. Whether this approach was reasonable or not, Galloway had no such patience or hope. But if the bulk of the state's ex-slaves were not yet ready for a more radical path, he had little choice but to wait for the day, should it come, when African Americans again saw the need for his unrestrained spirit and insistent demands for equality.

❧

Galloway returned to Wilmington at least in part for family reasons. After the war, his mother had left her refuge in Boston and rejoined Amos Galloway, Abraham's stepfather, as well as her younger son, Abraham's half-brother John, in Wilmington.[2] His mother and stepfather soon married under state law, a right that had been denied them before the war, and they settled in a house on North Fourth Street, across the street from Galloway's former owner, the master railroad mechanic Marsden Milton Hankins. Abraham and Martha Ann eventually made their home there as well. They already had one son, John, and looked forward to having more children in the coming years. Galloway had never owned a house or land, had never had much money, and had to have grown more concerned about his family's future as he and his wife began to raise a child.[3]

Galloway might have tried to make a living as a brick mason again in Smithville or Wilmington, though that remains highly unlikely. White employers blacklisted and boycotted local black builders who had fought against the Confederacy or rebelled against slavery in visible ways. Galloway's involvement with the Union army was widely known. A family story also insists that Galloway never depended on white patronage once he returned to the land of his birth. As a brick mason, he would have had no choice. According to descendants of John Wesley Galloway, the region's African American churches supported Abraham Galloway financially during Reconstruction so that he would not have to rely on white patrons, creditors, or employers. After the war, many of Wilmington's black political leaders did rely one way or another on white goodwill, usually that of white Republicans. The Galloway family story indicates that local blacks wanted Abraham, at least, to be unencumbered by that kind of economic dependence on those outside the African American community, even their political allies. Whether the story is true or not, Galloway certainly retained his fierce independence all his life. That came with a cost, however; he and his family always lived on the edge of poverty.[4]

When he decided to relocate to Wilmington, Galloway also anticipated that the city would once again become the center of African American political life in North Carolina.[5] Wilmington was the state's largest city and had a majority-black population, and its large number of black artisans and maritime laborers formed the core of a politically militant class that attracted Galloway. By 3 January 1866, the North Carolina Equal Rights League had also conspicuously moved its office out of Raleigh and opened in Wilmington. Galloway's relocation to Wilmington and the opening of the Equal Rights League's office may not have been coincidental.[6]

Another consideration may have influenced Galloway's departure from Beaufort and New Bern. In the fall of 1865, Galloway had a falling out with Mary Ann Starkey, the boardinghouse keeper and community activist who had been for so long one of his closest advisors and confidantes. Whether their quarrel influenced his decision to move home is far from clear, but according to Starkey, the conflict involved a disagreement over financial matters: Galloway had not accounted to her satisfaction for what he did with her personal savings of $141 in gold and silver. Starkey had entrusted him to deposit those funds into a New York bank, and she had also given him $168 in cash belonging to the Colored Ladies Relief Association to place in the hands of Edward Kinsley when Galloway was next in Boston. In Starkey's eyes, Galloway had betrayed her trust, at the very least, and, at worst, had committed thievery and turned out, in her words, "a scamp of the grosser dye."[7]

Without doubt, the incident deeply shook Starkey's faith in Galloway and tarnished the heroic image of him that she had held throughout the war. As recently as January 1865, she had called him "our noble president"— referring to his leadership in the John Brown Equal Rights League. In April, she had trusted him to escort her only daughter, Nancy, back to her as the war came to a close. At Starkey's request, Galloway had traveled 150 miles inland, to Hillsborough, North Carolina, deep inside the old Confederacy, where Nancy Starkey was a slave owned by a New Bern family that had fled the Union invasion. She was engaged to be married, and Galloway brought her home to prepare for the wedding, a dangerous journey through a virtu-ally lawless no-man's-land of returning war veterans, deserters, and refu-gees.[8] After having been so close to Galloway and having entrusted him with so many of the things that she held dearest, Starkey felt bitter and gravely disappointed about the financial disagreement and that their mu-tual friends in New England did not intervene on her behalf.[9] Yet she may have owed Galloway a significant sum of money as well, which contributed to their disagreement.[10]

Galloway's failure to respond to her queries stoked Starkey's worst fears about the loss of her savings. Because she had not spoken with him directly at that point, however, Galloway may have provoked Starkey's anxiety by failing to communicate with her effectively, not by venality. Perhaps, once they finally discussed the matter face-to-face, they reached a mutually satisfactory resolution to the financial disagreement. But Starkey's disap-pointment in Galloway lasted at least from July to October 1865. Unfor-tunately, Starkey did indeed descend into poverty after the war, and she continued to feel largely forsaken by the circle of Union soldiers and New England abolitionists who had befriended her during the conflict.[11] Of course, that was not unusual: many former slaves felt abandoned by the North in the difficult first years of freedom.[12]

Whatever motives led to his return to Wilmington, once back eating at his mother's dinner table, Galloway tried to give his life a semblance of normality. He and Martha Ann went about raising their newborn son. They attended St. Paul's Episcopal Church, an interracial congregation, and Abraham joined the newly founded Masonic Lodge, one of the centers of African American political activism.[13] Reconstruction was not an ordinary time, however, and a quiet life was hardly his destiny. Immediately after Appomattox, the city's black population found themselves in an often violent conflict over the shape of the postwar society. Nothing was certain: not their rights to vote, to own land, to attend school, to earn wages, to claim civil rights, or to enjoy equal protection under the law. Those issues were all being worked out on the streets of towns like Wilmington just as surely as in the halls of the U.S. Congress. Every encounter between a black person and a white person was fraught with danger. "They perceive insolence in a tone, a glance, a gesture, or failure to yield enough by two or three inches in meeting on the sidewalk," a visitor noted of Wilmington's white citizens.[14] Cape Fear conservatives sought to reestablish their antebellum power, while blacks sought to assert their new rights of freedom and citizenship. The talents for covert organizing and self-defense that Galloway had honed as a runaway slave, a fugitive abolitionist, and a Union spy would be put to good use in Reconstruction Wilmington.

Galloway was mistaken, however, if he believed that Wilmington blacks were better prepared for his militancy than the majority of delegates at the freedpeople's convention in Raleigh. At least at first, they were not. By the time that Galloway returned home, he probably suspected that he had moved too precipitously in Wilmington the previous year, when he had helped Equal Rights Leagues to blossom in the first days of freedom and encouraged their bold demands for suffrage and a role in the affairs of city government. He knew that the seaport had its own homegrown tradition of black revolutionary activism—indeed, he himself formed part of that tradition. But unlike their neighbors in New Bern, Wilmington's former slaves had not yet had the chance to allow that tradition of dissent to grow from a clandestine way of surviving slavery—and sometimes undermining slavery from within—into a popular movement of protest and rebellion strong enough to overcome vehement white opposition to African American political equality.

As white opposition grew more intense, many of Wilmington's black residents proved unprepared to defend themselves. Galloway discovered that their new political institutions did not yet have the fortitude to endure an organized white backlash against black empowerment. For three years during the war, the freedpeople in New Bern had built their political activism on a foundation of mass schooling, community institution building, and grassroots political organizing; Wilmington blacks had not had that experience. Many local blacks were still ready to fight. On 3 January 1866, the local Equal Rights League, in an address published in the *New York Times*, offered "our arms . . . and our lives, if necessary, to quell and crush insurrection," by which they meant Rebels who persisted in defying the U.S. government and continued to insist on black subjugation. But more than a hint of deference ran through the same address. "We ask an opportunity to be shown worthy to be free," league members wrote, and "propose to attain the condition and privileges of freemen by becoming intelligent, by industry, by virtue, by piety." They even felt compelled to reassure whites that they need not fear for their personal safety or the violent overthrow of the government. "Does any suggest insurrection, we frown upon him, denounce him!" they declared.

Not surprisingly, strands of militancy and deference, caution and bold self-assertion, coexisted in the African American community, and often in the breast of a single individual. What a person said in public might also differ from what he or she said in private. Most of the former slaves, however, were not yet ready for Galloway. Although he had strong roots in Wilmington, most local black activists believed that he moved too hastily, expected too much, and pushed whites too hard. They feared that his stridency endangered black neighborhoods and poisoned the sympathy of local whites, to whom most black residents still looked for jobs, credit, or other kinds of patronage. As Galloway settled back into Wilmington, he consequently found himself marginalized in the city's black political culture.

In the meantime, white conservatives gradually regained power in Wilmington, in large part due to Union military commanders who sympathized more with the Cape Fear aristocrats than with the former slaves. "The true soldiers, whether they wore the gray or the blue are now united in their opposition . . . to negro government and negro equality," gloated a local newspaper, adding, "Blood is thicker than water."[15] Nightriders, black-faced "Regulators," and white militias beat, killed, and otherwise terrorized African Americans who dared to act like free citizens. They strove to reimpose control over the freedpeople's lives, including control over whom they worked for, what wages they commanded, where they lived, and how they raised their children.[16]

For a time, the presence of black troops among the Federal occupying forces in Wilmington inhibited that kind of violence, but Union commanders showed a lack of resolve in supporting the black troops, even refusing to intervene when white militia groups targeted black soldiers. Increasingly, the black troops realized that they were on their own in postwar Wilmington. They mutinied against their white officers that September. They later laid siege to the city jail in order to halt the public whipping of black prisoners convicted in a trial in which a judge had refused to allow black testimony. After that incident, Union commanders withdrew all black troops from the Lower Cape Fear and replaced them with white soldiers.[17]

White terror reigned throughout the Cape Fear Valley. "The fact is," a freedman reported, "it's the first notion with a great many of these people, [that] if a Negro says anything or does anything that they don't like, [they] take a gun and put a bullet into him."[18] Not far from Wilmington, in Duplin County, police captain J. N. Stallings gave orders to shoot without trial blacks who had been accused of minor theft.[19] Galloway himself reported a white mob attacking a black Union army veteran when he was in Goldsboro in early June. As he and other blacks gathered to protest the assault, city police attempted to arrest all those who, in his words, expressed "any thing in the shape of indignation." Two of the protesters refused to be taken prisoner. "One of them was shot dead," Galloway wrote officials at the Freedmen's Bureau in Washington, D.C., "one mortally wounded." An angry crowd of whites then attacked Galloway. "I was compelled to flee for my life," he declared. He added, "There is no protection for the colored people. . . . Our lives are always in danger."[20]

Most often local African Americans had to fight their own battles. The Reverend Henry M. Turner, an African American army chaplain who had come to know Galloway during the war, expressed outrage that "a certain white man" in eastern North Carolina whipped freedpeople to remind them of their servile status. He heartily approved when two black men "apprehended this thug" and "confiscated his weapons." Elsewhere, black Union army veterans organized a militia to protect African American communities. The state's conservative governor, Jonathan Worth, observed that blacks in Edgecombe County "drill and go through all the military evolution." He reported that their mass meetings were ostensibly for planning "a strike for higher wages," but he suspected that they were "directed by some who have served in the Federal army."[21] The former slaves did much to protect their homes and communities, but violence by conservative whites still raged throughout the region.

Finally, persistent white terror and the passage of the notorious Black Codes across the South, as well as Andrew Johnson's apparent satisfaction with both developments, inspired the Republican Congress to pass the Reconstruction Acts of 1867. With this legislation, Radical Republicans wrestled control of Reconstruction in the South away from Johnson, and blacks in Wilmington and elsewhere gained a crucial new political opportunity. The Reconstruction Acts restored Federal military authority in the South and required states in the former Confederacy to pass constitutions that guaranteed universal male suffrage before they could be readmitted into the Union. The laws also opened the polls to black voters for the first time, while banning from political life all antebellum officeholders who had taken an oath to uphold the U.S. Constitution but sided with the Confederacy.[22] The long-awaited window for black citizenship had arrived.

Seizing the moment, Galloway began working toward the constitutional convention slated to occur in Raleigh early in 1868. He first turned to the founding of the state's Republican Party and building support among Wilmington's blacks for it. On 20 July 1867, Galloway gave an hour-long speech to a mass gathering at Thalian Hall, the city's antebellum opera house, in which he called for local blacks to make the Republican Party their own. As usual, Galloway did not mince words, and his daring drew notice in the press. "He confessed himself wholly devoted to the Republican Party," white opponents at the *Daily Journal* observed, "even to the extent which we call radical."[23]

For the next six weeks, Galloway espoused the Republican cause to anyone who would listen. In Wilmington, he gave rousing speeches at the meeting of the First Ward Republican Club, to the Fourth Ward Republicans, and at a mass meeting called to nominate local delegates to the founding convention of the state's Republican Party. He also canvassed in Brunswick County, his birthplace, as well in several neighboring counties. Galloway addressed a Republican gathering in Whiteville, forty-five miles west, and made another speech in Wilmington at the founding meeting of the state Colored Soldiers' and Sailors' League, a group established in

Philadelphia by black Union veterans for the support of war widows and orphans, but which also served as a vehicle for a strong militant politics. The speech, the *Wilmington Daily Post* noted, was "interrupted by rapturous applause."[24]

On 27 August, in a letter to the *Daily Post*, the city's Republican newspaper, Galloway laid out his vision of the Republican Party, or in his words, a plan for "a complete public political organization, in order that when the time shall arrive we may be fully prepared for any emergency." Using the organizing model that the state's Equal Rights Leagues had deployed during the war, and already adopted by the city's First Ward Republican Club, he recommended that each of the city's wards have a "Campaign Club" that would meet weekly and provide an opportunity for "remarks on the political questions of the day." He proposed a plan for each ward's residents to nominate aldermen and other elected officials and to elect delegates to carry those nominations forward to a citywide nominating convention. Eschewing "secret orders" and political cliques, Galloway demanded that the party's business be conducted "with the doors open to all who favor the cause." At the end of his letter, Galloway admonished Republican voters, "You see, fellow-citizens, the necessity for such an organization in each of your Wards. Now go to work!"[25]

On 4 September 1867, Galloway gave the opening address at the founding convention of the state Republican Party at Tucker Hall in Raleigh, delivering what others interpreted as a conciliatory speech aimed at building broad, biracial support for the Republicans. He exhorted his audience to "go everywhere there is a black man or a poor white man and tell him the true condition of the Republican Party."[26] He referred obliquely to his service as a Union spy and more directly to the leadership of Brigadier General Joseph C. Abbott at the Battle of Fort Fisher; Abbott had been nominated as the convention's president. Galloway indicated that he was proud to serve with white men who had taken part in the African American freedom struggle. "I stand here today as a representative of the Republican Party," Galloway shouted, "neither Republican black man nor Republican white man, but the Republican Party."[27]

His words reached out to poor whites, stressing that they would benefit as well from the Republican Party's commitment to free schools and that working-class blacks and whites had much else in common as well. To the consternation of some of his black colleagues, he also showed a willingness to overlook the Civil War allegiances of white men if they now showed a willingness to stand with the Republicans. "A man may be a Dutchman or an Irishman; a Yankee or a Southerner, and I tell you I will give him a hearty shake and a warm welcome upon the Republican platform," Galloway exclaimed.[28]

A few days later, on his return to Wilmington, Galloway acknowledged that he had clashed with some of the other black Republicans who had been in Raleigh. He assured a mass meeting held to welcome home the returning delegates that he stood prepared to "bury all our difficulties now and commence afresh." Though the Republican convention had not put forward any black candidates for statewide office, apparently in order not to provoke conservatives further, Galloway resolutely supported the party. "The half Negro that was in him loved *liberty*," the *Wilmington Daily Post* quoted him, "and he believed that it could be obtained only through the Republican Party."[29] Later that month, "after loud calls for Galloway," he addressed a torch-lit procession of black citizens from the top of Wilmington's market house. "My people stand here tonight fettered, bound hand [and] foot by a Constitution that recognizes them as chattel [and] that says [there are] no rights for negroes that white men shall respect," Galloway shouted, literally, from the rooftop.[30] He went on to predict that, within six months, African Americans would have the opportunity to vote for a new state constitution that had the potential to give them the full rights of suffrage and political equality. "In this," he challenged the crowd, "it will be left to them whether or not they will voluntarily remain where they are."[31]

That fall Galloway continued his political activism at a fever pitch while he waited for the constitutional convention. He addressed political gatherings of all sorts, ranging from a mass meeting of the "friends of Education, Temperance and Suffrage" in early September to a gathering at St. Stephen's African Methodist Episcopal church in Wilmington, where he presented an ornate chandelier to the congregation, a gift from the Vigilant Fire Company, one of the city's new, all-black firefighting brigades.[32] On 17 October, the New Hanover County Republican convention elected him one of three local candidates to run as delegates to the constitutional convention. The convention delegates also elected two white northerners, or in the term white conservatives preferred, "carpetbaggers": Brigadier General Joseph C. Abbott and the Reverend S. S. Ashley. After the election, Galloway offered a resolution defending himself from slurs made against him by conservative newspapers in Raleigh and reiterated his support for "equal and just taxation for the establishment . . . of a free school system." He later closed the county convention with a short speech.[33]

A sense of the substance of Galloway's political speeches that autumn appears in a surviving excerpt of an oration that he gave on 14 November. A Republican mass meeting at Camp Lamb, in Wilmington, provided the occasion, as well as the opportunity to welcome a visiting dignitary, John Mercer Langston, the black abolitionist, lawyer, and founding president of the National Equal Rights League, who was touring eastern North Carolina as part of his new duties as the Federal government's inspector general of the Freedmen's Schools. Galloway's remarks argued for supporting the new constitutional convention—the first question on the ballot in the approaching election—and then for supporting the Republican candidates to the convention. "They call us to sustain them as they were our best friends," he said of conservative leaders. But, he continued, "what kind of friends are those who propose to re-enslave us? . . . We know who are our friends. We knew them in war—we know them in peace."

To loud cheers, Galloway argued that "the proposition of the Republican party is to allow every man in the nation to be his own *master*." Putting aside his own struggles to compel the Union army, the Lincoln administration, and the Republican Party to treat the South's slaves with dignity and respect, he told his audience that the North had waged a war for their freedom and that now they should stand by the Republican Party. Galloway's words reflected a clear resolve for a biracial democratic politics, based on citizenship for all. The *Wilmington Daily Post* recorded his vision: "There is a bright future before us—the day of rejoicing is at hand—Let us stand united—let there be no divisions. Let us shout that we are a people, and that our freedom is not a bar to our advancement. Let the work go on, and be hopeful, for the Great Jehovah still hears the prayers of the downtrodden." He left the stage to wild cheers and applause.[34]

New Hanover County voted nearly three to one in favor of holding the constitutional convention and elected Galloway as one of its three delegates, along with Ashley and Abbott, to the convention. After the election, the young black leader—Galloway had only just turned thirty—caucused with local and state Republican leaders over the key issues that the new state constitution should address. He consulted as well with Thaddeus Stevens, the Radical Republican leader in the U.S. Senate, at his home in Washington, D.C., as part of a delegation of black and white southern Unionists. Amid that frenzy of activity, he also led a protest against the replacement of a well-respected Freedmen's Bureau agent with a new agent, in Galloway's words, "totally disinterested as to whether the negro gets justice or not." On New Year's Day 1868, Galloway gave a keynote address at an Emancipation Day celebration in Wilmington. He then headed to Raleigh two weeks later for the constitutional convention.[35]

Once in Raleigh, Galloway was, in the words of the foremost historian of the Cape Fear region, W. McKee Evans, one of "a small group of active delegates who largely dominated the life of the convention."[36] The *Wilmington Daily Journal* reported, "Two of our delegates, Galloway and Abbott, are running the machine," noting that Galloway had placed in nomination the president, secretary, and doorkeeper on the convention's first day. Between them, the two men spoke from the floor a total of eighteen times on the convention's second day, which was the first full day of business. Crowds of black women watched the proceedings from the gallery.[37]

During the constitutional convention, which ran from January to March 1868, Galloway served on the powerful rules-of-order committee, a five-member body that ran the convention's daily business, as well as on the judiciary committee and, under the chairmanship of the well-known white lawyer and newspaper editor—and later judge and novelist—Albion Tourgée, on the committee for local government.[38] As one of only 13 blacks out of 120 delegates elected to the constitutional convention, he felt a special responsibility to represent the political concerns of the state's African American population. Even so, he repeatedly went out of his way to say that he advocated for the workingman and the oppressed, whatever their color. A Republican newspaper quoted him saying, "I came here to help the poor white man, as well as the colored man, and to do justice to all men."[39]

Galloway sauntered through the convention with both fire and humor. He proposed articles outlining suffrage rights and banning discrimination against passengers on railroads and ships and played an active role in almost every floor debate.[40] At one point, on 20 February, Galloway explained his support for the popular election of the judiciary by saying, in a newsman's paraphrase, that "the Judiciary in New Hanover was a bastard, born in sin and secession." As he saw it, it was "a crime to be a black or a loyal man," he continued, and he denounced conservative judges whom he accused of imprisoning blacks solely to keep them from voting.[41] At another point, Galloway vehemently opposed public support of a railroad that, in his words, "did not employ a single colored man," and he refused to support a request by the YMCA to use the convention hall unless "no distinction be made between the races."[42]

The unlettered young leader showed no fear of going head-to-head with the convention's most brilliant legal minds, including the formidable

Tourgée, with whom Galloway tussled repeatedly. On 12 February, most memorably, Galloway challenged Tourgée from the convention floor for producing a judiciary committee report on a rather obscure reform to the state's legal code regarding civil suits without the advisement of the committee's dissenters. Galloway declared that he "knew no more about the report than what was in Heaven, and God knows he was not in the right road to know what that was." To make sure that conservatives back home did not feel spared of his wrath, he presented a petition to the constitutional convention calling for new municipal elections in Wilmington, after accusing the city's current mayor and city aldermen of being "disloyal."[43]

ᘓᘔ

At the constitutional convention, Galloway routinely endured lengthy arguments about black inferiority from conservative delegates, and the partisan press proved quick to adopt similar lines. The *Raleigh Sentinel*, for example, opined that true North Carolinians would blush "that a set of apes and hybrids should be holding a brutal carnival in her halls of legislation."[44] The *Daily Journal*, one of Galloway's hometown newspapers, viewed the proceedings in a similar vein, referring to the constitutional convention as a "Kangaroo Konvenshun" and "Grand Reconstrucshun Managerie" that would write a "Gorilla Constitution."[45] Conservative delegates and newspaper editors alike would discover that such remarks inspired Galloway's most cutting rhetoric. At the end of one harangue on the unfitness of blacks for suffrage and the "moral impossibility of the negro's ability to qualify himself as a voter," Galloway responded by saying "that the best blood in Brunswick County flowed in my veins," a reference to his own mixed-race heritage. "And if I could do it," he added, "in justice to the African race, I would lance myself and let it out."[46]

While in Raleigh, Galloway immersed himself in the practical issues of crafting a new state constitution. Writing the constitution, a remarkably complex endeavor, involved a fundamental rethinking of tax law, the legal code, the relationship between state and local governments, and a host of other issues far removed from those that most of the general public recognized as directly related to the end of slavery. Yet the enduring power of race and the dawn of African American freedom shaped those issues, too, and proved no less significant to his constituents.

On a personal level, Galloway could also not avoid the unique dilemmas of being a black delegate. He refused to obey the traditional, antebellum code of deference that white men expected on the streets and in public establishments. Inevitably, by refusing to step aside for a white man on a sidewalk or not waiting until white customers had finished their business to make his purchases, he drew glares of reprobation or awe, depending on whether the observer was white or black. Sometimes he was controversial simply by being himself. He provoked an uproar and a minor scandal, for instance, when he was seen sharing a dinner table at one of Raleigh's leading inns with Calvin J. Cowles, the convention's president, a white man, and one of his closest political allies in Raleigh.[47]

Then there was the morning of 31 January, when Galloway opened the convention's business by raising a copy of a Raleigh conservative newspaper over his head and damning the editors for their insistence on using the epithet "nigger" to describe black delegates. That morning Galloway had had enough. At the start of the day's business, he announced, in a journalist's paraphrase, that "if he could not obtain redress here, he would seek it elsewhere." Threatening to challenge his adversaries in the press to a duel made for a remarkable moment in the assembly. Galloway's outrage led to a lengthy deliberation over the proper and acceptable way to address a black leader—colored, Afro-American, black? The delegates also debated whether the Constitution's First Amendment sheltered a reporter from being barred from the gallery for using a racial epithet. Galloway threw grease on the fire more than once, saying, after a conservative delegate protested the convention's ultimate expulsion of the reporter, that "the gentleman had protested against the advance of the Union army [too], but failed to do anything [about it]."[48]

Despite all the rancor, conservatives represented a small minority at the convention. On 16 March 1868, the delegates approved a new state constitution that introduced universal male suffrage, removed all property and religious qualifications for holding office, endorsed the popular election of county officials, improved women's property and domestic rights, laid a foundation for mass public schooling, and made the state's penal code more humane.[49] Galloway returned home in time for the baptism of his first son, John, on 22 March.[50]

⇛

Once back in Wilmington, Galloway found that the Republican Party had nominated him to run for the state senate, in the first election in which African Americans were eligible to hold state office. Only eleven years earlier, he had fled the state, huddled behind barrels of turpentine in the hold of a ship. Now he was being considered for the legislature. Running for office in postwar North Carolina, however, may have seemed nearly as risky. As Galloway soon discovered, Cape Fear conservatives had launched a vicious campaign to intimidate blacks and prevent their voting to ratify the new constitution or elect Radical candidates in the upcoming April election. The former secessionists organized White Men's Clubs in Wilmington, and the city's conservative newspapers bristled with headlines such as "Shall White Children be Apprenticed to Negro Masters?!" Conservative newspaper editors railed against Republican leaders "who would convert four millions of happy laborers into savages by bestowing on them privileges which providence never intended them to possess." Such "wicked and cruel people," the *Wilmington Daily Journal* opined, "will be foiled and driven back." Reprinting an article from the *New York Herald*, the same newspaper warned that the preoccupation with African American equal rights "cannot be obliterated except by the stern and bloody experiences of the battlefield."[51]

Under the leadership of Colonel Roger Moore, a wealthy commission merchant and owner of a brick company, the newly founded Ku Klux Klan attempted to frighten blacks away from the polls.[52] Klansmen drove a cartload of bones through the city's streets in broad daylight, and "a skeleton, phantom, Ku Klux, or whatever it might be," was seen one night in an alley by the city post office. In large capital letters, the conservative *Daily Journal* reported the phantom's parting words: "THE KU KLUX ARE ABROAD! THE AVENGER COMETH WITH THE NIGHT WHEN MAN SLEEPTH! BEWARE! THE HOUR IS NEAR AT HAND!" The newspaper's editors nevertheless pronounced themselves astonished the next day that "there are many Negroes in this city who . . . almost constantly go armed."[53]

Klan terrorism would rage out of control during Reconstruction in many other parts of North Carolina, but it encountered a stubborn militancy among African Americans in Wilmington. Black men patrolled the city's streets, firing their guns in the air and wielding fence rails to intimidate Klansmen, daring them to do battle. Shots and scuffles shattered the evening quiet on the downtown streets repeatedly on the nights of 18 to 21 April. Exactly what happened in that darkness is not known, but the Ku Klux Klan was never a force in Wilmington again during Reconstruction.[54] In all likelihood, Galloway did not sit quietly at his mother's fireside while his allies fought the Klan in the darkened streets.

Defying nightriders and assassins, Galloway campaigned steadily in Wilmington and in outlying parts of New Hanover and Brunswick Counties that composed his senatorial district. To assist other Republican candidates, he also gave fiery orations at political meetings in two counties to the west, Columbus and Sampson, both outside his district. The dangers there were greater than in Wilmington. In Clinton, in Sampson County, a would-be assassin attacked Galloway with a bowie knife while he spoke. The candidate escaped injury but only avoided a lynch mob with the help, Galloway recalled, of "a Conservative—an honest man—Mr. T. Jeff Lee," the white editor of a local newspaper who had never been Galloway's friend. Putting their political differences aside, Galloway gave Lee unreserved credit for his escape: "If never before, he did at that time save the life of a fellow-man."[55]

In the spring 1868 election, voters overwhelmingly chose Galloway to represent New Hanover and Brunswick Counties in the state senate. He received 3,569 votes to his opponent's 2,235. That summer Galloway prepared for his first session of the North Carolina General Assembly, which convened in July. He continued to keep a high profile in Wilmington, speaking frequently at African American churches and Republican Party events. He also served as the marshal of a Memorial Day parade sponsored by the Grand Army of the Republic, a local branch of the national organization of Union army veterans. The next month, he addressed the annual celebration of the Union Brothers Society, a gathering of all the African American political and fraternal societies in Wilmington, of which there were an astonishing number by 1868.[56]

With the elections for the General Assembly done, Galloway supported other Republican candidates running in local, state, and national elections that fall. Though he already held his seat in the state senate, he found himself on the ballot again. At a Republican nominating convention in Robeson County that included, by one estimate, 600 to 800 blacks, half of them women, the delegates put forward the new state senator Galloway as the Third District's candidate for presidential elector. At that time, the election of electors proceeded by statewide, popular ballot, and a party's candidates for presidential electors appeared alongside its candidates for governor and president. Galloway thus became the first black man in North Carolina history to appear on a statewide ballot, a historic achievement that became a source of great pride among the legions of African American voters going to the polls for the first time.[57]

The fall electoral campaign was ugly. Across the state, conservative editors filled their pages with stories of alleged black outrages committed against white women and taunted southern white men for failing to "protect" white womanhood by allowing blacks access to the voting booth.

Their campaign propaganda managed to imply that allowing black men to vote lay one step shy of their invading white women's bedrooms.[58] They also circulated rumors that black militias stood ready "to make war" and waited in readiness to assemble quickly at the sound of a bugle. Those rumors may have had more than a grain of truth. "A company numbering about forty . . . passed by us in regular military order, officered by one who gave commands with a voice as if regularly authorized," a conservative newspaper editor noted that September, calling it "a nightly practice."[59] In the November election, bolstered by the ballots of newly enfranchised blacks, voters elected a local board of alderman that was half black and under Republican control. They also chose Galloway as the first black elector in the state's history. In early December, he conveyed the Third District's vote for the Republican ticket of Ulysses S. Grant and Schuyler Colfax to Washington, D.C.[60] In an open letter to the black voters of New Hanover County, Galloway, along with other Republican leaders, announced that the election affirmed that "we are men, and a part of the body politic."[61]

By that time, Galloway understood all too well that armed self-defense was crucial to political survival in Wilmington. Conservative leaders held him in contempt, Democratic editors parodied him mercilessly, and the threat of assassination dogged his every step. Wherever he went in the port city, Galloway conspicuously wore a pistol in his belt, a noteworthy symbol of defiance only two years after Wilmington's white leaders had organized house searches to disarm the black population. Black militiamen also stood by his side. In the coming year, a local militia, one of several organized by Wilmington blacks to defend themselves against white terrorists, elected Galloway their commander.[62] Organized under state law, Galloway's militia was called the 1st Regiment, North Carolina Defense Militia, and the newly elected governor, William W. Holden, commissioned him a lieutenant colonel and its commanding officer. Nobody understood better than former slaves and black army veterans that a constitution was only as strong as the military power available to defend it.[63]

❧

Galloway was one of three black senators and seventeen black representatives in a North Carolina General Assembly dominated by Republicans in 1868. When he first arrived at the General Assembly on 7 July, he was only thirty-one years old, poor, and still could not read or write.[64] He had, however, extraordinary gifts as an orator and instantly became an influential legislator. An intelligent, ferocious debater, Galloway was the kind of man whose biting sense of humor and sharp eye for hypocrisy inspired senate conservatives to steer away from a direct argument with him. Few of his fellow senators had ever been compelled to confront a black man as an equal, much less a black man as fearless and battle-tested as Galloway. The *Wilmington Daily Journal*, a Democratic newspaper apparently still squeamish about Galloway's mixed-race parentage, once referred to him as "the pugilistic 'Indian Senator.'" He inspired more grandiose comparisons as well. A correspondent for the *Brooklyn Daily Eagle*, in New York, referred to him as "the colored Napoleon."[65]

Political sympathizers turned Galloway's combativeness and readiness to take on all comers into endearing traits, but none denied them. After the editor of Wilmington's Republican newspaper, the *Post*, received a tour of the state senate, he wrote an article that highlighted several of its leaders, concluding with Galloway. "Last, but not least," he wrote, tongue in cheek, "we see the 'gentle Galloway' pitching into the enemy, and ever ready to oblige friend or foe." He added, with a note of playful affection, "Busy and studious[,] we see a great future for New Hanover's favorite— A. H. Galloway."[66]

The *Post*'s editor did not exaggerate the young senator's inclination to "oblige friend or foe" with a good fight. As he had all his life, Senator Galloway often seemed at war with the whole world. "If white people [in the state] don't like their legislation," Galloway was quoted as saying, obviously intent on rankling conservative leaders, "*they can leave*."[67] But senate Democrats were not his only foes. At one point, he called for the appointment of a joint senate-house committee to investigate a fellow Republican accused of taking bribes, saying that the committee should determine "whether the Senator from Craven [County] had sold himself to the Democrats." He argued so fiercely with one of the legislature's other black Republicans, Isham Swett of Cumberland County, that the two almost came to fisticuffs when they later met on a Wilmington street.[68] And nothing provoked his wrath more than the railroad interests and their senate backers. Throughout his legislative career, Galloway denounced, lambasted, and filibustered against what he considered abuses of power by the state's publicly supported railroads, those, in his words, "opulent and influential corporations." He maintained an especially contentious public feud with William A. Smith, the president of the North Carolina Railroad Company.[69]

His fellow senators gave Galloway plenty of grist for his mill. On 16 July 1868, as a prime example, one of his archenemies in the senate, R. G. Robbins, introduced a resolution against racial intermixing, proposing, in his words, "that we recognize the radical distinctions of color, blood, physical form, and peculiarities of intellect between the white and Negro races, and [that] all efforts to destroy or abridge these distinctions are crimes not only against society and civilization, but against God himself." The resolution went on to say that "the common rule, as well as the experience of mankind, proves that the white race is superior to the Negro in physical and intellectual endowment, and that civilization and its future successful progress are safe only in the hands of the white race." In addition, "the governments of the United States and of the several states were instituted by white men, have been administered by white men, and ought to be administered by white men, forever hereafter."[70]

Those sorts of proposals and comments were not uncommon during Galloway's first summer in the state senate. At times, he responded to them with anger but, just as often, with a teasing, playful humor that often infuriated his opponents more than his outbursts did. One such incident occurred that August, during a debate over a bill adding a two-cent tax on all passengers traveling on railroads in which the state had a financial interest. Railroad executives had recently raised ticket prices, Galloway argued, because they sought to discourage black citizens from purchasing first-class tickets in order to keep their trains segregated by race as much as possible. He feared that the new tax would prevent many black travelers from taking trains at all. "They would have to walk," he was quoted, "and, when tired, would be tempted to steal a horse." "Pass this bill," Galloway warned his fellow senators, tongue deep in his cheek, "and you encourage horse-stealing."[71]

On the occasion of Senator Robbins's resolution in defense of white supremacy, the senate simply ignored the resolution and adjourned. On other days, however, Galloway did lose patience. A long debate over increasing the strength of Governor Holden's militias to confront Ku Klux Klan nightriders was one such moment. At the time of the debate—the end of 1869—Klan terrorism raged in many piedmont and eastern North Carolina counties. During 1869–70, Klansmen committed hundreds of acts of violence against African Americans. Often they dragged black victims from their homes and beat, whipped, or lynched them. At other times they burned the homes of African Americans. They used the rape of black women to assail black political empowerment, and they killed without mercy, at times including pregnant women and children. The Freedmen's Bureau's campaign to educate African Americans offered another special target: Klansmen beat and killed Freedmen's Bureau teachers and students and burned their schools.[72]

The Klan terrorists also targeted Republican leaders and other elected officials who opposed the Klan, including, of course, Galloway. In some cases, they succeeded; a Republican state senator in Yanceyville, a county commissioner in Jones County, and a sheriff in Lenoir County can all be counted among their victims. The Federal army offered little protection. In fact, when Galloway entered the debate in the General Assembly, an episode in Goldsboro had recently raised questions about the dangers that white Union troops posed to African Americans. In Goldsboro, white soldiers had beaten a black couple on their way home from night classes at an African American school. The incident had led to a pitched gun battle between black men and the soldiers.[73]

Galloway had no patience with white legislators who defended the Klan. As conservative senators rose repeatedly to defend the Klan as a necessary evil for assuring order and opposing black criminality, Galloway fairly jumped from his seat and roared that he could not understand how the Democratic Party could continue "to justify the deeds and outrages of this miserable and contemptible organization!" Accusing the Klan of a murder "every other day," he declared that he could come to only one conclusion. Glaring icily at the bill's opponents, he said that "it was the purpose and understanding of the Democratic Party to oppose everything for the benefit of society and give more power to these miserable murderers who are now troubling the entire country."[74]

Galloway often took conservative attitudes toward the mixing of blacks and whites as a personal insult, whether the debate hinged on schools or jury boxes. On one occasion, after a white senator from Craven County had made racial slurs in the midst of a floor debate over the racial makeup of New Bern's city council, Galloway declared "that he would hold the Senator from Craven responsible for his language, outside of this Hall; and . . . that, if hereafter, the Senator from Craven insulted him, he would prove to him the blood of a true Southron."[75] That was hardly the only incident in which Galloway reminded conservative Democrats that he was at least as aristocratic by birth as most of them—or that he threatened to take up firearms when he felt his dignity insulted or his reputation besmirched.

Galloway had long claimed to be "a true Southron" and brazenly touted his racially mixed parentage.[76] No senate floor debate could examine the "color line" or antiblack laws without Galloway taunting conservatives for their hypocrisy in language that reminded the Democrats that they were ultimately talking about family. Repeatedly, when a conservative called black men sexual predators posing threats to "white womanhood," Galloway reminded the senators how commonly white men pursued black women. He was probably well enough acquainted with the conservative Democrats' private lives to make more than a few of them nervous with a wink or a whisper. No wonder Galloway attracted such venomous editorials in Democratic newspapers. The *Wilmington Journal* referred to Galloway's flaunting of his "bastardy" as "disgusting vulgarity [that] . . . was a disgrace to any civilized community." Another time, the *Journal*'s editors seem to have nearly fainted at his mention of his parentage and interracial sex, referring obliquely to "some indelicate remarks [by Galloway] in regard to . . . white men mingling with negroes which we omit for the sake of decency."[77]

For all his tempestuousness, Galloway also proved an able, savvy legislator who exercised considerable power within the legislative body. Particularly in 1868, he played an integral part in the senate leadership and was widely recognized as being the senate Republicans' liaison to the state's black voters. Galloway gained plum committee assignments, always obtained the floor when he sought to enter a debate or propose a resolution or bill, and was a key figure among the small circle of Republican leaders who caucused nightly at a Raleigh hotel and laid out the next day's legislative agenda. Galloway used his influence not only to confront the great issues of the day related to the aftermath of the war and the end of slavery, but also to support issues unique to his constituents in New Hanover and Brunswick Counties. Many of those issues were as mundane as harbor channel dredging, setting rates of pilotage, and other acts related to Wilmington's competitiveness as a commercial seaport.[78]

The codifying of a new color line occupied the senate repeatedly during Galloway's first term. That was true even with respect to the conduct of the General Assembly. On 8 July 1868, as a typical example, Galloway successfully amended a proposal to segregate the senate galleries by race to allow for a middle section where blacks and whites could voluntarily sit together.[79] Such a racial "middle ground" had been unimaginable before the war and would become unthinkable again after the white supremacy campaigns of 1898 and 1900, but for a generation, individuals such as Galloway drew a more fluid boundary between blacks and whites.

Galloway's adversaries pushed diligently to maintain a hard divide between the races, however, as can be seen from a floor debate on 26 February 1869 over racial segregation in public schools. Senator W. Levi Love introduced an amendment requiring that no black teacher be employed in a school that had white students. In response, Senator Orlin S. Hayes, with Galloway's support, moved to amend Love's amendment to say, "or employ white teachers to serve in any school wherein colored children are to be instructed." This second amendment unnerved conservatives who feared the political implications of black control over black schooling. To make the point stronger, Galloway moved next to amend Love's and Hayes's amendments, facetiously adding a provision "that no white Democrat should teach any colored girl." Ruled out of order, Galloway had won the day if not the war. Under Republican leadership, the full senate rejected Love's amendment and later created a state board of education and North Carolina's first statewide system of public schooling. Not even Galloway's white Republican allies, however, supported the call by him and other black legislators for racially integrated public schools or for equal funding of black schools.[80]

Much of Galloway's senate career addressed the most fundamental rights of freedmen and freedwomen. He voted for the Fourteenth Amendment to the U.S. Constitution, extending citizenship to former slaves and affirming their right to due process and equal protection of the law. He voted as well for the Fifteenth Amendment, guaranteeing black men the right to vote and asserting that that right could not be abridged on the basis of race, color, or previous condition of servitude. He introduced a successful bill to help former slaves hold on to land and homes given them while in bondage even if they did not have written title, and he backed several measures to curtail the Ku Klux Klan, including a bill to create a state militia to combat white terrorism. Galloway strongly supported Governor Holden's ill-fated attempts to crack down on the Ku Klux Klan in the state's piedmont, where by mid-1870 hundreds of Klan atrocities had been documented. He also pushed to guarantee that blacks serve on juries, a right granted by the 1868 constitution, but one that Galloway contended county commissioners often ignored.[81]

Galloway steadfastly advocated for labor rights as well. The first piece of legislation that he introduced on the senate floor was a bill for a law, ultimately defeated, that would have limited laborers to a ten-hour workday. He supported the founding of black labor groups, such as the Coopers' Association of Wilmington—cooperage, or barrel making, was an essential part of the naval stores industry—as well as the New Hanover Laborers' and Farmers' Association and the Wilmington Laborers' Protective Association, the latter of which was said to include both black and white workingmen.[82] In the fall of 1869, he joined a national committee that included Frederick Douglass, Henry Highland Garnet, and John Mercer Langston that called for a "Colored Labor Convention" to protest the importation of Chinese immigrant labor as a way of "forcing American laborers to work at Coolie wages or starve."[83]

More than any other elected leader in North Carolina, Galloway also fought for women's rights. The rights of women had become an important political issue in the Reconstruction South, as well as in the North, with former slaves and suffragists briefly finding common cause in an advocacy of universal voting rights. Black southerners supported women's suffrage far more strongly than whites did, perhaps a sign of the relatively higher status that black women had held in slave families and of a more collective sensibility toward voting among the ex-slaves.[84] Black women did not hold voting rights at Republican Party meetings, but they were welcomed into the political process in a way that would have been unimaginable for women of any race prior to the Civil War. The senate galleries overflowed with black women during Galloway's tenure in the General Assembly, and black women also participated in large numbers in Republican ward, city, and district meetings in Galloway's Third District. In fact, at the Republicans' Third District nominating convention in Lumberton in the fall of 1868, estimates of the numbers of black women in attendance ranged from 250 to 400, or roughly half of those in attendance.[85]

Galloway's legislative agenda clearly reflected the importance of African American women in Reconstruction politics. Twice he introduced bills to amend the state's constitution to allow women's suffrage, the first time on 1 February 1869 and again in 1870. Outraged by an 1868 state supreme court ruling that men had a right to beat their wives, he sought unsuccessfully to force the senate judiciary committee to report a bill against domestic violence. He also supported a bill that gave women a greater right to sign deeds, and another to protect married women from willful abandonment or neglect by their husbands.[86] Women's suffrage and many other pioneering women's rights laws advocated by Galloway would not become law in North Carolina for half a century.

⚬∫⚬

With respect to his legislative support for women's suffrage, as for most issues for which he fought, Galloway should not be seen as ahead of his time.

He had emerged out of an African American intellectual culture deeply committed to egalitarian values and a revolutionary struggle for freedom. That culture of slave resistance had arisen over generations in the maritime districts of the American South, and in spirit at least, Galloway was heir to Denmark Vesey, David Walker, and other black radicals raised in southern seaports in the late eighteenth and early nineteenth centuries. Galloway's years as a fugitive slave, renegade abolitionist, and Union spy had enlarged his world and his political vision, while they strengthened his commitment to the African American men and women back home in the American South. His experience of grassroots organizing and political struggle in the freedpeople's camps along the Carolina coast influenced him deeply. Remarkably, after all the bloody struggles of the war and its aftermath, the racial contempt of his enemies, and the attempts to kill him, Galloway also embodied a persistent willingness to make common cause across the color line, to remain "the warm friend of the laboring classes," black or white.[87] But if Galloway embodied the spirit of democracy and black radicalism that emerged onto the world stage in the Reconstruction South, he certainly did not invent it. That tradition grew from a collective experience. He translated and enlarged it, and it would surely outlive him. To his credit, he found within himself the strength of will and the raw courage to carry that collective vision of racial justice and political equality out into a world that was not ready for it.

Epilogue

GALLOWAY DIED UNEXPECTEDLY ON 1 SEPTEMBER 1870 AT HIS MOTHER'S
home in Wilmington. Most reports indicate that he succumbed to "fever
and jaundice," but many years later his wife, Martha Ann, recalled that he
had long suffered from chronic rheumatism and "heart troubles."[1] One of
his obituaries refers to a lingering illness, but he died so quickly that Martha Ann could not return from a visit to New Bern in time to be at his
side. His mother tended to him in his last hours.[2] At the time of his death,
Galloway was only thirty-three years old. He and Martha Ann had had
their second son, Abraham Jr., only six months earlier. He had just been
reelected to the state senate, still held together a fragile biracial coalition
in the local Republican Party, and had recently survived another assassination attempt.[3] Given the hostile political climate and the repeated threats
on his life, many of his supporters must have suspected foul play, but no
historical evidence can confirm such suspicions.

Galloway died on the cusp of a conservative resurgence that prevailed
across the South from 1870 to 1877. That resurgence, which white southerners called "Redemption," occurred in North Carolina barely two years
after African Americans first gained access to the ballot box. Racial violence, official corruption, and the Republican Party's own internal divisions, including those grounded in racial prejudice and a growing cyni-
cism, paved the way for Democratic triumph in 1870. At the national level,
the spirit of abolition that had prevailed after the war, the ardent quest
for "Liberty and Union," was cast aside in the spirit of commerce and by
the revelation that the Grand Old Party did not need black southerners
to hold national dominion. Reminding white voters in the North of their
sacrifices during the Civil War—"waving the bloody shirt," as it was called

at the time—and doing the bidding of the railroad trusts proved sufficient in the new era.[4]

The collapse of North Carolina's Republican Party no doubt disappointed Galloway as much as the national party's abandonment of southern blacks. In the 4 August elections, the Democratic Party won most local and state contests. Shortly thereafter, the Democratic victors converged in Wilmington. Galloway may not have stood among the local blacks who pelted the visiting Democrats with stones, but he could not have welcomed the sight of the celebrating conservatives parading through the city.

To the end, Galloway railed against the coming darkness. Unlike almost all the other black men elected to the North Carolina General Assembly in 1868, he did not go down to defeat in the state elections in 1870. He did not accept the Republican Party's misfortunes gracefully, either. Throughout the summer of 1870, he had unleashed his fury against the rise of the state's new reactionary political leadership. The *Wilmington Daily Journal*, the city's most conservative newspaper, bemoaned how "the disgusting vulgarity, intermingled with profanity, which characterized the harangue of A. H. Galloway in front of the Market House . . . was a disgrace to any civilized community." The newspaper's editors lambasted him, as they always had, referring to "the Indian senator, who vaunts himself upon his popularity and who seems to think he can control the whole Republican party of New Hanover county." The *Journal* had been warring with Galloway for years, and Galloway had certainly given as good as he had got. By the summer of 1870, however, the newspaper's tone grew more ominous, reflecting a change in political winds. "We hope," the editors wrote, "the city authorities will hereafter put a stop to such exhibitions on the public streets, no matter who may attempt it. The peace and good order of the city demand it at their hands." A few days later, Galloway narrowly averted another attempt on his life.[5]

Galloway had to have seen the Democratic resurgence coming, however. He had been putting fingers in the dike that was the Third District's Republican Party for more than a year. Deep rifts had developed between local black factions, grounded most irreconcilably in differing stances toward their alliance with white Republicans. Many black leaders had grown disenchanted with what they considered the reluctance of local white Republicans to support the candidacy of a more significant number of blacks. More than a year earlier, Galloway had felt it necessary to deliver a major speech defending the Republican Party from disaffected black voters. "There is not a black man in the State," he had told a mass meeting at

Wilmington's city hall in May 1869, "who does not owe his freedom to that party, and what do we place ahead of the gift of freedom?" As the national political climate grew harsher for black aspirations, however, his defense of local white Republicans grew more difficult.

At a Wilmington celebration of the passage of the Fifteenth Amendment a few months before his death, Galloway was on hand to hear one of the city's foremost black leaders, John P. Sampson, who had moved home from Ohio after the war, angrily take the stage to criticize white Republican leaders. A few days later, on 8 May 1870, the Third Congressional District's Republican Party convention in Lumberton fell into disarray. The New Hanover County delegation, of which Galloway was the chairman, split its support for an electoral slate, with a faction led by George Price, who had left New Bern and also returned home, turning back his attempt to unify the delegation. The next day, Galloway and two other black colleagues withdrew from the convention. Three weeks later, the party's Wilmington convention proved nearly as contentious and also splintered. In the face of conservative violence, the election on 4 August would have been difficult for local Republicans under any circumstances, but they stood little chance of victory if not united.[6]

Compared with the rest of North Carolina, however, Wilmington remained a stronghold of African American political power, economic self-sufficiency, and working-class militancy long after Galloway's passing. Historian W. McKee Evans has argued, in fact, that the unique ability of Wilmington Republicans to maintain significant numbers of black policemen and militia units preserved the relative peace of Cape Fear society from 1868 to 1877. At one point in 1875, the *Wilmington Journal* even alleged that "there are now nearly, or quite as many negro [militia] companies in this city, as there are white companies throughout the limits of North Carolina."[7] Wilmington blacks continued to embrace Galloway's spirit of political militancy long after his death.

Galloway's obituaries were surprisingly respectful and sometimes reverential. Close to home, even the *Wilmington Journal*'s editors, his long-standing foes, held their tongues. They gave Galloway credit for having been "very popular with the colored people" and "a bold defender of the principles of the [Republican] Party."[8] Across the state, newspapers of all political stripes marked his passing, as did newspapers in Washington, D.C., Philadelphia, and New York City. The *Christian Recorder*, the AME Church's national journal, called him "bold, brave, defiant, and patriotic" and a "guiding star." "He was full of charity—kind, benevolent, liberal, with a disposition to help the poor," said Washington's *New National Era*, adding, "He commanded attention and respect from political friends and foes." The author of the newspaper's obituary frowned, though, on Galloway's poverty, as if he did not know what to make of an American political leader who did not have the station in life to attain at least a significant measure of wealth. "He was poor, very poor," the newspaper lamented.[9]

The most insightful obituary appeared in Raleigh, his home state's capital. Appearing without attribution, the obituary was penned by someone who had known Galloway well and who had seriously pondered his complexity. "A telegram from Wilmington announces the death of this great man," the correspondent for the *Raleigh Weekly Standard* began. The writer extolled Galloway's intelligence and lambasted the institution of slavery for preventing such a mind from being fully cultivated when he was a child. "Had he enjoyed the advantage of an early education, he would have exhibited one of the brightest intellects that North Carolina ever produced," the obituary concluded. Lauding Galloway's accomplishments during the war and his political career during Reconstruction, the newspaper's correspondent made special issue of Galloway's ability to hold together the various factions of the Republican Party across racial and class lines and to win reelection to the state senate a month earlier. The author remarked upon Galloway's moral courage but also noted fondly his impetuousness and passion. The obituary closed simply, saying, "He leaves an affectionate wife and two children, with a confiding constituency, to mourn his loss."[10]

At the time of his death, the forces of counterrevolution were indeed afoot. The Democratic Party's political triumph marked the beginning of a new age of white rule across the old Confederacy. In Wilmington, the struggle ahead would be among the most difficult. A generation later, in the fall of 1898, Galloway's hometown was the site of one of the century's worst racial atrocities, a massacre and political revolt that has been called the only coup d'état in U.S. history. Those events overthrew the local government in Wilmington and destroyed a unique coalition of blacks and whites that had been elected to govern across North Carolina in 1894. In its wake, white supremacy ruled the land. "The Party of White Supremacy," as the Democrats proudly called their party at the time, reigned for more than two generations.[11] For all that Galloway and his comrades had accomplished, their children, grandchildren, and great-grandchildren would battle for many of the things they once had imagined were close at hand.

Galloway himself never expressed publicly a concern for his legacy or how posterity might remember him. Throughout his life, he seemed to live each day as if history was being made now, that the moment upon which history would judge him was that very moment. At some level, Galloway acted as if he could not live in the world into which he was born without fighting with his every breath, as if the fight itself fired his blood and kept him alive, no matter the odds against him. How he would have fared, or how long he would have survived, in the coming era of white supremacy is hard to imagine.

Near the end of his life, Galloway did contemplate, if not his legacy exactly, then at least the time after his own passing. In the spring of 1869, a year before his death, he told a mass meeting in Wilmington, "I am looking for the rising generation. I care not for the living present, but there must be a deep foundation laid for the coming generation."[12] Perhaps the births of his sons compelled him to lift his eyes toward the future. History, though, would not be kind to his memory. As the forces of white supremacy triumphed across the South, they banished Galloway from the region's history. In the coming years, no books recalled him; no monuments marked his life. The memory of a black insurgent like him became a dangerous apostasy in the mythic story of slavery and the Lost Cause around which the white South built its new social order and sense of identity. The history of the Civil War's generals and their battles was told and retold, in literally thousands of books, but the memory of Galloway and the slaves' Civil War grew cold. No school child uttered Abraham Galloway's name, it is safe to say, for more than 125 years. Even his final resting place alongside other African Americans at the Pine Forest Cemetery in Wilmington would eventually, mysteriously, disappear.[13]

Though Galloway died a pauper, an estimated 6,000 mourners gathered at his funeral.[14] Legions of ex-slaves from miles around walked into town to stand at his coffin. They came from every Wilmington neighborhood as well. Others arrived on the old river packet from Smithville, and others came by train. The funeral procession stretched half a mile through a downtown Wilmington draped with American flags at half-mast. Even the city courts closed for the morning.[15] The Masons in their finery, the black firefighters' brigades, the political and fraternal societies, 100 carriages, and throngs of people on horseback and on foot marched the eight blocks from his home on North Fourth Street to St. Paul's Episcopal Church.

His closest friends and a dozen Masonic brothers escorted the horse-drawn hearse to the church. The lead carriages conveyed his family, a delegation of members from the North Carolina General Assembly, and local ministers. Behind them came African American army veterans, the black firefighters' brigades, policemen, the rest of the Masons, a Christian association, a temperance league, and a host of city, county, and Federal officials. All of black Wilmington turned out, but hundreds of white citizens also attended the ceremony. The Reverend George Patterson, the rector at St. John's Episcopal Church and evidently a close friend to the Galloway family, officiated at the funeral, though he had served as a chaplain in the Confederate army during the war. The multitude could not fit into St. Paul's and crowded the streets nearby. One newspaper called it the largest funeral in the state's history.[16]

As the mass of men, women, and children left the church and accompanied his coffin to the cemetery, they held a deep conviction that the larger significance of Galloway's life would not be lowered into a grave but would walk away from it in their minds and hearts. Their young native son had played a leading role in an extraordinary generation of African American activists within the South. Together they had fought to end slavery, bring down the Confederacy, and imagine a United States that lived up to its most democratic ideals.

Above all, on that late summer day in 1870, those who gathered to mourn Abraham Galloway cherished him for the "unquenchable fire of freedom" that burned so brightly within him. They realized that a meteoric life such as Galloway's, though its light illuminates larger truths, also has a singular arc of fire. His is the oft-told story of the rebel hero who lives a life so deeply unreconciled to tyranny that even the most downtrodden and despised are moved to believe, at least for that brilliant moment of its flashing across the night sky, that freedom and justice may not be just a dream.

Notes

NHCPL	North Carolina Room, New Hanover County Public Library, Wilmington
NYPL	New York Public Library, New York
RG	Record Group
SHC	Southern Historical Collection, University of North Carolina at Chapel Hill
UMA	W. E. B. Du Bois Library, University of Massachusetts, Amherst
UNCW	Special Collections, William Madison Randall Library, University of North Carolina at Wilmington
USMA	Special Collections, United States Military Academy Cadet Library, West Point, N.Y.
USMHI	United States Army Military History Institute, Carlisle Barracks, Pa.
VA	Veterans Administration Hospital, Winston-Salem, N.C.

Prologue

1. The broad picture that I have drawn of occupied New Bern and the specific incidents that I have mentioned are derived from a variety of primary and secondary sources. See John G. Barrett, *The Civil War in North Carolina* (Chapel Hill: University of North Carolina Press, 1963), 93–113; Joe A. Mobley, *James City: A Black Community in North Carolina, 1863–1900* (Raleigh: North Carolina Department of Cultural Resources, Division of Archives and History, 1981), 1–25; John S. Carbone, *The Civil War in Coastal North Carolina* (Raleigh: North Carolina Department of Cultural Resources, Division of Archives and History, 2001); and Judkin Browning, *Shifting Loyalties: The Union Occupation of Eastern North Carolina* (Chapel Hill: University of North Carolina Press, 2011). Among the most interesting of the many published reminiscences and diaries written by Union soldiers in New Bern, see W. P. Derby, *Bearing Arms in the Twenty-Seventh Massachusetts Regiment of Volunteer Infantry during the Civil War, 1861–1865* (Boston: Wright & Potter, 1883), esp. 94–95; James A. Emmerton, *A Record of the Twenty-Third Regiment, Mass. Vol. Infantry, in the War of the Rebellion, 1861–1865* (Boston: William Ware & Co., 1886); "Corporal" [Z. T. Haines], *Letters from the Forty-fourth Regiment M.V.M.: A Record of the Experience of a Nine Months' Regiment in the Department of North Carolina in 1862–3* (Boston: Herald Job Office, 1863); Vincent Colyer, *Brief Report of the Services Rendered by the Freed People to the United States Army, in North Carolina, in the Spring of 1862, after the Battle of Newbern* (New York: Vincent Colyer, 1864); J. Waldo Denny, *Wearing the Blue in the 25th Mass. Volunteer Infantry* (Worcester, Mass.: Putnam & Davis, 1879); Thomas Kirwan, *Soldiering in North Carolina* (Boston: T. Kirwan, 1864); John J. Wyeth, *Leaves from a Diary, Written While Serving in Co. #44 Mass. From September, 1862, to June, 1863* (Boston: L. F. Lawrence & Co., 1878); Madison Drake, *The History of the Ninth New Jersey Volunteers* (Elizabeth, N.J.: Journal Printing House, 1889); Herbert E.

Valentine, *Story of Co. F, 23d Massachusetts Volunteers in the War for the Union, 1861–1865* (Boston: W. B. Clarke & Co., 1896); D. L. Day, *My Diary of Rambles with the 25 Mass. Volunteer Infantry, with Burnside's Coast Division: 18th Army Corp and Army of the James* (Milford, Mass.: King & Billings, 1884); and Albert W. Mann, *History of the Forty-Fifth Regiment Massachusetts Volunteer Militia* (Jamaica Plain, Mass.: Brookside Print, 1908).

2. Mann, *History of the Forty-Fifth Regiment*, 300–302, and Reminiscences, chap. 2, pp. 5–9, Edward W. Kinsley Papers, UMA. Kinsley later related the story of his first encounter with Galloway to the thirtieth reunion of the 45th Regiment, Massachusetts Volunteer Infantry, which had been stationed in New Bern. That account was described in Mann's regimental history. In addition, Kinsley gave a fuller description of his time in New Bern in an unpublished memoir that he penned for his family and friends late in his life. The two accounts differ in some respects, but the essential parts of Kinsley's story—including his role in the recruitment of African American soldiers in New Bern, his acquaintance with Galloway and Mary Ann Starkey, and his ongoing efforts to support Galloway and Starkey's political activism later in the war—are confirmed in wartime records, but especially in a long series of wartime letters among Starkey, Kinsley, Union officers stationed in New Bern (and sometimes their wives), and other New England abolitionists, in collections of Kinsley's papers at Duke University, the Library of Congress, Howard University, and the University of Massachusetts, Amherst.

3. Lt. George F. Woodman to Lt. Col. Hoffman, 19 Feb. 1863, W-31 1863, Letters Received, ser. 3238, Dept. of NC and Virginia, 18th A.C., RG 393, pt. 1, NA, published in *Freedom: A Documentary History of Emancipation, 1861–1867*, ed. Ira Berlin, Barbara Fields, Thavolia Glymph, Joseph P. Reidy, and Leslie S. Rowland, ser. 1, vol. 2, *The Black Military Experience* (Cambridge: Cambridge University Press, 1982), 129; Foster to Stanton, 5 May 1863, Executive Papers, Gov. John A. Andrew, Incoming Correspondence, MA; Andrew to Foster, 14 May 1863, Registrar of Letters Received, Department of North Carolina and Virginia (1863), RG 393, NA; William H. Singleton, *Recollections of My Slavery Days*, ed. Katherine Mellen Charron and David S. Cecelski (Raleigh: North Carolina Department of Cultural Resources, Division of Archives and History, 1999), 48–49, 95–97; Mann, *History of the Forty-Fifth Regiment*, 446–49.

4. Reminiscences, chap. 2, pp. 2, 5, Kinsley Papers, UMA.

5. Mann, *History of the Forty-Fifth Regiment*, 300–302.

6. Ibid., 301.

7. Reminiscences, chap. 2, pp. 5–7, Kinsley Papers, UMA.

8. Ibid., pp. 6–9.

9. Ibid., p. 7.

10. Mann, *History of the Forty-Fifth Regiment*, 301–2, 446–49.

11. For a thorough overview of the recruitment of the African Brigade in New Bern, and for references to more general works on the recruitment of black sol-

diers into the Union army, see Richard M. Reid, *Freedom for Themselves: North Carolina's Black Soldiers in the Civil War Era* (Chapel Hill: University of North Carolina Press, 2008). An early, shorter version of Reid's scholarship on the African Brigade can be found in "Raising the African Brigade: Early Black Recruitment in Civil War North Carolina," *NCHR* 70, no. 3 (July 1993): 266–97. For a thought-provoking overview of black military service in the Civil War, see the essays collected in John David Smith, ed., *Black Soldiers in Blue: African American Troops in the Civil War Era* (Chapel Hill: University of North Carolina Press, 2002).

12. Quoted in Stephanie McCurry, *Confederate Reckoning: Power and Politics in the Civil War South* (Cambridge, Mass.: Harvard University Press, 2010), 11–12.

13. Ibid., 14–18. Jefferson Davis quote on 14.

14. *Raleigh Confederate*, 23 Nov. 1864, quoted in ibid., 311.

15. W. E. B. Du Bois, *Black Reconstruction: An Essay Toward a History of the Part which Black Folk Played in the Attempt to Reconstruct Democracy in America, 1860–1880* (New York: Harcourt, Brace, 1935).

16. Among this latest generation of scholarly works that highlight African American militancy and political activism in the South during the Civil War, see especially Steven Hahn, *A Nation under Our Feet: Black Political Struggles in the Rural South from Slavery to the Great Migration* (Cambridge, Mass.: Harvard University Press, 2003); Steven Hahn, *The Political Worlds of Slavery and Freedom* (Cambridge, Mass.: Harvard University Press, 2009); McCurry, *Confederate Reckoning*; and on a more local scale, David S. Cecelski, *The Waterman's Song: Slavery and Freedom in Maritime North Carolina* (Chapel Hill: University of North Carolina Press, 2001). All of these works build on the extraordinary, multivolume collection of documents and essays in *Freedom: A Documentary History of Emancipation, 1861–1867*, produced by Ira Berlin and his colleagues at the Freedmen and Southern Society Project at the University of Maryland. While not focusing on the South, other recent scholarship on the African American freedom struggle during the war and the way it has subsequently been marginalized in historical works has been fundamental to my placing Galloway in a broader context of black activism and to understanding his historical legacy. See, in particular, Stephen Kantrowitz, *More Than Freedom: Fighting for Black Citizenship in a White Republic, 1829–1889* (New York: Penguin, 2012); David W. Blight, *Race, Memory, and the American Civil War* (Amherst: University of Massachusetts Press, 2002), 28–90; David W. Blight, *Race and Reunion: The Civil War in American Memory* (Cambridge, Mass.: Belknap Press of Harvard University Press, 2001); and Manisha Sinha, "Black Abolitionism: The Assault on Southern Slavery and the Struggle for Racial Equality," in *Slavery in New York*, ed. Ira Berlin and Leslie M. Harris (New York: New Press, 2005), 239–62. See also the essays in Timothy Patrick McCarthy and John Stauffer, eds., *Prophets of Protest: Reconsidering the History of American Abolitionism* (New York: New Press, 2006).

17. I first laid out the broad outlines of Galloway's life in David S. Cecelski, "Abraham H. Galloway: Wilmington's Lost Prophet and the Rise of Black Radi-

calism in the American South," in *Democracy Betrayed: The Wilmington Race Riot of 1898 and Its Legacy*, ed. David S. Cecelski and Timothy B. Tyson (Chapel Hill: University of North Carolina Press, 1998), 43–72. A nearly identical version of that essay later appeared as a chapter in my study of the African American maritime culture in which Galloway was born and raised; see Cecelski, *Waterman's Song*. Prior to those works, the few books and articles that discussed Galloway refer mainly to his political life during Reconstruction, and that only briefly. See William McKee Evans, *Ballots and Fence Rails: Reconstruction on the Lower Cape Fear* (Chapel Hill: University of North Carolina Press, 1967), 87–91; Leonard Bernstein, "The Participation of Negro Delegates in the Constitutional Convention of 1868 in North Carolina," *Journal of Negro History* 34, no. 4 (Oct. 1949): 390–409; Elizabeth Balanoff, "Negro Legislators in the North Carolina General Assembly, July, 1868–February, 1872," *NCHR* 49, no. 1 (Jan. 1972): 23–24, 27; William S. Powell, ed., *Dictionary of North Carolina Biography* (Chapel Hill: University of North Carolina Press, 1979–96), 2:271–72; and Eric Foner, *Freedom's Lawmakers: A Directory of Black Officeholders during Reconstruction* (Baton Rouge: Louisiana State University Press, 1996), 81–82. For an earlier era, see J. G. de Roulhac Hamilton, *Reconstruction in North Carolina* (New York: Columbia University Press, 1914), esp. 150, 254, 263, 363, 366, 418.

18. Du Bois, *Black Reconstruction*, 528–29; Evans, *Ballots and Fence Rails*, 87–91.

19. John Hope Franklin, *Reconstruction: After the Civil War* (Chicago: University of Chicago Press, 1961), 89; Leon F. Litwack, *Been in the Storm So Long: The Aftermath of Slavery* (New York: Vintage, 1980), 266, 503, 507; Eric Foner, *Reconstruction: America's Unfinished Revolution, 1863–1877* (New York: Harper & Row, 1988), 305, 376; Hahn, *Nation under Our Feet*, 202–3.

Chapter 1

1. Burial Records, 1870, Vestry Minutes, 1858–1917, St. Paul's Episcopal Church, Wilmington, N.C.; *New National Era*, 4 Sept. 1870; William Still, *The Underground Railroad: A Record of Facts, Authentic Narratives, Letters, etc., Narrating the Hardships, Hair-Breadth Escapes, and Death Struggles of the Slaves in their Efforts for Freedom* (Philadelphia: Porter & Coates, 1872), 150–52.

2. Fifth and Sixth Federal Censuses of the United States (1830, 1840): Brunswick County, N.C., Population and Slave Schedules, NA.

3. 5 Oct. 1830 entry, personal diary, 1830–36, Moses Ashley Curtis Correspondence and Diary, SHC.

4. In a little-known memoir published in 1896, a Union navy veteran named Allen Parker, who grew up in slavery in Chowan County, North Carolina, remembered night as "the slave's holiday" (Allen Parker, *Recollections of Slavery Times* [Worcester, Mass.: Chas. W. Burbank & Sons, 1895], 63). For a broader discussion on the ways that maritime slaves took advantage of nights to gain a measure of independence and to feed themselves and their families, see David S. Cecelski,

The Waterman's Song: Slavery and Freedom in Maritime North Carolina (Chapel Hill: University of North Carolina Press, 2001), 70–71.

5. Douglass, a ship's caulker by trade, escaped from slavery in Baltimore, Maryland, disguised as a sailor and carrying forged seaman's protection papers. Though he fled by train, Douglass had dreamed as a young man that he would one day escape by ship. See Frederick Douglass, *Narrative of the Life of Frederick Douglass, an American Slave*, ed. Deborah E. McDowell (New York: Oxford University Press, 1999), 62–63, and Eighth Federal Census of the United States (1860): Brunswick County, N.C., Population and Slave Schedules, NA.

6. Still, *Underground Railroad*, 150–52; Petition of Lewis A. Galloway for Division of Negroes (Mar. 1837), Lewis A. Galloway Estate Record, Brunswick County Estate Records, NCSA; Lewis Galloway Will (1826), Brunswick County Wills, 1765–1912, NCSA.

7. Martha A. Little deposition, 22 Sept. 1927, Celie Galloway Pension Application File (1927), U.S. Department of the Interior: Bureau of Pensions, VA; 15 Oct. 1866 entry, New Hanover County: Record of Cohabitation, 1866–1868, NCSA; Ninth Federal Census of the United States (1870): New Hanover County, N.C., Population Schedule, NA; *Wilmington Daily Journal*, 20 July 1869 (Galloway speaking on the darkness of his mother's skin). In 1927 Celie Galloway, the widow of another Abraham (or Abram) Galloway, also of Brunswick County, North Carolina, applied for veteran's benefits based on her husband's military service in the Union army. The Federal pension office ruled against her application because the pension board suspected that she was attempting to gain benefits for Abraham H. Galloway, the subject of this book. Confronted with a rejection of her pension application, Celie Galloway hired an attorney to establish that her husband was not Abraham H. Galloway, but an African American soldier also from Brunswick County. On her behalf, an attorney visited Beaufort, North Carolina, to take depositions from surviving family of Abraham H. Galloway that might indicate details about his personal appearance, military career, and death that would distinguish the two men and justify the widow's claims for pension benefits. The attorney interviewed Abraham H. Galloway's widow, Martha Ann Little, who still lived in her native Beaufort; she had remarried in 1887.

8. Nine years later, in April 1846, Hester Hankins took a husband, Amos Galloway, a slave owned by John Wesley Galloway. See Seventh Federal Census of the United States (1850): Brunswick County and New Hanover County, N.C., Population and Slave Schedules, NA. Amos Galloway belonged to Lewis Galloway at the time of Lewis's death in 1826 and was apportioned to his son John Wesley legally by 1837 and in practice probably sometime before that date. Amos and Hester Hankins considered themselves married as of April 1846, though it is doubtful that they shared a household at that time. They were living together in Wilmington as of the 1870 federal census. See Petition of Lewis A. Galloway for Division of Negroes (Mar. 1837), Lewis A. Galloway Estate Record, Brunswick County Estate Records, NCSA; 15 Oct. 1866 entry, New Hanover County: Rec-

ord of Cohabitation, 1866–1868, NCSA; and Ninth Federal Census of the United States (1870): New Hanover County, N.C., Population Schedule, NA.

9. Seventh, Eighth, and Ninth Federal Censuses of the United States (1850, 1860, 1870): Brunswick County, N.C., Population and Slave Schedules, NA.

10. John Wesley Galloway's closest neighbors were households headed by four ship's pilots, a boat captain, and a nautical surveyor. Like all seaports, Smithville was not an insular community; John Wesley's other neighbors included an Irish merchant, Catharine Corlette, a single mother of children born in Mexico and Florida (probably a widow). Similarly, another neighbor, Catharine Richards, was a school and music teacher born in Massachusetts. See Eighth Federal Census of the United States (1860): Brunswick County, N.C., Population and Slave Schedules, NA.

11. *Semi-Weekly Messenger* (Wilmington, N.C.), 26 Aug. 1898, copy in the Galloway Family File, Bill Reaves Collection, NHCPL.

12. David Cecelski, interview with Robert Wilkinson, Brunswick County, N.C., Fall 2005.

13. Sixth, Seventh, and Eighth Federal Censuses of the United States (1840, 1850, 1860): Brunswick County, N.C., Population and Slave Schedules, NA; Seventh and Eighth Federal Censuses of the United States (1850, 1860): New Hanover County, N.C., Population and Slave Schedules, NA; John W. Galloway (1864), Brunswick County Estate Records, NCSA. See also *Wilmington Daily Journal*, 15 Oct. 1864, cited in Helen Moore Sammons, *Marriage and Death Notices from Wilmington, North Carolina, Newspapers, 1860–1865* (Wilmington, N.C.: North Carolina Room, New Hanover County Public Library, 1987), 76.

14. Quote is from Still, *Underground Railroad*, 150–52.

15. Martha A. Little deposition, Celie Galloway Pension File, VA.

16. Three accounts written by former slaves shed unique light on African American life in the Lower Cape Fear: Thomas H. Jones, *The Experience of Thomas H. Jones, Who Was a Slave for Forty-Three Years* (Boston: Bazin & Chandler, 1862); James Johnson, *The Life of the Late James Johnson (Colored Evangelist), an Escaped Slave from the Southern States of America* (Oldham, England: W. Galley, n.d.); and William H. Robinson, *From Log Cabin to the Pulpit; or, Fifteen Years in Slavery*, 3rd ed. (Eau Claire, Wisc.: James H. Tifft, 1913). The only known original copy of Johnson's narrative is at the Oldham Metropolitan Borough Council Archives, Oldham, England, but the North Carolina State Archives in Raleigh has recently obtained a photocopy. For background on Johnson and his narrative, see David S. Cecelski and Alex Christopher Meekins, "*The Life of the Late James Johnson*: An American Slave Narrative from Oldham, England," *Carolina Comments* 56, no. 3 (July 2008), 108–13. For a discussion of several other slave narratives from eastern North Carolina, see Cecelski, *Waterman's Song*, 25–81. See also Jean Yellin, *Harriet Jacobs: A Life* (New York: Basic Civitas Books, 2004).

17. Robinson, *From Log Cabin to the Pulpit*, esp. 16–44.

18. Ibid., 42–44.

19. *Standard Laconic* (Snow Hill, N.C.), 10 Dec. 1909. Walter Gilman Curtis was a native of Massachusetts, trained at Harvard Medical School, and moved south to Smithville (later renamed Southport) in 1848 to serve as a tutor and eventually to establish a medical practice. He was a physician in Smithville and Wilmington, where he also served as state quarantine officer for the port from 1868 to 1895. His brother, Moses Ashley Curtis (1808–72), was an important botanist who did pioneering research in Appalachia and the Carolina coastal plain. He had originally come south in 1830 to serve as a tutor for the children of Edward Dudley in Wilmington. See Walter Gilman Curtis Papers, SHC, and Curtis Correspondence and Diary, SHC. See also James Sprunt, *Chronicles of the Cape Fear River, 1660–1916* (Raleigh: Edwards & Broughton, 1916), 680–82; Walter Gilman Curtis, *Reminiscences of Wilmington and Southport, 1848–1900* (Wilmington, N.C., 1905; republished by Southport Historical Society, 1999); Edmund Berkeley and Dorothy Smith Berkeley, *A Yankee Botanist in the Carolinas: The Reverend Moses Ashley Curtis* (Berlin: J. Kramer, 1986); and William S. Powell, *Moses Ashley Curtis (1808–1872): Teacher, Priest, Scientist* (Chapel Hill: University of North Carolina Library, 1958).

20. William Still incorrectly indicates that a Milton Hawkins owned Galloway, but the mistake was presumably a typographical error. See Martha A. Little deposition, Celie Galloway Pension File, VA; Still, *Underground Railroad*, 150–52; and Eighth and Ninth Federal Censuses of the United States (1860, 1870): New Hanover County, N.C., Population Schedules, NA.

21. Eighth, Ninth, and Tenth Federal Censuses of the United States (1860, 1870, 1880): New Hanover County, N.C., Population Schedules, NA; *Register of Deaths and Births, Bellevue Cemetery, Wilmington, N.C.* (Wilmington: University of North Carolina at Wilmington Printing Services, 1999; distributed by William Madison Randall Library).

22. Bill Reaves, *Southport (Smithville): A Chronology* (Southport, N.C.: Southport Historical Society, 1978), 78; Louis Philip Hall, *Land of the Golden River: Historical Events and Stories of Southeastern North Carolina and the Lower Cape Fear*, vol. 2, *This Fair Land of Ours* (Wilmington, N.C.: Hall, 1975), 32–33.

23. Seventh Federal Census (1850): Brunswick County, N.C., Population and Slave Schedules, NA; *Wilmington Daily Journal*, 21 May 1857; Brunswick County Will Book B, NCSA, 10.

24. Catherine W. Bishir, "Black Builders in Antebellum North Carolina," *NCHR* 61, no. 4 (Oct. 1984): esp. 431–33.

25. Born a slave ca. 1801 in Sampson County, N.C., James D. Sampson was given his freedom by his owner, who was also his father, in 1819. After settling in Wilmington, he became an accomplished carpenter and minister. He apparently taught his slave apprentices to read and write, and he established a school on his property where a Massachusetts tutor and later his daughters taught both free blacks and slaves. See Bill Reaves, *"Strength through Struggle": The Chronological and Historical Record of the African-American Community in Wilmington, North*

Carolina, 1865–1950 (Wilmington, N.C.: New Hanover County Public Library, 1998), 460–61.

26. *Wilmington Dispatch*, 2 Nov. 1897, and *Wilmington Star*, 3 Nov. 1897, in Reaves Collection, NHCPL. The year in which Milton and Mary Ann Hankins relocated to Wilmington is unclear. Church records indicate that they were married in Wilmington at Front Street Methodist Church on 24 December 1851 but do not confirm their residence in the city. Wills and deeds indicate that they bought their lot on North Fourth Street (their longtime residence) in 1855, but of course they may have been renting or living at one of Miles Potter's townhouses or with other relatives or friends prior to that time. See Record of Births, Baptisms and Burials, Front Street Methodist Church, Wilmington, N.C., and Marsden Milton Hankins will (1897), New Hanover County Wills, NCSA. Chartered in 1846, the Wilmington & Manchester Railroad ran from Wilmington to Camden Crossing, S.C., beginning in 1853.

27. *Insurance Maps of Wilmington, New Hanover County, North Carolina* (New York: Sanborn Map Co., 1904); Eighth Federal Census of the United States (1860): New Hanover County, N.C., Population Schedule, NA.

28. Still, *Underground Railroad*, 150–52; Fugitive Slave Ledger, William Still Papers, HSP; *Wilmington Daily Journal*, 20 July 1869 ("rocked in a Republican cradle" quote); *Wilmington Messenger*, 1 Feb. 1895 (obituary), in Reaves Collection, NHCPL; Eighth Federal Census of the United States (1860): New Hanover County, N.C.: Population and Slave Schedules, NA.

29. Still *Underground Railroad*, 150–52. For background on slave life in antebellum Wilmington, see esp. Peter P. Hinks, *To Awaken My Afflicted Brethren: David Walker and the Problem of Antebellum Slave Resistance* (University Park: Pennsylvania State University Press, 1997), 1–21; Alan D. Watson, *Wilmington: Port of North Carolina* (Columbia: University of South Carolina Press, 1992), 46–52; and James Howard Brewer, "Legislation Designed to Control Slavery in Wilmington and Fayetteville," *NCHR* 30, no. 2 (Apr. 1953): 155–66.

30. Robinson, *From Log Cabin to the Pulpit*, 30–32. On slaves in Wilmington and other parts of coastal North Carolina carving out a political sphere via family, church, community, illicit trading, and wage earning, see Cecelski, *Waterman's Song*, 126–33. For a broader and pathbreaking conceptual look at daily acts of slave resistance and their importance to fostering a political sphere within the slave South, see Steven Hahn, *A Nation under Our Feet: Black Political Struggles in the Rural South from Slavery to the Great Migration* (Cambridge, Mass.: Harvard University Press, 2003), 13–61.

31. Hinks, *To Awaken My Afflicted Brethren*.

32. Guion Griffis Johnson, *Ante-Bellum North Carolina: A Social History* (Chapel Hill: University of North Carolina Press, 1937), 577–78.

33. Hinks, *To Awaken My Afflicted Brethren*, 137–38; David Walker, *David Walker's Appeal to the Coloured Citizens of the World*, ed. Peter P. Hinks (University Park: Pennsylvania State University Press, 2000).

34. Hinks, *To Awaken My Afflicted Brethren*, 1–21, 173–236. On the emergence of this radical ideology out of the Black Atlantic, see also Cecelski, *Waterman's Song*. See also Julius S. Scott, "The Common Wind: Currents of Afro-American Communication in the Era of the Haitian Revolution" (Ph.D. diss., Duke University, 1986); W. Jeffrey Bolster, *Black Jacks: African American Seamen in the Age of Sail* (Cambridge, Mass.: Harvard University Press, 1997), esp. 190–214; Elizabeth Raul Bethel, *The Roots of African-American Identity: Memory and History in the Antebellum Free Communities* (New York: St. Martin's Press, 1997), 53–79; and Sterling Stuckey, *Slave Culture: Nationalist Theory and the Foundations of Black America* (New York: Oxford University Press, 1987), 98–137.

35. Cecelski, *Waterman's Song*, 143–48; Johnson, *Ante-Bellum North Carolina*, 577–78 (*Wilmington Aurora* quote).

36. Charles Edward Morris, "Panic and Reprisal: Reaction in North Carolina to the Nat Turner Insurrection, 1831," *NCHR* 62, no. 1 (Jan. 1985): 35–48.

37. Ibid.; 9–13 and 21 Sept. 1831 entries, personal diary, 1830–36, Curtis Correspondence and Diary, SHC.

Chapter 2

1. William Still, *The Underground Railroad: A Record of Facts, Authentic Narratives, Letters, etc., Narrating the Hardships, Hair-Breadth Escapes, and Death Struggles of the Slaves in their Efforts for Freedom* (Philadelphia: Porter & Coates, 1872), 151–52.

2. Ibid.

3. *National Era*, 3 Sept. 1857 (reprinted from the *Milwaukee Free Democrat*, 21 Aug. 1857).

4. See esp. Walter Johnson, *Soul by Soul: Life inside the Antebellum Slave Market* (Cambridge, Mass.: Harvard University Press, 1999).

5. The Post Road, also referred to as the King's Highway, the "Old Trading Path," and various other local names, was a cart road that was the main north-south corridor out of Wilmington and passed up and down the eastern seaboard.

6. Thomas Fanning Woods, "Some Recollections of My Life" (1886), UNCW.

7. Ibid. On the efforts of slaves to learn to read and write generally, see Heather Williams, *Self-Taught: African American Education in Slavery and Freedom* (Chapel Hill: University of North Carolina Press, 2005).

8. Woods, "Some Recollections of My Life," UNCW.

9. Don Fehrenbacher, *The Dred Scott Case: Its Significance in American Law and Politics* (New York: Oxford University Press, 1978); Earl M. Maltz, *Dred Scott and the Politics of Slavery* (Lawrence: University Press of Kansas, 2007). Black reaction to the case can be followed closely in William Lloyd Garrison's newspaper, the *Liberator*. See, among many others, the issues of 3 and 10 April 1857.

10. Woods, "Some Recollections of My Life," UNCW.

11. A net export of slaves from North Carolina had existed since 1800. The

number of enslaved blacks sold out of North Carolina peaked at approximately 50,000 in the 1830s, and a total in the neighborhood of 100,000 was sent out of the state between 1830 and 1860. Many, probably the large majority, went to the Deep South. See Michael Tadman, "The Interregional Slave Trade in the History and Myth-Making of the U.S. South," in *The Chattel Principle: Internal Slave Trades in the Americas*, ed. Walter Johnson (New Haven: Yale University Press, 2005), 117–42; for North Carolina slave export figures, see 118–20.

12. David S. Cecelski, *The Waterman's Song: Slavery and Freedom in Maritime North Carolina* (Chapel Hill: University of North Carolina Press, 2001), 121–51.

13. William H. Robinson, *From Log Cabin to the Pulpit; or, Fifteen Years in Slavery*, 3rd ed. (Eau Claire, Wisc.: James H. Tifft, 1913), 12–27.

14. Still, *Underground Railroad*, 151.

15. "List of Vessels Searched and Fumigated, 1858–1862" and "Account Records with Wm. J. Love," Board of Commissioners of Navigation and Pilotage for the Cape Fear River and Bar Papers, DU; Still, *Underground Railroad*, 151–52.

16. Still, *Underground Railroad*, 151–52.

17. Ibid., 152.

18. Paul Finkelman, ed., *Encyclopedia of African-American History, 1619–1895: From the Colonial Period to the Age of Frederick Douglass* (New York: Oxford University Press, 2006), 3:206–8.

19. Ibid. See also James Oliver Horton, "A Crusade for Freedom: William Still and the Real Underground Railroad," in *Passages to Freedom: The Underground Railroad in History and Memory*, ed. David W. Blight (Washington, D.C.: Smithsonian Books, 2004), 174–93.

20. Finkelman, *Encyclopedia of African-American History*, 3:206–8.

21. George Hendrick and Willene Hendrick, eds., *Fleeing for Freedom: Stories of the Underground Railroad as Told by Levi Coffin and William Still* (Chicago: Ivan R. Dee, 2004), 15–23; Julie Winch, *A Gentleman of Color: The Life of James Forten* (New York: Oxford University Press, 2002), esp. 142, 351–57.

22. Gary B. Nash and Jean R. Soderlund, *Freedom by Degrees: Emancipation in Pennsylvania and Its Aftermath* (New York: Oxford University Press, 1991), 75.

23. Joseph A. Borome, "Vigilant Committee of Philadelphia," *Pennsylvania Magazine of History and Biography* 92, no. 3 (July 1968): 320–51.

24. Still, *Underground Railroad*, 152.

25. Milton C. Sernett, *North Star Country: Upstate New York and the Crusade for African American Freedom* (Syracuse, N.Y.: Syracuse University Press, 2002), esp. 166–68, 174–79. See also Jermain Wesley Loguen, *The Reverend J. W. Loguen, as a Slave and as a Freeman: A Narrative of Real Life* (Syracuse, N.Y.: J. G. K. Truair and Co., 1859).

26. Charles B. Sedgwick to Dora Sedgwick, 11 Apr. 1851, Charles Baldwin Sedgwick Papers, Special Collections Research Center, Syracuse University, Syracuse, N.Y.

27. Quoted in Merrill D. Peterson, *The Great Triumvirate: Webster, Clay, and Calhoun* (New York: Oxford University Press, 1987), 482.

28. William Henry Pearson, *Recollections and Records of Toronto of Old, with References to Brantford, Kingston and other Canadian Towns* (Toronto: William Briggs, 1914), 133–41.

29. Robin W. Winks, *The Blacks in Canada—A History* (New Haven: Yale University Press, 1971), 30.

30. An African American man named Josiah Henson was the Dawn Settlement's best-known leader. An American runaway and abolitionist leader, he is often thought to have been Harriet Beecher Stowe's inspiration for Uncle Tom in *Uncle Tom's Cabin*. Henson related the story of his life in Josiah Henson, *The Life of Josiah Henson, Formerly a Slave, Now an Inhabitant of Canada, as Narrated by Himself* (Boston: Arthur D. Phelps, 1849), and in at least two subsequent memoirs.

31. Rick Neilson, "George Mink: A Black Businessman in Early Kingston," *Historic Kingston* 46 (1998): 111–29; *1857 Ontario Business Directory*. See also Winks, *Blacks in Canada*, 96–99, and Allen P. Stouffer, *The Light of Nature and the Law of God—Antislavery in Ontario, 1833–1877* (Montreal: McGill-Queen's University Press, 1992), 12–14.

32. *Globe* (Toronto, Canada West), 22 July, 10 Aug. 1857.

33. C. Peter Ripley, ed., *The Black Abolitionists Papers*, vol. 2, *Canada, 1830–1865* (Chapel Hill: University of North Carolina Press, 1987), 20.

34. Ibid., 9–12.

35. Still, *Underground Railroad*, 151–52.

36. Thomas Flynn, ed., *Directory of the city of Kingston for 1857–1858; with Statistical and General Information Respecting the United Counties of Frontenac, Lennox and Addington, and Descriptive Notices of the Towns and Villages Therein* (Kingston, Canada West: T. W. Robison, 1857), ii–iv.

37. *Daily News* (Kingston, Ontario), 31 July 1857.

38. Benjamin Drew, *The Refugee: Narratives of Fugitive Slaves in Canada* (Toronto: Dundurn Press, 2008), 52; originally published in 1856.

39. Pearson, *Recollections and Records of Toronto of Old*, 63–64.

40. *Provincial Freeman and Weekly Advertiser* (Chatham, Ontario), 27 June 1857; *Chatham Weekly Planet*, 5, 12, 19 Nov. 1857.

41. Delany has attracted a considerable body of scholarly interest in recent years, including two engaging works by Robert S. Levine: Levine, ed., *Martin R. Delany: A Documentary Reader* (Chapel Hill: University of North Carolina Press, 2003), and *Martin Delany, Frederick Douglass, and the Politics of Representative Identity* (Chapel Hill: University of North Carolina Press, 1997). For a thoughtful and nuanced discussion on the transition of black emigration into the mainstream of African American political thought between the late 1840s and the Civil War, see Rita Roberts, *Evangelicalism and the Politics of Reform in Northern Black Thought, 1776–1863* (Baton Rouge: Louisiana State University Press, 2010), 167–99.

42. On the Liberian emigration movement, see esp. Claude A. Clegg III, *The Price of Liberty: African Americans and the Making of Liberia* (Chapel Hill: University of North Carolina Press, 2004).

43. David G. Hill, *The Freedom-Seekers: Blacks in Early Canada* (Agincourt: Book Society of Canada Ltd., 1981), 24–61; Ken Alexander and Aris Glaze, *Towards Freedom: The African-Canadian Experience* (Toronto: Umbrella Press, 1996), 51.

Chapter 3

1. *Anglo-African*, 16 Jan. 1864.

2. During Reconstruction, Galloway credited his experience in Ohio with shaping his willingness to support political coalitions across racial lines, a willingness not shared by many of his compatriots at the time. See *Wilmington Daily Journal*, 20 July 1869.

3. Wild to Kinsley, 30 Nov. 1863, Edward W. Kinsley Papers, DU. This is a reference to Boston abolitionist John H. Stephenson (1820–88), who is described more fully in Chap. 7, n. 2.

4. Richard Hinton, *John Brown and His Men* (New York: Funk & Wagnalls, 1894), 171–75.

5. Ibid.

6. Douglass did not find the mob so varied as the *Tribune*; the journal that he published, *Douglass' Monthly*, referred to the assailants as "the gentleman's mob" and observed that "its rank and file, not less than its leaders, claim position with the upper classes of Boston society" (*Douglass' Monthly*, Jan. 1861).

7. Circular, 2 Nov. 1860, signed by James Redpath and others, Massachusetts Anti-Slavery Society Records, New-York Historical Society. The political atmosphere was similar throughout New York and New England. That winter, proslavery demonstrations and riots occurred in Utica, Buffalo, Rochester, Auburn, and at least a dozen other towns. See Benjamin Quarles, *Allies for Freedom: Blacks and John Brown* (New York: Oxford University Press, 1974), 156.

8. *Douglass' Monthly*, Jan. 1861; circular, Boston, 16 Nov. 1860, Samuel J. May Anti-Slavery Collection, CU.

9. Francis Jackson to William Lloyd Garrison, 13 Jan. 1861, BPL; Account Book of Francis Jackson, Treasurer, Vigilance Committee of Boston, facsimile of original manuscript, Bostonian Society, Boston, Mass.

10. James Redpath, *The Public Life of Captain John Brown* (Boston: Thayer and Eldridge, 1860); Charles F. Horner, *The Life of James Redpath and the Development of the Modern Lyceum* (New York: Barse & Hopkins, 1926); Willis D. Boyd, "James Redpath and American Negro Colonization in Haiti, 1860–1862," *The Americas* 12, no. 2 (Oct. 1855): 169–82; John McKivigan, *Forgotten Firebrand: James Redpath and the Making of Nineteenth-Century America* (Ithaca, N.Y.: Cornell University Press, 2008), esp. 19–50.

11. William Lloyd Garrison to William Lloyd Garrison Jr., June 1856 and 7 Jan. 1858, in William Lloyd Garrison, *The Letters of William Lloyd Garrison*, ed. Walter M. Merrill and Louis Ruchames (Cambridge, Mass.: Belknap Press of Harvard University Press, 1975), 4:394, 502–3 (originals in the Smith College Library).

12. Francis Jackson to William Lloyd Garrison, 13 Jan. 1861, BPL.

13. A good description of a similar voyage from Boston to Haiti a month earlier than Galloway's passage can be found in a letter from a black emigrant to St. Marc, William H. Ardin, 25 Feb. 1861, in *Weekly Anglo-African*, 13 Apr. 1861. See also letter from John H. Rapier, another Haitian emigrant, 18 Jan. 1861, ibid.

14. A. E. Newton to the Rev. Mr. Davis [Edgertown, Mass.], 18 Feb. 1861, and James Redpath to Mrs. Leary, 24 May 1861, James Redpath Letter Press Book, DU.

15. *New York Daily Tribune*, 3 Apr. 1861.

16. Frank Sanborn, "John Brown and His Friends," *Atlantic Monthly* 30 (July 1872): 52–54; Frank Sanborn, *Life and Letters of John Brown, Liberator of Kansas, and Martyr of Virginia* (Concord, Mass.: F. Sanborn, 1885), 548; Ralph Keeler, "Owen Brown's Escape from Harpers Ferry," *Atlantic Monthly* 33 (Mar. 1874): 342; Frank Sanborn, "Henry David Thoreau," *Harvard Register* 3 (Apr. 1881): 215.

17. Mary Stearns, the wife of George Stearns, had turned her attention to Kansas as early as 1856, when she tried to rouse enthusiasm for a Free Kansas meeting in Medford. See Mary Stearns to Augusta King, 16 Sept. 1856, BSC/OHS. See also Charles E. Heller, *Portrait of an Abolitionist: A Biography of George Luther Stearns, 1809–1867* (Westport, Conn.: Greenwood, 1996), 137–39.

18. Thomas J. Marsh to George Stearns, 2 Sept. 1857, and George Stearns to E. B. Whitman, 14 Nov. 1857, George L. Stearns Papers, KSHS. The extensive correspondence in this collection for 1857 provides a detailed account of Stearns's support for the Free State Party in Kansas.

19. A. L. Reed to George Stearns, 25 Mar. 1861, George L. Stearns Papers, KSHS.

20. T. W. Carter to Stearns, 29 May 1857, and Stearns to John Brown, 18 Jan., 15 Apr. 1857, 15 May 1858, all in BSC/OHS. Stearns enjoyed close ties with many of New England's wealthiest abolitionists, including the Lodges, Howes, and Forbeses. Drawing on those individuals, he leveraged his status within Boston's business community to raise tremendous sums of money. At times of emergency, he did so with rather remarkable dispatch. Among the prominent donors who answered Stearns's appeals were L. B. Howe, John Carter Brown, John E. Lodge, George W. Bond, Francis Bird, and Amos Lawrence. See "Kansas Organization Fund," 14 Nov. 1857, George L. Stearns Papers, KSHS.

21. Heller, *Portrait of an Abolitionist*. See also David S. Reynolds, *John Brown, Abolitionist: The Man Who Killed Slavery, Sparked the Civil War, and Seeded Civil Rights* (New York: Knopf, 2005), 209–10, 218–19; on Brown and the antislavery struggle in the Kansas Territory, see 138–205.

22. Quoted in John Stauffer, *The Black Hearts of Men: Radical Abolitionists and the Transformation of Race* (Cambridge, Mass.: Harvard University Press, 2002), 37.

23. Stearns to John Brown, 12 Feb., 14 May 1858, and H. Wilson to Stearns, 9 May 1858, BSC/OHS. On Stearns and his support for Brown and the Free Soil movement in the Kansas Territory, see A. L. Reed to George Stearns, 25 Mar. 1861, George L. Stearns Papers, KSHS, as well as T. W. Carter to Stearns, 29 May 1857, and Stearns to John Brown, 18 Jan., 15 Apr., 15 May 1858, all in BSC/OHS.

24. Stearns to John Brown, 12 Feb., 14 May 1858, and H. Wilson to Stearns, 9 May 1858, BSC/OHS.

25. *Le Moniteur Haitien*, esp. 23 Mar., 20, 27 Apr. 1861.

26. Letter from Louis H. Armand, 24 Jan. 1860, *Weekly Anglo-African*, 3 Mar. 1860; *Weekly Anglo-African*, 25 Feb. 1860. On Haitians raising funds for John Brown's family, see American Anti-Slavery Society, *Anti-Slavery History of the John Brown Year, Being the Twenty-Seventh Annual Report of the American Anti-Slavery Society* (New York: American Anti-Slavery Society, 1861), 163–65; John E. Baur, "The Presidency of Geffrard of Haiti," *The Americas* 10, no. 4 (Apr. 1954): 425–61; George Stearns to Wendell Phillips, 17 June 1860, Crawford Blagden Collection, HL; letter from Louis H. Armand, 24 Jan. 1860, *Weekly Anglo-African*, 3 Mar. 1860. Mary Brown and John Brown Jr., John Brown's widow and oldest son, later requested that George Stearns act as trustee for the Haitian funds. See Mary A. Brown to George L. Stearns, 23 Oct. 1861, 14 May 1862, George L. Stearns Papers, KSHS.

27. The term's more current usage, as a congressional debate tactic, hijacking or "pirating" debate by refusing to give up the floor, evolved from that earlier meaning of filibustering.

28. James M. McPherson, *Battle Cry of Freedom: The Civil War Era* (New York: Oxford University Press, 1988), 103–16; Basil Rauch, *American Interest in Cuba, 1848–1855* (New York: Columbia University Press, 1948); Robert E. May, *The Southern Dream of a Caribbean Empire, 1854–1861* (Baton Rouge: Louisiana State University Press, 1973); Amy S. Greenberg, *Manifest Manhood and the Antebellum American Empire* (New York: Cambridge University Press, 2005), esp. 18–32, 135–96.

29. 1861 correspondence, Redpath Letter Book, DU.

30. *Weekly Anglo-African*, 27 Apr. 1861.

31. McKivigan, *Forgotten Firebrand*, 61–83.

32. Ibid., 64–68. Redpath may have gotten the idea for a Haitian colony from a black minister named James Theodore Holly, a former shoemaker, teacher, and principal from New Haven. Frustrated at the prospects for people of color in the United States, Holly toured Haiti with an eye toward establishing a colony there in 1855. Holly's plan for African American emigration eventually stalled, but he and Redpath later worked together; Holly led a black delegation from New Haven to St. Marc in May 1861. On Holly's life, see David M. Dean, *Defender of the Race: James Theodore Holly, Black Nationalist Bishop* (Boston: Lambeth Press, 1979). Other black emigration movements had focused on Haiti earlier in the century. On one such movement in the 1820s, see Richard S. Newman, *Freedom's*

Prophet: Bishop Richard Allen, the AME Church, and the Black Founding Fathers (New York: New York University Press, 2008), 253–63.

33. McKivigan, *Forgotten Firebrand*, 46–47. McKivigan notes that Francis Merriam remained in Haiti between Redpath's two visits.

34. James Redpath, *Guide to Hayti* (New York: G. Woolworth Colton, 1861).

35. On Redpath, the Haitian Bureau of Emigration, and the St. Marc colony, see the Redpath Letter Book, DU; Letters and Reports of James Redpath, LC; James Redpath Letter Copy Book and James Redpath Correspondence and Clippings Scrapbook, Schomburg Center for Research in Black Culture, NYPL; and Haitian Bureau of Emigration, Reports and Correspondence, 1860–1861, BPL. His journal, *The Pine and the Palm*, published 1861–62, is also an excellent source. See also Boyd, "James Redpath and the American Negro Colonization in Haiti," 169–82; Chris Dixon, *African Americans and Haiti: Emigration and Black Nationalism in the Nineteenth Century* (Westport, Conn.: Greenwood, 2000); Alfred N. Hunt, *Haiti's Influence on Antebellum America: Slumbering Volcano in the Caribbean* (Baton Rouge: Louisiana State University Press, 1988); and John McKivigan, "James Redpath and Black Reaction to the Haitian Emigration Bureau," *Mid-America* 69 (1987): 139–53. On abolitionists in the United States evoking the legacy of the Haitian Revolution in their battles against slavery, see Matthew J. Clavin, *Toussaint Louverture and the American Civil War* (Philadelphia: University of Pennsylvania Press, 2010), esp. 33–73.

36. Douglass and his daughter were planning a tour of Haiti, as Redpath's guests, when the Civil War intervened. By July 1861, he was again adamantly opposed to Redpath's plans in Haiti. See *Douglass' Monthly*, Jan., May, July 1861.

37. Since Redpath's first visit to Port-au-Prince in 1859, he and Haitian president Fabre-Nicholas Geffrard had forged a close relationship, and Geffrard had appointed Redpath the director of a new government agency, the Haiti Emigration Fund. Based in Washington, D.C., the fund had two public goals: encouraging the emigration of U.S. and Canadian blacks to St. Marc and lobbying for formal recognition of Haiti by the U.S. government. Whether Geffrard knew anything about Redpath's more revolutionary ambitions is not known. More likely, he looked at his alliance with Redpath and his support for St. Marc primarily as a way of obtaining support for U.S. diplomatic recognition of Haiti. Certainly neither Geffrard nor Redpath seemed to make the exile community a priority. The community's emigrants were chosen with little thought for having the trades or backgrounds necessary for building a successful agrarian community. Though the community's population peaked at approximately a thousand settlers early in the Civil War, the lack of investment in agricultural implements, fertilizer, or infrastructure bled St. Marc's chances for success. Infectious diseases killed many settlers. Religious strife with their Haitian neighbors and the dangers of war with Spain also contributed to the community's demise. See Thomas C. Miller to Wm. H. Seward, Sec. of State, 19 Nov. 1861, Despatches from United States Consuls in St. Marc, Haiti, 1861–1891 (vol. 1), NA. See also Hinton, *John Brown*

and His Men, 575; Boyd, "James Redpath and American Negro Colonization in Haiti," 178; and Albert J. von Frank, "John Brown, James Redpath, and the Idea of Revolution," *Civil War History* 52, no. 2 (June 2006): 142–60. In the spring of 1861, in a letter to encourage the invocation of the Monroe Doctrine to contest Spanish colonial policy in the West Indies, Redpath wrote, "We need Cuba, Hayti and Porto Rico as the future England, Scotland and Ireland of our colored races" (*New York Daily Tribune*, 20 May 1861).

38. In his recent biography of Redpath, John McKivigan describes him as an "intermediary" between John Brown and Stearns and the other five members of the "Secret Six." He also notes that Redpath was able to pay his agents in the summer of 1861 only because of a loan from Stearns. See McKivigan, *Forgotten Firebrand*, 50, 79.

39. John A. Andrew to George L. Stearns, 21 Oct. 1859, Collected Manuscripts Relating to John Brown, BSC/OHS.

40. Stearns to Pres. Geffrard, 11 Apr. 1860, George L. Stearns Papers, KSHS; Stearns to Wendell Phillips, 17 June 1860, Crawford Blagden Papers, HL.

41. Stearns to Pres. Geffrard of Haiti, 11 Apr. 1860, George L. Stearns Papers, KSHS.

42. *Liberator*, 15 Mar. 1861.

43. Ibid.

44. Ibid.; *Chicago Times* article reprinted in Frederick Douglas, "The Wicked Flee When No man Pursueth," *Douglass' Monthly* 3 (Apr. 1861), 438.

45. *Liberator*, 15 Mar. 1861; *Chicago Times* article reprinted in Douglas, "Wicked Flee When No man Pursueth."

46. *Liberator*, 15 Mar. 1861; *Chicago Times* article reprinted in Douglas, "Wicked Flee When No man Pursueth."

47. *Liberator*, 2 July 1861.

48. Ibid.

49. Ibid.

50. Ibid.

51. Ibid.

52. Laflin, Smith to Thomas Carnet, 29 Apr. 1861, George L. Stearns Papers, KSHS. The gunpowder was not necessarily destined for Haiti. Stearns was also supplying guns, ammunition, and other material to Kansas abolitionists well into 1861. See James Montgomery to Stearns, 23 Apr. 1861; George M. Collamore to Stearns, 2 May 1861; James Montgomery to Stearns, 8 May, 21 June 1861; J. W. Carter to Stearns, 13 Apr. 1860; and J. T. Ames to Stearns, 26 Apr. 1860, all in George L. Stearns Papers, KSHS.

53. George Stearns to Frank Sanborn, 26 Apr. 1861, Franklin Sanborn Papers, Concord Free Public Library, Concord, Mass.

54. John Brown Jr. to Stearns, 29 Apr. 1861, George L. Stearns Papers, KSHS.

55. Unsigned letter to "Dear friend," 14 May 1861, George L. Stearns Papers, KSHS.

56. John Brown Jr. to Stearns, 14 May 1861, George L. Stearns Papers, KSHS. The list provided Stearns included fifty-eight individuals, including nationally prominent abolitionists such as Frederick Douglas and Parker Pillsbury, but mainly local abolitionist leaders in Ohio, Pennsylvania, and upstate New York.

57. *Liberator*, 12 July 1861.

Chapter 4

1. *Weekly Anglo-African*, 6 Apr. 1861.

2. A Union general, Edward A. Wild, later noted that Galloway served as a spy from "the commencement of the war" (Wild to Kinsley, 30 Nov. 1863, Edward W. Kinsley Papers, DU). See also *New National Era*, 22 Sept. 1870.

3. George Stearns to Franklin Sanborn, 26 Apr. 1861, Franklin Sanborn Papers, Concord Free Public Library, Concord, Mass.

4. Stephanie McCurry, *Confederate Reckoning: Power and Politics in the Civil War South* (Cambridge, Mass.: Harvard University Press, 2010), 11–12.

5. Born in Windham, Maine, on 31 May 1818, Andrew graduated from Bowdoin College in 1837, studied law in Boston, and was admitted to the bar in 1840. He was involved in the legal defense of fugitive slave Anthony Burns in 1854, as well as in other antislavery cases, and he helped to arrange counsel for John Brown in 1859. He was elected to the Massachusetts House in 1858. On Andrew, Stearns, and African American recruitment, see Peleg W. Chandler, *Memoir of Governor Andrew, with Personal Reminiscences* (Boston: Roberts Brothers, 1880), 31–37; John A. Andrew, *Sketch of the Official Life of John A. Andrew, as Governor of Massachusetts* (New York: Hurd & Houghton, 1868), 103–15; Henry Greenleaf Pearson, *The Life of John A. Andrew, Governor of Massachusetts, 1861–1865* (Boston: Houghton, Mifflin, 1904); William Schouler, *A History of Massachusetts in the Civil War* (Boston: E. P. Dutton, 1868); Charles E. Heller, *Portrait of an Abolitionist: A Biography of George Luther Stearns, 1809–1867* (Westport, Conn.: Greenwood, 1996), 123–59; Dudley Cornish, *The Sable Arm: Negro Troops in the Union Army, 1861–1865* (New York: Longmans, Green, 1956); James M. McPherson, *The Negro's Civil War: How American Negroes Felt and Acted during the War for the Union* (New York: Pantheon, 1965); Benjamin Quarles, *The Negro in the Civil War* (Boston: Little, Brown, 1953); and John A. Andrew and Benjamin F. Butler, *Correspondence between Gov. Andrew and Major General Butler* (Boston: J. J. Dyer & Co., 1862).

6. Butler to Gov. John A. Andrew, 19 Apr. 1861, Correspondence, 1861–1862, Benjamin F. Butler Papers, LC.

7. *Raleigh Weekly Standard*, 7 Sept. 1870. The following National Archives records have been consulted for mention of Galloway without success: RG 110, Scouts, Guides, Spies, and Detectives; Secret Service Accounts; RG 109, Union Provost Marshal's Files of Papers Relating to Citizens or Business Firms (M345); RG 92, index to scouts in Reports of Persons and Articles Hired and the index to Quartermaster Claims; RG 59, Letters of Application and Recommendation

During the Administrations of Abraham Lincoln and Andrew Johnson; RG 94, indexes to Letters Received by the Adjutant General's Office, 1861–65 (M725) and General Information Index.

8. Wild to Kinsley, 30 Nov. 1863, Kinsley Papers, DU.

9. Richard Weinert and Robert Arthur, *Defender of the Chesapeake: The Story of Fort Monroe* (Annapolis, Md.: Leeward Publications, 1978).

10. Butler to Lewis Tappan, 10 Aug. 1861, Correspondence, 1861–62, Butler Papers, LC.

11. Montgomery Blair to Butler, 8 June 1861, in Benjamin F. Butler, *Private and Official Correspondence of Gen. Benjamin F. Butler, during the Period of the Civil War* (Norwood, Mass.: Plimpton Press, 1917), 1:130; Redpath to Auguste Elie, 15 June 1861, James Redpath Papers, 1861, LC; Butler to Lewis Tappan, 10 Aug. 1861, Correspondence, 1861–1862, Butler Papers, LC. For more on Butler's policies toward the freedpeople, see U.S. Adjutant General's Office, *The Negro in the Military Service of the United States, 1639–1886* (Washington, D.C.: Adjutant General's Office, 1973), NA microfilm publication 858, roll 1, vol. 2: 1860–1862, esp. Butler to Lt. Gen. Winfield Scott, 24 May 1861; Butler to Scott, 27 May 1861; and Simon Cameron to Butler, 8 Aug. 1861.

12. George McClellan to the Union Men of Western Virginia, 26 May 1861, in U.S. War Department, *The War of the Rebellion: A Compilation of the Official Records of the Union and Confederate Armies* (Washington, D.C.: Government Printing Office, 1880–1901), ser. 2, 1:753.

13. Butler to Winfield Scott, 24, 27 May 1861, in U.S. War Department, *War of the Rebellion*, ser. 2, 1:752, 754.

14. Testimony accompanying Final Report of the American Freedmen's Inquiry Commission, 15 May 1864, in U.S. Adjutant General's Office, *Negro in the Military Service*, roll 3, vol. 4: Military Employment, 1864.

15. Few incidents capture the talent for disguise better than that of the remarkable and very romantic saga of a fugitive slave woman, Lucilla Mosely (Hall), in the fall of 1862. According to a report written by African American sailor and mason William Gould I, she escaped from her owner in Hillsborough, N.C., and traveled home to Wilmington and then into Union lines disguised as a Confederate soldier, all in order to be reunited with her lover and future husband, Joseph Hall. With Gould, Hall had already escaped to a Union ship. See William Gould, *Diary of a Contraband: The Civil War Passage of a Black Sailor*, ed. William Gould IV (Stanford: Stanford University Press, 2002), 73–75.

16. W. E. B. Du Bois, *Black Reconstruction: An Essay Toward a History of the Part which Black Folk Played in the Attempt to Reconstruct Democracy in America, 1860–1880* (New York: Harcourt, Brace, 1935), 57; McCurry, *Confederate Reckoning*, 31 (*Charleston Mercury* quote), 82 (McCurry quote), 222–25.

17. Quarles, *Negro in the Civil War*, 78–79.

18. On the fluid nature of a contraband's involvement in gathering military intelligence, see, for example, the testimony of Hugh Cale in his 1871 file for

the Southern Claims Commission. Arrested by Confederate troops as a spy "up the Chowan River" in 1862, the former slave "did all I could to get other colored people to leave home and to go to the places held by the United States authorities." Cale also piloted Union troops, led them to Confederate blockade-runners, and "did all I could for them." Typical of the freedpeople who reached Federal lines, he played many roles in his service to the Union army, including those of scout, guide, spy, and probably manual laborer. "I was always a Union man and did all I could for the cause of the Union," he testified. See claim of Hugh Cale of Pasquotank County, State of North Carolina, Summary Report, Southern Claims Commission, Approved Files, Hugh Cale, 3 Mar. 1871 (no. 12688), NA.

19. *Richmond Daily Dispatch*, 8 Aug. 1861; Quarles, *Negro in the Civil War*, 78–79; Lee to Critcher, 22 May 1863, in U.S. War Department, *War of the Rebellion*, 25(2):826. Spying was of course not a one-way street. The Confederacy also had spies around Fortress Monroe. "The rebel authorities were advised of your intentions before I was," Major General John Peck complained to Butler in November 1863. "Norfolk is one city of spies and communication is kept up day and night, by land and water, with the Rebel army," he added. See Peck to Butler, 14 Nov. 1863, General Correspondence, Butler Papers, LC.

20. Edmund Cleveland Diary, 24 Nov. 1864, SHC; Wild to Kinsley, 30 Nov. 1863, Kinsley Papers, DU; *New National Era*, Sept. 4, 1870. For a riveting, first-hand account of the Burnside expedition, see Alfred S. Roe, *The Twenty-Fourth Regiment Massachusetts Volunteers, 1861–1866* (Worcester, Mass.: Twenty-Fourth Veterans Association, 1907), esp. 60–62, 94–100.

21. David S. Cecelski, *The Waterman's Song: Slavery and Freedom in Maritime North Carolina* (Chapel Hill: University of North Carolina Press, 2001), 153–58.

22. H. E. Paine to Maj. Gen. O. O. Howard, 13 June 1866, Series 15: Letters Received (G-210 1866), Washington Headquarters, RG 105, M752, roll 32, NA. One of Galloway's obituaries indicated an awareness that Galloway had served with Paine and the 4th Wisconsin, but the obituary's author mistakenly believed that Galloway had actually enlisted in the regiment. See *New National Era*, 22 Sept. 1870.

23. Halbert Paine, "Manuscripta Minora" (1901), Halbert Paine Papers, Center for Southeast Louisiana Studies Archive, University of Southeast Louisiana, Hammond. See also William Deloss Love, *Wisconsin in the War of the Rebellion: A History of All Regiments and Batteries the State Has Sent to the Field, and deeds of her Citizens, Governors, and other Military Officers, and State and National Legislators to Suppress the Rebellion* (Chicago: Church and Goodman, 1866).

24. Michael J. Martin, *A History of the 4th Wisconsin Infantry and Cavalry in the Civil War* (New York: Savas Beatie, 2006), 43–61. On Butler's command in New Orleans, see John W. Blassingame, *Black New Orleans, 1860–1880* (Chicago: University of Chicago Press, 1973), 24–47.

25. Martin, *History of the 4th Wisconsin Infantry*, 62–73.

26. Ibid., 62–76.

27. Paine, "Manuscripta Minora," 24–33.

28. Martin, *History of the 4th Wisconsin Infantry*, 78–83.

29. Ibid., 82.

30. James Parton, *General Butler in New Orleans: History of the Administration of the Department of the Gulf in the Year 1862* (New York: Mason Brothers, 1864), 491–516.

31. H. E. Paine to Maj. Gen. O. O. Howard, 13 June 1866, Series 15: Letters Received (G-210 1866), Washington Headquarters, RG 105, M752, roll 32, NA.

32. Martin, *History of the 4th Wisconsin Infantry*, 83.

33. Ibid., 87.

34. Ibid., 93. On the Vicksburg incident, see also Richard Biddle Irwin, *History of the Nineteenth Army Corps* (New York: G. P. Putnam's Sons, 1893), 20–26; J. E. Kaufman and H. W. Kaufman, *Fortress America: The Forts That Defended America, 1600 to the Present* (Cambridge, Mass.: Da Capo Press, 2004), 260; and Ira Berlin, Barbara Fields, Thavolia Glymph, Joseph P. Reidy, and Leslie S. Rowland, eds., *Freedom: A Documentary History of Emancipation, 1861–1867*, ser. 1, vol. 1, *The Destruction of Slavery* (Cambridge: Cambridge University Press, 1985), 187–99.

35. H. E. Paine to Maj. Gen. O. O. Howard, 13 June 1866, Series 15: Letters Received (G-210 1866), Washington Headquarters, RG 105, M752, roll 32, NA.

Chapter 5

1. Gen. Ambrose E. Burnside to Hon. E. M. Stanton, Secretary of War, 21 Mar. 1862, in U.S. War Department, *The War of the Rebellion: A Compilation of the Official Records of the Union and Confederate Armies* (Washington, D.C.: Government Printing Office, 1880–1901), ser. 1, 9:199–200.

2. Quoted in David S. Cecelski, "A Thousand Aspirations," *Southern Exposure* 18, no. 1 (Spring 1990): 22–25.

3. William Wells Brown, *The Negro in the American Rebellion* (Boston: n.p., 1867), 212–16.

4. James Rumley diary, Dec. 1862, Levi W. Pigott Collection, NCSA.

5. Beth Gilbert Crabtree and James W. Patton, eds., *Journal of a Secesh Lady: The Diary of Catherine Ann Devereux Edmondston, 1860–1866* (Raleigh: North Carolina Department of Cultural Resources, Division of Archives and History, 1979), 670.

6. Henry Jones to John R. Donnell, 12, 22 Sept. 1862, Dec. 1863, James West Bryan Family Papers, DU.

7. *New York Herald*, 17 Nov. 1862.

8. William Loftin to his mother, 18 Mar., 5 Sept., Oct. 1862, 22 Jan. 1863, William F. Loftin Papers, SHC.

9. *Anglo-African*, 16 Jan. 1864.

10. An excerpt of a later speech, to the Republican State Convention in Raleigh, N.C., in September 1867, is typical of Galloway's oblique manner of discussing his service as a Union spy: "I rendered good service to this government—if I

didn't do it publicly, I did it privately" (*Weekly North-Carolina Standard*, 11 Sept. 1867).

11. For a good overview of the Union occupation in New Bern and other parts of eastern North Carolina, see Judkin Browning, *Shifting Loyalties: The Union Occupation of Eastern North Carolina* (Chapel Hill: University of North Carolina Press, 2011). See also David S. Cecelski, *The Waterman's Song: Slavery and Freedom in Maritime North Carolina* (Chapel Hill: University of North Carolina Press, 2001), 153–77.

12. *Douglass' Monthly*, Apr. 1863.

13. The body of regimental histories, private correspondence, and Union soldiers' diaries describing society and camp life in wartime New Bern is voluminous. In addition to the works cited at the beginning of this book's prologue, some of the other more useful sources include Samuel H. Putnam, *The Story of Company A, Twenty-Fifth Regiment, Mass. Vols., in the War of the Rebellion* (Worcester, Mass.: Putnam, Davis, & Co., 1886), esp. 113–15, 168–76; Edward H. Rogers, *Reminiscences of Military Service in the Forty-Third Regiment, Massachusetts Infantry, during the Great Civil War, 1862–63* (Boston: Franklin Press, 1883); *Record of the Service of the Forty-Fourth Massachusetts Volunteer Militia in North Carolina, August 1862 to May 1863* (Boston: n.p., 1887), esp. 75–97; Alfred S. Roe, *The Twenty-Fourth Regiment Massachusetts Volunteers, 1861–1866* (Worcester, Mass.: Twenty-Fourth Veterans Association, 1907); John K. Burlingame, ed., *History of the Fifth Regiment of Rhode Island Heavy Artillery during Three Years and a Half of Service in North Carolina* (Providence: Snow & Farnham, 1892); and Henry A. Clapp, *Letters to the Home Circle: The North Carolina Service of Pvt. Henry A. Clapp*, ed. John R. Barden (Raleigh: North Carolina Department of Cultural Resources, Division of Archives and History, 1998). Among the more interesting collections of correspondence from Union soldiers stationed in New Bern in 1862–63 are the William Wallace Davis Letters, the Edward Jarvis Bartlett Correspondence, the Henry F. Wellington Correspondence and Diary, and perhaps most engaging, the Charles E. Briggs Letters, all in MHS.

14. Letter from George Nelson Williams, 19 May 1863, *Christian Recorder*, 30 May 1863.

15. William Wallace Davis to his Aunt Margaret, 31 Oct. 1862, Davis Letters, MHS; Mary Peabody to F. H. Peabody, 19 Feb. 1863, Everett-Peabody Family Papers, MHS; John A. Hedrick to Benjamin Hedrick, 10 June 1862, Benjamin Sherwood Hedrick Papers, DU.

16. Browning, *Shifting Loyalties*, 55–80.

17. See esp. Vincent Colyer, *Brief Report of the Services Rendered by the Freed People to the United States Army, in North Carolina, in the Spring of 1862, after the Battle of Newbern* (New York: Vincent Colyer, 1864), 29–51; Joe A. Mobley, *James City: A Black Community in North Carolina, 1863–1900* (Raleigh: North Carolina Department of Cultural Resources, Division of Archives and History, 1981), 5–13, 29–46; and *Anglo-African*, 23 Apr. 1864.

18. The single most insightful source on African American life in antebellum New Bern is probably John P. Green, *Fact Stranger than Fiction: Seventy-Five Years of a Busy Life with Reminiscences of Many Great and Good Men and Women* (Cleveland: Riehl Printing Co., 1920), esp. 12–52.

19. Cecelski, *Waterman's Song*, esp. 124, 135–36.

20. John Hope Franklin, *The Free Negro in North Carolina, 1790–1860* (Chapel Hill: University of North Carolina Press, 1943), 107–8, 149–50, 161–62, 191–92; Loren Schweninger, "John Carruthers Stanly and the Anomaly of Black Slaveholding," *NCHR* 67, no. 2 (Apr. 1990): 159–92; Loren Schweninger, *Black Property Owners in the South, 1790–1915* (Urbana: University of Illinois Press, 1997), 108–11.

21. On antebellum New Bern from an African American perspective, see Green, *Fact Stranger than Fiction*, 12–52 (see pp. 41–42 regarding John Stuart Stanly's school). John P. Green was a free black who was born in New Bern in 1845. After his father died in 1857, he and his mother moved north to Cleveland, an especially common destination, along with Oberlin, Ohio, for New Bern's free black emigrants. He later became a lawyer and served in the Ohio state legislature. In another memoir, Green describes an incident of white violence against a free black man in New Bern that he indicates prompted him to encourage his mother to leave the city for the North. See John P. Green, *Recollections of the Inhabitants, Localities, Superstitions and KuKlux Outrages of the Carolinas. By a "Carpet-Bagger" who was Born and Lived there* ([Cleveland?], 1880), 195–97.

22. *Philadelphia Inquirer*, 17 July 1862.

23. Testimony of Vincent Colyer, Superintendent of the Poor, Department of North Carolina, accompanying Final Report of the American Freedmen's Inquiry Commission, 15 May 1864, in U.S. Adjutant General's Office, *The Negro in the Military Service of the United States, 1639–1886* (Washington, D.C.: Adjutant General's Office, 1973), NA microfilm publication 858, roll 3, vol. 4: Military Employment 1864); Colyer, *Brief Report of the Services Rendered by the Freed People*, 9–10. Colyer describes a number of intelligence missions conducted by former slaves in Confederate territory; see *Brief Report*, 10–22. While black spies provided a unique source of military intelligence, the observations and knowledge culled from fugitive slaves who traveled into New Bern probably proved more comprehensive. The thoroughness with which they might inform Union army plans could be seen the following year, when a Union colonel proposed an attack on Rebel forces in Swansboro, N.C. Referring to Swansboro as "the nest of spies and scouts and confederate agents and home guards," he informed Major General John J. Peck that "I have competent guides who know where every home guard keeps his rifle and where every man is to be found" (Col. E. H. Ripley to Peck, 18 Apr. 1864 [telegram], John James Peck Papers, USMA).

24. John Richard Dennett, *The South as It Is, 1865–1866*, ed. Henry M. Christman (New York: Viking, 1965), 151–53.

25. Ibid. Quote is from the *Colored American* (Augusta, Ga.), 30 Dec. 1865.

26. William McKee Evans, *Ballots and Fence Rails: Reconstruction on the Lower*

Cape Fear (Chapel Hill: University of North Carolina Press, 1967), 111–12; Dennett, *South as It Is*, 151–53.

27. Mary Ann Starkey was born into slavery in New Bern ca. 1827. A longtime member of Christ Episcopal Church in New Bern, she married James R. Starkey on 24 May 1843. They had two children, Alexander and Nancy. Nancy was baptized on 17 October 1846. Little is known about Mary Ann's parents. Their names were Israel and Mary Bryan, presumably also slaves of the wealthy Craven County family of merchants, lawyers, and planters by that name. She had at least one brother, Henry. See Register of Baptisms, Burials, and Marriages, Christ Episcopal Church, New Bern, N.C.; Ninth Federal Census of the United States (1870): Craven County, N.C., Population Schedule, NA; "Freedman's Bank Records, 1865–1874," from Freedman's Savings and Trust Company, *Registers of Signatures of Depositors in Branches of the Freedman's Savings and Trust Company, 1865–1874* (Washington, D.C.: National Archives and Records Service, 1969), Record for Mary Ann Starkey, no. 3009, Branch Location: New Bern, NC, App. Year: 1872, and Record for Nancy Kennedy Moore, no. 2533, Branch Location: New Bern, NC, App. Year 1871; and database heritagequestonline.com (accessed 29 November 2011). See also Kinsley to F. E. Wild, 17 May 1865, and Correspondence, and Reminiscences, chap. 7, Edward W. Kinsley Papers, UMA. The only scholarly work with which I am familiar that has looked at Starkey's leadership in the African American freedom struggle in New Bern is Thavolia Glymph, *Out of the House of Bondage: The Transformation of the Plantation Household* (New York: Cambridge University Press, 2008), 212–13.

28. F. E. Wild to Kinsley, 17 May 1865, Correspondence, and Reminiscences, chap. 2, p. 3, Kinsley Papers, UMA. Starkey's mother, Mary Bryan, was born ca. 1787 and died in 1889, age 102; see *New Bern Daily Journal*, 23 July 1889.

29. Andrew J. Wolbrook to Edward W. Kinsley, 3, 12 Sept. 1863, and Lt. Andrew J. Holbrook to Kinsley, 3 Sept. 1863, all in Edward W. Kinsley Papers, DU.

30. Starkey could not read and write well, if at all, and dictated her letters to Union officers. The identities of her scribes are usually not indicated, but in September 1863 at least one Union officer, Lieutenant A. J. Holbrook, noted on several occasions that he was writing letters on her behalf. In one such letter to Edward Kinsley, Holbrook explained that "I am requested by Mrs. Mary Ann Starkie, after reading your letters to her, to answer them for her, she giving me the sentiment of her heart." See Mary Ann Starkie to Edward Kinsley, 12 Sept. 1863; Andrew J. Holbrook to Kinsley, 3 Sept. 1863; Holbrook to Mrs. Kinsley, 12 Sept. 1863; and Holbrook to Kinsley, 13 Sept. 1863, all in Kinsley Papers, DU. In the 3 September letter, Lieutenant Holbrook explains that his wife, Susie, has "instituted a writing school and she now has 16 scholars, all grown up women," as well as "a Sabbath morning Bible class," both apparently held at Starkey's home. As of May 1864, Starkey remarked to Kinsley that she still could not "wield the pen myself" and lamented that she had "to wait the opportunity of some friend"

in order to send him a letter. See Starkey to Kinsley, 31 May 1864, Kinsley Papers, DU.

31. Born in Boston in 1836, Thomas G. Stevenson commanded the 24th Regiment, Massachusetts Volunteer Infantry, at the battles of Roanoke Island and New Bern early in 1862. Later that year, he served as a brigade commander, based in New Bern. He was promoted to brigadier general that December. The following year, he served as a brigade commander in Alfred H. Terry's X Army Corps in South Carolina. He died, the victim of a sniper's bullet, while in command of the 1st Division, IX Army Corps, at Spotsylvania, on 10 May 1864. See *General Stevenson* (Cambridge, Mass.: Welch, Bigelow & Co., date uncertain), esp. 7–32. Hartwell's ardent abolitionism and his devotion to the rights of African American soldiers can be seen throughout his correspondence in the Alfred S. Hartwell Papers, Massachusetts State Library, Boston, Mass., and in his "Personal Reminiscences of the Civil War" (ca. 1903), series I, Alfred Stedman Hartwell Papers, Hawaii State Archives, Honolulu.

32. Starkey was hardly the only African American woman in New Bern who befriended Union soldiers and played complex roles in shaping their attitudes toward race, the war, and abolition. For others, see the reference to Hannah Robinson in Herbert E. Valentine, *Story of Co. F, 23d Massachusetts Volunteers in the War for the Union, 1861–1865* (Boston: W. B. Clarke & Co., 1896), 139; the comments regarding "Aunt Dinah Holmes" and "Aunt 'Nicey Lucky'" in James A. Emmerton, *A Record of the Twenty-Third Regiment, Mass. Vol. Infantry, in the War of the Rebellion, 1861–1865* (Boston: William Ware & Co., 1886), 95–97; and most especially, the letters mentioning Mary Jane Connor, who, like Starkey, was also a famed cook and boardinghouse keeper with strong political opinions, in Clapp, *Letters to the Home Circle*, esp. 82–83, 129, 165, 175–76.

33. Born in Nashua, New Hampshire, in 1829, Edward W. Kinsley was raised in Springfield, Massachusetts, where his father, Rhodolphus Kinsley, was a cabinet-maker and apparently something of an inventor. His father was also a dedicated abolitionist who, his son recalled, played a role in a local branch of the Underground Railroad. Edward moved to the Boston area in 1848 and was engaged in the wholesale woolen business with Blake, Patterson & Company. Through his father's abolitionist friends, he became associated with Charles Sumner, John A. Andrew, and other antislavery political leaders in and around Boston. Declared unfit for active duty by a Cambridge surgeon for "hernia of the right side," Kinsley undertook a number of special assignments on behalf of Governor Andrew during the war. In his unpublished memoir, he indicates that he was offered but refused commissions in the U.S. Army on more than one occasion, in order that he might avoid the constraints of the military bureaucracy. See Bowdoin S. Parker, *What One Grand Army Post Has Accomplished: History of Edward W. Kinsley Post, No. 113, Department of Massachusetts, Grand Army of the Republic, Boston, Mass.* (Norwood, Mass.: Norwood Press, 1913), 6, 143–44; Albert W. Mann, *History*

of the *Forty-Fifth Regiment Massachusetts Volunteer Militia* (Jamaica Plain, Mass.: Brookside Print, 1908), 446–51; and Reminiscences, esp. chap. 1, and "Calista A. Kinsley: Notes from her diary, 1862–1864," Kinsley Papers, UMA.

34. Reminiscences, chap. 1, p. 6, Kinsley Papers, UMA.

35. On Edward A. Wild, see Bradford Kingman, *Memoir of Gen. Edward Augustus Wild* (Boston: D. Clapp & Son, 1895), and Francis Harding Casstevens, *Edward A. Wild and the African Brigade in the Civil War* (Jefferson, N.C.: McFarland, 2003). A useful group of papers on his early life is the Edward Augustus Wild Papers, Brookline Public Library, Brookline, Mass. On Wild and the recruitment of the African Brigade, see esp. Richard M. Reid, *Freedom for Themselves: North Carolina's Black Soldiers in the Civil War Era* (Chapel Hill: University of North Carolina Press, 2008), 19–65. Of the toll that his wartime injuries had already taken on him by the summer of 1863, Wild wrote Kinsley, "I must raise my brigade . . . and show them how to fight; before I can with any decency retire from the field into any civil employment. I only fear that my broken constitution will compel me to back out prematurely. . . . I am not the man I was a year ago" (Wild to Kinsley, 28 July 1863, Kinsley Papers, DU).

36. Reminiscences, chap. 1, pp. 8–10, Kinsley Papers, UMA.

37. James M. McPherson, *Ordeal by Fire: The Civil War and Reconstruction* (New York: Knopf, 1982), 399.

38. Mann, *History of the Forty-Fifth Regiment*, 300–302.

39. Wild to Kinsley, 30 Nov. 1863, Kinsley Papers, DU (copy in the Kinsley Papers at UMA as well). The reasons behind Galloway no longer serving as a Union army spy are not known, but several possibilities exist. The opportunity to play a more central role in African American political organizing might well have been the most important. He may have had other reasons as well: disillusionment with the Union army's treatment of slaves and contrabands that he had witnessed in both the Deep South and the Upper South; changes in the organization of the Union spy service that made it more bureaucratic and centralized in Washington, D.C.; and the absence in North Carolina and Virginia of commanding officers such as Butler and Paine, who were comfortable working with a black man like him and who shared his commitment to the African American freedom struggle.

40. Reminiscences, chap. 2, pp. 3–4, Kinsley Papers, UMA.

41. Ibid., pp. 2–3. A rather different account of this incident, in which Kinsley is described as "Mr. X" and as a "Massachusetts gentleman," appeared in *Douglass' Monthly*, Aug. 1863.

42. Reminiscences, chap. 2, p. 2, Kinsley Papers, UMA.

43. "Diary of Edward W. Kinsley during his First Visit to the South," Kinsley Papers, UMA.

44. Reminiscences, chap. 2, p. 2, Kinsley Papers, UMA.

45. Ibid., p. 5.

46. Born into slavery on 18 October 1827 in or near Washington, N.C., John Randolph Jr. was an important African American political, religious, and civic leader in New Bern during and after the Civil War. Census records indicate that he was illiterate, but these were almost surely in error: he was noted for his intelligence and political sophistication, and an 1867 account describes him reading the Declaration of Independence aloud at a political rally in New Bern. His daughter, Fannie, later married George White, a local teacher, principal, and lawyer who was later elected to the U.S. House of Representatives. On Randolph's family life and political career, see *Daily Journal* (New Bern, N.C.), 25 Nov. 1890 (containing his obituary); *Christian Recorder*, July 1864; Alan D. Watson, *A History of New Bern and Craven County* (New Bern, N.C.: Tryon Palace Commission, 1987), 449; Ninth and Tenth Censuses of the United States (1870, 1880): Craven County, N.C., Population Schedules, NA; *North Carolina Times*, 28, 31 Jan. 1865; Lachlan Cumming Vass, *History of the First Presbyterian Church in New Bern, N.C., with a Resume of Early Ecclesiastical Affairs in Eastern North Carolina, and a Sketch of the Early Days of New Bern, N.C., 1817–1886* (Richmond, Va.: Whittet and Shepperson, 1886), 184; signature records no. 1464 (31 Jan. 1870), no. 1526 (9 Mar. 1870), and no. 2306 (18 Sept. 1871), New Bern, North Carolina, in *Registers of Signatures of Depositors in Branches of the Freedman's Savings and Trust Company, 1865–1874*, NA microfilm publication M816, roll 18, Records of the Office of the Comptroller of the Currency, RG 101; 28 Aug. 1866 entry, Marriages of Craven County, 1851–1905, vol. 2, page 186, NCSA; Register of Registrars (2 vols.), Records of the Assistant Commissioner for the State of North Carolina, Bureau of Refugees, Freedmen, and Abandoned Lands, 1865–1870, RG 105, NA; and Reminiscences, chap. 2, Kinsley Papers, UMA.

47. Reminiscences, chap. 2, p. 7, Kinsley Papers, UMA. As with the preponderance of men and women born in slavery, little is known about Rev. Isaac Felton. He appears again in our story in Chapters 8 and 12 but has not been identified in census records, business directories, or other public documents before, during, or after the Civil War.

48. Robert Dale Owen, James McKaye, and Samuel G. Howe, "Preliminary Report of the American Freedmen's Inquiry Commission," to E. M. Stanton, 30 June 1863, in U.S. Adjutant General's Office, *Negro in the Military Service*, roll 2, vol. 3, pt. 1: Military Employment 1863.

49. *Douglass' Monthly*, June, July 1862. See also Browning, *Shifting Loyalties*, 76–80. For an insightful discussion of Stanly, his race politics, and his political stewardship during the war, see Joe A. Mobley, *"War Governor of the South": North Carolina's Zeb Vance in the Confederacy* (Gainesville: University of Florida Press, 2005), 99–106.

50. Mobley, *"War Governor of the South,"* 99–106.

51. W. P. Derby, *Bearing Arms in the Twenty-Seventh Massachusetts Regiment of Volunteer Infantry during the Civil War, 1861–1865* (Boston: Wright & Potter, 1883),

110–11. For Stanly's view of this incident, see Edward Stanly to Stanton, 12 June 1862, in U.S. Adjutant General's Office, *Negro in the Military Service*, roll 1, vol. 2: 1860–62.

52. *Christian Recorder*, 21 June 1862.

53. Ibid.

54. Ibid. Among Union leaders in New Bern, Stanly's appointment as military governor—and his interference in army policies toward the contrabands—was widely viewed as a bureaucratic hindrance. Both Horace James and Ambrose Burnside met with Lincoln regarding Stanly's tenure as governor and his policies toward the contrabands. See Horace James to friends of the Old South Sabbath School, 21 June 1862, Horace James Correspondence and Papers, AAS. See also *Douglass' Monthly*, June, July 1862.

55. William H. Singleton, *Recollections of My Slavery Days*, ed. Katherine Mellen Charron and David S. Cecelski (Raleigh: North Carolina Department of Cultural Resources, Division of Archives and History, 1999), 48–49, 95–97. The pamphlet was originally published in Peekskill, N.Y., in 1922.

56. Emancipation Proclamation, 1 Jan. 1863, Presidential Proclamations, 1791–1991, RG 11, NA (original copy).

57. The racist conduct of Union servicemen is one of the most persistent themes in both the private papers and the published works by Federal soldiers stationed in North Carolina during the Civil War. See, among many other sources, Arthur M. Schlesinger, ed., "A Blue Bluejacket's Letters Home, 1863–1864," *New England Quarterly* 1, no. 4 (Oct. 1928): 562, 565; Emmerton, *Record of the Twenty-Third Regiment*, 135–36; James Rumley diary, 15 Aug. 1863, 17 Aug. 1864 entries, Pigott Collection, NCSA; and John David Smith, *Black Voices from Reconstruction, 1865–1877* (Gainesville: University of Florida Press, 1997), 34–39.

58. Lt. George F. Woodman to Lt. Col. Hoffman, 19 Feb. 1863, W-31 1863, Letters Received, ser. 3238, Dept. of NC and Virginia, 18th A.C., RG 393, pt. 1, NA, published in *Freedom: A Documentary History of Emancipation, 1861–1867*, ed. Ira Berlin, Barbara Fields, Thavolia Glymph, Joseph P. Reidy, and Leslie S. Rowland, ser. 1, vol. 2, *The Black Military Experience* (Cambridge: Cambridge University Press, 1982), 129.

59. Samuel Storrow to his parents, Apr. 1863, Samuel Storrow Correspondence and Diaries, MHS.

60. Ibid. Storrow apparently sent his letters home through Confederate lines to New Bern in the hands of an African American courier accustomed to passing through enemy territory. "Last night," he wrote on 13 April, "I dispatched a voluminous missive of 38 pages by the underground railroad, in other words a darkie of Lieut. Johnson who started down the river for New Bern" (Storrow to his parents and sister, 13 Apr. 1863, Storrow Correspondence and Diaries, MHS).

61. Reminiscences, chap. 2, p. 7, Kinsley Papers, UMA.

62. Brigadier General Foster's racial views and his relationships with black soldiers were somewhat nuanced. Militant abolitionists such as James Montgomery

and George Stearns grew frustrated at what they considered his lukewarm support for black recruiting in North Carolina. On the other hand, Foster was among the first Union generals to arm black spies and scouts, and he armed contrabands on an emergency basis when Rebel troops attempted to retake Elizabeth City and Washington, N.C. "They did fine, and fought well," Foster reported to the secretary of war, "but did not want to enlist." Foster went on to say that the ex-slaves "wish to *work* for the Government, but to live with their families." He later made clear that he did not doubt the ability of former slaves to become good soldiers so much as their interest in fighting for the Union army. At the time that Foster wrote Stanton, he was, however, considering a petition from 120 blacks in New Bern "for arms and organization in the U.S. Service." See Montgomery to Stearns, 18 June 1864, George L. Stearns Papers, KSHS; Foster to Stanton, 5 May 1863, Executive Papers, Gov. John A. Andrew, Incoming Correspondence, MA; Andrew to Foster, 14 May 1863, Registrar of Letters Received, Department of North Carolina and Virginia (1863), RG 393, NA; and Stearns to Stanton, 17 Aug. 1863, in U.S. War Department, *The War of the Rebellion: A Compilation of the Official Records of the Union and Confederate Armies* (Washington, D.C.: Government Printing Office, 1880–1901), ser. 3, 3:682–85.

63. Reminiscences, chap. 1, pp. 5–7, Kinsley Papers, UMA.

64. Ibid., chap. 2, pp. 7–9.

65. Mann, *History of the Forty-Fifth Regiment*, 301–2, 446–49.

66. *New Bedford Mercury*, n.d., letter dated New Bern, 29 May 1863, clipping in Norwood P. Hallowell Papers, MHS. See also Rogers, *Reminiscences of Military Service*, 162.

67. On the service of the 1st North Carolina Colored Volunteers during the war, see Reid, *Freedom for Themselves*, esp. 67–109, 161–62. Though the black regiments never fully reached brigade status, they existed as the African Brigade well into 1864, when the 37th United States Colored Troops was reorganized with three other African American regiments as the First Brigade in General Edward Hinks's Third Division. In the Army of the James, they were for the first time assigned leading roles in combat, serving with distinction particularly (and again under Wild's command) in the advance on Richmond. See ibid., 87, 161–62.

68. Leon F. Litwack, *Been in the Storm So Long: The Aftermath of Slavery* (New York: Vintage, 1980), 69–71, 98.

69. Maj. Franklin Stratton to Maj. Gen. John J. Peck, 29 Jan., 26 Apr. 1863, Peck Papers, USMA. To get an inkling of the rather mysterious way that the department's Secret Service operated later in the war, when again under Butler's command, see the lists of Secret Service expenditures and vouchers in the Charles M. Whelden Papers, MHS. On Foster's detectives in New Bern, see Edward Bartlett to "Martha," 12 May 1863, Bartlett Correspondence, MHS. Union generals also employed special agents to ferret out Confederate smugglers, undercover detectives to expose Rebel spies, and clandestine patrols to shadow enemy troops. Most were paid out of "Secret Service funds" at the disposal of every Union gen-

eral. Others were discreetly financed from the local provost marshal's budget or out of a general's own pockets, a practice that helped assure a general that his covert affairs would go unquestioned. See Butler to Salmon P. Chase, 31 Dec. 1863, and Butler to Stanton, 2 Feb. 1864, Letter book, 1863–65, Benjamin F. Butler Papers, LC.

Chapter 6

1. Reminiscences, chap. 2, pp. 10–12, Edward W. Kinsley Papers, UMA. Kinsley may have misremembered one part of what Mariah Hargett told him; the 55th Regiment, Massachusetts Volunteer Infantry, did not arrive in New Bern until later that summer. However, Hargett may have heard about the 55th's flag from Union soldiers who had recently come from Boston. A more contemporary but secondhand account of this incident, also apparently originating with Kinsley, appeared in *Douglass' Monthly*, Aug. 1863. That account refers to "Marian Haight" and identifies her as a cook.

2. James Rumley diary, 30 May, 1, 18 June 1863, Levi W. Pigott Collection, NCSA.

3. Wild to Kinsley, 30 Nov. 1863, Edward W. Kinsley Papers, DU.

4. Rumley diary, 1 Jan. 1864, Pigott Collection, NCSA; *Proceedings of the National Convention of the Colored Citizens of the United States, 1864*, reprinted in *A Documentary History of the Negro People in the United States*, ed. Herbert Aptheker (New York: Citadel Press, 1951), 1:511–13.

5. Aptheker, *Documentary History*, 1:522–23.

6. Rumley diary, 1 Jan. 1864, Pigott Collection, NCSA.

7. *Raleigh Weekly Standard*, 7 Sept. 1870.

8. John K. Burlingame, ed., *History of the Fifth Regiment of Rhode Island Heavy Artillery during Three Years and a Half of Service in North Carolina* (Providence: Snow & Farnham, 1892), 184.

9. John A. Hedrick to Benj. S. Hedrick, 5 July 1863, Benjamin Sherwood Hedrick Papers, DU.

10. 1 June 1863 entry, minutes of meetings, Records of the Educational Committee, 1862–1874, New England Freedmen's Aid Society, MHS; Kinsley to Gov. Andrew, 26 Aug. 1863, Executive Papers, Gov. John A. Andrew, Incoming Correspondence (vol. 102, no. 91), MA; *Anglo-African*, 30 July 1864. Quote is from *Anglo-African*, 23 Apr. 1864.

11. Edward Kinsley to James Beecher, 10 July 1863, James C. Beecher Papers, Schlesinger Library, Radcliffe Institute for Advanced Study, Harvard University, Cambridge, Mass.

12. Mariah Hargit and Harriett Filmore, 25 July 1863, Kinsley Papers, UMA.

13. *New York Times*, 5 Aug. 1865; *Christian Recorder*, 15 Aug. 1863. Harriet Beecher Stowe's involvement in the design of the African Brigade's flag led to correspondence between her and Starkey, which apparently has not survived.

However, in a letter to her brother, Stowe indicated that she planned "to send Marianne" a copy of *Uncle Tom* "as soon as I can get time to go into Boston and see about it." Starkey's correspondence apparently impressed Stowe. "Our friend Marianne is a trump," she wrote Kinsley. She later sent a note to Starkey via Kinsley. See James C. Beecher to Kinsley, 27 July 1863, Kinsley Papers, UMA. See also Harriet Beecher Stowe to Kinsley, 14 July, 7 Sept. 1863, Kinsley Papers, UMA, and Stowe to James Beecher, 26 June 1863, Beecher Papers, Harvard University.

14. *New York Times*, 5 Aug. 1863; *Christian Recorder*, 15 Aug. 1863. The source of Wild's reference to "the widow's mite" can be found in the Gospels of Luke 20:45–47 and 21:1–4 and Mark 12:28–34.

15. Beecher to Kinsley, 27 July 1863, Kinsley Papers, UMA.

16. *New York Times*, 5 Aug. 1863; Beecher to Kinsley, 27 July 1863, Kinsley Papers, UMA.

17. The Lincoln administration first contemplated the use of black troops in mid-1862. "Limited and unauthorized" use of black troops had actually occurred in at least Kansas, Louisiana, and South Carolina before August 1862, when the War Department finally authorized the recruitment of the first slave regiment into the Union army—the 1st South Carolina Volunteers, recruited from the occupied portion of the Sea Islands. In September 1862, Lincoln issued the "Preliminary Proclamation of Emancipation" that stated that as of 1 January 1863, slaves in the Confederate states would be "forever free." Once the proclamation went into effect, black recruitment occurred on a mass scale. Six months later, thirty black regiments had been organized. More than 186,000 blacks enlisted in the Union army by war's end. See Leon F. Litwack, *Been in the Storm So Long: The Aftermath of Slavery* (New York: Vintage, 1980), 69–71, 98.

18. Rumley diary, 4 Aug. 1863, Pigott Collection, NCSA; Edmund Cleveland diary, 24 Nov. 1864, SHC.

19. Andrew to Stearns, 10 July 1863, Gov. John A. Andrew Files, MA, and Receipt from Geo. L. Stearns, 13 July 1863, Executive Papers, Gov. John A. Andrew, Incoming Correspondence (vol. 102, no. 87), MA.

20. Born and raised in New York City, John V. DeGrasse earned his medical degree from Bowdoin in 1849 and was the first black man admitted to the Massachusetts Medical Society. Commissioned assistant surgeon, he served as one of a small number of black surgeons in Union regiments. On DeGrasse's background and Brigadier General Wild's efforts to commission African Americans as officers in the African Brigade, see Richard M. Reid, *Freedom for Themselves: North Carolina's Black Soldiers in the Civil War Era* (Chapel Hill: University of North Carolina Press, 2008), 21–27. Reid notes that other early efforts to commission blacks as officers in Kansas and Louisiana in 1862 had been overturned or denied and that even Governor Andrew had not been able to get approval for black officers to serve in the 54th or 55th Regiment, Massachusetts Volunteers. Reid also emphasizes that the commissioning of black officers did not grow any easier as the war progressed and that Wild's brigade was one of the last where the commanding

general had the authority to pick his officers, black or white, with a relatively free hand.

21. Warren Lee Goss, *The Soldier's Story of His Captivity at Andersonville, Belle Isle, and Other Rebel Prisons* (Boston: Lee and Shepard, 1867), 55.

22. Brig.-Gen. Wild to Gen. Westle, 12 July 1863, Military Order of the Loyal Legion of the United States Collection, USMHI.

23. Ibid.

24. Ibid.

25. Ibid.

26. Ibid.

27. Ibid.

28. Ibid.

29. Ibid.

30. Ibid.

31. The U.S. Congress finally equalized pay for black and white Union troops in mid-1864, though black soldiers did not receive retroactive pay due them until the following year. See Reid, *Freedom for Themselves*, 16–17.

32. Butler to Stanton, 29 Nov., 4, 7, 14 Dec. 1863, Letter Book, 1863–1865, and telegram, James H. Hardie to Butler, 29 Nov. 1863, General Correspondence, all in Benjamin F. Butler Papers, LC.

33. Lincoln's General Order No. 252 insisted that the U.S. government would protect Union prisoners of war, black or white, and threatened that "for every soldier of the U.S. killed in violation of the laws of war, a rebel soldier shall be executed, and for every one enslaved by the enemy or sold into slavery, a rebel soldier shall be placed in hard labor." On the disparate treatment of black troops, including pay, see Reid, *Freedom for Themselves*, 16–17, 27.

34. Peck to Butler, 3 Dec. 1863, General Correspondence, Butler Papers, LC. Another important factor in the decline of black recruiting stemmed from Brigadier General Wild's transfer out of North Carolina in July 1863, the deployment of the 1st North Carolina Colored Volunteers to South Carolina, and Peck's reassignment of the state's other black troops to Virginia. Those actions left a vacuum in Union army leadership that was committed to African American recruiting in North Carolina, as well as removed the motivational presence of black troops on potential enlistees. Though the 3rd North Carolina Colored Volunteers was then headquartered in Norfolk, black men were still able to enlist in its ranks and those of the 2nd North Carolina Colored Volunteers at recruiting stations in North Carolina. See Reid, *Freedom for Themselves*, 153.

35. *National Anti-Slavery Standard*, 28 Mar. 1864. On Stearns's travails as the Union army's commissioner of Negro recruiting, see especially Amos Lawrence to Sen. Henry Wilson, 20 Aug. 1863; J. M. Forbes to Edwin M. Stanton, 24 Aug. 1863; Stearns to Amos Lawrence, 3 Aug. 1863; Amos Lawrence to Stanton, 26 Aug. 1863; and Andrew Johnson to Stanton, 17 Sept. 1863, all in U.S. Adjutant General's

Office, *The Negro in the Military Service of the United States, 1639–1886* (Washington, D.C.: Adjutant General's Office, 1973), NA microfilm publication 858, roll 2, vol. 3, pt. 1: Military Employment 1863.

36. *Beaufort (S.C.) Cor. Tribune*, reprinted in *Anglo-African*, 16 Apr. 1864, and Andrew to Kinsley, 25 Apr. 1864, Correspondence, Kinsley Papers, UMA. Emphasis in quote is in the original.

37. Maj. Gen. John J. Peck to Maj. Gen. Pickett (CSA), Petersburg, 11 Feb. 1864, Letters Sent, 1864, Department of Virginia and North Carolina, RG 393, NA; Wild to Capt. George H. Johnston, 28 Dec. 1863, Edward Augustus Wild Papers, SHC. Regarding Wild's understanding of his tactics in relation to black recruitment and morale, see the series of letters, orders, and notes in Correspondence File, Edward Augustus Wild Papers, SHC. On Wild and the guerrilla war in northeastern North Carolina, see Barton A. Myers, *Executing Daniel Bright: Race, Loyalty, and Guerrilla Violence in a Coastal Carolina Community, 1861–1865* (Baton Rouge: Louisiana State University Press, 2009), 31–98.

38. Benjamin F. Butler, *Private and Official Correspondence of Gen. Benjamin F. Butler, during the Period of the Civil War* (Norwood, Mass.: Plimpton Press, 1917), 3:269–70; Kinsley to Gov. Andrew, 8 Jan. 1864, Executive Papers, Gov. John A. Andrew, Incoming Correspondence (vol. 102, no. 90), MA; Butler to Stanton, 31 Dec. 1863, Letter Book, 1863–1865, Butler Papers, LC.

39. On Wild's views of the African Brigade's fighting ability and tactics, see Wild to Gov. Andrew, 14 July 1863, Executive Papers, Gov. John A. Andrew, Incoming Correspondence (vol. 10, no. 88), MA, and Wild to Kinsley, 27 Oct. 1864, Edward W. Kinsley Papers, LC. Embracing Wild's tactics as his own, Butler reported in October 1864 that he was ordering Confederate prisoners of war put to hard labor in Union prison camps in numbers equal to those that his spies had reported of black prisoners of war in Richmond prison camps. See Butler to Robert Ould, Agent of Exchange, Richmond, Va., 12 Oct. 1864, printed in *New Orleans Tribune*, 23 Oct. 1864.

40. Lincoln to Hon. James C. Conkling, 26 Aug. 1863, in U.S. Adjutant General's Office, *Negro in the Military Service*, roll 2, vol. 3, pt. 1: Military Employment 1863.

41. *Christian Recorder*, 16 Apr. 1864. The same edition of the *Christian Recorder* printed a letter from another black sergeant serving in the 1st U.S. Colored Troops, George W. Hatton: "We are too patriotic to our race not to distinguish ourselves when opportunity is offered," he wrote. He made no attempt to conceal his dismay at the unequal treatment of black soldiers in the Union army, however, rhetorically asking, "Have we not proved ourselves soldiers in every respect? Patriotic and true when a dark cloud was hanging over our country; and when her Capitol was threatened with conflagration, did we not come forward to assist in protecting her without meditating for a moment on days gone by, and how our forefathers and mothers had been treated beneath that glorious flag— the Star-Spangled Banner—the flag of the free?"

Chapter 7

1. Wild to Kinsley, 30 Nov. 1863, Edward W. Kinsley Papers, DU.

2. Ibid. In this letter, Wild refers to Galloway's contact as "Mr. Stevenson—of Boston—No. 12 Arch St." This was John Hubbard Stephenson (1820–88), who resided in West Newton, at the western end of Boston's trolley line, and was a partner in the Boston Silk and Woolen Mills, located at 12 Arch Street, Boston. A determined antislavery man, he was a close friend of William Lloyd Garrison's and worked closely with George Stearns, Francis Bird, Lewis Hayden, and Boston's other leading abolitionists. In 1863, Massachusetts governor John A. Andrew appointed him one of the thirty-eight members of a committee charged with raising $50,000 for Stearns to recruit black troops nationally. See *Directory of the City of Boston: Embracing the City Record, General Directory of the Citizens and a Special Directory of Trades, Professions, Etc.* (Boston: George Adams, 1850); Real and Personal State Tax List, 1860–1862, Newton Collection, Newton Free Library, Newton, Mass.; death certificate, John H. Stephenson, Office of the City Clerk, Newton, Mass.; *Boston Evening Transcript*, 22 Dec. 1888; *New York Post*, 22 Dec. 1888. On his relationships with New England abolitionists, see Stephenson to E. H. Heywood, 8 Apr. 1861, and Stephenson to Mary May, 18 May 1863, Anti-Slavery Collection, BPL; Stephenson to Edward Kinsley (date uncertain, probably 1863), John A. Andrew Papers, MHS; Stephenson to William Lloyd Garrison, 29 Nov. 1864, Anti-Slavery Collection, BPL; Stephenson to Wendell Phillips, 15 Aug. 1864, 4 May 1865, HL; Account Book of Francis Jackson, Treasurer, Vigilance Committee of Boston, 56, 58, Bostonian Society, Boston, Mass. On Newton's abolitionist legacy, see Ellen Jackson, "Annals from the Old Homestead," unpublished manuscripts, 1894, Jackson Homestead Collection, Jackson Homestead Museum/Newton History Museum and Historical Society, Newton, Mass.; Alice Jackson and Bettina Jackson, *Three Hundred Years of America* (Madison: Historical Society of Wisconsin, 1951); and William I. Bowditch to Wilbur H. Siebert, undated 1893, W. H. Siebert Papers, OHS.

3. Stephenson also served as one of the fourteen executive board members in charge of raising funds for the recruitment of the 54th Massachusetts Volunteers. See "Subscription levee of the friends of Massachusetts volunteers," Scrapbook, Norwood P. Hallowell Papers, MHS. Stephenson first offered his services to Governor John A. Andrew in April 1861, writing, "What I desire is not pecuniary remuneration but an opportunity to render my aid in my capacity where it can be made available" (John H. Stephenson to Andrew, 27 Apr. 1861, Executive Papers, Gov. John A. Andrew, MA). On Stephenson and Garrison, see William Lloyd Garrison to Oliver Johnson, 9 Aug. 1860, in William Lloyd Garrison, *The Letters of William Lloyd Garrison*, ed. Walter M. Merrill and Louis Ruchames (Cambridge, Mass.: Belknap Press of Harvard University Press, 1975), 4:685–87.

4. The only known source for Galloway undertaking a mission to the Point Lookout prison camp is an obituary published at the time of his death in the

New National Era, a Washington, D.C., newspaper that at that time was edited by Frederick Douglass. The obituary was not signed; but the author obviously knew Galloway intimately, and other parts of the obituary provide unique, and generally verifiable, insights into Galloway's life. See *New National Era*, 22 Sept. 1870.

5. Ibid.

6. Rev. A. B. Cross, "Map of Hospital and Military Prison at Point Lookout," in Edwin Warfield Beitzell, *Point Lookout Prison Camp for Confederates* (Abell, Md., 1972), 105.

7. G. W. Jones, *In Prison at Point Lookout* (Martinsville, Va.: n.p., n.d.), 2–3, in Point Lookout, Md., Prison Camp Records, Schoff Civil War Collections, William C. Clements Library, University of Michigan, Ann Arbor.

8. Ibid.

9. 1 Jan., 18 Feb. 1864 entries in "The Diary of Bartlett Yancey Malone," ed. William Whatley Pierson Jr., *James Sprunt Historical Publications* (Chapel Hill: University of North Carolina, 1919), vol. 16, no. 2, pp. 45–46; "Diary of Charles Warren Hutt," 17 Feb. 1864, in Beitzell, *Point Lookout Prison Camp for Confederates*, 65–87; Jones, *In Prison at Point Lookout*, 5.

10. J. G. De Roulhac Hamilton, "The Prison Experiences of Randolph Shotwell," *NCHR* 2, no. 2 (Apr. 1925): 160; 10 Jan. 1864 entry in "Diary of Bartlett Yancey Malone," 45. Quotes are from "Diary of Charles Warren Hutt," 8 Feb. 1864, and Jones, *In Prison at Point Lookout*, 1–5.

11. "Diary of Charles Warren Hutt," 24, 25 Feb. 1864; "War Diary of Robert Emory Park," *Southern Historical Society Papers* 26 (1898): 9 Dec., 18, 21, 29 Apr., 24 May, 7 Aug. 1864, 22 Jan. 1865; "Official Inquiry into Prisoner Shooting," Mar. 1864, cited in Beitzell, *Point Lookout Prison Camp for Confederates*, 38; Mar. 1864 entry in "Diary of the Rev. A. B. Cross," in Beitzell, *Point Lookout Prison Camp for Confederates*, 108.

12. Earlier in the war, before significant numbers of black Union soldiers enlisted in the Union army, prisoner exchanges were often strikingly civil affairs conducted in a gentlemanly manner that gave both Confederate and Union generals a chance to display an enduring sense of honor even after hard-fought battles with large losses. By the fall of 1863, however, prisoner exchanges had ground to a halt over the Confederate treatment of black soldiers. The Confederacy was willing to trade prisoners "man for man and officer for officer except blacks and officers in command of black troops. These they absolutely refuse to exchange," Secretary of War Stanton wrote Butler on 17 November. That policy ultimately led Butler and Stanton to suspend all prisoner exchanges. Grant proved even more adamant than Butler. In April 1864, Butler, who was by then commissioner of prisoner exchanges in Virginia, assumed that the Federal army would make an exception for the sick and wounded. Grant, in reply, said in a telegram to Butler, "Receive all the sick and wounded the Confederate authorities will send you, but send no more in return."

The collapse of the prisoner exchange system had far-ranging implications.

One of the most tragic was that large numbers of Union and Confederate prisoners of war that might otherwise have been released remained in custody during a smallpox epidemic in the winter of 1863 and during the great yellow fever epidemic of 1864. Stanton's appointment of Butler as commissioner of prisoner exchanges did not help negotiations to settle the stalemate, either. In December 1862, Jefferson Davis had pronounced Butler "to be a felon, deserving of capital punishment"—and hence himself not eligible for parole or exchange if captured—because of his treatment of Confederate civilians and his support for slaves in New Orleans. A rich historical record on the impact of race on prisoner exchanges in Butler's department can be found in U.S. Adjutant General's Office, *The Negro in the Military Service of the United States, 1639–1886* (Washington, D.C.: Adjutant General's Office, 1973), NA microfilm publication 858, roll 5, vol. 7. See esp. S. A. Meredith to Robert Ould, 29 Oct., 2 Nov. 1863; Stanton to Butler, 17 Nov. 1863; Ould to Maj.-Gen. E. A. Hitchcock, 27 Dec. 1863; U.S. Grant to Butler, 17, 20 Apr. 1864; Butler to Grant, 20 Apr. 1864; Stanton to Lincoln, 5 May 1864; J. B. Door et al. to Lincoln, 14 Aug. 1864; Adjutant and Inspector General's Office (Confederate), Richmond, 24 Dec. 1862, General Orders, No. 111; James Seddon to Robert Ould, 24 June 1863; and Lee to Grant, 19 Oct. 1864. On the nature of prisoner exchanges before the deployment of black Union troops, see a series of letters between Confederate major general B. Huger and Union brigadier general John E. Wool, Sept. 1861–May 1862, John E. Wool Papers, box 30, folders 10–19, esp. Huger to Wool, 24 Apr. 1862, Manuscripts and Special Collections, New York State Library, Albany. On prisoner exchanges and an outbreak of a smallpox epidemic in Confederate prison camps near Richmond, see Butler to Stanton, 7 Dec. 1863, Letter Book, 1863–1865, Benjamin F. Butler Papers, LC.

13. D. Alexander Brown, *The Galvanized Yankees* (Urbana: University of Illinois Press, 1963), 65–66.

14. At first Stanton recommended only enlisting Point Lookout prisoners into the Union navy. He did not want to put them into a position where they might have to confront their former Confederate comrades in close battle. After further correspondence with Butler, however, Stanton took the matter to Lincoln, who gave his approval for enlisting the Rebel prisoners into either the Union army or navy. See Brown, *Galvanized Yankees*, 65–66.

15. Michèle Tucker Butts, "Trading Gray for Blue: Ex-Confederates Hold the Upper Missouri for the Union," *Prologue* 37, no. 4 (Winter 2005): 14–21.

16. Many of the 1st U.S. Volunteers died of scurvy, starvation, and pneumonia at Fort Connor, in the Powder River territory of Wyoming, where the great Lakota warrior Red Cloud blockaded their fort and cut off their supply lines that next winter. At the end of the Civil War, when Union authorities released their comrades from Point Lookout, the survivors of Red Cloud's assault received orders to remain in the West. Many deserted for home or the gold fields rather than face another winter in a Union regiment. Union officials halted all recruitment at Point Lookout at the end of June 1864, though other such companies of

Galvanized Yankees were later organized at Rock Island Prison in Illinois. Army leaders promised them, as they did the 4th U.S. Volunteers (the second regiment of Galvanized Yankees recruited at Point Lookout), that they would never have to fight Confederate soldiers. See Michèle Tucker Butts, *Galvanized Yankees on the Upper Missouri: The Face of Loyalty* (Boulder: University Press of Colorado, 2003), 12, 35, 52, 57; Brown, *Galvanized Yankees*, 67–69

17. The Hamilton brothers originally called their newspaper the *Weekly Anglo-African* but had changed its name to *Anglo-African* by 1863. On the Hamiltons and the *Anglo-African*, see Paul Finkelman, ed., *Encyclopedia of African-American History, 1619–1895: From the Colonial Period to the Age of Frederick Douglass* (New York: Oxford University Press, 2006), 2:71. On Robert Hamilton's activism in New York City, see Manisha Sinha, "Black Abolitionism: The Assault on Southern Slavery and the Struggle for Racial Equality," in *Slavery in New York*, ed. Ira Berlin and Leslie M. Harris (New York: New Press, 2005), 239–62. For copies of the *Anglo-African Magazine*, see the C. Fiske Harris Collection on the Civil War and Slavery, Special Collections Department, Providence Public Library, Providence, R.I.

18. C. Peter Ripley, ed., *The Black Abolitionists Papers*, vol. 2, *Canada, 1830–1865* (Chapel Hill: University of North Carolina Press, 1987), 27–29.

19. Robert F. Engs, *Freedom's First Generation: Black Hampton, Virginia, 1861–1890* (New York: Fordham University Press, 2004), 8–10; Ervin L. Jordan, *Black Confederates and Afro-Yankees in Civil War Virginia* (Charlottesville: University of Virginia Press, 1995), 70.

20. *Syracuse Daily Journal*, 6, 7 Oct. 1864.

21. *Anglo-African*, 22 Oct. 1864; *Christian Recorder*, 15 Oct. 1864.

22. *Anglo-African*, 26 Dec. 1863. On the black community in Hampton, see Engs, *Freedom's First Generation*.

23. *Anglo-African*, 26 Dec. 1863.

24. Ibid., 2, 16 Jan. 1864.

25. Ibid.

26. Martha A. Little deposition, 22 Sept. 1927, Celie Galloway Pension Application File (1927), U.S. Department of the Interior: Bureau of Pensions, VA.

27. Marriage Register, Carteret County, 29 Dec. 1863, NCSA.

28. *Anglo-African*, 16 Jan. 1864; Twelfth Federal Census of the United States (1900): Carteret County, N.C., NA.

29. Twelfth, Thirteenth, and Fourteenth Federal Censuses of the United States (1900, 1910, 1920): Carteret County, N.C., NA.

30. *Anglo-African*, 6 Feb. 1864, 1 Apr. 1865. In emphasizing the rights of African American women to stand up to their former owners, Martha Ann Galloway may well have been referencing a recent local incident involving the whipping of a mother seeking her daughter's return. See Capt. Wm. B. Fowle Jr. to Maj. Southard Hoffman, [14 Jan. 1863], F-6 1863, Letters Received, ser. 3238, Dept. of NC and Virginia, 18th A.C., RG 393, pt. 1, NA, in *Freedom: A Documentary History of Eman-*

cipation, 1861–1867, ed. Ira Berlin, Barbara Fields, Thavolia Glymph, Joseph P. Reidy, and Leslie S. Rowland, ser. 1, vol. 1, *The Destruction of Slavery* (Cambridge: Cambridge University Press, 1985), 86–87.

31. David S. Cecelski, *The Waterman's Song: Slavery and Freedom in Maritime North Carolina* (Chapel Hill: University of North Carolina Press, 2001), 203–12.

32. *Anglo-African*, 16 Jan. 1864.

33. Ibid.

34. Ibid.; Ninth Federal Census of the United States (1870): Craven County, N.C., Mortality Schedule, NA; Eric Foner, *Freedom's Lawmakers: A Directory of Black Officeholders during Reconstruction* (Baton Rouge: Louisiana State University Press, 1996), 88–89, 170.

35. John A. Hedrick to Benj. S. Hedrick, 13 Dec. 1863, 17 Jan. 1864, Benjamin Sherwood Hedrick Papers, DU.

36. *Anglo-African*, 16 Jan. 1864.

37. Ibid., 16 Jan., 23 Apr. 1864. Born ca. 1815, John R. Good had been a free person of color before the war and made his living as a barber. He was a stalwart among the city's black leaders during the war, as evidenced by this leadership in refugee relief efforts and his election, in January 1865, as head of one of two African American firefighting companies organized in the city. After the war, he served as a justice of the peace in New Bern and represented Craven County in the N.C. House of Representatives in 1874–75. See Seventh, Eighth, and Ninth Federal Censuses of the United States (1850, 1860, 1870): Craven County, N.C., Population Schedules, NA; *North Carolina Times* (New Bern, N.C.), 28, 31 Jan. 1865; *Anglo-African*, 30 July 1864; and Foner, *Freedom's Lawmakers*, 88–89.

On Hill, Johnson, and the Harris brothers, see Seventh, Eighth, Ninth, and Tenth Federal Censuses of the United States (1850, 1860, 1870, 1880): Craven County, N.C., Population and Mortality Schedules, NA, and *New Bern Weekly Journal*, 23 Feb. 1888 (Hill's obituary).

38. *Anglo-African*, 9 Jan. 1864.

39. Ibid.

40. Ibid. "Copperheads" was the name that Republicans had given antiwar Democrats in the northern states, likening them to the poisonous snakes.

41. James Rumley diary, 1 Jan. 1864, Levi W. Pigott Collection, NCSA; *American Missionary* 8, no. 3 (Mar. 1864): 64–67, microfilm S305 (1864–70) in Duke University Divinity School Library, Durham, N.C. In that issue of *American Missionary*, Rev. E. J. Comings, who was under the misapprehension that Galloway was a Union soldier, writes, "The speech of the day was made by a Mr. Galloway, a soldier whose mother was a slave and whose father is now an officer in the rebel army. Such a speech it was, as would do honor to any man of common advantages, be he black or white. As to himself, he remarked, he did not know what to call himself. He was such a mixture of races that he did not know whether he was black or white."

42. Capt. John J. Bomen, A.Q.M.'s Office, Sub-district of Beaufort, 18th Army Corps, to Pero Henry *with others on Committees*, 1 Jan. 1864, in *Anglo-African*, 16 Jan. 1864; *American Missionary* 8, no. 3 (Mar. 1864): 64–67.

43. *Anglo-African*, 16 Jan. 1864.

44. Ibid.

45. Ibid.

46. Ibid., 20 Feb. 1864.

47. Ibid.

48. Ibid.

49. Ibid., 16 Jan. 1864.

Chapter 8

1. *North Carolina Times*, 21 May 1864.

2. On Lincoln's meeting with Frederick Douglass, see David W. Blight, *Race and Reunion: The Civil War in American Memory* (Cambridge, Mass.: Belknap Press of Harvard University Press, 2001), 15–18. Douglass described the encounter in his *Life and Times of Frederick Douglass* (Boston: De Wolfe and Fiscke, 1892), 421–24. On Lincoln's meeting with African American leaders in Washington, D.C., in August 1862, see Kate Masur, "The African American Delegation to Abraham Lincoln: A Reappraisal," *Civil War History* 56, no. 2 (June 2010): 117–44.

3. The petition presented to Lincoln, at least as published in the *Anglo-African*, does not include Edward H. Hill's name, but that newspaper later reports Hill at the Zion Church in New York City as one of the delegates describing their visit with the president. See *Anglo-African*, 14 May 1864.

4. Eighth Federal Census of the United States (1860): Beaufort County, N.C., Population Schedule, NA.

5. Frederick Douglass, "Lincoln and the Colored Troops," in *Reminiscences of Abraham Lincoln by Distinguished Men of His Time*, ed. Allen Thorndike Rice (New York: Harper and Brothers, 1909), 323.

6. *Anglo-African*, 2 July 1864.

7. Ibid., 14 May 1864.

8. Ibid.; *North Carolina Times*, 21 May 1864.

9. Official Confederate policy toward white officers captured while commanding black troops was even grimmer. The Confederacy's president, Jefferson Davis, had warned the U.S. Congress the previous year that his army would treat those white officers as "criminals engaged in exciting servile insurrection" and would refer them to the states for punishments befitting traitors and revolutionaries, which usually meant hanging. A few months later, the Confederate Congress advised that they should be "put to death or be otherwise punished." In practice, however, Confederate troops showed leniency toward white Union officers serving in African American regiments, but far less mercy to their solders. See U.S.

War Department, *The War of the Rebellion: A Compilation of the Official Records of the Union and Confederate Armies* (Washington, D.C.: Government Printing Office, 1880–1901), ser. 2, 5:808, 844–55, 940.

10. James A. Seddon to Robert Ould, 24 June 1863, in U.S. Adjutant General's Office, *The Negro in the Military Service of the United States, 1639–1886* (Washington, D.C.: Adjutant General's Office, 1973), NA microfilm publication 858, roll 5, vol. 7.

11. Brig.-Gen. John P. Hatch (headquarters, District of Florida, Jacksonville, Fla.), to Maj.-Gen. E. A. Hitchcock, 23 Sept. 1864, in U.S. Adjutant General's Office, *Negro in the Military Service*, roll 5, vol. 7.

12. Maj.-Gen. John C. Peck to Maj.-Gen. Pickett (CSA), 17 Feb. 1864, Letters Sent, 1864, Dept. of Virginia and North Carolina (RG 393), NA. On the treatment of black prisoners after the Battle of Olustee, see also Richard M. Reid, *Freedom for Themselves: North Carolina's Black Soldiers in the Civil War Era* (Chapel Hill: University of North Carolina Press, 2008), 93–97.

13. Weymouth T. Jordan Jr. and Gerald W. Thomas, "Massacre at Plymouth: April 20, 1864," *NCHR* 75, no. 2 (Apr. 1995): 125–27, 133–45; Joseph E. Fiske, "An Involuntary Journey through the Confederacy," in *Civil War Papers Read before the Commandery of the State of Massachusetts, Military Order of the Loyal Legion of the United States* (Boston: F. H. Gilson Co., 1900), 2:514.

14. Jordan and Thomas, "Massacre at Plymouth," 152–53, 158–59. Quotes are from *Charlotte Daily Bulletin*, 18 Mar. 1864; J. W. Graham to W. A. Graham, 13 Mar. 1864, in William Alexander Graham, *The Papers of William Alexander Graham*, ed. Max R. Williams (Raleigh: North Carolina Department of Cultural Resources, Division of Archives and History, 1984), 6:43; and *Daily Confederate*, 8 May 1864.

15. A black soldier, Sergeant Samuel Johnson, provided the most detailed account of the Plymouth massacre. He apparently served in the 2nd Regiment, U.S. Colored Cavalry. After being held in a Confederate prison camp and escaping near Richmond, Johnson reported that, at Plymouth, "all the negroes found in blue uniform . . . was killed." He testified that Rebel soldiers took some blacks into the woods and hanged them and stripped others of their clothing and shot them on the banks of the Roanoke River. "Still others," he swore, "were killed by having their brains beaten out by the butt end of the muskets in the hands of the rebels." The southern troops allegedly dragged some of the white officers of black troops through the streets with ropes around their necks. The next day, they executed more black prisoners, evidently by firing squad, according to Johnson. He stated that he escaped only because he had shed his Union blues and donned a civilian suit before the town's surrender and was consequently only taken prisoner. See Jordan and Thomas, "Massacre at Plymouth," 165, 170–92. Quote is from U.S. War Department, *War of the Rebellion*, ser. 2, 7:459–60. Another telling firsthand source is the diary of a first sergeant in Company F, 16th Connecticut Regiment of Infantry. See Oliver W. Gates Diary, CHS.

16. David Heaton to Salmon P. Chase, 23 Apr. 1864, Abraham Lincoln Papers, ser. 1, General Correspondence, 1833–1916, LC.

17. Lincoln articulated one of his most powerful defenses of the Emancipation Proclamation in a letter declining an invitation to "a mass meeting of unconditional Union men" adamantly opposed to the enlistment of black troops and African American emancipation. Lincoln told them that most Union field commanders reported strong support for the use of black troops and the importance of black soldiers to recent Union victories. "Among the commanders holding these views," the president wrote, "are some who have never had an affinity with what is called Abolitionism, or with Republican party politics, but who hold them purely as military opinions. . . . You say you will not fight to free negroes. Some of them seem to be willing enough to fight for you. . . . But negroes, like other people, act upon motive. Why should they do anything for us, if we will do nothing for them?" (Lincoln to James C. Conklin, 26 Aug. 1863, in U.S. Adjutant General's Office, *Negro in the Military Service*).

18. On Lincoln's thinking on how best to respond to Fort Pillow and other Confederate massacres of black Union troops, see Abraham Lincoln, *The Collected Works of Abraham Lincoln* (Washington, D.C.: Lincoln Sesquicentennial Commission, 1959), vol. 7, esp. his Address at Sanitary Fair, Baltimore, Md., 18 Apr. 1864, 302–3, and Lincoln to Stanton, 17 May 1864.

19. *Anglo-African*, 14 May 1864. For an early history of AME Zionism and the Zion Church in New York City, by one of the church's bishops, see John Jamison Moore, *History of the A.M.E. Zion Church in America, Founded in 1796, in the City of New York* (York, Pa.: Teachers' Journal Office, 1884), esp. 53–105. Christopher Rush's own account of the church's early years in New York City can be found in his *A Short Account of the Rise and Progress of the African M.E. Church in America* (New York: the author, 1843), which he wrote "with the aid of" George Collins.

20. Moore, *History of the A.M.E. Zion Church in America*, 349–53.

21. *Anglo-African*, 14 May 1864; *North Carolina Times*, 21 May 1864.

22. *Anglo-African*, 14 May 1864.

23. Ibid.; *North Carolina Times*, 21 May 1864.

24. *Anglo-African*, 14 May 1864; *North Carolina Times*, 21 May 1864.

25. Mary Ann Starkey to Edward Kinsley, 21 May 1864, Edward W. Kinsley Papers, DU.

26. William Gould, *Diary of a Contraband: The Civil War Passage of a Black Sailor*, ed. William Gould IV (Stanford: Stanford University Press, 2002), 169, 187. See also *Anglo-African*, 14 May 1864.

27. *Anglo-African*, 2 July 1864.

28. Ibid.

29. Amos York (1818–85) was an African American cooper, preacher, and civic leader in New Bern. Apparently born into slavery, he was said, by Vincent Colyer, to be "a leading man among his people" and "an intelligent and worthy Christian." Colyer employed him as a personal secretary during his service as super-

intendent of the poor in New Bern. In the 1870s, New Bern city directories and census accounts listed him as a city councilman, as a Methodist minister, and as "a barrel manufacturer." See Eula Pearl Beauchamp, *Craven County, North Carolina Cemeteries* (New Bern: Eastern North Carolina Genealogical Society, [1995?]), vol. 2; Levi Branson, *Branson's North Carolina Business Directory* (Raleigh: L. Branson, 1877); Vincent Colyer, *Brief Report of the Services Rendered by the Freed People to the United States Army, in North Carolina, in the Spring of 1862, after the Battle of Newbern* (New York: Vincent Colyer, 1864), 41, 59–60; J. Henry Chataigne, *Chataigne's Raleigh City Directory: Containing a general directory of the citizens of Raleigh, together with a complete business directory of the cities of Raleigh, Charlotte, Durham, Fayetteville, Greensboro', Newbern and Wilmington; also a list of post offices of the states of North Carolina, Virginia and West Va.* (Raleigh: J. H. Chataigne, 1875); and the Eighth, Ninth, and Tenth Federal Censuses of the United States (1860, 1870, 1880): Craven County, N.C., Population Schedules, NA.

30. *Anglo-African*, 2 July 1864.

31. Ibid.

32. Ibid.

33. Ibid.

34. Ibid.

35. Ibid.

36. Ibid.

Chapter 9

1. Galloway's letter to the *Liberator* mistakenly refers to the drilling soldiers as the 5th Rhode Island Heavy Artillery. That regiment's officers did take the lead in recruiting, outfitting, and training the 1st North Carolina Colored Heavy Artillery, but the 5th Rhode Island was a white regiment, unlike the 1st North Carolina. The leadership of the 5th Rhode Island's officers in raising the 1st North Carolina might also explain the red coats to which Galloway refers. On the 1st North Carolina Colored Heavy Artillery, see Richard M. Reid, *Freedom for Themselves: North Carolina's Black Soldiers in the Civil War Era* (Chapel Hill: University of North Carolina Press, 2008), 187–214.

2. *Liberator*, 22 July 1864. For a fuller sense of African American striving for education in the Civil War South, see Heather Williams, *Self-Taught: African American Education in Slavery and Freedom* (Chapel Hill: University of North Carolina Press, 2005).

3. *Liberator*, 22 July 1864.

4. On Garnet, see Martin Pasternak, *Rise Now and Fly to Arms: The Life of Henry Highland Garnet* (New York: Garland Publishing, 1995); Joel Schor, *Henry Highland Garnet: A Voice of Black Radicalism in the Nineteenth Century* (Westport, Conn.: Greenwood, 1977); and Earl Ofari, *"Let Your Motto Be Resistance": The Life and Thought of Henry Highland Garnet* (Boston: Beacon Press, 1972).

5. Henry Highland Garnet, "Let Your Motto Be Resistance!" in *Let Nobody Turn Us Around: Voices of Resistance, Reform, and Renewal: An African-American Anthology*, ed. Manning Marable and Leith Mullings (Lanham, Md.: Rowman & Littlefield, 1999), 56–62 (quote on 62).

6. *Syracuse Journal*, 19 Jan., 29 Apr., 3 May, 16 July, 1 Aug., 12 Nov. 1864; *Syracuse Daily Standard*, 14 May, 28 Sept. 1864.

7. *Anglo-African*, 20 Aug. 1864.

8. Kinsley to "My dear [general?]," 29 July 1864, Correspondence File, Edward W. Kinsley Papers, MSRC/HU.

9. Lt. Col. Godfrey Ryder Jr. to Col. Joseph M. Day, 18 Dec. 1864, Correspondence, Provost Marshal Papers, MA.

10. Galloway may also have met with Butler when the major general visited New Bern in November. See Wild to Kinsley, 19 Nov. 1864, Special Collections Department, Alderman Library, University of Virginia, Charlottesville.

11. *Anglo-African*, 8 Oct. 1864. Bishop J. J. Clinton, the leader of AME Zion's New England Annual Conference, had appointed Hood to relocate from a church in Bridgeport, Connecticut, and serve as a missionary in North Carolina in December 1863. Hood had arrived in New Bern on 20 January 1864. After also considering alignment with the AME Church, the congregation at Andrew Chapel voted instead to affiliate with the AME Zion denomination later that spring. On Hood and the rise of AME Zionism in North Carolina, see Sandy Dwayne Martin, *For God and Race: The Religious and Political Leadership of AMEZ Bishop James Walker Hood* (Columbia: University of South Carolina Press, 1999), 15–79. Established as a mission of Centenary Methodist Church in 1802, Andrew Chapel had become one of the largest black Methodist congregations in North Carolina prior to the Civil War. A leading historian of the state's Methodist congregations wrote in 1925 that the church had 1,000 members before the war, second in size only to the black congregation at Front Street Methodist Church in Wilmington. Andrew Chapel's congregation voted to leave the Methodist Episcopal Church, South, earlier in 1864 and affiliate with the AME Zion Church. The congregation changed the church's name to St. Peter AME Zion Church in 1879. See Rev. Robert H. Willis, "Methodist Missions in North Carolina," in *Historical Papers of the North Carolina Conference Historical Society and the Western North Carolina Conference Historical Society* (Greensboro: North Carolina Christian Advocate, 1925), 110–25; Barbara W. Howlett, "St. Peter's AME Zion Church," *Journal of the New Bern Historical Society* 1 (May 1988): 31–34; and Martin, *For God and Race*, 51–59.

12. *Anglo-African*, 20 Aug., 17 Sept. 1864.

13. Letter from J. Randolph Jr., John R. Good, and Clinton D. Pearson, 24 Sept. 1864, in *Anglo-African*, 8 Oct. 1864; Capt. Henry W. Gore to Col. Joseph M. Day, 5 Sept. 1864, and F. P.[?] Richmond to Day, 8 Aug. 1864, Reports Concerning Southern Recruitment, Provost Marshal Papers, MA. For a more far-ranging discussion of Union profiteering, corruption, and brutality during the end of the war in eastern North Carolina, see Judkin Browning, *Shifting Loyalties: The Union Occu-*

pation of Eastern North Carolina (Chapel Hill: University of North Carolina Press, 2011), 149–66.

14. Thomas J. Farnham and Francis P. King, "'The March of the Destroyer': The New Bern Yellow Fever Epidemic," *NCHR* 76, no. 4 (Oct. 1996): 435–83; Benjamin F. Butler, *Autobiography and Personal Reminiscences of Major-General Benj. F. Butler* (Boston: A. M. Thayer & Co., 1892), 411–12.

15. Starkey to Kinsley, 7 Oct. 1864, Correspondence, Edward W. Kinsley Papers, UMA.

16. Joseph Kittinger, *Diary, 1861–1865: Joseph Kittinger, 23rd New York Independent Battery* (Buffalo, N.Y.: Kittinger Co. and Buffalo and Erie County Historical Society, 1963), 190.

17. Earlier in the war, a Union corporal in New Bern, Z. T. Haines, commented how the contrabands "render night so hideous by their songs and shoutings that the guard is attracted to the scene of the spiritual orgies, to enforce order" ("Corporal" [Z. T. Haines], *Letters from the Forty-Fourth Regiment M.V.M.: A Record of the Experience of a Nine Months' Regiment in the Department of North Carolina in 1862–3* [Boston: Herald Job Office, 1863], 14).

18. F. Lyman to George Whipple, 19 Dec. 1864, 1 Feb. 1865, AMAA. The missionaries' frustration at black resistance to what Lyman referred to as "a truer, more reasoned, less emotional Christianity" is a central theme in Maxine D. Jones, "'A Glorious Work': The American Missionary Association and Black North Carolinians, 1863–1880" (Ph.D. diss., Florida State University, 1982).

19. W. S. Benjamin, *The Great Epidemic in New Berne and Vicinity, September and October 1864, By One who Passed through it* (New Bern, N.C.: Geo. Mills Joy, 1865), 4–17. A good overview of the epidemic can be found in Farnham and King, "'March of the Destroyer,'" 435–83.

20. Farnham and King, "'March of the Destroyer,'" 452–53.

21. Kittinger, *Diary*, 190–91.

22. Benjamin, *Great Epidemic*, 20–26. A soldier's-eye view of the yellow fever epidemic can be found in the letters from Joel Griswold, in the 15th Connecticut Infantry, to his sister Mary. See 1864 correspondence, Griswold Family Letters, Manuscripts Division, NYPL. See also summer and fall entries, 1864, in the Martin Webster Journal, Manuscript Division, William C. Clements Library, University of Michigan, Ann Arbor, and Hale Wesson to Calvin Wesson, 21 Sept., 27 Oct. 1864, Hale Wesson Papers, Manuscript, Archives, and Rare Book Library, Emory University, Atlanta, Ga. Webster was a sergeant in the 3rd New York Light Artillery Regiment at the time; Wesson served in the 25th Massachusetts Infantry.

23. Starkey to Kinsley, 6 Dec. 1864, Correspondence File, Kinsley Papers, MSRC/HU.

24. Rev. T. Lyman to George Whipple, 1 Feb. 1865, AMAA.

25. A compilation of the men in "Galloway's Coast Guard," as well as their occupations and service records, can be found at http://rootsweb.com/pub/usgenweb/nc/brunswick/military/galowy01.text. Greene County, N.C., historian

Mike Edge compiled the roster from Confederate Military Service Records at the National Archives.

26. *Wilmington Daily Journal*, cited in Helen Moore Sammons, *Marriage and Death Notices from Wilmington, North Carolina, Newspapers, 1860–1865* (Wilmington, N.C.: North Carolina Room, New Hanover County Public Library, 1987), 76.

27. *Anglo-African*, 8 Oct. 1864.

Chapter 10

1. The presence of Rev. Samuel J. Williams as a delegate representing Roanoke Island, N.C., is rather mysterious. A large contraband colony did exist on Roanoke Island, but no individual of that name is known to have been associated with the colony or African American communities elsewhere in North Carolina. A newspaper account also indicates that Galloway later told an audience at the Zion Church in New York City that he served in Syracuse as "the only member from the old North State" (*Anglo-African*, 29 Oct. 1864). On the Roanoke Island contraband camp, see Patricia C. Click, *Time Full of Trial: The Roanoke Island Freedmen's Colony, 1862–1867* (Chapel Hill: University of North Carolina Press, 2001).

2. *Syracuse Daily Journal*, 3 Oct. 1864. Born a slave in Charlotte, North Carolina, in 1832, John Sella Martin escaped from the South while a boatman on the Mississippi River, and by the time of the Syracuse convention, he was minister at the Joy Street Baptist Church in Boston. Charles Lenox Remond, a free black who was a native of Salem, Massachusetts, had been the first black lecturer for the American Anti-Slavery Society. See William Wells Brown, *The Black Man: His Antecedents, His Genius, and His Achievements* (Boston: James Redpath, 1863), 241–50, and George A. Levesque, "Inherited Reformers–Inherited Orthodoxy: Black Baptists in Boston, 1800–1873," *Journal of Negro History* 60, no. 4 (Oct. 1975): 491–525.

3. *Liberator*, 1, 8 Feb. 1861.

4. *Syracuse Courier and Union*, 4 Oct. 1864.

5. *Anglo-African*, 29 Oct. 1864.

6. James M. McPherson, *Ordeal by Fire: The Civil War and Reconstruction* (New York: Knopf, 1982), 399; Leslie M. Harris, *In the Shadow of Slavery: African Americans in New York City, 1626–1863* (Chicago: University of Chicago Press, 2003), 279–88.

7. *Anglo-African*, 22, 29 Oct. 1864.

8. Ibid., 8 July 1865.

9. *Liberator*, 9 Sept. 1864.

10. I. Garland Penn, *The Afro-American Press and Its Editors* (Springfield, Mass.: Wiley & Co, 1891), 90–91; William Cheek and Aimee Lee Cheek, *John Mercer Langston and the Fight for Black Freedom, 1829–65* (Urbana: University of Illinois Press, 1996); Martin Robison Delany, *The Condition, Elevation, Emigration and Destiny of the Colored People of the United States* (Philadelphia: the author, 1852),

5–9; Charles Mercer Langston, *From the Virginia Plantation to the Nation's Capital* (Hartford, Conn.: American Publishing Co., 1894); Bill Reaves, *"Strength through Struggle": The Chronological and Historical Record of the African-American Community in Wilmington, North Carolina, 1865–1950* (Wilmington, N.C.: New Hanover County Public Library, 1998), 460–61.

11. *Syracuse Daily Journal*, 6, 7 Oct. 1864; John W. Cromwell, "The First Negro Churches in the District of Columbia," *Journal of Negro History* 7, no. 1 (Jan. 1922): 76–78; J. Merton England, "The Free Negro in Antebellum Tennessee," *Journal of Southern History* 9, no. 1 (Feb. 1943): 37–58; John Cimprich, "The Beginning of the Black Suffrage Movement in Tennessee," *Journal of Negro History* 65, no. 3 (Summer 1980): 185–95.

12. *Syracuse Daily Journal*, 6, 7 Oct. 1864; William Wells Brown, *The Narrative of William W. Brown, a Fugitive Slave, Written by Himself* (Boston: Anti-Slavery Office, 1847); J. W. C. Pennington, *The Fugitive Blacksmith* (London: Charles Gilpin, 1849).

13. Isaac Mason, *Life of Isaac Mason, as a Slave* (Worcester, Mass.: n.p., 1893), 56–57; Daniel R. Mandell, "Shifting Boundaries of Race and Ethnicity: Indian-Black Intermarriage in Southern New England, 1760–1880," *Journal of American History* 85, no. 2 (Sept. 1998): 466–501.

14. W. B. Hartgrove, "The Story of Maria Louise Moore and Fannie M. Richards," *Journal of Negro History* 1, no. 1 (Jan. 1916): 23–33.

15. *Syracuse Daily Journal*, 6, 7 Oct. 1864.

16. Born free in Virginia, Randolph became a spiritualist, clairvoyant, and trance-medium who embraced the occult, sex magic, and hashish. He was also a respected abolitionist lecturer and had occasionally served as a spiritual advisor to Mary Todd Lincoln. See John Patrick Deveney, *Paschal Beverly Randolph: A Nineteenth-Century Black American Spiritualist, Rosicrucian, and Sex Magician* (Albany: State University of New York Press, 1997).

17. William J. Simmons, *Men of Mark: Eminent, Progressive, and Rising* (Cleveland: Geo. M. Rewell & Co., 1887), 1003–7; Joe M. Richardson, "Francis Cardozo: Black Educator during Reconstruction," *Journal of Negro History* 48, no. 1 (Winter 1979): 73–83.

18. *Syracuse Daily Journal*, 6 Oct. 1864.

19. *Proceedings of the National Convention of Colored Men, Held in the City of Syracuse, N.Y., Oct. 4, 5, 6 and 7, 1864; With the Bill of Wrongs and Rights and the Address to the American People* (Boston: J. S. Rock & Geo. L. Ruffin, 1864), 29–30 (original copy at Boston Athenaeum, Boston, Mass.).

20. *New Orleans Tribune*, 25 Oct. 1864. On James Ingraham and the Louisiana Native Guards, see James G. Hollandsworth Jr., *The Louisiana Native Guards: The Black Military Experience during the Civil War* (Baton Rouge: Louisiana State University Press, 1995), esp. 78, 105–9; Charles Vincent, *Black Legislators in Louisiana during Reconstruction* (Baton Rouge: Louisiana State University Press, 1976); David C. Rankin, "The Origins of Black Leadership in New Orleans during Reconstruction," *Journal of Southern History* 40, no. 3 (Aug. 1974): 417–40; and Ted

Tunnel, *Crucible of Reconstruction: War, Radicalism, and Race in Louisiana* (Baton Rouge: Louisiana State University Press, 1992), 76–77. Cailloux was the first black officer to die during the war. His body lay on the battlefield for forty-one days, as Confederate riflemen refused to allow Union soldiers to retrieve black corpses and bury them even during cease-fires held for that purpose. See Drew Gilpin Faust, *This Republic of Suffering: Death and the American Civil War* (New York: Knopf, 2008), 49–51. While Cailloux died heroically at Port Hudson, the story of his bearing the regiment's flag in battle, a compelling detail for speeches, was something of a folktale. In actuality, the 1st Regiment's color sergeant, Anselmas Planciancois, was hit by a shell in the battle, and his blood, not Cailloux's, stained the flag. Two corporals caught the flag before it hit the ground and carried it during the battle. See Hollandsworth, *Louisiana Native Guards*, 54–55.

21. *Proceedings of the National Convention of Colored Men*, 12–13.

22. *New Orleans Tribune*, 25 Oct. 1864; *Proceedings of the National Convention of Colored Men*, 7–13. Lyrics can be found in *The John Brown Song, or Glory Hallelujah* (Chicago: Root & Cady, 1861).

23. Frederick Douglass, *Narrative of the Life of Frederick Douglass, an American Slave*, ed. Deborah E. McDowell (New York: Oxford University Press, 1999). See also Frederick Douglass, *Life and Times of Frederick Douglass: His Early Life as a Slave, His Escape from Bondage, and His Complete History to the Present Time* (Hartford, Conn.: Park, 1881); William McFeely, *Frederick Douglass* (New York: Norton, 1995); and John Stauffer, *Giants: The Parallel Lives of Frederick Douglass and Abraham Lincoln* (New York: Twelve, 2009).

24. *Proceedings of the National Convention of Colored Men*, 13–14.

25. Ibid., 41–43.

26. Ibid.

27. Ibid.

28. Ibid.

29. Ibid.

30. Ibid.

31. Ibid., 42–43.

32. The convention's published proceedings do not refer to Douglass as the author, but James McPherson indicates that Frederick Douglass had written the "Address to the People of the United States," which was then adopted by the delegates in Syracuse. See James M. McPherson, *Marching toward Freedom: Blacks in the Civil War, 1861–1865* (New York: Facts on File, 1991), 111. See also David W. Blight, *Frederick Douglass's Civil War: Keeping Faith in Jubilee* (Baton Rouge: Louisiana State University Press, 1989), 181.

33. *Proceedings of the National Convention of Colored Men*, 44.

34. Ibid., 45.

35. Ibid., 47–48.

36. Ibid., 61.

37. Ibid., 61–62.

38. Ibid., 62.

39. Ibid.

40. Ibid., 33–36.

41. Ibid., 46–59.

42. Ibid., 16–31; *Syracuse Daily Journal*, 7 Oct. 1864.

43. *Anglo-African*, 29 Oct. 1864.

44. Ibid.

45. Ibid.

46. Ibid. On the Twelfth Baptist Church and black Boston's support for fugitive slaves, see James Oliver Horton, *Free People of Color: Inside the African American Community* (Washington, D.C.: Smithsonian Institution Press, 1993), 36–39.

47. *Anglo-African*, 29 Oct. 1864.

48. Ibid.

49. Ibid.

50. Ibid.

51. Michael Vorenberg, *The Final Freedom: The Civil War, the Abolition of Slavery and the Thirteenth Amendment* (Cambridge: Cambridge University Press, 2001), 160–63.

52. *Syracuse Daily Journal*, 7 Oct. 1864; *Commonwealth* (Boston, Mass.), 29 Oct. 1864.

53. *New Orleans Tribune*, 25, 26, 27, 28 Oct. 1864.

54. Vincent, *Black Legislators in Louisiana during Reconstruction*; Hollandsworth, *Louisiana Native Guards*, 78, 105–9.

Chapter 11

1. *Anglo-African*, 25 Jan. 1865.

2. Lucy Chase to Sarah Chase, 15 Jan. 1865, Chase Family Papers, AAS; *Statistics of the operations of the Executive Board of the Friends' Association of Philadelphia and Its Vicinity, for the Relief of the Colored Freedmen* (Philadelphia: Inquirer Printing Office, 1864), Pamphlet Collection, Samuel J. May Anti-Slavery Collection, CU.

3. Earlier that year, as one example, an African American man, "Dr. Waters," posed as the agent of a company that could relocate former slaves to the northern states and swindled a number of contrabands in the New Bern–Beaufort area. Galloway eventually tracked him to Alexandria, Virginia, and apparently pursued him in a chase. The man eluded Galloway but was caught by Union army guards. See Wild to Andrew, 24 Apr. 1864, Executive Papers, Gov. John A. Andrew, MA, and *Anglo-African*, 21 May 1864. See also A. H. Galloway to Gen. Palmer, 28 Nov. 1864, Letters Received, District of North Carolina, 18 Oct. 1864–1 Mar. 1865, RG 393, NA, and Lt. Col. Godfrey Ridger to Col. Joseph M. Day, 18 Dec. 1864, Correspondence, Provost Marshal Papers, MA.

4. A. G., "Anniversary Celebration of the President's Proclamation at New-

bern, by an Eyewitness," *Freedmen's Journal* 1, no. 1 (Jan. 1865), copy, CU. The New England Freedman's Aid Society published this journal between 1865 and 1868.

5. *Christian Recorder*, 4 Feb. 1865. Bishop Joseph Jackson Clinton (1823–81) served as AME Zion's third bishop. He had appointed Hood as a missionary to New Bern in January 1864. See J. W. Hood, *One Hundred Years of the African Methodist Episcopal Zion Church* (New York: AME Zion Book Concern, 1895), 172–74. For a history of the AME Zion's founding and early work in North Carolina, see John Jamison Moore, *History of the A.M.E. Zion Church in America, Founded in 1796, in the City of New York* (York, Pa.: Teachers' Journal Office, 1884), 162–68.

6. Edmund Cleveland diary, 24 Nov. 1864, SHC.

7. Other African American leaders began organizing state and local auxiliaries of the National Equal Rights League later in 1864 and early in 1865. Galloway's colleague Captain James Ingraham and his compatriots in New Orleans organized a Louisiana Equal Rights League and a number of local leagues nearly as quickly as Galloway and his brethren organized their chapters in North Carolina. Black leaders in Pennsylvania shared their enthusiasm for the founding of the new national political group; they organized a state league, based in Philadelphia, by Christmas 1864. Three weeks later, on 16 January, the black citizens of Boston finally held a mass meeting to establish a state league for Massachusetts. Ohio's black leaders met in Xenia, Ohio, 10–12 February, and founded a state Equal Rights League. By the middle of March 1865, black citizens had also organized state leagues in Tennessee, Missouri, Michigan, and New York. See *Christian Recorder*, 24 Dec. 1864, 15 Apr. 1865; *Anglo-African*, 4, 18 Feb. 1865. On the leagues in Beaufort and Morehead City, N.C., see also *Old North State*, 7 June 1865.

8. James M. McPherson, *Battle Cry of Freedom: The Civil War Era* (New York: Oxford University Press, 1988), 825–30.

9. *Anglo-African*, 28 Jan. 1865.

10. Anne C. G. Canedy, *Freedmen's Journal* 1, no. 2 (Mar. 1865), copy, CU.

11. *Anglo-African*, 28 Jan. 1865.

12. *Old North State*, 7 Jan. 1865; *Anglo-African*, 28 Jan. 1865; *North Carolina Times*, 7 Jan. 1865.

13. Isaac Watts, "Am I a Soldier of the Cross?" ca. 1721–24. A final verse reads, *When that illustrious day shall rise, / And all Thy armies shine / In robes of victory through the skies, / The glory shall be Thine.*

14. On the role of African American theology in shaping political activism in North Carolina, see Mathew J. W. Harper, "Living in God's Time: African-American Faith and Politics in Post-Emancipation North Carolina" (Ph.D. diss., University of North Carolina, Chapel Hill, 2009).

15. *Anglo-African*, 28 Jan. 1865.

16. Ibid.; *Old North State*, 7 Jan. 1865; A. G., "Anniversary Celebration of the President's Proclamation."

17. *Anglo-African*, 28 Jan. 1865.

18. Ibid., 4 Feb. 1865.

19. Horace James, *Annual Report of the Superintendent of Negro Affairs in North Carolina, 1864* (Boston: W. F. Brown & Co., 1865), 41–43; Patricia C. Click, *Time Full of Trial: The Roanoke Island Freedmen's Colony, 1862–1867* (Chapel Hill: University of North Carolina Press, 2001), 85.

20. *Anglo-African*, 28 Jan. 1865; *Old North State*, 7 Jan. 1865.

21. *Anglo-African*, 28 Jan. 1865; *Old North State*, 7 Jan. 1865.

22. Bruce A. Ragsdale and Joel D. Treese, *Black Americans in Congress, 1870–1989* (Washington, D.C.: Office of the Historian, U.S. House of Representatives, 1990), 105–6.

23. Jonathan C. Gibbs, one of Dartmouth College's first black graduates, was a Presbyterian minister who had worked closely with William Still, the African American leader in Philadelphia who helped Galloway escape from slavery. At the time of the second anniversary of Emancipation Day, Gibbs had recently resigned his pastorship at the First African Presbyterian Church in Philadelphia and announced that he intended to come south to work with the freedpeople in the Carolinas. Senator Samuel C. Pomeroy had originally gone to the Kansas Territory as the general agent for the New England Emigrant Aid Company, of which Galloway's old ally George Stearns was a driving force. Stearns had largely been responsible for Pomeroy's election as mayor of Atchison, Kansas, in 1859 and as U.S. senator in 1861. Pomeroy is best-remembered as the inspiration for the pompous, corrupt, and dim-witted Senator Dilworthy in Mark Twain's novel *The Gilded Age*. See Shelton B. Waters, *We Have This Ministry: A History of the First African Presbyterian Church, Philadelphia, Pennsylvania, the Mother Church of African American Presbyterians* (Philadelphia: Winchell, 1994), 30; "Letter from Rev. J. C. Gibbs," *Christian Recorder*, Apr. 15, 1865; Learotha Williams, "'Leave the pulpit and go into the . . . school room': Jonathan Clarkson Gibbs and the Board of Missions for Freedmen in North and South Carolina, 1865–1866," *Southern Studies* 13, no. 1/2 (Spring/Summer 2006): 89–104; and Mark A. Plummer, "Samuel Clarke Pomeroy," *American National Biography* (New York: Oxford University Press, 1999).

24. *Anglo-African*, 28 Jan. 1865; *Old North State*, 7 Jan. 1865. See also *Journal of the Forty-Ninth Annual Council of the Protestant Episcopal Church in the State of North Carolina* (Raleigh: J. C. Gorman, 1865), 13–14; J. W. Hood, *Sketch of the Early History of the African Episcopal Methodist Church* (Charlotte, N.C.: A.M.E. Zion Publishing House, 1914), 84; and James, *Annual Report*, 12–13.

25. *Anglo-African*, 28 Jan. 1865.

Chapter 12

1. *Anglo-African*, 11 Mar. 1865.

2. After the founding of a state AME Zion conference during a nine-day convocation in New Bern in December 1864, the church had grown into an increasingly potent political force. That was especially true in New Bern, the home of Andrew Chapel, but also in nine other black communities between Roanoke Is-

land and western Craven County. The original North Carolina Conference of the AME Zion Church included congregations at Andrew Chapel, Clinton Chapel (also in New Bern), Beaufort, Roanoke Island, Plymouth, Hull Swamp, Macedonia, Carolina City, Morehead City, Brice's Creek, Slocum's Creek, and what church leaders called "the Red Hill circuit," west of New Bern. See ibid., 28 Jan. 1865.

3. Ibid., 11 Mar. 1865.

4. W. E. B. Du Bois, *Black Reconstruction in America, 1860–1880* (New York: Touchstone, 1935), 124. See also Mathew J. W. Harper, "Living in God's Time: African-American Faith and Politics in Post-Emancipation North Carolina" (Ph.D. diss., University of North Carolina, Chapel Hill, 2009).

5. *Anglo-African*, 11 Mar. 1865.

6. Ibid.

7. Ibid., 25 Mar. 1865. On Wilmington's fall, see Chris E. Fonvielle Jr., *The Wilmington Campaign: Last Rays of Departing Hope* (Mechanicsburg, Pa.: Stackpole Books, 1997), esp. 385–438.

8. *Anglo-African*, 25 Mar. 1865.

9. Ibid. One of the liberated slaves' first mass meetings focused on organizing schools for the city's black children. One account indicates that 400 children showed up for the first day of classes in early March. See *North Carolina Times*, 17 Mar. 1865.

10. James M. McPherson, *Battle Cry of Freedom: The Civil War Era* (New York: Oxford University Press, 1988), 830.

11. Starkey to Kinsley, 4 Jan. 1865, Correspondence, Edward W. Kinsley Papers, UMA; Minutes, 16 Jan. 1865, Union League of America, Council No. 13 (Boston Ward 11) Papers, MHS; Martha Ann Little pension claim, 30 Jan. 1894, William L. Horner Collection, Frederick C. Douglass Papers, ECU (on John D. Galloway's birthday). Church records indicate that Abraham and Martha Ann Galloway named their first son John Deabiron Galloway. The church secretary probably recorded the middle name incorrectly, however. More likely, the Galloways gave their son a middle name in memory of local African American leader James Drawborn Sampson, the carpenter and minister who had established a clandestine school that served free and enslaved blacks prior to the war. He died ca. 1863. See entry for 22 Mar. 1868, Record of Burials and Baptisms, St. Paul's Episcopal Church archives, Wilmington, N.C., and Bill Reaves, *"Strength through Struggle": The Chronological and Historical Record of the African-American Community in Wilmington, North Carolina, 1865–1950* (Wilmington, N.C.: New Hanover County Public Library, 1998), 460–61.

12. Starkey to Kinsley, 10 Mar. 1865, Kinsley Papers, UMA.

13. A recently discharged Union serviceman, one of Mary Ann Starkey's friends, attended the meeting and later wrote to Edward Kinsley expressing his wish that Starkey receive similar accolades: "I went last night and saw the presentation of the Bible. It was a big thing. Why don't the people send Mary Ann a

present of a . . . dress and some shoes and such things[?] She does more work for the Negroes than anyone in the country of her means" (Alfred [surname illegible] to Edward Kinsley, 10 Mar. 1865, Correspondence, Edward W. Kinsley Papers, MSRC/HU).

14. Starkey to Kinsley, 10 Mar. 1865, Kinsley Papers, UMA.

15. McPherson, *Battle Cry of Freedom*, 844–52; Mark L. Bradley, *This Astounding Close: The Road to Bennett Place* (Chapel Hill: University of North Carolina Press, 2006).

16. *North Carolina Times*, 25 Apr. 1865. In addition to praising Lincoln, Felton was, the newspaper correspondent observed, "unfriendly toward rebels." Felton "stated that if he had a drop of rebel blood in his veins he would 'give a doctor five dollars to pull it out.' He believed that treason should be punished and that 'we must kill the nits to kill the lice.'"

17. Starkey to Kinsley, 20 Apr. 1865, Kinsley Papers, UMA.

18. Ibid. See also Starkey to Kinsley, 5 July 1865, Kinsley Papers, UMA.

19. Starkey to Kinsley, 5 July 1865, Kinsley Papers, UMA. For an insightful overview of liberated slaves searching for their families across the South, see Heather Williams, *Help Me to Find My People: The African American Search for Family Lost in Slavery* (Chapel Hill: University of North Carolina Press, 2012).

20. The turmoil that surrounded Mary Ann Starkey was also personal. On 28 April 1865, her daughter, Nancy, wrote from Hillsborough, N.C., where she was still a slave, to inform her that she was engaged and asked her to send "some underclothing or some bleach homespun and some fine unbleached, also some dark calico to make a dress, and some stockings and a pair of Morocco boots." She continued: "I hope you will not think that I am intruding upon you for asking you to send me so much for I am ashamed to send the letter because I am asking so much. . . . I hope it will not be long before we shall be together and I will be able to return as much to you. Give my love to Cousin Hagar and all enquiring friends. Tell them that I have grown so much that I don't believe they will know me when I return home." Though money was very scarce in New Bern, few mothers could turn down such a request after not seeing their daughter for three years of war. See Nancy Starkey to Mary Ann Starkey, 28 Apr. 1865, Kinsley Papers, UMA.

21. *Anglo-African*, 3 July 1865.

22. Eric Foner, *Reconstruction: America's Unfinished Revolution, 1863–1877* (New York: Harper & Row, 1988), 178–81.

23. Chase referred to these local groups alternately as the "Union League of America" and the "Union Colored League," but by indicating in his diary that they traced their origins to the 1864 National Convention of Colored Men in Syracuse, New York, he made clear that he was referring to local auxiliaries of the National Equal Rights League.

24. John Niven, ed., *The Salmon P. Chase Papers*, vol. 1, *Journals, 1829–1872* (Kent, Ohio: Kent State University Press, 1993), 542–44.

25. Memorandum from C. C. Emerson, 3 June 1865, and John Dawson et al. to W. W. Holden, 12 July 1865, Governors Papers, W. W. Holden, NCSA.

26. William Woods Holden, a printer by trade, was onetime editor of the *North Carolina Standard*, vocal critic of the war, and unsuccessful "peace candidate" in the 1864 gubernatorial election. Appointed governor by President Johnson, he lost a special election for governor in 1865 to Jonathan Worth but was elected to the office in 1868. The leader of the state's Republican Party, he was impeached, convicted, and removed from office in 1871 principally for alleged abuses related to his campaign against the Ku Klux Klan. See William C. Harris, *William Woods Holden: Firebrand of North Carolina Politics* (Baton Rouge: Louisiana State University Press, 1987).

27. John Dawson et al. to W. W. Holden, 3, 4 Aug. 1865, Governors Papers, W. W. Holden, NCSA. Holden sent a copy of the petition to President Johnson and requested that he order the removal of all black soldiers from Wilmington. See W. W. Holden to Pres. Andrew Johnson, 10 Aug. 1865, Governors Papers, W. W. Holden, NCSA.

28. W. W. Holden to Pres. Andrew Johnson, 10 Aug. 1865, Governors Papers, W. W. Holden, NCSA.

29. Foner, *Reconstruction*, 176–227.

30. Roberta Sue Alexander, *North Carolina Faces the Freedmen: Race Relations during Presidential Reconstruction, 1865–67* (Durham, N.C.: Duke University Press, 1985), esp. 1–17, 99–100.

31. Joe A. Mobley, *James City: A Black Community in North Carolina, 1863–1900* (Raleigh: North Carolina Department of Cultural Resources, Division of Archives and History, 1981), 66–91. Regarding an outbreak of violence between Union occupying forces and black army veterans in James City in 1868, see Mark L. Bradley, *Bluecoats and Tar Heels: Soldiers and Civilians in Reconstruction North Carolina* (Lexington: University Press of Kentucky, 2009), 196–98.

32. Willie Lee Rose, *Rehearsal for Reconstruction: The Port Royal Experiment* (Indianapolis: Bobbs-Merrill, 1964).

33. Sidney Andrews, *The South Since the War; As Shown by Fourteen Weeks of Travel and Observation in Georgia and the Carolinas* (Boston: Ticknor & Fields, 1866), 125.

34. Alexander, *North Carolina Faces the Freedmen*, 16; James Rumley diary, 4 July 1865, Levi W. Pigott Collection, NCSA.

35. *New York Times*, 17 Sept. 1865.

36. Ibid.

37. Ibid.

38. Ibid.

39. Ibid.

40. Born ca. 1843–44, George W. Price Jr. was one of eight slaves who escaped from Wilmington in September 1862 by rowing out to a Union gunboat, the USS *Cambridge*. Along with William Gould I (see Chap. 8), Price enlisted in the Union

navy but seems to have deserted that November, an incident that Galloway raised in a political argument with Price after the war. He apparently moved to New Bern sometime in 1865 but soon returned home to Wilmington. He worked as a plasterer but was also a merchant and businessman. For more than three decades, Price was one of the city's most important African American civic leaders, especially active in local fraternal lodges and the Republican Party. He served in the N.C. House of Representatives in 1869–70 and the state senate in 1870–72. In 1889 he was elected president of the North Carolina State Emigration Bureau, which advocated mainly for impoverished African American farmers to leave North Carolina in search of greater opportunities elsewhere. See William Gould, *Diary of a Contraband: The Civil War Passage of a Black Sailor*, ed. William Gould IV (Stanford: Stanford University Press, 2002), 29, 113, and Reaves, *"Strength through Struggle,"* esp. 449–51, 492–93.

41. Starkey to Kinsley, 10 Mar. 1865, Kinsley Papers, UMA.

42. *Wilmington Herald*, 8 Sept. 1865.

43. Ibid.

44. *Christian Recorder*, 28 Oct. 1865.

45. Ibid.

46. Ibid., 28 Aug., 9 Sept. (letter from Rev. G. A. Rue), 28 Oct. 1865. Though not elected a delegate at this gathering, another New Bern leader, Rev. James W. Hood, also attended the Raleigh convention.

47. Ibid., 28 Oct. 1865.

48. William McKee Evans, *Ballots and Fence Rails: Reconstruction on the Lower Cape Fear* (Chapel Hill: University of North Carolina Press, 1967), 87–91.

49. *Christian Recorder*, 28 Aug. 1865.

50. Ibid.

51. *Anglo-African*, 9 Dec. 1865.

52. Herbert Aptheker, ed., *A Documentary History of the Negro People in the United States* (New York: Citadel Press, 1951), 1:546.

53. *Christian Recorder*, 28 Oct. 1865. For background on James Harris, see James Harris Papers, NCSA.

54. John Richard Dennett, *The South as It Is, 1865–1866*, ed. Henry M. Christman (New York: Viking, 1965), 151–53. Quote is from the *Colored American* (Augusta, Ga.), 30 Dec. 1865.

55. *Journal of Freedom* (Raleigh, N.C.), 7 Oct. 1865 (copy, NCC). The quoted passage also refers to speeches that evening by James Harris and Isham Swett of Cumberland County. Both later served in the N.C. House of Representatives.

56. Ibid.

57. Ibid.; *Christian Recorder*, 28 Oct. 1865; *Anglo-African*, 11 Nov. 1865. The open letter appeared in all three newspapers.

58. On the centrality of domestic rights to African American political aspirations in postwar North Carolina, see especially Laura F. Edwards, *Gendered Strife*

and Confusion: The Political Culture of Reconstruction (Urbana: University of Illinois Press, 1997).

59. *Journal of Freedom*, 7 Oct. 1865.

60. Ibid. For a pivotal discussion of violence directed against African American homes and the use of rape as a weapon of political terrorism across the South, see Hannah Rosen, *Terror in the Heart of Freedom: Citizenship, Sexual Violence, and the Meaning of Race in the Postemancipation South* (Chapel Hill: University of North Carolina Press, 2009), esp. 179–221.

61. *Journal of Freedom*, 7 Oct. 1865.

62. Ibid.

63. By the middle of March 1865, African American leaders had organized statewide chapters of the National Equal Rights League in at least North Carolina, Louisiana, Pennsylvania, Massachusetts, Ohio, Tennessee, Missouri, Michigan, and New York. As the war ended, the headquarters of the national league had few resources to dedicate to organizing in the former Confederacy, however, and the league's northern leaders seemed cut off from their brethren in the South. The league's national office had no field organizers or lecturers and no publication. Drawing mainly on northern black activists, the governing board struggled even to get a quorum at quarterly meetings in 1864–65. At the league's first annual convention in Cleveland on 19 September 1865, only forty-one delegates attended; two-thirds came from Ohio or Pennsylvania. Only eight delegates represented the South. A second national convention, held in Washington, D.C., in January 1867, attempted to renew the organization's standing and reach out more wholeheartedly to ex-slaves in the South, but it had limited success. The organization gradually faded away at a national level, surviving, though, in a host of local auxiliaries, usually under different names, that took on lives of their own. Galloway is not known to have been at a national-level league meeting after the Syracuse convention. The last known mention of any of the Equal Rights Leagues in North Carolina is a reference to the Abraham Lincoln Equal Rights League in the *New Bern Republican*, 2 May 1867. See *Christian Recorder*, 24 Dec. 1864, 18 Feb., 14 Mar., 21 Oct. 1865, 21 Apr., 28 Aug., 3 Sept., 20 Nov., 2, 22 Dec. 1866, 2 Feb. 1867; *Anglo-African*, 4, 18 Feb. 1865; and *Proceedings of the First Annual Meeting of the National Equal Rights League, Held in Cleveland, Ohio, October 19, 20, and 21, 1865* (Philadelphia: E. C. Markey & Son, 1865).

64. *Journal of Freedom*, 7 Oct. 1865.

Chapter 13

1. *Minutes of the Freedmen's Convention, held in the City of Raleigh, on the 2nd, 3rd, 4th, and 5th of October, 1866* (Chapel Hill: Academic Affairs Library, University of North Carolina, 2001); *Proceedings of the First Annual Meeting of the National Equal Rights League, Held in Cleveland, Ohio, October 19, 20, and 21, 1865* (Philadelphia: E. C. Markeley & Son, 1865).

2. Born ca. 1852, Galloway's half-brother John W. Galloway was the son of his mother, Hester Hankins, and his stepfather, Amos Galloway. He may have been named after John Wesley Galloway, Abraham's father and Amos's owner prior to the war. The 1870 federal census lists John W. living at his parents' home in Wilmington and his occupation as "laborer." By 1900 the federal census lists him as a house carpenter. See Ninth and Twelfth Federal Censuses of the United States (1870, 1900): New Hanover County, N.C., Population Schedules, NA.

3. Ninth Federal Census of the United States (1870): New Hanover County, N.C., Population Schedule, NA.

4. David Cecelski, telephone interview with Charles Galloway, Brunswick County, N.C., 21 Sept. 2005.

5. *New National Era*, 22 Sept. 1870. Galloway is not listed in the city directories of New Bern or Wilmington in 1865–66. See Frank D. Smaw Jr., *Smaw's Wilmington Directory* (Wilmington, N.C.: Frank D. Smaw Jr., [ca. 1866]), and R. A. Shotwell, *New Bern Mercantile and Manufacturers' Business Directory and North Carolina Farmers Reference Book* (New Bern, N.C.: W. I. Vestal, 1866).

6. William McKee Evans, *Ballots and Fence Rails: Reconstruction on the Lower Cape Fear* (Chapel Hill: University of North Carolina Press, 1967), 93. How long the local Equal Rights Leagues remained active in Wilmington or elsewhere in North Carolina is not clear. The last known reference to the John Brown Equal Rights League, in New Bern, appears in the *New Bern Republican*, 2 May 1867.

7. Starkey to Kinsley, 27 July 1865, Correspondence, Edward W. Kinsley Papers, UMA.

8. Nancy Starkey to Mary Ann Starkey, 28 Apr. 1865, and Mary Ann Starkey to Kinsley, 5 May 1865, Kinsley Papers, UMA. Nancy Starkey's intended was Columbus Moore, who was, in her mother's words, "an industrious and honorable young man."

9. During the last part of the war and throughout 1865, Mary Ann Starkey stayed in touch with her friends from the North who had already departed New Bern, including Edward A. Wild and his wife but also Edward Kinsley and his wife and brother. They corresponded, exchanged gifts and birthday greetings, and did errands for one another. At Starkey's request, for instance, Kinsley purchased American flags for the Emancipation Day celebration in New Bern in January 1865, and Wild's wife acquired a wedding gown and other items for Nancy Starkey's wedding later that spring. Starkey paid for the items herself, though in the case of Mrs. Wild's errands, Kinsley assured Starkey that "we have purchased these of people who are of our way of thinking, and who put the prices below their regular selling price." See Kinsley to Starkey, 19 May 1865, Letter book, Edward W. Kinsley Papers, MSRC/HU; Starkey to Kinsley, 6 Dec. 1864, 4 Mar. 1865, Correspondence, Kinsley Papers, MSRC/HU; and F. E. Wild to Kinsley, 17 May 1865, Kinsley Papers, UMA.

10. Starkey to Kinsley, 27 July 1865, Kinsley Papers, UMA.

11. Ibid., 7 Sept. 1866.

12. No letters from Mary Ann Starkey after 1866 are known to have survived. The federal census still listed her as a boardinghouse keeper in New Bern in 1880, and she still resided in the city at the time of her mother's death. Her mother, Mary Bryan, died on 22 July 1889, at the age of 102. See Ninth and Tenth Federal Censuses of the United States (1870, 1880): Craven County, N.C., Population Schedules, NA, and *New Bern Daily Journal*, 23 July 1889.

13. Founded in 1858, St. Paul's Protestant Episcopal Church sat on the corner of South Fourth and Orange Streets. The church had black and white members from the beginning, though they sat apart or had separate worship services. After the war, the congregation remained interracial until the African American members left to establish St. Mark's Episcopal Church in 1871. The church also hosted a Freedmen's Bureau school during Reconstruction. See Bill Reaves, *"Strength through Struggle": The Chronological and Historical Record of the African-American Community in Wilmington, North Carolina, 1865–1950* (Wilmington, N.C.: New Hanover County Public Library, 1998), 125–26. On the Masonic orders and African American political activism more generally, see Peter P. Hinks, "John Marrant and the Meaning of Early Black Freemasonry," *William and Mary Quarterly*, 3rd ser., 64, no. 1 (Jan. 2007): 105–16, and Stephen Kantrowitz, "'Intended for the Better Government of Man': The Political History of African American Freemasonry in the Era of Emancipation," *Journal of American History* 96, no. 4 (Mar. 2010): 1001–26.

14. John Richard Dennett, *The South as It Is, 1865–1866*, ed. Henry M. Christman (New York: Viking, 1965), 42.

15. Quoted in Leon F. Litwack, *Been in the Storm So Long: The Aftermath of Slavery* (New York: Vintage, 1980), 271.

16. Allan Rutherford, "Annual Report of the 4th Sub-district of N.C., Wilmington," 25 Sept. 1867, and "Reports on the Orphan Asylum at Middle Sound," in Reports of Operations (1867–68), Records of the Assistant Commissioner for the State of North Carolina, Bureau of Refugees, Freedmen, and Abandoned Lands, 1865–70, RG 105, NA. See also "Reports of Outrages and Arrests: Reports of Outrages, June 1866–Dec. 1868," and "Reports of Arrest, Aug. 1866–Dec. 1868," ibid. For an overview of white terrorism and the racism prevalent among Union occupying forces in Reconstruction North Carolina, see Mark L. Bradley, *Bluecoats and Tar Heels: Soldiers and Civilians in Reconstruction North Carolina* (Lexington: University Press of Kentucky, 2009), esp. 195–99.

17. Evans, *Ballots and Fence Rails*, 64–81; Litwack, *Been in the Storm So Long*, 289.

18. Dennett, *South as It Is*, 110.

19. Evans, *Ballots and Fence Rails*, 83–85.

20. Abraham Galloway to Maj. Gen. O. O. Howard, 16 June 1866, Series 15: Letters Received (G-210 1866), Washington Headquarters, RG 105, M752, roll 32, NA.

21. Stephen Ward Angell, *Bishop Henry Turner and African-American Religion*

in the South (Knoxville: University of Tennessee Press, 1992), 61. On Turner's travails in locating Galloway during a visit to New Bern in 1864, see *Christian Recorder*, 14 Jan. 1865. On black organizing in Edgecombe County, N.C., see Gov. Jonathan Worth to Col. Bernford, Dec. 1866, Records of the Assistant Commissioner for the State of North Carolina, Bureau of Refugees, Freedmen, and Abandoned Lands, RG 105, Letters Received, roll 13, NA, cited in Steven Hahn, *A Nation under Our Feet: Black Political Struggles in the Rural South from Slavery to the Great Migration* (Cambridge, Mass.: Harvard University Press, 2003), 174.

22. Eric Foner, *Reconstruction: America's Unfinished Revolution, 1863–1877* (New York: Harper & Row, 1988), 228–80.

23. *Daily Journal* (Wilmington, N.C.), 20 July, 16 Nov. 1867.

24. *Wilmington Daily Post*, 13, 15, 23, 27 Aug. 1867; *Weekly North-Carolina Standard*, 21 Aug. 1867.

25. *Wilmington Daily Post*, 8 Sept. 1867.

26. *Tri-Weekly Standard* (Raleigh, N.C.), 7 Sept. 1867.

27. On the founding of the state's Republican Party, see Richard Lee Hoffman, "The Republican Party in North Carolina, 1867–1871" (M.A. thesis, University of North Carolina, Chapel Hill, 1960), esp. 13, 17–18. The seeds for the party's founding seem to have been sown first at a meeting in New Bern in August 1866, followed by a black mass meeting in Raleigh on 6 March 1867, then by what was described as the first "mixed meeting of colored and white" in the state capital on 27 March 1867. See *North Carolina Standard*, 13 Mar. 1867, and Hoffman, "Republican Party," 17–18.

28. *Weekly North-Carolina Standard*, 9, 11 Sept. 1867; *Tri-Weekly Standard* (Raleigh, N.C.), 7 Sept. 1867.

29. *Wilmington Daily Post*, 8 Sept. 1867.

30. *Wilmington Evening Star*, 25 Sept. 1867; *New National Era*, 22 Sept. 1870.

31. *New National Era*, 12 Sept. 1870.

32. On black firefighting companies in postwar Wilmington, see Reaves, "*Strength through Struggle,*" 185–98. On black firefighting brigades in the Reconstruction South, see Amy S. Greenberg, *Cause for Alarm: The Volunteer Fire Department in the Nineteenth-Century City* (Princeton, N.J.: Princeton University Press, 1998).

33. *Wilmington Daily Post*, 13 Sept., 12, 18 Oct. 1867. S. S. Ashley was a native of Rhode Island and a graduate of Oberlin College who entered the ministry in 1849 and served a church in Northboro, Massachusetts, until the Civil War. He first came to Wilmington in 1865 to do relief work among the former slaves and was an agent for the American Missionary Association and, later, the Freedmen's Bureau. See ibid., 3 May 1868.

34. Ibid., 15 Nov. 1867; *New Bern Republican*, 7 Nov. 1867 (cited in Hahn, *Nation under Our Feet*, 202–3).

35. *Wilmington Daily Post*, 19 Dec. 1867, 2 Jan. 1868. For a fuller account of the meeting with Thaddeus Stevens at his home on Capitol Hill, see the *Daily*

Evening Bulletin (Philadelphia, Pa.), 14 Dec. 1867. On the Freedmen's Bureau incident, see A. H. Galloway to O. O. Howard, 22 Dec. 1867, Letters Received, 2nd Military District, RG 393, NA, cited in Bradley, *Bluecoats and Tar Heels*, 179–81.

36. Evans, *Ballots and Fence Rails*, 95–97. On the constitutional convention in North Carolina and other southern states, see Richard L. Hume and Jerry B. Gough, *Blacks, Carpetbaggers, and Scalawags: The Constitutional Conventions of Radical Reconstruction* (Baton Rouge: Louisiana State University Press, 2008).

37. *Daily Journal*, 15 Feb., 18 Jan. 1868.

38. On Tourgée, see especially Mark Elliott, *Color-Blind Justice: Albion Tourgée and the Quest for Racial Equality from the Civil War to* Plessy v. Ferguson (New York: Oxford University Press, 2006). For insight into the convention's judiciary committee business, from the point of view of the committee's chairman, see the William Blount Rodman Papers, NCSA.

39. *Wilmington Daily Post*, 22 Jan. 1868. Two of Galloway's former political colleagues from New Bern, James W. Hood and Clinton D. Pierson, were also among the black delegates to the constitutional convention. See Leonard Bernstein, "The Participation of Negro Delegates in the Constitutional Convention of 1868 in North Carolina," *Journal of Negro History* 34, no. 4 (Oct. 1949): 390–409.

40. *Wilmington Daily Post*, 23, 25 Jan. 1868; *Weekly North-Carolina Standard*, 22 Jan. 1868.

41. *Wilmington Journal*, 14 Feb. 1868.

42. *Standard* (Raleigh, N.C.), 25 Jan., 17 Feb. 1868, cited in Bernstein, "Participation of Negro Delegates," 399, 407.

43. *Daily Journal*, 9, 15 Feb. 1868.

44. Quoted in Evans, *Ballots and Fence Rails*, 98.

45. *Daily Journal*, 19, 26 Feb. 1868.

46. *Wilmington Weekly Journal*, 28 Feb. 1868; *Daily Journal*, 23 Feb. 1868.

47. Calvin J. Cowles (1821–1907) was a Wilkes County, N.C., merchant who had strongly opposed secession, remained a Unionist throughout the war, and supported peace movements. Exempted from the Confederate army because of a lame leg, he was threatened with conscription, arrested at one point under charges of disloyal activities, and compelled to resign as postmaster of the little community of Walkerton for refusing to sign a loyalty oath. After the war, he became a Republican and served on the Council of State from May to December 1865. He lost elections to the constitutional convention of 1865 and the state senate in 1866. For a good survey of his political views and his service at the constitutional convention of 1868, see his personal correspondence in the Calvin J. Cowles Papers, NCSA.

48. *Wilmington Daily Post*, 4 Feb., 4 Apr. 1868. On antebellum debates over what to call free people of color in the northern states, see Patrick Rael, *Black Identity and Black Protest in the Antebellum North* (Chapel Hill: University of North Carolina Press, 2002), 82–117.

49. Evans, *Ballots and Fence Rails*, 95–97; *Daily Journal*, 3 Mar. 1867; Karin Zipf,

"No Longer under Cover[ture]: Marriage, Divorce, and Gender in the 1868 Constitutional Convention," in *North Carolinians in the Era of the Civil War and Reconstruction*, ed. Paul D. Escott (Chapel Hill: University of North Carolina Press, 2008), 193–219.

50. Entry for 22 Mar. 1868, Record of Burials and Baptisms, St. Paul's Episcopal Church archives, Wilmington, N.C.

51. *Daily Journal*, 17, 26 Mar., 14 Apr. 1868.

52. J. Kenneth Davis Jr., *Patriarch of the Lower Cape Fear: Governor James Moore and Descendants* (Wilmington, N.C.: New Hanover County Public Library, 2006), 70, 119–20; William Lord De Rossett, *Pictorial and Historical New Hanover County and Wilmington, North Carolina, 1723–1938* (Wilmington, N.C.: n.p., 1938), 30.

53. *Daily Journal*, 18, 19 Apr. 1868; *Wilmington Daily Post*, 7 Apr. 1868.

54. Evans, *Ballots and Fence Rails*, 98–102.

55. *Wilmington Daily Post*, 9, 10, 14, 16, 17 (letter from Galloway), 21 Apr. 1868 (letter from Galloway).

56. *Daily Journal*, 31 May 1868; *Weekly North-Carolina Standard*, 24 June 1868; *Wilmington Post*, 31 May 1868.

57. *Daily Journal*, 27 Sept. 1868.

58. For a thought-provoking analysis of the struggle for black voting rights and the perceived threat to white women in the South in a somewhat later era, see Jane Dailey, "The Limits of Liberalism in the New South: The Politics of Race, Sex, and Patronage in Virginia, 1879–1883," in *Jumpin' Jim Crow: Southern Politics from Civil War to Civil Rights*, ed. Jane Dailey, Glenda Elizabeth Gilmore, and Bryant Simon (Princeton, N.J.: Princeton University Press, 2000), 88–114.

59. *Weekly North-Carolina Standard*, 20 Aug. 1870; *Wilmington Daily Journal*, 13 Sept. 1868.

60. On conservative reaction to Galloway being placed on the statewide ballot, see the *Eagle* (Fayetteville, N.C.), 19 Oct. 1868, and William A. Graham to William A. Graham Jr., 28 Sept. 1868, in William Alexander Graham, *The Papers of William Alexander Graham*, ed. Max R. Williams (Raleigh: North Carolina Department of Cultural Resources, Division of Archives and History, 1984), 7:613.

61. *Wilmington Daily Post*, 25 Apr. 1868; Linda Gunter, "Abraham H. Galloway: First Black Elector," *North Carolina African-American Historical and Genealogical Society Quarterly*, Fall 1990, 9–10; *Eagle*, 1, 28 Oct., 16 Nov. 1868; *Wilmington Post*, 15 Nov. 1868 (circular letter to "Fellow Citizens" signed by Galloway), 7 Jan. 1869; *Weekly North-Carolina Standard*, 18 Nov. 1868.

62. *Christian Recorder*, 24 Sept. 1870. Commonly led by Union army veterans, the black militias had been sanctioned by state law to fight off foreign invasion or to quell domestic insurrections. During Reconstruction, however, Governor Holden authorized them as part of his efforts to quell Ku Klux Klan violence. In many ways, they acted as a military wing of the Republican Party. For background on black militias in the Reconstruction South, see Otis A. Singletary, *Negro Militia and Reconstruction* (Austin: University of Texas Press, 1957).

63. Allen W. Trelease, *White Terror: The Ku Klux Klan Conspiracy and Southern Reconstruction* (Baton Rouge: Louisiana State University Press, 1971), 189–225; Evans, *Ballots and Fence Rails*, 101–2, 145–48; William C. Harris, *William Woods Holden: Firebrand of North Carolina Politics* (Baton Rouge: Louisiana State University Press, 1987), 287–307.

64. Elizabeth Balanoff, "Negro Legislators in the North Carolina General Assembly, July, 1868–February, 1872," *NCHR* 49, no. 1 (Jan. 1972): 23–24, 27.

65. *Wilmington Daily Journal*, 20 July 1869; *Brooklyn Daily Eagle*, 15 June 1870.

66. *Wilmington Post*, 28 Nov. 1869.

67. *Wilmington Daily Journal*, 28 June 1868.

68. Ibid., 21 July 1868; *Weekly North-Carolina Standard*, 9, 23 Dec. 1868.

69. On Galloway's legislative battles with the state's railroad interests, see *Wilmington Post*, 28 Nov., 2, 9 (quote), 19 Dec. 1869.

70. *Wilmington Daily Journal*, 19 July 1868.

71. Ibid., 23 Aug. 1868.

72. Bradley, *Bluecoats and Tar Heels*, 196–223; Hannah Rosen, *Terror in the Heart of Freedom: Citizenship, Sexual Violence, and the Meaning of Race in the Postemancipation South* (Chapel Hill: University of North Carolina Press, 2009), 179–242.

73. *Wilmington Post*, 19 Dec. 1869. For more on Ku Klux Klan violence in North Carolina in 1868–70, see Bradley, *Bluecoats and Tar Heels*, 196–223 (see 213–14 for the Goldsboro incident).

74. *Wilmington Post*, 19 Dec. 1869.

75. *Wilmington Weekly Journal*, 2 Apr. 1869.

76. *New York Times*, 17 Sept. 1865.

77. *Wilmington Daily Journal*, 20 July 1869; *Wilmington Journal*, 4 Aug. 1870, in Bill Reaves Collection, NHCPL.

78. *Wilmington Post*, 30 July, 23 Aug., 24 Dec. 1868, 15 Apr. 1869.

79. *Wilmington Daily Journal*, 11 July 1868; *Journal of the Senate of the General Assembly of the State of North Carolina at Its 1868 Session* (Raleigh: M. S. Littlefield, 1869), 41–42.

80. *Journal of the Senate of the General Assembly of the State of North Carolina at Its Session of 1868–'69* (Raleigh: M. S. Littlefield, 1869), 360–61; Balanoff, "Negro Legislators," 34–36.

81. Balanoff, "Negro Legislators," 41–42, 44–48; *North Carolina Standard*, 21 Jan. 1868, 10 Feb. 1870; *Laws of North Carolina, 1868–69–70*, c. 77; letter from A. H. Galloway, George Z. French, and J. S. W. Eagles to Governor Holden, 10 Aug. 1869, Governors Papers, W. W. Holden, NCSA.

82. *Wilmington Daily Journal*, 30 July 1868; *Wilmington Post*, 7, 25 Feb., 18 Mar. 1869.

83. *Wilmington Post*, 16 July 1868. The introduction of Chinese laborers as a replacement for slave labor was being widely discussed in the Deep South but had also been proposed as a way of supplying labor for rice plantations near Wilming-

ton. See Moon-Ho Jung, *Coolies and Cane: Race, Labor, and Sugar in the Age of Emancipation* (Baltimore: Johns Hopkins University Press, 2006); *Carolina Farmer* (Wilmington, N.C.), 5 Nov. 1869; *Weekly North-Carolina Standard*, 29 Sept. 1869, 4 May 1870 (Galloway letter); *Wilmington Daily Journal*, 1 Sept. 1868.

84. An informative discussion of the collective outlook toward voting held by Reconstruction blacks is Elsa Barkley Brown, "Negotiating and Transforming the Public Sphere: African American Political Life in the Transition from Slavery to Freedom," *Public Culture* 7, no. 1 (Fall 1994): 107–46.

85. *Wilmington Daily Journal*, 27 Sept. 1868.

86. *Journal of the Senate of the General Assembly of the State of North Carolina at Its Session of 1868-'69*, 209, 223, 648; *Journal of the Senate of the General Assembly of the State of North Carolina at Its Session of 1869-'70* (Raleigh: M. S. Littlefield, 1870), 466; *Wilmington Journal*, Feb. 1869, in Bill Reaves Collection, NHCPL; *Wilmington Post*, 4 Feb. 1869; Balanoff, "Negro Legislators," 42–44.

87. *New National Era*, 22 Sept. 1870 (quote).

Epilogue

1. Martha Ann Little pension claim, 30 Jan. 1894, William L. Horner Collection, Frederick C. Douglass Papers, ECU.

2. Galloway's wife and sons returned to her family's home in Beaufort, N.C., sometime in the first decade after his death. In the 1880 federal census, Martha [Ann] Galloway is listed as the head of a Beaufort household that also included their sons, John, age fifteen, and Abraham, age ten. She remarried on 26 December 1887. Her new husband, Bright Little, died less than six years later. Thereafter she resided alone and made her living as a dressmaker and seamstress. She applied for a pension as the widow of Abraham Galloway in 1894 but was denied, as he was never enrolled in the regular army or navy. In September 1927, she gave a deposition regarding a pension claim made by the widow of another Abraham Galloway, also of Brunswick County, N.C., who had served in the Union army. Martha Ann died sometime between that deposition and 1930, as she is not listed in the 1930 federal census. The uncertainty of her year of death derives from the absence of either a will or a death certificate.

The adult lives of Abraham and Martha Ann's sons are obscure after 1880. The names of both disappeared from local and state censuses by 1900. The 1900 census listing for Martha Ann indicates that she still had two living children, though neither resided with her in Beaufort at the time. Her 1910 census listing indicates that she was the mother of only one living child by that time, though it does not say whether she lost John or Abraham Jr. A brief notice in the *Wilmington Star* in 1895 indicates that an "Abram Galloway (colored)" had been elected chairman of the Republican Party's executive committee in Brunswick County, N.C.; whether this refers to Martha Ann and Abraham's younger son is not clear. See Tenth, Twelfth, Thirteenth, Fourteenth, and Fifteenth Federal Censuses of the United

States (1880, 1900, 1910, 1920, 1930): Carteret County, N.C., NA; Martha A. Little, Widow's Declaration of Pension, 1 Feb. 1894, War Department: Adjutant General's Office, and Martha Annes [*sic*] Little deposition, 22 Sept. 1927, both in Celie Galloway Pension Application File (1927), U.S. Department of the Interior: Bureau of Pensions, VA; Carteret County: Index to Wills, 1745–1961, NCSA; Carteret County: Index to Vital Statistics, 1913–57, NCSA; and *Wilmington Star*, 6 July 1895.

3. *Raleigh Weekly Standard*, 7 Sept. 1870; *Wilmington Daily Journal*, 2–4, 10 Sept. 1870, 23 Apr. 1871, in Bill Reaves Collection, NHCPL; *Christian Recorder*, 24 Sept. 1870. According to his mother's affidavit, Abraham Jr. was born on 25 February 1870. See Martha Ann Little pension claim, 30 Jan. 1894, Horner Collection, Douglass Papers, ECU.

4. Eric Foner, *Reconstruction: America's Unfinished Revolution, 1863–1877* (New York: Harper & Row, 1988), 449–50.

5. *Wilmington Daily Journal*, 4 Aug. 1870.

6. *Wilmington Post*, 5 May, 9, 12, 16 June 1870.

7. William McKee Evans, *Ballots and Fence Rails: Reconstruction on the Lower Cape Fear* (Chapel Hill: University of North Carolina Press, 1967), 137–41.

8. *Wilmington Daily Journal*, 2, 3, 4 Sept. 1870.

9. *Christian Recorder*, 24 Sept. 1870; *New National Era*, 22 Sept. 1870. For a variety of other obituaries from Galloway's home state, see the *People's Press* (Salem, N.C.), 9 Sept. 1870; *Wilmington Morning Star*, 4 Sept. 1870; *Greensboro Patriot*, 8 Sept. 1870; and *Tarboro Southerner*, 8 Sept. 1870.

10. *Raleigh Weekly Standard*, 7 Sept. 1870.

11. On the white supremacy campaigns of 1898 and 1900 and their enduring consequences, see Glenda Elizabeth Gilmore, *Gender and Jim Crow: Women and the Politics of White Supremacy in North Carolina, 1896–1920* (Chapel Hill: University of North Carolina Press, 1996), and David S. Cecelski and Timothy B. Tyson, eds., *Democracy Betrayed: The Wilmington Race Riot of 1898 and Its Legacy* (Chapel Hill: University of North Carolina Press, 1998).

12. *Wilmington Post*, 1 July 1869.

13. The Wilmington City Council created Pine Forest Cemetery for the city's blacks in 1860. Sometime after Galloway's burial there in 1870, the section of the cemetery where his grave lay as marked on the cemetery's surviving maps disappeared. What happened to that section of the cemetery is unclear. Expansion of neighboring Oakdale and Bellevue cemeteries took up large portions of the land originally allotted to Pine Forest. Fences did not clearly demarcate the cemetery boundaries until the mid-twentieth century. Differences in Pine Forest Cemetery's boundaries are also evident in Sanborn Fire Insurance maps drawn between 1915 and 1946. The cemetery's internal maps are also inconclusive and do not agree with one another. Thus the section of the graveyard where Galloway was buried may now be a parking lot or a paved road, or it might have been taken up by an adjacent cemetery. See Pine Forest cemetery records, Pine Forest

Cemetery, Wilmington, N.C., and Sanborn Fire Insurance Maps, Wilmington, N.C., 1915, 1946 (microfilm, NCC).

14. The *Wilmington Journal* claimed that Galloway had insured his life for $10,000 but that the policy had lapsed because he could not afford to make the payments. The following spring, the newspaper reported that African American state senator George Mabson had created a fund to benefit Galloway's family, "who were left entirely destitute by this death." See *Wilmington Daily Journal*, 10 Sept. 1870, 23 Apr. 1871.

15. *Wilmington Morning Star*, 4 Sept. 1870.

16. *Christian Recorder*, 24 Sept. 1870; *Wilmington Journal*, 2–4 Sept. 1870, in Reaves Collection, NHCPL; *Raleigh Weekly Standard*, 17 Sept. 1870. A native of Boston, Rev. George Patterson had originally come to North Carolina before the war, as chaplain for Josiah Collins's plantation at Lake Phelps in Washington County. See J. G. de Roulhac Hamilton, ed., *The Papers of Thomas Ruffin* (Raleigh: N.C. Historical Commission, 1920), 3:486.

Bibliography

Primary Sources

MANUSCRIPT COLLECTIONS

Albany, N.Y.
  New York State Library/Archives
    John E. Wool Papers
Amherst, Mass.
  University of Massachusetts, W. E. B. Du Bois Library, Special Collections
    Edward W. Kinsley Papers
Ann Arbor, Mich.
  University of Michigan, William C. Clements Library, Manuscript Division
    William H. and Edwin C. Burbank Papers
    Point Lookout, Md., Prison Camp Records
    Martin Webster Journal
Atlanta, Ga.
  Emory University
    Manuscript, Archives, and Rare Book Library
      Hale Wesson Papers
Boston, Mass.
  Bostonian Society
    Account Book of Francis Jackson, Vigilance Committee of Boston
    Subscription Book, Mass. Committee to Aid in the Enlistment of
      Colored Troops
  Boston Public Library, Rare Books and Manuscripts Division
    Anti-Slavery Collection
    Haitian Bureau of Emigration, Reports and Correspondence, 1860–61
  Massachusetts Archives
    Gov. John A. Andrew: Executive and Official Files
    Massachusetts State Census, 1865
    Provost Marshal Papers

Massachusetts Historical Society
  John A. Andrew Papers
  Edward Jarvis Bartlett Correspondence
  John E. Bassett Diary
  Boston Anti-Man-Hunting League Records
  Henry I. Bowditch Papers
  Charles E. Briggs Letters
  Charles H. Dalton Official Correspondence
  Charles H. Dalton Papers
  William Wallace Davis Letters
  DeGrasse-Howard Family Papers
  Everett-Peabody Family Papers
  Norwood P. Hallowell Papers
  Hartwell-Clark Family Papers
  John Hay Diaries
  Samuel Gridley Howe Letters
  Edward Kinsley Papers
  New England Emigrant Aid Company Records
  New England Freedmen's Aid Society Records
  George L. Stearns Papers
  Samuel Storrow Correspondence and Diaries
  John W. Trafton Papers
  Troup Family Papers
  Union League of America, Council No. 13 Papers
  Henry F. Wellington Correspondence and Diary
  Charles M. Whelden Papers
Massachusetts State Library
  Alfred S. Hartwell Papers
Brookline, Mass.
  Brookline Public Library
    Edward Augustus Wild Papers
Cambridge, Mass.
  Harvard University, Houghton Library
    Crawford Blagden Collection
    William Lloyd Garrison Papers
    Wendell Phillips Collection
  Harvard University, Schlesinger Library, Radcliffe Institute for
      Advanced Study
    James C. Beecher Papers
Carlisle Barracks, Pa.
  United States Army Military History Institute
    Military Order of the Loyal Legion of the United States Collection
    Miscellaneous Civil War Collection

Chapel Hill, N.C.
    University of North Carolina at Chapel Hill, Southern Historical Collection
            at the Wilson Library
        Edmund Cleveland Diary
        Moses Ashley Curtis Correspondence and Diary
        Walter Gilman Curtis Papers
        William F. Loftin Papers
        New Bern Occupation Papers
        Edward Augustus Wild Papers
    University of North Carolina at Chapel Hill, Wilson Library, North Carolina
            Collection
        Newspaper Collection
Charleston, S.C.
    Charleston County Public Library
        Newspaper Collection
Charlottesville, Va.
    University of Virginia, Alderman Library, Special Collections Department
        Edward A. Wild Letter
Columbus, Ohio
    Ohio Historical Society
        Wilbur H. Siebert Collection
        Boyd B. Stutler Collection of John Brown Papers
Concord, Mass.
    Concord Free Public Library
        Franklin Sanborn Papers
Durham, N.C.
    Duke University, David M. Rubenstein Rare Book and Manuscript Library
        Board of Commissioners of Navigation and Pilotage for the Cape Fear
            River and Bar Papers
        James West Bryan Family Papers
        Benjamin Sherwood Hedrick Papers
        Edward W. Kinsley Papers
        James Redpath Letter Press Book
        David P. Reynolds Papers
Freemont, Ohio
    Rutherford B. Hayes Presidential Center
        John Brown Jr. Papers, Charles E. Frohman Collection
Greenville, N.C.
    East Carolina University, J. Y. Joyner Library, Manuscripts and Rare Books
            Department
        Frederick C. Douglass Papers
        Gooding Family Papers
        New Bern Historical Society Papers

Hammond, La.
   University of Southeast Louisiana, Center for Southeast Louisiana
       Studies Archive
      Halbert Paine Papers
Hartford, Conn.
   Connecticut Historical Society
      Andrews Folder
      Charles A. Boyle Letters
      Civil War Papers
      Oliver W. Gates Diary
      Tracey Collection
Honolulu, Hawaii
   Hawaii State Archives
      Alfred Stedman Hartwell Papers
Ithaca, N.Y.
   Cornell University, Carl Kroch Library, Rare and Special Collections
      Samuel J. May Anti-Slavery Collection
Kingston, Ontario
   Kingston-Frontenac County Public Library
      Kingston Historical Society Papers
New Orleans, La.
   Tulane University, Amistad Research Center
      American Missionary Association Archives
Newton, Mass.
   Jackson Homestead Museum/Newton History Museum and Historical
      Society
      Jackson Homestead Collection
   Newton Free Public Library
      Newton Collection
New York, N.Y.
   New-York Historical Society
      Theodore S. Billings Diary
      Massachusetts Anti-Slavery Society Records
   New York Public Library, Manuscripts Division
      Griswold Family Letters
      Elizabeth Van Lew Papers
      Maloney Collection of McKim-Garrison Family Papers
      Charles Alexander Nelson Papers
   New York Public Library, Schomburg Center for Research in Black Culture,
      Manuscript, Archives and Rare Books Division
      James Redpath Letterbook
Philadelphia, Pa.
   Historical Society of Pennsylvania

    Pennsylvania Society for Promoting the Abolition of Slavery Papers
    William Still Papers
Providence, R.I.
  John Hay Library, Brown University
    John Hay Papers
  Providence Public Library, Special Collections Department
    C. Fiske Harris Collection on the Civil War and Slavery
  Rhode Island Historical Society
    Ambrose E. Burnside Collection
Raleigh, N.C.
  North Carolina State Archives
    Brunswick County Estate Records
    Brunswick County Wills, 1765–1912
    Carteret County: Index to Vital Statistics, 1913–1957
    Carteret County: Index to Wills, 1745–1961
    Calvin J. Cowles Papers
    Governors Papers, W. W. Holden
    James Harris Papers
    Marriages of Craven County, 1851–1905
    New Hanover County: Record of Cohabitation, 1866–1868
    New Hanover County Wills
    Levi W. Pigott Collection
Richmond, Va.
  Virginia Historical Society
    C. J. Paine Papers
    Franz Wilhelm von Schilling Papers
St. Louis, Mo.
  Missouri Historical Society
    Lucien Eaton Papers
Syracuse, N.Y.
  Onondaga County Public Library
    Local History Collection
  Onondaga Historical Association Research Center
  Syracuse University, Special Collections Research Center
    Charles Baldwin Sedgwick Papers
    Gerrit Smith Broadside and Pamphlet Collection
    Gerrit Smith Papers
Topeka, Kans.
  Kansas State Historical Society
    Thomas Wentworth Higginson Papers
    James Montgomery Papers
    George and Mary Stearns Papers
    George L. Stearns Papers

Washington, D.C.
  Howard University, Moorland-Spingarn Research Center
    George Downing Papers
    Edward W. Kinsley Papers
  Library of Congress, Manuscripts Division
    Benjamin F. Butler Papers
    Frederick Douglass Papers
    Edward W. Kinsley Papers
    Abraham Lincoln Papers
    James Redpath Papers
    Edwin M. Stanton Papers
    Lewis Tappan Papers
  National Archives
    Adjutant General's Office, Division of Colored Troops, Record Group 94
    Bureau of Refugees, Freedmen, and Abandoned Lands, Records of the
      Assistant Commissioner for the State of North Carolina, Record
      Group 105
    Presidential Proclamations, 1791–1991, Record Group 11
    State of North Carolina, Southern Claims Commission, Summary Report,
      Treasury Department, Special Agents Records, Record Group 366
    U.S. Army, Dept. of Virginia and North Carolina, Letters Sent, 1864, Record
      Group 393
    U.S. Army, Dept. of Virginia and North Carolina, Registrar of Letters
      Received, 1863, Record Group 393
    U.S. Army, District of North Carolina, Letters Received, 18 Oct. 1864–1
      Mar. 1865, Record Group 393
    U.S. Army, Washington Headquarters (Record Group 105), Letters Received
      (G-210), 1866
    U.S. Consulate, Despatches from United States Consuls in St. Marc, Haiti,
      1861–1891 (NA microform publication T-486)
West Point, N.Y.
  United States Military Academy Cadet Library at West Point,
      Special Collections
    John James Peck Papers
Wilmington, N.C.
  Front Street Methodist Church
    Record of Births, Baptisms and Burials
  Lower Cape Fear Historical Society
    Genealogical Collections
    B. Frank Hall Memoirs
  New Hanover County Public Library, North Carolina Room
    Lola James Collection
    Bill Reaves Collection

Pine Forest Cemetery
    Pine Forest Cemetery Records
St. Paul's Episcopal Church
    Burial Records, Vestry Minutes, 1858–1917
University of North Carolina at Wilmington, William Madison Randall
        Library, Special Collections
    Nicholas W. Schenck Diary
    Wood Family Papers
Winston-Salem, N.C.
  Veterans Administration Hospital
    Pension Files
Worcester, Mass.
  American Antiquarian Society
    Chase Family Papers
    Horace James Correspondence and Papers
    Pamphlet Collection
    Samuel Staples Papers

NEWSPAPERS AND PERIODICALS

American Missionary

Boston Evening Transcript

British Whig (Kingston, Ontario)

Carolina Farmer (Wilmington, N.C.)

Charlotte Daily Bulletin (N.C.)

Chatham Weekly Planet (Ontario)

Christian Recorder (Philadelphia)

Colored American (Augusta, Ga.)

Colored Tennessean (Nashville)

Commonwealth (Boston)

Daily Dispatch (Richmond, Va.)

Daily Evening Bulletin (Philadelphia, Pa.)

Daily Journal (Wilmington, N.C.)

Daily News (Kingston, Ontario)

Douglass' Monthly (Rochester, N.Y.)

Eagle (Fayetteville, N.C.)

Free Democrat (Milwaukee, Wisc.)

Freedmen's Journal (Boston)

Freedmen's Reporter (Cincinnati/
    Indianapolis)

Globe (Boston)

Globe (Toronto, Canada West)

Greensboro Patriot (N.C.)

Harvard Register (Cambridge, Mass.)

Journal of Freedom (Raleigh, N.C.)

Liberator (New York, N.Y.)

Le Moniteur Haitien (Port-au-Prince)

National Anti-Slavery Standard
    (New York, N.Y.)

National Era (Washington, D.C.)

National Freedman (New York, N.Y.)

New Bedford Mercury (Mass.)

New Bern Daily Journal

New Bern Republican

New Bern Weekly Times

New National Era (Washington, D.C.)

New Orleans Tribune

New York Daily Tribune

New York Express

New York Herald

New York Post

New York Times

New York Tribune

North Carolina Times (New Bern)

North Carolinian (Raleigh)

Old North State (Beaufort, N.C.)

Onondaga Standard (Syracuse, N.Y.)
People's Press (Salem, N.C.)
Philadelphia Inquirer
Pine and Palm (Boston, Mass., and New York, N.Y.)
Post (Wilmington, N.C.)
Provincial Freeman (Toronto)
Provincial Freeman and Weekly Advertiser (Chatham, Ontario)
Raleigh Weekly Standard (N.C.)
Richmond Daily Dispatch (Va.)
Right Way (Boston)
Semi-Weekly Messenger (Wilmington, N.C.)
Sentinel (Raleigh, N.C.)
Standard Laconic (Snow Hill, N.C.)
Syracuse Courier and Union (N.Y.)

Syracuse Daily Standard (N.Y.)
Syracuse Journal (N.Y.)
Tarboro Southerner (N.C.)
Tribune (Beaufort, N.C.)
Tri-Weekly Standard (Raleigh, N.C.)
L'Union (New Orleans)
Weekly Anglo-African/Anglo-African (New York, N.Y.)
Weekly North-Carolina Standard (Raleigh)
Wilmington Daily Journal (N.C.)
Wilmington Herald
Wilmington Journal
Wilmington Messenger
Wilmington Post
Wilmington Star

OTHER PUBLISHED PRIMARY SOURCES

American Anti-Slavery Society. *Anti-Slavery History of the John Brown Year, Being the Twenty-Seventh Annual Report of the American Anti-Slavery Society.* New York: American Anti-Slavery Society, 1861.

Andrew, John A. *Sketch of the Official Life of John A. Andrew, as Governor of Massachusetts.* New York: Hurd & Houghton, 1868.

Andrew, John A., and Benjamin F. Butler. *Correspondence between Gov. Andrew and Major General Butler.* Boston: J. J. Dyer & Co., 1862.

Andrews, Sidney. *The South Since the War; As Shown by Fourteen Weeks of Travel and Observation in Georgia and the Carolinas.* Boston: Ticknor & Fields, 1866.

Aptheker, Herbert, ed. *A Documentary History of the Negro People in the United States.* New York: Citadel Press, 1951.

Beauchamp, Eula Pearl. *Craven County, North Carolina Cemeteries.* New Bern: Eastern North Carolina Genealogical Society, [1995?].

Beitzell, Edwin Warfield. *Point Lookout Prison Camp for Confederates.* Abell, Md., 1972.

Benjamin, W. S. *The Great Epidemic in New Berne and Vicinity, September and October 1864, By One who Passed through it.* New Bern, N.C.: Geo. Mills Joy, 1865.

Berlin, Ira, Barbara Fields, Thavolia Glymph, Joseph P. Reidy, and Leslie S. Rowland, eds. *Freedom: A Documentary History of Emancipation, 1861–1867.* Cambridge: Cambridge University Press, 1982–2010.

Branson, Levi. *Branson's North Carolina Business Directory.* Raleigh: L. Branson, 1877.

Brown, William Wells. *The Narrative of William W. Brown, a Fugitive Slave, Written by Himself.* Boston: Anti-Slavery Office, 1847.

Burlingame, John K., ed. *History of the Fifth Regiment of Rhode Island Heavy Artillery during Three Years and a Half of Service in North Carolina.* Providence: Snow & Farnham, 1892.

Butler, Benjamin F. *Autobiography and Personal Reminiscences of Major-General Benj. F. Butler.* Boston: A. M. Thayer & Co., 1892.

———. *Private and Official Correspondence of Gen. Benjamin F. Butler, during the period of the Civil War.* Norwood, Mass.: Plimpton Press, 1917.

Chandler, Peleg W. *Memoir of Governor Andrew, with Personal Reminiscences.* Boston: Roberts Brothers, 1880.

Chataigne, J. Henry. *Chataigne's Raleigh City Directory: Containing a general directory of the citizens of Raleigh, together with a complete business directory of the cities of Raleigh, Charlotte, Durham, Fayetteville, Greensboro', Newbern and Wilmington; also a list of post offices of the states of North Carolina, Virginia and West Va.* Raleigh: J. H. Chataigne, 1875.

Clapp, Henry A. *Letters to the Home Circle: The North Carolina Service of Pvt. Henry A. Clapp.* Edited by John R. Barden. Raleigh: North Carolina Department of Cultural Resources, Division of Archives and History, 1998.

Colyer, Vincent. *Brief Report of the Services Rendered by the Freed People to the United States Army, in North Carolina, in the Spring of 1862, after the Battle of Newbern.* New York: Vincent Colyer, 1864.

Crabtree, Beth Gilbert, and James W. Patton, eds. *Journal of a Secesh Lady: The Diary of Catherine Ann Devereux Edmondston, 1860–1866.* Raleigh: North Carolina Department of Cultural Resources, Division of Archives and History, 1979.

Curtis, Walter Gilman. *Reminiscences of Wilmington and Southport, 1848–1900.* Wilmington, N.C.: n.p., 1905. Republished by Southport Historical Society, 1999.

Day, D. L. *My Diary of Rambles with the 25 Mass. Volunteer Infantry, with Burnside's Coast Division: 18th Army Corps and Army of the James.* Milford, Mass.: King & Billings, 1884.

Dennett, John Richard. *The South as It Is, 1865–1866.* Edited by Henry M. Christman. New York: Viking, 1965.

Denny, J. Waldo. *Wearing the Blue in the 25th Mass. Volunteer Infantry.* Worcester, Mass.: Putnam & Davis, 1879.

Derby, W. P. *Bearing Arms in the Twenty-Seventh Massachusetts Regiment of Volunteer Infantry during the Civil War, 1861–1865.* Boston: Wright & Potter, 1883.

Directory of the City of Boston: Embracing the City Record, General Directory of the Citizens and a Special Directory of Trades, Professions, Etc. Boston: George Adams, 1850.

Douglass, Frederick. *The Frederick Douglass Papers.* Series 1, *Speeches, Debates and Interviews.* Vol. 3, *1855–63.* Edited by John W. Blassingame. New Haven: Yale University Press, 1985.

———. *Life and Times of Frederick Douglass*. Boston: De Wolfe and Fiscke, 1892.

———. *Life and Times of Frederick Douglass: His Early Life as a Slave, His Escape from Bondage, and His Complete History to the Present Time*. Hartford, Conn.: Park, 1881.

———. "Lincoln and the Colored Troops." In *Reminiscences of Abraham Lincoln by Distinguished Men of His Time*, edited by Allen Thorndike Rice, 315–25. New York: Harper and Brothers, 1909.

———. *Narrative of the Life of Frederick Douglass, an American Slave*. Edited by Deborah E. McDowell. New York: Oxford University Press, 1999.

Drake, Madison. *The History of the Ninth New Jersey Volunteers*. Elizabeth, N.J.: Journal Printing House, 1889.

Drew, Benjamin. *The Refugee: Narratives of Fugitive Slaves in Canada*. Toronto: Dundurn Press, 2008. Originally published in 1856.

Emmerton, James A. *A Record of the Twenty-third Regiment, Mass. Vol. Infantry, in the War of the Rebellion, 1861–1865*. Boston: William Ware & Co., 1886.

Fiske, Joseph E. "An Involuntary Journey through the Confederacy." In *Civil War Papers Read before the Commandery of the State of Massachusetts, Military Order of the Loyal Legion of the United States*, 2:513–29. Boston: F. H. Gilson Co., 1900.

Flynn, Thomas, ed. *Directory of the city of Kingston for 1857–1858; with Statistical and General Information Respecting the United Counties of Frontenac, Lennox and Addington, and Descriptive Notices of the Towns and Villages Therein*. Kingston, Canada West: T. W. Robison, 1857.

Freedman's Savings and Trust Company. *Registers of Signatures of Depositors in Branches of the Freedman's Savings and Trust Company, 1865–1874*. Washington, D.C.: National Archives and Records Service, 1969.

Gardner, James Brown. *Record of the Forty-Fourth Massachusetts Volunteer Militia in North Carolina, August 1862 to May 1863*. Boston: privately printed, 1887.

Garrison, Wendell Phillips, and Francis Jackson Garrison. *William Lloyd Garrison, 1805–1879: The Story of His Life Told By His Children*. 4 vols. Boston: Houghton, Mifflin, 1894.

Garrison, William Lloyd. *The Letters of William Lloyd Garrison*. 6 vols. Edited by Walter M. Merrill and Louis Ruchames. Cambridge, Mass.: Belknap Press of Harvard University Press, 1971–81.

Gen. Stevenson. Cambridge, Mass.: Welch, Bigelow & Co., 1864[?].

Goss, Warren Lee. *The Soldier's Story of His Captivity at Andersonville, Belle Isle, and Other Rebel Prisons*. Boston: Lee and Shepard, 1867.

Gould, William. *Diary of a Contraband: The Civil War Passage of a Black Sailor*. Edited by William Gould IV. Stanford: Stanford University Press, 2002.

Graham, William Alexander. *The Papers of William Alexander Graham*. Edited by Max R. Williams. Raleigh: North Carolina Department of Cultural Resources, Division of Archives and History, 1984.

Green, John P. *Fact Stranger than Fiction: Seventy-Five Years of a Busy Life with Reminiscences of Many Great and Good Men and Women*. Cleveland: Riehl Printing Co., 1920.

———. *Recollections of the Inhabitants, Localities, Superstitions and KuKlux Outrages of the Carolinas. By a "Carpet-Bagger" who was Born and Lived there*. [Cleveland?], 1880.

Haines, Zenas T. *"In the Country of the Enemy": The Civil War Reports of a Massachusetts Corporal*. Edited by William C. Harris. Gainesville: University of Florida Press, 1999.

[———] *"Corporal." Letters from the Forty-fourth Regiment M.V.M.: A Record of the Experience of a Nine Months' Regiment in the Department of North Carolina in 1862-3*. Boston: Herald Job Office, 1863.

Hall, Louis Philip. *Land of the Golden River: Historical Events and Stories of Southeastern North Carolina and the Lower Cape Fear*. Vol. 2, *This Fair Land of Ours*. Wilmington, N.C.: Hall, 1975.

Hamilton, J. G. de Roulhac, ed. *The Papers of Thomas Ruffin*, vol. 3. Raleigh: N.C. Historical Commission, 1920.

Hendrick, George, and Willene Hendrick, eds. *Fleeing for Freedom: Stories of the Underground Railroad as Told by Levi Coffin and William Still*. Chicago: Ivan R. Dee, 2004.

Henson, Josiah. *The Life of Josiah Henson, Formerly a Slave, Now an Inhabitant of Canada, as Narrated by Himself*. Boston: Arthur D. Phelps, 1849.

Holden, William Woods. *The Papers of William Woods Holden*, vol. 1 (1841–68). Edited by Horace W. Raper. Raleigh: North Carolina Department of Cultural Resources, Division of Archives and History, 2000.

Hood, J. W. *One Hundred Years of the African Methodist Episcopal Zion Church*. New York: AME Zion Book Concern, 1895.

———. *Sketch of the Early History of the African Episcopal Methodist Church*. Charlotte, N.C.: A.M.E. Zion Publishing House, 1914.

Hutt, Charles Warren. "Diary of Charles Warren Hutt." In Beitzell, *Point Lookout Prison Camp for Confederates*, 65–87.

Insurance Maps of Wilmington, New Hanover County, North Carolina. New York: Sanborn Map Co., 1904.

Irwin, Richard Biddle. *History of the Nineteenth Army Corps*. New York: G. P. Putnam's Sons, 1893.

James, Horace. *Annual Report of the Superintendent of Negro Affairs in North Carolina, 1864*. Boston: W. F. Brown & Co., 1865.

The John Brown Song, or Glory Hallelujah. Chicago: Root & Cady, 1861.

Johnson, James. *The Life of the Late James Johnson (Colored Evangelist), an Escaped Slave from the Southern States of America*. Oldham, England: W. Galley, n.d.

Jones, George W. *In Prison at Point Lookout*. Martinsville, Va.: n.p., n.d.

Jones, Thomas H. *The Experience of Thomas H. Jones, Who Was a Slave for Forty-Three Years*. Boston: Bazin & Chandler, 1862.

Journal of the Forty-Ninth Annual Council of the Protestant Episcopal Church in the State of North Carolina. Raleigh: J. C. Gorman, 1865.

Journals of the Senate of the General Assembly of the State of North Carolina. Raleigh: M. S. Littlefield, 1868–70.

Keeler, Ralph. "Owen Brown's Escape from Harpers Ferry." *Atlantic Monthly* 33 (March 1874): 342–66.

Kingman, Bradford. *Memoir of Gen. Edward Augustus Wild.* Boston: D. Clapp & Son, 1895.

Kirwan, Thomas. *Soldiering in North Carolina.* Boston: T. Kirwan, 1864.

Kittinger, Joseph. *Diary, 1861–1865: Joseph Kittinger, 23rd New York Independent Battery.* Buffalo, N.Y.: Kittinger Co. and Buffalo and Erie County Historical Society, 1963.

Langston, John Mercer. *From the Virginia Plantation to the Nation's Capital.* Hartford, Conn.: American Publishing Co., 1894.

Levine, Robert S., ed. *Martin R. Delany: A Documentary Reader.* Chapel Hill: University of North Carolina Press, 2003.

Lincoln, Abraham. *The Collected Works of Abraham Lincoln.* Washington, D.C.: Lincoln Sesquicentennial Commission, 1959.

Loguen, Jermain Wesley. *The Reverend J. W. Loguen, as a Slave and as a Freeman: A Narrative of Real Life.* Syracuse, N.Y.: J. G. K. Truair and Co., 1859.

Mann, Albert W. *History of the Forty-Fifth Regiment Massachusetts Volunteer Militia.* Jamaica Plain, Mass.: Brookside Print, 1908.

Marable, Manning, and Leith Mullings, eds. *Let Nobody Turn Us Around: Voices of Resistance, Reform, and Renewal: An African-American Anthology.* Lanham, Md.: Rowman & Littlefield, 1999.

Mason, Isaac. *Life of Isaac Mason, as a Slave.* Worcester, Mass.: n.p., 1893.

Minutes of the Freedmen's Convention, held in the city of Raleigh, on the 2nd, 3rd, 4th, and 5th of October, 1866. Chapel Hill: Academic Affairs Library, University of North Carolina, 2001.

Moore, John Jamison. *History of the A.M.E. Zion Church in America, Founded in 1796, in the City of New York.* York, Pa.: Teachers' Journal Office, 1884.

National Equal Rights League. *Proceedings of the first annual meeting of the National Equal Rights League held in Cleveland, Ohio, October 19, 20, and 21, 1865.* Philadelphia: E. C. Markey and Son, 1865.

Niven, John, ed. *The Salmon P. Chase Papers.* Kent, Ohio: Kent State University Press, 1993.

North Carolina Constitutional Convention. *Journal of the Constitutional Convention of the State of North Carolina, at Its Session 1868.* Raleigh, N.C.: Printed by Joseph W. Holden, 1868.

Park, Robert Emory. "War Diary of Robert Emory Park." *Southern Historical Society Papers* 26 (1898): 1–31.

Parker, Allen. *Recollections of Slavery Times.* Worcester, Mass.: Chas. W. Burbank & Sons, 1895.

Parker, Bowdoin S. *What One Grand Army Post Has Accomplished: History of Edward W. Kinsley Post, No. 113, Department of Massachusetts, Grand Army of the Republic, Boston, Mass.* Norwood, Mass.: Norwood Press, 1913.

Parton, James. *General Butler in New Orleans: History of the Administration of the Department of the Gulf in the Year 1862.* New York: Mason Brothers, 1864.

Pearson, William Henry. *Recollections and Records of Toronto of Old, with References to Brantford, Kingston and other Canadian Towns.* Toronto: William Briggs, 1914.

Pennington, J. W. C. *The Fugitive Blacksmith.* London: Charles Gilpin, 1849.

Proceedings of the First Annual Meeting of the National Equal Rights League, Held in Cleveland, Ohio, October 19, 20, and 21, 1865. Philadelphia: E. C. Markey & Son, 1865.

Proceedings of the National Convention of Colored Men, Held in the City of Syracuse, N.Y., Oct. 4, 5, 6 and 7, 1864; With the Bill of Wrongs and Rights and the Address to the American People. Boston: J. S. Rock & Geo. L. Ruffin, 1864.

Proceedings of the National Convention of the Colored Citizens of the United States, 1864. Reprinted in Herbert Aptheker, *A Documentary History of the Negro People in the United States,* vol. 1. New York: Citadel Press, 1951.

Putnam, Samuel H. *The Story of Company A, Twenty-Fifth Regiment, Mass. Vols., in the War of the Rebellion.* Worcester, Mass.: Putnam, Davis, & Co., 1886.

Redpath, James. *Guide to Hayti.* New York: G. Woolworth Colton, 1861.

———. *The Public Life of Captain John Brown.* Boston: Thayer and Eldridge, 1860.

Register of Deaths and Births, Bellevue Cemetery, Wilmington, N.C. Wilmington: University of North Carolina at Wilmington Printing Services, 1999.

Registers of Signatures of Depositors in Branches of the Freedman's Savings and Trust Company, 1865–1874, heritagequestonline.com. Accessed 29 November 2011.

Ripley, C. Peter, ed. *The Black Abolitionist Papers.* Vol. 2, *Canada, 1830–1865.* Chapel Hill: University of North Carolina Press, 1987.

Robinson, William H. *From Log Cabin to the Pulpit; or, Fifteen Years in Slavery.* 3rd ed. Eau Claire, Wisc.: James H. Tifft, 1913.

Roe, Alfred S. *The Twenty-Fourth Regiment Massachusetts Volunteers, 1861–1866.* Worcester, Mass.: Twenty-Fourth Veterans Association, 1907.

Rogers, Edward H. *Reminiscences of Military Service in the Forty-Third Regiment, Massachusetts Infantry, during the Great Civil War, 1862–63.* Boston: Franklin Press, 1883.

Rush, Christopher, and George Collins. *A Short Account of the Rise and Progress of the African M.E. Church in America.* New York: the author, 1843.

Sammons, Helen Moore. *Marriage and Death Notices from Wilmington, North Carolina, Newspapers, 1860–1865.* Wilmington, N.C.: North Carolina Room, New Hanover County Public Library, 1987.

Sanborn, Frank. "Henry David Thoreau." *Harvard Register* 3 (April 1881): 215.

———. "John Brown and His Friends." *Atlantic Monthly* 30 (July 1872): 52–54.

———. *Life and Letters of John Brown, Liberator of Kansas, and Martyr of Virginia.* Concord, Mass.: F. Sanborn, 1885.

Schlesinger, Arthur M., ed. "A Blue Bluejacket's Letters Home, 1863–1864." *New England Quarterly* 1, no. 4 (October 1928): 554–67.

Shotwell, R. A. *New Bern Mercantile and Manufacturers' Business Directory and North Carolina Farmers Reference Book.* New Bern, N.C.: W. I. Vestal, 1866.

Singleton, William H. *Recollections of My Slavery Days.* Edited by Katherine Mellen Charron and David S. Cecelski. Raleigh: North Carolina Department of Cultural Resources, Division of Archives and History, 1999.

Smaw, Frank D., Jr. *Smaw's Wilmington Directory.* Wilmington, N.C.: Frank D. Smaw Jr., [ca. 1866].

Sprunt, James, *Chronicles of the Cape Fear River, 1660–1916.* Raleigh: Edwards & Broughton, 1916.

Statistics of the operations of the Executive Board of the Friends' Association of Philadelphia and Its Vicinity, for the Relief of the Colored Freedmen. Philadelphia: Inquirer Printing Office, 1864.

Still, William. *The Underground Railroad: A Record of Facts, Authentic Narratives, Letters, etc., Narrating the Hardships, Hair-Breadth Escapes, and Death Struggles of the Slaves in their Efforts for Freedom.* Philadelphia: Porter & Coates, 1872.

U.S. Adjutant-General's Office. *The Negro in the Military Service of the United States, 1639–1886.* Washington, D.C.: Adjutant General's Office, 1973. NA microfilm publication 858.

U.S. Army. Dept. of Virginia and North Carolina. Dept. of Negro Affairs. *Report of the Superintendent of Negro Affairs in North Carolina, 1864.* Boston: W. F. Brown & Co., printers, 1865.

U.S. Bureau of Refugees, Freedmen, and Abandoned Lands. *Reports of Operations (1867–1868), Records of the Assistant Commissioner for the State of North Carolina.* Washington, D.C.: National Archives and Records Service, 1972 (microfilm).

U.S. Bureau of the Census. Fourth through Fifteenth Federal Censuses of the United States (1830–1930): Population and Slave Schedules. Washington, D.C.: National Archives and Records Service, 1820–1930 (microfilm).

U.S. War Department. *The War of the Rebellion: A Compilation of the Official Records of the Union and Confederate Armies.* 70 vols. Washington, D.C.: Government Printing Office, 1880–1901.

Valentine, Herbert E. *Story of Co. F, 23d Massachusetts Volunteers in the War for the Union, 1861–1865.* Boston: W. B. Clarke & Co., 1896.

Walker, David. *David Walker's Appeal to the Coloured Citizens of the World.* Edited by Peter P. Hinks. University Park: Pennsylvania State University Press, 2000.

Wyeth, John J. *Leaves from a Diary, Written While Serving in Co. #44 Mass. From September, 1862, to June, 1863.* Boston: L. F. Lawrence & Co., 1878.

Secondary Sources

Alexander, Ken, and Aris Glaze. *Towards Freedom: The African-Canadian Experience*. Toronto: Umbrella Press, 1996.

Alexander, Roberta Sue. *North Carolina Faces the Freedmen: Race Relations during Presidential Reconstruction, 1865–67*. Durham, N.C.: Duke University Press, 1985.

Angell, Stephen Ward. *Bishop Henry Turner and African-American Religion in the South*. Knoxville: University of Tennessee Press, 1992.

Balanoff, Elizabeth. "Negro Legislators in the North Carolina General Assembly, July, 1868–February, 1872." *North Carolina Historical Review* 49, no. 1 (January 1972): 23–24, 27.

Barrett, John G. *The Civil War in North Carolina*. Chapel Hill: University of North Carolina Press, 1963.

Baur, John E. "The Presidency of Geffrard of Haiti." *The Americas* 10, no. 4 (April 1954): 452–61.

Beckel, Deborah. "Roots of Reform: The Origins of Populism and Progressivism as Manifest in Relationships among Reformers in Raleigh, North Carolina, 1850–1905." Ph.D. diss., Emory University, 1998.

Berkeley, Edmund, and Dorothy Smith Berkeley. *A Yankee Botanist in the Carolinas: The Reverend Moses Ashley Curtis*. Berlin: J. Kramer, 1986.

Bernstein, Leonard. "The Participation of Negro Delegates in the Constitutional Convention of 1868 in North Carolina." *Journal of Negro History* 34, no. 4 (October 1949): 390–409.

Bethel, Elizabeth Raul. *The Roots of African-American Identity: Memory and History in the Antebellum Free Communities*. New York: St. Martin's Press, 1997.

Bishir, Catherine W. "Black Builders in Antebellum North Carolina." *North Carolina Historical Review* 61, no. 4 (October 1984): 423–61.

Blassingame, John W. *Black New Orleans, 1860–1880*. Chicago: University of Chicago Press, 1973.

Blight, David W. *Frederick Douglass's Civil War: Keeping Faith in Jubilee*. Baton Rouge: Louisiana State University Press, 1989.

———. *Race and Reunion: The Civil War in American Memory*. Cambridge, Mass.: Belknap Press of Harvard University Press, 2001.

———. *Race, Memory, and the American Civil War*. Amherst: University of Massachusetts Press, 2002.

Bolster, Jeffrey. *Black Jacks: African American Seamen in the Age of Sail*. Cambridge, Mass.: Harvard University Press, 1997.

Borome, Joseph A. "Vigilant Committee of Philadelphia." *Pennsylvania Magazine of History and Biography* 92, no. 3 (July 1968): 320–51.

Boyd, Willis D. "James Redpath and American Negro Colonization in Haiti, 1860–1862." *The Americas* 12, no. 2 (October 1855): 169–82.

Bradley, Mark L. *Bluecoats and Tar Heels: Soldiers and Civilians in Reconstruction North Carolina*. Lexington: University Press of Kentucky, 2009.

———. *This Astounding Close: The Road to Bennett Place*. Chapel Hill: University of North Carolina Press, 2006.

Brewer, James Howard. "Legislation Designed to Control Slavery in Wilmington and Fayetteville." *North Carolina Historical Review* 30, no. 2 (April 1953): 155–66.

Brown, D. Alexander. *The Galvanized Yankees*. Urbana: University of Illinois Press, 1963.

Brown, Elsa Barkley. "Negotiating and Transforming the Public Sphere: African American Political Life in the Transition from Slavery to Freedom." *Public Culture* 7, no. 1 (Fall 1994): 107–46.

Brown, William Wells. *The Black Man: His Antecedents, His Genius, and His Achievements*. Boston: James Redpath, 1863.

———. *The Negro in the American Rebellion*. Boston: n.p., 1867.

Browning, Judkin. *Shifting Loyalties: The Union Occupation of Eastern North Carolina*. Chapel Hill: University of North Carolina Press, 2011.

Butts, Michèle Tucker. *Galvanized Yankees on the Upper Missouri: The Face of Loyalty*. Boulder: University Press of Colorado, 2003.

———. "Trading Gray for Blue: Ex-Confederates Hold the Upper Missouri for the Union." *Prologue* 37, no. 4 (Winter 2005): 14–21.

Camp, Stephanie M. H. *Closer to Freedom: Enslaved Women and Everyday Resistance in the Plantation South*. Chapel Hill: University of North Carolina Press, 2004.

Carbone, John S. *The Civil War in Coastal North Carolina*. Raleigh: North Carolina Department of Cultural Resources, Division of Archives and History, 2001.

Casstevens, Francis Harding. *Edward A. Wild and the African Brigade in the Civil War*. Jefferson, N.C.: McFarland, 2003.

Cecelski, David S. "A Thousand Aspirations." *Southern Exposure* 18, no. 1 (Spring 1990): 22–25.

———. *The Waterman's Song: Slavery and Freedom in Maritime North Carolina*. Chapel Hill: University of North Carolina Press, 2001.

Cecelski, David S., and Alex Christopher Meekins. "*The Life of the Late James Johnson*: An American Slave Narrative from Oldham, England." *Carolina Comments* 56, no. 3 (July 2008): 108–13.

Cecelski, David S., and Timothy B. Tyson, eds. *Democracy Betrayed: The Wilmington Race Riot of 1898 and Its Legacy*. Chapel Hill: University of North Carolina Press, 1998.

Cheek, William, and Aimee Lee Cheek. *John Mercer Langston and the Fight for Black Freedom, 1829–65*. Urbana: University of Illinois Press, 1996.

Cimprich, John. "The Beginning of the Black Suffrage Movement in Tennessee." *Journal of Negro History* 65, no. 3 (Summer 1980): 185–95.

Clavin, Matthew J. *Toussaint Louverture and the American Civil War.* Philadelphia: University of Pennsylvania Press, 2010.

Clegg, Claude A., III. *The Price of Liberty: African Americans and the Making of Liberia.* Chapel Hill: University of North Carolina Press, 2004.

Click, Patricia C. *Time Full of Trial: The Roanoke Island Freedmen's Colony, 1862–1867.* Chapel Hill: University of North Carolina Press, 2001.

Cornish, Dudley. *The Sable Arm: Negro Troops in the Union Army, 1861–1865.* New York: Longmans, Green, 1956.

Cromwell, John W. "The First Negro Churches in the District of Columbia." *Journal of Negro History* 7, no. 1 (January 1922): 76–78.

Crow, Jeffrey J., Paul D. Escott, and Flora J. Hatley Wadelington. *A History of African Americans in North Carolina.* Raleigh: North Carolina Department of Cultural Resources, Division of Archives and History, 1992.

Dailey, Jane. "The Limits of Liberalism in the New South: The Politics of Race, Sex, and Patronage in Virginia, 1879–1883." In *Jumpin' Jim Crow: Southern Politics from Civil War to Civil Rights,* edited by Jane Dailey, Glenda Elizabeth Gilmore, and Bryant Simon, 88–114. Princeton, N.J.: Princeton University Press, 2000.

Davis, J. Kenneth, Jr. *Patriarch of the Lower Cape Fear: Governor James Moore and Descendants.* Wilmington: New Hanover County Public Library, 2006.

Dean, David M. *Defender of the Race: James Theodore Holly, Black Nationalist Bishop.* Boston: Lambeth Press, 1979.

Delany, Martin Robison. *The Condition, Elevation, Emigration and Destiny of the Colored People of the United States.* Philadelphia: the author, 1852.

De Rossett, William Lord. *Pictorial and Historical New Hanover County and Wilmington, North Carolina, 1723–1938.* Wilmington, N.C.: n.p., 1938.

Deveney, John Patrick. *Paschal Beverly Randolph: A Nineteenth-Century Black American Spiritualist, Rosicrucian, and Sex Magician.* Albany: State University of New York Press, 1997.

Dixon, Chris. *African Americans and Haiti: Emigration and Black Nationalism in the Nineteenth Century.* Westport, Conn.: Greenwood, 2000.

Du Bois, W. E. B. *Black Reconstruction: An Essay Toward a History of the Part which Black Folk Played in the Attempt to Reconstruct Democracy in America, 1860–1880.* New York: Harcourt, Brace, 1935.

Edwards, Laura F. *Gendered Strife and Confusion: The Political Culture of Reconstruction.* Urbana: University of Illinois Press, 1997.

Elliott, Mark. *Color-Blind Justice: Albion Tourgée and the Quest for Racial Equality from the Civil War to* Plessy v. Ferguson. New York: Oxford University Press, 2006.

England, J. Merton. "The Free Negro in Antebellum Tennessee." *Journal of Southern History* 9, no. 1 (February 1943): 37–58.

Engs, Robert F. *Freedom's First Generation: Black Hampton, Virginia, 1861–1890.* New York: Fordham University Press, 2004.

Evans, William McKee. *Ballots and Fence Rails: Reconstruction on the Lower Cape Fear*. Chapel Hill: University of North Carolina Press, 1967.

Farnham, Thomas J., and Francis P. King. "'The March of the Destroyer': The New Bern Yellow Fever Epidemic." *North Carolina Historical Review* 76, no. 4 (October 1996): 435–83.

Faust, Drew Gilpin. *This Republic of Suffering: Death and the American Civil War*. New York: Knopf, 2008.

Fehrenbacher, Don. *The Dred Scott Case: Its Significance in American Law and Politics*. New York: Oxford University Press, 1978.

Finkelman, Paul, ed. *Encyclopedia of African-American History, 1619–1895: From the Colonial Period to the Age of Frederick Douglass*. 3 vols. New York: Oxford University Press, 2006.

Fishel, Edwin C. *The Secret War for the Union: The Untold Story of Military Intelligence in the Civil War*. Boston: Houghton, Mifflin, 1996.

Foner, Eric. *Freedom's Lawmakers: A Directory of Black Officeholders during Reconstruction*. Baton Rouge: Louisiana State University Press, 1996.

———. *Reconstruction: America's Unfinished Revolution, 1863–1877*. New York: Harper & Row, 1988.

Fonvielle, Chris E., Jr. *The Wilmington Campaign: Last Rays of Departing Hope*. Mechanicsburg, Pa.: Stackpole Books, 1997.

Franklin, John Hope. *The Free Negro in North Carolina, 1790–1860*. Chapel Hill: University of North Carolina Press, 1943.

———. *Reconstruction: After the Civil War*. Chicago: University of Chicago Press, 1961.

Gilmore, Glenda Elizabeth. *Gender and Jim Crow: Women and the Politics of White Supremacy in North Carolina, 1896–1920*. Chapel Hill: University of North Carolina Press, 1996.

Glymph, Thavolia. *Out of the House of Bondage: The Transformation of the Plantation Household*. New York: Cambridge University Press, 2008.

Greenberg, Amy S. *Cause for Alarm: The Volunteer Fire Department in the Nineteenth-Century City*. Princeton, N.J.: Princeton University Press, 1998.

———. *Manifest Manhood and the Antebellum American Empire*. New York: Cambridge University Press, 2005.

Gunter, Linda. "Abraham H. Galloway: First Black Elector." *North Carolina African-American Historical and Genealogical Society Quarterly*, Fall 1990, 9–10.

Hahn, Steven. *A Nation under Our Feet: Black Political Struggles in the Rural South from Slavery to the Great Migration*. Cambridge, Mass.: Harvard University Press, 2003.

———. *The Political Worlds of Slavery and Freedom*. Cambridge, Mass.: Harvard University Press, 2009.

Hamilton, J. G. de Roulhac. "The Prison Experiences of Randolph Shotwell." *North Carolina Historical Review* 2, no. 2 (April 1925): 160.

———. *Reconstruction in North Carolina*. New York: Columbia University Press, 1914.

Harper, Mathew J. W. "Living in God's Time: African-American Faith and Politics in Post-Emancipation North Carolina." Ph.D. diss., University of North Carolina, Chapel Hill, 2009.

Harris, Leslie M. *In the Shadow of Slavery: African Americans in New York City, 1626–1863*. Chicago: University of Chicago Press, 2003.

Harris, William C. *William Woods Holden: Firebrand of North Carolina Politics*. Baton Rouge: Louisiana State University Press, 1987.

Hartgrove, W. B. "The Story of Maria Louise Moore and Fannie M. Richards." *Journal of Negro History* 1, no. 1 (January 1916): 23–33.

Heller, Charles E. *Portrait of an Abolitionist: A Biography of George Luther Stearns, 1809–1867*. Westport, Conn.: Greenwood, 1996.

Hildebrand, Reginald F. *The Times Were Strange and Stirring: Methodist Preachers and the Crisis of Emancipation*. Durham, N.C.: Duke University Press, 1995.

Hill, David G. *The Freedom-Seekers: Blacks in Early Canada*. Agincourt: Book Society of Canada, 1981.

Hinks, Peter P. "John Marrant and the Meaning of Early Black Freemasonry." *William and Mary Quarterly*, 3rd ser., 64, no. 1 (January 2007): 105–6.

———. *To Awaken My Afflicted Brethren: David Walker and the Problem of Antebellum Slave Resistance*. University Park: Pennsylvania State University Press, 1997.

Hinton, Richard. *John Brown and His Men*. New York: Funk & Wagnalls, 1894.

Hoffman, Richard Lee. "The Republican Party in North Carolina, 1867–1871." M.A. thesis, University of North Carolina, Chapel Hill, 1960.

Hollandsworth, James G., Jr. *The Louisiana Native Guards: The Black Military Experience during the Civil War*. Baton Rouge: Louisiana State University Press, 1995.

Horner, Charles F. *The Life of James Redpath and the Development of the Modern Lyceum*. New York: Barse & Hopkins, 1926.

Horton, James Oliver. "A Crusade for Freedom: William Still and the Real Underground Railroad." In *Passages to Freedom: The Underground Railroad in History and Memory*, edited by David W. Blight, 174–93. Washington, D.C.: Smithsonian Books, 2004.

———. *Free People of Color: Inside the African American Community*. Washington, D.C.: Smithsonian Institution Press, 1993.

Howlett, Barbara W. "St. Peter's AME Zion Church." *Journal of the New Bern Historical Society* 1 (May 1988): 31–34.

Hume, Richard L., and Jerry B. Gough. *Blacks, Carpetbaggers, and Scalawags: The Constitutional Conventions of Radical Reconstruction*. Baton Rouge: Louisiana State University Press, 2008.

Hunt, Alfred N. *Haiti's Influence on Antebellum America: Slumbering Volcano in the Caribbean*. Baton Rouge: Louisiana State University Press, 1988.

Jackson, Alice, and Bettina Jackson. *Three Hundred Years of America*. Madison: Historical Society of Wisconsin, 1951.

Johnson, Guion Griffis. *Ante-Bellum North Carolina: A Social History*. Chapel Hill: University of North Carolina Press, 1937.

Johnson, Walter. *Soul by Soul: Life inside the Antebellum Slave Market*. Cambridge, Mass.: Harvard University Press, 1999.

———, ed. *The Chattel Principle: Internal Slave Trades in the Americas*. New Haven: Yale University Press, 2005.

Jones, Maxine D. "'A Glorious Work': The American Missionary Association and Black North Carolinians, 1863–1880." Ph.D. diss., Florida State University, 1982.

Jordan, Ervin L. *Black Confederates and Afro-Yankees in Civil War Virginia*. Charlottesville: University Press of Virginia, 1995.

Jordan, Weymouth T., Jr., and Gerald W. Thomas. "Massacre at Plymouth: April 20, 1864." *North Carolina Historical Review* 75, no. 2 (April 1995): 125–97.

Jung, Moon-Ho. *Coolies and Cane: Race, Labor, and Sugar in the Age of Emancipation*. Baltimore: Johns Hopkins University Press, 2006.

Kantrowitz, Stephen. "'Intended for the Better Government of Man': The Political History of African American Freemasonry in the Era of Emancipation." *Journal of American History* 96, no. 4 (March 2010): 1001–26.

———. *More Than Freedom: Fighting for Black Citizenship in a White Republic, 1829–1889*. New York: Penguin, 2012.

Kaufman, J. E., and H. W. Kaufman. *Fortress America: The Forts That Defended America, 1600 to the Present*. Cambridge, Mass.: Da Capo Press, 2004.

Khan, Larry. *One Day, Levin . . . He Be Free*. New York: E. P. Dutton, 1972.

Levesque, George A. "Inherited Reformers–Inherited Orthodoxy: Black Baptists in Boston, 1800–1873." *Journal of Negro History* 60, no. 4 (October 1975): 491–525.

Levine, Robert S. *Martin Delany, Frederick Douglass, and the Politics of Representative Identity*. Chapel Hill: University of North Carolina Press, 1997.

Lewis, Daniel Levering. *W. E. B. Du Bois, 1868–1919: Biography of a Race*. New York: Henry Holt, 1994.

Litwack, Leon F. *Been in the Storm So Long: The Aftermath of Slavery*. New York: Vintage, 1980.

Love, William Deloss. *Wisconsin in the War of the Rebellion: A History of All Regiments and Batteries the State Has Sent to the Field, and deeds of her Citizens, Governors, and other Military Officers, and State and National Legislators to Suppress the Rebellion*. Chicago: Church and Goodman, 1866.

Maltz, Earl M. *Dred Scott and the Politics of Slavery*. Lawrence: University Press of Kansas, 2007.

Mandell, Daniel R. "Shifting Boundaries of Race and Ethnicity: Indian-Black Intermarriage in Southern New England, 1760–1880." *Journal of American History* 85, no. 2 (September 1998): 466–501.

Martin, Michael J. *A History of the 4th Wisconsin Infantry and Cavalry in the Civil War*. New York: Savas Beatie, 2006.

Masur, Kate. "The African American Delegation to Abraham Lincoln: A Reappraisal." *Civil War History* 56, no. 2 (June 2010): 117–44.

May, Robert E. *The Southern Dream of a Caribbean Empire, 1854–1861*. Baton Rouge: Louisiana State University Press, 1973.

McCarthy, Timothy Patrick, and John Stauffer, eds. *Prophets of Protest: Reconsidering the History of American Abolitionism*. New York: New Press, 2006.

McCurry, Stephanie. *Confederate Reckoning: Power and Politics in the Civil War South*. Cambridge. Mass.: Harvard University Press, 2010.

McFeely, William. *Frederick Douglass*. New York: Norton, 1995.

McGuire, Danielle. *At the Dark End of the Street: Black Women, Rape and Resistance*. New York: Knopf, 2010.

McKivigan, John. *Forgotten Firebrand: James Redpath and the Making of Nineteenth-Century America*. Ithaca, N.Y.: Cornell University Press, 2008.

———. "James Redpath and Black Reaction to the Haitian Emigration Bureau." *Mid-America* 69 (1987): 139–53.

McPherson, James M. *Battle Cry of Freedom: The Civil War Era*. New York: Oxford University Press, 1988.

———. *Marching toward Freedom: Blacks in the Civil War, 1861–1865*. New York: Facts on File, 1991.

———. *The Negro's Civil War: How American Negroes Felt and Acted during the War for the Union*. New York: Pantheon, 1965.

———. *Ordeal by Fire: The Civil War and Reconstruction*. New York: Knopf, 1982.

Mobley, Joe A. *James City: A Black Community in North Carolina, 1863–1900*. Raleigh: North Carolina Department of Cultural Resources, Division of Archives and History, 1981.

Morris, Charles Edward. "Panic and Reprisal: Reaction in North Carolina to the Nat Turner Insurrection, 1831." *North Carolina Historical Review* 62, no. 1 (January 1985): 29–52.

Myers, Barton A. *Executing Daniel Bright: Race, Loyalty, and Guerrilla Violence in a Coastal Carolina Community, 1861–1865*. Baton Rouge: Louisiana State University Press, 2009.

Nash, Gary B., and Jean R. Soderlund. *Freedom by Degrees: Emancipation in Pennsylvania and Its Aftermath*. New York: Oxford University Press, 1991.

Neilson, Rick. "George Mink: A Black Businessman in Early Kingston." *Historic Kingston* 46 (1998): 111–29.

Ofari, Earl. *"Let Your Motto Be Resistance": The Life and Thought of Henry Highland Garnet*. Boston: Beacon Press, 1972.

Pearson, Henry Greenleaf. *The Life of John A. Andrew, Governor of Massachusetts, 1861–1865*. Boston: Houghton, Mifflin, 1904.

Penn, I. Garland. *The Afro-American Press and Its Editors*. Springfield, Mass.: Wiley & Co., 1891.

Peterson, Merrill D. *The Great Triumvirate: Webster, Clay, and Calhoun*. New York: Oxford University Press, 1987.

Plummer, Mark A. "Samuel Clarke Pomeroy." In *American National Biography*. New York: Oxford University Press, 1999.

Powell, William S. *Moses Ashley Curtis: Teacher, Priest, Scientist*. Chapel Hill: University of North Carolina Library, 1958.

——, ed. *Dictionary of North Carolina Biography*. 6 vols. Chapel Hill: University of North Carolina Press, 1979–96.

Quarles, Benjamin. *Allies for Freedom: Blacks and John Brown*. New York: Oxford University Press, 1974.

——. *The Negro in the Civil War*. Boston: Little, Brown, 1953.

Rael, Patrick. *Black Identity and Black Protest in the Antebellum North*. Chapel Hill: University of North Carolina Press, 2002.

Ragsdale, Bruce A., and Joel D. Treese. *Black Americans in Congress, 1870–1989*. Washington, D.C.: Office of the Historian, U.S. House of Representatives, 1990.

Rankin, David C. "The Origins of Black Leadership in New Orleans during Reconstruction." *Journal of Southern History* 40, no. 3 (August 1974): 417–40.

Rauch, Basil. *American Interest in Cuba, 1848–1855*. New York: Columbia University Press, 1948.

Reaves, Bill. *Southport (Smithville): A Chronology*. Southport, N.C.: Southport Historical Society, 1978.

——. *"Strength through Struggle": The Chronological and Historical Record of the African-American Community in Wilmington, North Carolina, 1865–1950*. Wilmington, N.C.: New Hanover County Public Library, 1998.

Reid, Richard M. *Freedom for Themselves: North Carolina's Black Soldiers in the Civil War Era*. Chapel Hill: University of North Carolina Press, 2008.

——. "Raising the African Brigade: Early Black Recruitment in Civil War North Carolina." *North Carolina Historical Review* 70, no. 3 (July 1993): 266–97.

Reynolds, David S. *John Brown, Abolitionist: The Man Who Killed Slavery, Sparked the Civil War, and Seeded Civil Rights*. New York: Knopf, 2005.

Richardson, Joe M. "Francis Cardozo: Black Educator during Reconstruction." *Journal of Negro History* 48, no. 1 (Winter 1979): 73–83.

Roberts, Rita. *Evangelicalism and the Politics of Reform in Northern Black Thought, 1776–1863*. Baton Rouge: Louisiana State University Press, 2010.

Rose, Willie Lee. *Rehearsal for Reconstruction: The Port Royal Experiment*. Indianapolis: Bobbs-Merrill, 1964.

Rosen, Hannah. *Terror in the Heart of Freedom: Citizenship, Sexual Violence, and the Meaning of Race in the Postemancipation South*. Chapel Hill: University of North Carolina Press, 2009.

Schor, John. *Henry Highland Garnet: A Voice of Black Radicalism in the Nineteenth Century*. Westport, Conn.: Greenwood, 1977.

Schouler, William. *A History of Massachusetts in the Civil War*. Boston: E. P. Dutton, 1868.

Schweninger, Loren. "John Carruthers Stanly and the Anomaly of Black Slaveholding." *North Carolina Historical Review* 67, no. 2 (April 1990): 159–92.

Scott, Julius S. "The Common Wind: Currents of Afro-American Communication in the Era of the Haitian Revolution." Ph.D. diss., Duke University, 1986.

Sernett, Milton C. *North Star Country: Upstate New York and the Struggle for African American Freedom*. Syracuse, N.Y.: Syracuse University Press, 2002.

Simmons, William J. *Men of Mark: Eminent, Progressive, and Rising*. Cleveland: Geo. M. Rewell & Co., 1887.

Singletary, Otis A. *Negro Militia and Reconstruction*. Austin: University of Texas Press, 1957.

Sinha, Manisha. "Black Abolitionism: The Assault on Southern Slavery and the Struggle for Racial Equality." In *Slavery in New York*, edited by Ira Berlin and Leslie M. Harris, 239–62. New York: New Press, 2005.

Smith, John David. *Black Voices from Reconstruction, 1865–1877*. Gainesville: University of Florida Press, 1997.

———, ed. *Black Soldiers in Blue: African American Troops in the Civil War Era*. Chapel Hill: University of North Carolina Press, 2002.

Stauffer, John. *The Black Hearts of Men: Radical Abolitionists and the Transformation of Race*. Cambridge, Mass.: Harvard University Press, 2002.

———. *Giants: The Parallel Lives of Frederick Douglass and Abraham Lincoln*. New York: Twelve, 2009.

Stouffer, Allen P. *The Light of Nature and the Law of God—Antislavery in Ontario, 1833–1877*. Montreal: McGill-Queen's University Press, 1992.

Stuckey, Sterling. *Slave Culture: Nationalist Theory and the Foundations of Black America*. New York: Oxford University Press, 1987.

Tadman, Michael. "The Interregional Slave Trade in the History and Myth-Making of the U.S. South." In Johnson, *Chattel Principle*, 117–42.

Trelease, Allen W. *White Terror: The Ku Klux Klan Conspiracy and Southern Reconstruction*. Baton Rouge: Louisiana State University Press, 1971.

Tunnel, Ted. *Crucible of Reconstruction: War, Radicalism, and Race in Louisiana*. Baton Rouge: Louisiana State University Press, 1992.

Vass, Lachlan Cumming. *History of the First Presbyterian Church in New Bern, N.C., with a Resume of Early Ecclesiastical Affairs in Eastern North Carolina, and a Sketch of the Early Days of New Bern, N.C., 1817–1886*. Richmond, Va.: Whittet and Shepperson, 1886.

Vincent, Charles. *Black Legislators in Louisiana during Reconstruction*. Baton Rouge: Louisiana State University Press, 1976.

von Frank, Albert J. "John Brown, James Redpath, and the Idea of Revolution." *Civil War History* 52, no. 2 (June 2006): 142–60.

Vorenberg, Michael. *The Final Freedom: The Civil War, the Abolition of Slavery and the Thirteenth Amendment*. Cambridge: Cambridge University Press, 2001.

Waters, Shelton B. *We Have This Ministry: A History of the First African Presbyterian Church, Philadelphia, Pennsylvania, the Mother Church of African American Presbyterians*. Philadelphia: Winchell, 1994.

Watson, Alan D. *A History of New Bern and Craven County*. New Bern, N.C.: Tryon Palace Commission, 1987.

———. *Wilmington: Port of North Carolina*. Columbia: University of South Carolina Press, 1992.

Weinert, Richard, and Robert Arthur. *Defender of the Chesapeake: The Story of Fort Monroe*. Annapolis, Md.: Leeward Publications, 1978.

White, Deborah Gray. *Ar'n't I A Woman? Female Slaves in the Plantation South*. New York: Norton, 1985.

Williams, Heather Andrea. *Help Me to Find My People: The African American Search for Family Lost in Slavery*. Chapel Hill: University of North Carolina Press, 2012.

———. *Self-Taught: African American Education in Slavery and Freedom*. Chapel Hill: University of North Carolina Press, 2005.

Williams, Learotha, "'Leave the pulpit and go into the . . . school room': Jonathan Clarkson Gibbs and the Board of Missions for Freedmen in North and South Carolina, 1865–1866." *Southern Studies* 13, no. 1/2 (Spring/Summer 2006): 89–104.

Willis, Rev. Robert H. "Methodist Missions in North Carolina." In *Historical Papers of the North Carolina Conference Historical Society and the Western North Carolina Conference Historical Society*, 110–25. Greensboro: North Carolina Christian Advocate, 1925.

Winch, Julie. *A Gentleman of Color: The Life of James Forten*. New York: Oxford University Press, 2002.

Winks, Robin W. *The Blacks in Canada—A History*. New Haven: Yale University Press, 1971.

Yellin, Jean. *Harriet Jacobs: A Life*. New York: Basic Civitas Books, 2004.

Zipf, Karin. "No Longer under Cover[ture]: Marriage, Divorce, and Gender in the 1868 Constitutional Convention." In *North Carolinians in the Era of the Civil War and Reconstruction*, edited by Paul D. Escott, 193–219. Chapel Hill: University of North Carolina Press, 2008.

Acknowledgments

MANY SCHOLARS CONTRIBUTED TO MY RESEARCH ON ABRAHAM GAL-loway's life and world. I especially want to thank Steve Kantrowitz at the University of Wisconsin–Madison, Thanayi Jackson at the Freedmen and Southern Society Project at the University of Maryland–College Park, and Chris Meekins and the late George Stevenson at the North Carolina State Archives. All brought crucial historical documents for understanding Galloway's life to my attention. In addition, at the New Hanover County Public Library, in Wilmington, North Carolina, Beverly Tetterton devoted long hours and her considerable talents to helping me unravel the mysteries of Galloway's family and early life. I cannot thank her enough—or her colleagues Joseph Sheppard and Greg Minerva and her able volunteer Michael Whaley. I also want to thank the scores of other archivists, librarians, and museum curators who supported my research on Galloway. That research led me to more than fifty archival collections, and at every one of them I found warm hospitality and extraordinarily helpful guidance—thank you all.

I am also grateful to Susan Holland, Chris Fonveille, Margaret Rogers, John David Smith, John Haley, Raymond Gavins, Joanna Stanbridge, Peter Sandbeck, William Harris, Richard Reid, William Gould IV, Kelly Navies, Melody Ivins, Alisa Harrison, Robert Anthony, and Catherine Bishir for their many contributions to my research on Galloway. I want to express my appreciation as well to Adriane Lentz-Smith, Lu Ann Jones, Joe Mobley, Peter Wood, and the University of North Carolina Press's outside readers, Edward Baptist and Jeffrey Crow, for their helpful comments on earlier drafts of the book. I count myself deeply blessed for the opportunity to work with David Perry and his colleagues at UNC Press, including Alison Shay, Stephanie Wenzel, and Caitlin Bell-Butterfield. I feel fortunate to have this book in such caring hands. I also know how lucky I am to have an agent like Charlotte Sheedy, who both looks after business and is a personal inspiration in her commitment to making this a better world.

From the bottom of my heart, I also want to express my thanks to Kat Charron, now at North Carolina State University, and Tim Tyson, at Duke University. Tim edited every draft of every chapter, and I had the unsurpassed pleasure of writing and editing side by side with him for most of a summer. Similarly, Kat's commitment to my telling Galloway's story buoyed my work at every stage, and she improved the book immeasurably with her gifts as a historian and poet. I likewise want to extend special thanks to my friend Jack Holtzman, a gifted amateur historian, for his strong faith in this book's importance and his very concrete help in thinking through the historical issues raised by Galloway's life.

Other friends helped in less tangible but no less important ways. I am deeply beholden in particular to Jack's wife, Pam Silberman; Bland and Ann Simpson; the Reverend Joe Harvard; Dub and Libby Gulley; Lanier and her late husband, Fred Blum; Paul Baldasare; Jane Wettach; Karen Amspacher; and Allan Gurganus. Occasionally they helped with historical research; more often they lent me a sunny room in which to write or patiently listened to my ideas on long walks in the woods. Every bit of their support means the world to me.

Finally, I am thankful beyond words for the support and encouragement of my brother and sisters and their families, my cousins, my dear mother, and my wife's parents, Karl and Pamela Hanson. Above all, I want to thank my wife, Laura Hanson, and our children, Vera and Guy. From beginning to end, they enthusiastically supported my labors on this book. They shared the thrill of discovery by my side, helped me to overcome many obstacles, and good-heartedly put up with family vacations planned around my visits to archives and libraries. Now I have a hundred sweet memories of those trips. Those memories fill my heart with delight, whether I am remembering our long days exploring the back roads of eastern North Carolina or the nights we swam at Walden Pond in the fading summer light.

Index

Burnside, Ambrose, 50–51, 58, 70
Butler, Benjamin F., 134; Galloway
and, 45–46, 50–52, 84, 132; at Fortress Monroe, 45–51; and contraband policy, 47–48; employing black
spies, 48–52; in the Deep South,
51–56, 144; and treatment of black
soldiers, 93; and black prisoners
of war, 94, 253–54 (n. 12); and Brig.
Gen. Wild, 96; and Point Lookout
prison camp, 100–102; affection
among black activists for, 104,
111–12, 151, 155
Butler's Ditch, 56

Cadogan's Hall (Syracuse), 139
Cailloux, André, 145, 155, 265 (n. 20)
Cambridge, Mass., 70
Cambridge (Union gunboat), 123
Camp Lamb, 198
Canada, xx, 15, 20, 21–26, 28, 30, 31, 34,
35, 36, 38, 41, 72, 94, 104, 105, 141,
142, 184
Canada West, 22–26, 27–28, 33, 34, 36,
43, 44, 67, 108, 184
Canedy, Anne C. G., 160, 161
Cape Fear, xix, 4, 5, 194, 199
Cape Fear Commissioners of Naviga-
tion and Pilotage, 17
Cape Fear River, xiv, 1, 3, 4, 5, 11, 13, 15,
51, 52, 100, 137; Galloway's escape
down, 18; and Fort Fisher, 58, 159,
170
Cape Hatteras, 105
Cape Haytien, Haiti, 32
Cape May, 18
Capitol Building (Washington, D.C.),
117, 174
Cardozo, Francis, 143
Caribbean, 34, 35, 64
Carolina Motel (Wilmington, N.C.), 14
Cary, Mary Ann Shadd, 23
Caswell County, N.C., 101

Catawba Indians, 1
Cedar Grove Cemetery, 135
Central America, 33, 34
Ceres (Union vessel), 53–54
Chancellorsville, Va., 71
Chapel Hill, N.C., 166
Charleston, S.C., 2–3, 7, 58, 71, 143
Charleston Mercury (newspaper), 49
Charlotte Observer, 119
Chase, Salmon P., 120, 176
Chatham, Canada West, 23, 25, 184
Chatham Vigilance Committee, 23
Chesapeake Bay, 18, 46, 100, 103, 105
Chicago, Ill., 24
Chicago Times, 36
Child, Lydia Maria, 31
Chinese immigrants, 210
Chowan River, 59, 90
Christian Church (New Bern, N.C.),
109
Christian Recorder (newspaper), 88,
181, 182, 215
Cincinnati, Ohio, 141, 142
Cincinnati Colored Citizen (newspaper),
141
Civil War: recruitment of black troops
during, xiii–xvi, 70–80, 83–85, 88–
89; Galloway and understanding of,
xvi–xviii; Haitian conspiracy and,
40–42; black Union army spies and
scouts during, 43–44, 49–51, 65–66,
82; beginning of, 43–46; Federal
contraband policy during, 47–48,
54–55; slaves escaping to Union
lines during, 47–48, 58–59, 61–62;
Galloway in Deep South during,
51–57; Burnside expedition, 58–59;
black quest for political equality
during, 89, 115–17, 121–23, 126–27;
black soldiers and struggle for
equal treatment in Union army,
90–98; "Galvanized Yankees" and,
100–102; Robert Hamilton's tour of

contraband communities during, 103–14; black southerners meeting with Lincoln during, 115–17, 124–26; Confederate army atrocities against black soldiers during, 118–21; Galloway's lecture tours of North during, 121–23, 153–57; final days of, 169–74. *See also* African Americans; National Convention of Colored Men of the United States; National Equal Rights League

Clark, Peter H., 141

Cleveland, Edmund J., 50

Cleveland, Ohio, 189

Clinton, J. J., 159, 261 (n. 11)

Clinton, N.C., 203

Clotel; or, The President's Daughter (novel), 142

Cocke School, 164

Colfax, Schuyler, 204

Colored Ladies Relief Association (New Bern, N.C.), 86–88, 191

Colored Soldiers' and Sailors' League, 195–96

Columbia, N.C., 59

Columbus County, N.C., 203

Colyer, Vincent, 66–67, 75

Comings, E. J., 111

Commodore Perry (Union vessel), 91

Confederacy, 28, 29, 49, 53, 58, 80, 88, 99, 125, 146, 150, 182, 190; slaves escaping from, xiii, 58–59, 61–62, 65–66, 79, 123; as enemy of African Americans, xiv, 80–82, 98; policy of on captured black soldiers, xv, 78–79, 96, 118, 120, 151; African American freedom struggle within, xvi; Galloway in, xvi, 42, 43–57, 62, 73, 79, 99–100, 154; founding principles of, xvii–xviii, 45; Constitution of, xviii; status of blacks in, xviii, 73; black spies in, 66–67; black scouts returning to, 75–76;

massacres of black prisoners of war in, 118–20; black leaders from, 138; decline and fall of, 158, 159, 169, 172, 173–74; Reconstruction in former parts of, 175–76, 178, 191, 195, 216

Confederate army, xiii, 6, 45, 54, 78, 86, 104, 169, 218; casualties of, 42; and use of black labor, 48; attempts of to recapture New Bern, N.C., 63, 114, 133, 166; atrocities against black soldiers by, 94, 95–96, 118–20; effect of emancipation and black soldiers on, 96–97; in Cape Fear, 100, 171; at Port Hudson, 145; at Bentonville, 172; veterans of, 182

Confederate blockade-runners, 137

Confederate coast guard, 137

Confederate guerrillas, 54, 64, 95–96

Confederate Home Guard, 66, 82

Confederate prisoners of war, 100–102

Confederate shipping, 63

Confederate States of America, 45, 74, 81. *See also* Confederacy

Confederate White House, 50

Congress of the Confederate States of America, xviii, 118

Congressional Globe, 108, 109

Congressional Record, 108

Connecticut, 89, 121

Contrabands: in Virginia, 48, 122; as spies, 48–50, 66–67; in Louisiana and Mississippi, 54–55, 155; on North Carolina coast, 59, 63–67, 83–89, 122; and decision to join Union army, 72–82; organizing militia, 76–77; desire of for freedom, 114, 115; conscription of, 133–34; and yellow fever epidemic, 134–37; organizing local Equal Rights Leagues, 158–59, 188; and celebration of Emancipation Day (1865), 160–68; disbanding of camps of, 177–78. *See also* Schools;

Emigration movements (black), 25–26, 29–42 passim, 130, 148, 233 (n. 32), 234–35 (n. 37)
Engels, Friedrich, 108
England, 141
Equal Rights League. *See* National Equal Rights League
Erie Canal, 21
Evans, W. McKee, xix, 199, 215

Farragut, David, 53, 54
Felton, Isaac K., xv–xvi, 74, 78–79, 110, 115–17, 124–25, 166, 169, 174, 270 (n. 16)
Fifteenth Street Presbyterian Church, 130
Filmore, Harriet, 88
First African Presbyterian Church, 167
First Baptist Church (Hampton, Va.), 104
First Ward Republican Club (Wilmington, N.C.), 195, 196
Florida, 95, 119, 154
Foner, Eric, xix
Ford's Theater, 174
Fort Fisher, 58, 136, 159, 169, 171, 196
Fort Henry, 22
Fort Johnston, 1, 11
Fort Pillow, 118
Fortress Monroe, 45–48, 50, 51, 52, 54, 93, 96, 104, 105, 132, 136, 144, 174
Fort Sumter, 6, 43, 45
Fort Totten, xvi, 163, 166
Fort Wagner, 118
Foster, John G., 75–76, 79, 88, 246–47 (n. 62)
Fourth Ward Republican Club (Wilmington, N.C.), 195
France, 32, 38
Franklin, John Hope, xix
Fredericksburg, Va., 142–43
Freedmen's Bureau, 55, 194, 198, 206–7
Freedmen's Journal, 161

Free Soil settlers, 30–31
From Log Cabin to the Pulpit (slave narrative), 5–6
Frying Pan Shoals, 3
Fugitive Aid Society (St. Catharines), 23
Fugitive Aid Society (Syracuse), 21
Fugitive Slave Act of 1850, 20, 22, 23, 28, 103

Galloway, Abraham H.: and founding of African Brigade, xiv–xvi, 70–82, 84; significance of for understanding Civil War, xvii–xx; childhood and early family life of, 1–12; escape of from slavery, 13–22; in Canada, 24–26, 27–28; in northern states, 27–28, 123; in Haiti, 28–30, 34–37, 39–40; in Confederacy, 42, 73, 79; recruitment of into Union spy service, 43–45; as a Union spy, 46–57, 67, 196, 239–40 (n. 10); in Louisiana and Mississippi, 51–57; capture of at Vicksburg, 56–57, 62; arrival of in New Bern, N.C., 62–63; description of, 67–69; and women's rights, 69, 210; and Mary Ann Starkey, 69–70, 172–73, 191–92; struggles of for justice with Union army, 78–79, 82, 90–94; as Union army recruiter, 84, 89, 90–93; on importance of African American military service, 84–85; oratory of, 85, 110, 122, 126–27, 166, 179–80, 185, 197, 198, 204–5, 256 (n. 41); fund-raising activities of, 86; quest of for voting rights and political equality during war, 89, 115–17, 126–27; in Plymouth, N.C., 90–93; rescuing mother, 99–100; at Point Lookout prison camp, 99–102; with Robert Hamilton in Virginia and North Carolina, 103–14; wed-

sympathy for John Brown in, 31–33; relations with United States, 32–33, 36–37, 39; abolitionists in, 33, 37, 39; relations with Spain, 38–39. *See also* St. Marc, Haiti

Haitian John Brown Committee, 37

Hamilton, Robert, 27, 103–14, 115, 121–22, 123, 131, 141, 146, 167, 170

Hamilton, Thomas, 103

Hampton, Va., 45, 104

Hampton Roads, Va., 46

Hankins, Hester, 2–4, 99–100, 224 (n. 8)

Hankins, Louisa, 2, 6, 8

Hankins, Marsden Milton, 6–8, 13, 190, 227 (n. 26)

Hankins, Mary Ann, 8

Hargett, Mariah, 83–84, 87, 88

Harland School, 164

Harper, Frances Ellen Watkins, 143

Harpers Ferry, 30, 31, 33, 34, 35, 36, 40, 41, 42, 184

Harper's Weekly, 83

Harris, D. H., 109

Harris, James H., 184–88

Harris, Thomas, 109

Hartwell, Alfred, 70, 90

Harvard College, 6, 70

Harvard Medical School, 71

Hatteras Inlet, 51, 58

Hatteras Island, 136

Hayes, Orlin S., 209

Heaton, David, 120

Hedrick, John A., 86

Hememway, Ebenezer, 142

Hemings, Sally, 142

Henderson, Morris, 141

Henry, William "Jerry," 21

Henry Highland Garnet Equal Rights League, 159, 164

Higginson, Thomas W., 49

Highgate, Edmonia, 104, 143, 146

Hill, Edward H., 109, 115–17, 121

Hillsborough, N.C., 191

Hinton, Richard, 28, 34–35

Hispaniola, 34, 38

Hoke, Robert F., 119–20

Holden, William Woods, 176–77, 182, 186–87, 204, 206, 209, 271 (n. 26)

Holly, James Theodore, 233 (n. 32)

Honduras, 33

Hood, James W., 131, 132, 137, 159, 166, 169, 183–84, 261 (n. 11), 277 (n. 39)

Hudson River, 21

Hughes, Edward, 99

Hyde County, N.C., 61

Ingraham, James H., 144–45, 152, 155, 157, 267 (n. 7)

Institute for Colored Youth, 141

Irish immigrants, 13, 24, 71, 139–40, 167

Isabella II (queen of Spain), 38, 39

Jackson, Francis, 30

Jacmel, Haiti, 32

Jamaica, 2, 25

James City, N.C., 177–78

James River, 94, 105

James School, 160, 164

Jamesville, N.Y., 139

Jefferson, Thomas, 142

John Brown Equal Rights League, 159, 163, 164, 172–75, 191, 273 (n. 63)

Johnson, Andrew, 175–76, 177, 189, 195

Johnson, Levin, 109

Johnson, William, 110

Johnston, Joseph, 172, 174

Jones, G. W., 100–101

Jones, Henry, 61

Jones County, N.C., 207

Journal of Freedom, 185

Joy Street Baptist Church, 29

Juno (enslaved woman), 59

Kansas Border Wars, 30, 31

Kansas Territory, 26, 28, 30–31, 44, 167

Kenansville, N.C., 11–12
Kent County, Md., 129
Kentucky, 28
Kingston, Canada West, 21–25, 26
Kingston Female Benevolent
   Society, 23
Kingston Hotel, 23
Kinsley, Edward W., 96, 99, 131, 175,
   243 (n. 33); in New Bern, xiii–xvii,
   70–74, 79–81, 83–84; first impres-
   sions of Galloway, xiv, xvi, xix;
   support of for freedpeople while
   in North, 86–87, 123, 173, 191
Kinston, N.C., 63
Ku Klux Klan, xx, 202, 206–7, 209

Labor and labor issues, 180, 183, 185,
   186–87, 209–10
Lake Erie, 142
Lake Ontario, 21, 22, 25
Lakin, John, 91–93
Lane, Annetta M., 104
Langston, John Mercer, 141, 147, 153,
   198, 210
Laurel Hill (Union steamboat), 55
League of Freedom, 28
Lee, Robert E., 71, 99, 113, 133, 158, 159,
   169, 172, 173
Lee, S. P., 120
Lee, T. Jeff, 203
Leggett, Robert, 76
Lenoir County, N.C., 207
Lewett, Mr. (black principal), 167
Liberator (newspaper), 27, 35–36,
   37–39, 128–29, 149
Liberators, 28
Liberia, 25, 151
Lincoln, Abraham, xiv, xviii, xx, 70,
   75, 80, 129, 149, 156, 175; and slavery, 41; and policy toward contrabands, 54–55; and black recruitment into Union army, 71–72, 77,
   94, 95; African American views of,
74, 118, 121, 134, 150, 159, 161, 170,
   174; and Emancipation Proclamation, 77, 86, 107, 111, 161; and
   Confederate treatment of black
   prisoners of war, 79, 94, 96, 120–21,
   250 (n. 33); and aims of war, 81, 122;
   defending importance of black
   military service, 96–97, 259 (n. 17);
   and Point Lookout prison camp,
   100–102; meeting of with Galloway, 115–17, 122, 124–26, 164, 187;
   support of for black civil rights,
   151; Equal Rights League chapter
   named after, 158–59; death of, 174
Lincoln, Mary Todd, 140
Lincoln School, 164
Litwack, Leon, xix
Liverpool, England, 8
Lockwood Folly River, 3
Loftin, William, 61–62
Loguen, Jermain Wesley, 21, 131
London, England, 142
López, Narciso, 32
Lorens, Mary, 14
Louisiana and Louisianans, 15, 34,
   52–55, 62, 118, 144–45, 155
Louisiana Native Guards, 144, 155
L'Ouverture, Toussaint, 170
Love, W. Levi, 209
Loyal African Methodist Church,
   182–83, 188
Lumberton, N.C., 210, 215

Maine, 155
Malone, B. Y., 101
Malvern Hill, Battle of, 6
Manhattan, 103, 109, 121–22
Maria Elena (blockade-runner), 137
Mars, John N., 89
Martin, J. Sella, 29, 139, 141, 143, 146,
   154, 263 (n. 2)
Martinsville, Va., 100
Marx, Karl, 108

North Carolina Equal Rights League, 188, 189–90
North Carolina General Assembly, 10, 203, 204–10, 214, 217
North Carolina Railroad Company, 205
North Star (newspaper), 146

Oak Island, 2, 6
Oberlin College, 104, 141, 184
Office of the Superintendent of the Freedmen, 79
O'Hara, James E., 166–67
Ohio, xix, 27, 28, 33, 141, 142, 189, 215
Ohio River, 28, 44
Old Benevolent Choir, 131
Old North State (newspaper), 161
Old Topsail Inlet, 50
Olustee, Battle of, 154
Olustee, Fla., 119
Oneida Theological Institute, 129
Ontario, Canada, 21, 22, 23. *See also* Canada West
Ormes, Mary, 14
Oswego Canal, 22
Ould, Robert, 118
Outer Banks, 51, 59, 105, 161

Paine, Halbert, 52–57
Paine, Tom, 170
Palmer School, 160, 164–65, 166
Pamlico Sound, 105
Pardee, B. S., 167
Parker School, 136
Patterson, George, 218
Peacocks, J. R., 91–93
Peake, Mary, 104
Peake, Thomas, 50, 104
Peck, John G., 94
Pennington, J. W. C., 141
Pennsylvania, 17, 20, 153
Pennsylvania Anti-Slavery Society, 19
Peter (slave pilot), 16–17, 18

Pettifoot, John Henry, 20–22, 24
Pettigrew, J. Johnston, 166
Philadelphia, Pa., 17, 18–20, 24, 88, 141, 148, 155, 156, 167, 196, 215
Phillips, Wendell, 29
Pierce, Franklin, 32, 33
Pierson, Clinton D., 108, 109, 115–17, 121–23, 131, 133, 134, 137, 277 (n. 39)
Pine and Palm (newspaper), 103
Pine Forest Cemetery, 217, 281 (n. 13)
Plane Street Presbyterian Church, 154
Plymouth, Battle of, 119
Plymouth, N.C., 51, 58, 59, 90–93, 119–20, 177, 258 (n. 15)
Point Frederick, 22
Point Lookout (Union prison camp), 100–102
Poison Springs, Ark., 118
Pomeroy, Samuel C., 167, 268 (n. 23)
Pompey (enslaved man), 61
Port-au-Prince, Haiti, 30, 32, 33, 37, 39, 43, 63
Port Hudson, La., 145, 155
Port Hudson, Siege of, 144–45
Portsmouth, Va., 87, 104, 143
Potomac River, 100
Potter, Miles, 6
Presidential Reconstruction, 177, 180
Price, George W., Jr., 180–81, 215, 271–72 (n. 40)
Prince Hall Masons, 64
Provincial Freeman (newspaper), 23, 25
Purvis, Robert, 20

Quakers, 17

Race riots, 29, 71, 140, 194, 216
Radical Republicans, 195, 198
Raleigh, N.C., 160, 173, 189, 190, 216; freedpeople's convention and, 180–88, 192; Galloway in, 184–88, 196–97, 199–201, 204–10; constitutional convention (1868) in, 195,

199–201; founding of state Republican Party in, 196–97; state legislature convening in, 204–10

Raleigh Sentinel, 200

Raleigh Weekly Standard, 216

Randolph, John, Jr., xv–xvi, 73–74, 78, 79, 131, 133, 134, 137, 180–81, 182, 183, 245 (n. 46)

Randolph, Paschal Beverly, 143, 264 (n. 16)

Ransom, Robert, 119

Ransom's Brigade, 119

Recollections of My Slavery Days (slave narrative), 76

Reconstruction, 177, 178–79, 190, 211, 216; white racial violence during, 180, 192–95, 202

Reconstruction Acts of 1867, 195

Redemption, 213

Redpath, James, 29–42 passim, 43, 103, 233 (n. 32), 234–35 (n. 37)

Remond, Charles, 139, 263 (n. 2)

Republic (Plato), 135

Republicans and Republican Party, 8, 149, 150, 156, 167, 190, 195–98, 201–4, 205, 207–10, 213–16, 276 (n. 27)

Richards, Adolphe, 142

Richards, John D., 142–43

Richmond, Va., 6, 20, 45, 50, 58, 84, 154, 173

Richmond Daily Dispatch, 50

Richmond-Petersburg Campaign, 133

Rikers Island, 130

Roanoke Island, 51, 58, 59, 105, 131, 132, 138, 158, 161, 166, 177, 182–83

Roanoke River, 59, 90

Robbins, R. G., 205–6

Robeson County, N.C., 203

Robinson, William H., 5–6, 16–17

Rochester, N.Y., 146

Rock, John S., 141, 147

Rodman's Point, 78

Rose, Willie Lee, 178

Rose (enslaved woman), 62

Rue, George A., 182

Rumley, James, 59, 84, 85, 111, 179

Rush, Christopher, 121

Russell School, 164

Russia, 71

St. Catharines, Canada West, 23, 24

St. Charles Hotel (New Orleans), 53

St. Charles Hotel (Syracuse), 139–40

St. James Episcopal Church (Smithville), 1

St. John's Episcopal Church (Wilmington, N.C.), 218

St. Lawrence River, 22

St. Louis, Mo., 28, 142

St. Marc, Haiti, 30, 34, 36, 37, 38–40, 234 (n. 37)

St. Paul's Episcopal Church, 192, 217–18, 275 (n. 13)

St. Peter's AME Zion Church. *See* Andrew Chapel

St. Stephen's African Methodist Episcopal Church, 197

Salisbury, N.C., 6

Salmon P. Chase Equal Rights League, 179

Sampson, Fannie, 172

Sampson, James D., 8, 226 (n. 25)

Sampson, John P., 141, 215

Sampson County, N.C., 203

Sanborn, Frank, 40, 44

San Francisco, Calif., 143

Sansom Street Hall (Philadelphia), 155

Savannah, Ga., 159, 169, 172

Schools (African American): in Wilmington, N.C., 8, 172, 226 (n. 25); in New Bern, N.C., 65, 74, 109, 128, 160, 161, 164–65, 166; in Tidewater Virginia, 104; in Beaufort, N.C., 107, 136; among freedpeople generally, 112–13; in Fredericksburg, Va., 142;